Contents

Part 3 Controlling IT facilities

Part 4 Aspects of IT management

Part 5 IT Management tomorrow

Appendix A. short case studies about the contents of a chapter

Appendix B.   Extended Case Studies for Group Assignments

Preface

This book came into being in the form of lecture notes for the subject Information technology management (IT management) at the Twente University in the Netherlands. Since 1995 this subject is part of the Master's degree of the course Business Management and Information Technology. Over a decade of teaching, this book developed into what it is today.

The book gives an idea of how organizations should organize their information and communication technology facilities in order to be able to say "IT does not matter." Management and the organization of IT are only conveniences within day-to-day operations and enablers, for organizations that want to supply other products and services.

The book has the following starting points:

(a) The IT support of products and services of organizations makes functional and performance demands on the IT facilities. In order to be able to meet these requirements optimally, an IT architecture is required. The IT services and products are supplied within this architecture.

(b) Controlling IT is part of normal operational management. This means that:
   - at setting up the IT facilities the principles of logistics and operations management apply;
   - the information, needed for controlling a process, makes demands on the set-up of the information service process.

   The question is:
   - whether someone is authorized to supply the data;
   - whether the data corresponds with the physically present objects and
   - whether the given data is correct and complete.

(c) A distinction is made between both the IT demand and the IT supply organization. Both organizations have to be set up. Methods indicate, which processes have to be in place in these organizations and each of these processes has financial, personnel, legal and security aspects.

This results in a book, in which IT management is placed amongst other disciplines within an organization. The book discusses most methods and standards in the field of IT management, such as the Microsoft Operations Framework (MOF) method, the eTOM standard in the telecommunications industry and the new Data centre mark-up language (DCML).

I would like to thank all that contributed to the theories as mentioned in this book. My special thanks go to Remko van der Pols. In the late eighties it was already a joy to teach him the subject IT management. It is an even greater joy to see how he and his group at Getronics elaborate on this subject.

Theo Thiadens,
Doorn, April 2005

Introduction

The field

IT management is the control of IT facilities within an organization. This control is exercised on various levels, by various parties concerned. It results in the support of the processes in the organization by IT complying with the functional and performance requirements as stated. These requirements are called for by the party paying for the use of the IT facility. This party can be the owner of an IT object, like the owner of a tailor made application; it could be someone that owns the right for using an IT object, like a license holder for the use of Microsoft Office and it could be the manager that hires an IT service for his organization from a third party.

Importance of the field

IT management has become important to organizations. With the change from the industrial to the network economy, many organizations are aware that being able to obtain and use information quickly has many advantages. These advantages could be gained from being able to work more cheaply, producing new services and products faster, arriving at better control of the organization or in simply being able to work more effectively. Better use of information usually demands the use of IT facilities. It also often results in higher demands on the facilities already in place.

Limits of the field

IT management includes tasks in the fields of exploitation, developing and maintenance of IT facilities. It can be split into facilities in the field of the infrastructure, the applications and the organization. This book discusses the tasks that have to be carried out for IT facilities that are procured from a third party or the ones that are already in production. It speaks about the activities necessary for ongoing development and exploitation of IT facilities. The book deals so with all subjects related to the field of IT service management or management of IT facilities. It also means that the book does not go into building of entirely new IT facilities for the organization or supply chain, in which there is yet no trace of an infrastructure, an application or organization.

Characteristics of the tasks

The tasks to be performed for the control of IT facilities within an organization have an operational, as well as a tactical and a strategic characteristic. The allocation of these tasks to organization units may differ, depending on

- the size of the organization;
- the history of the organization with regard to the IT support of company processes;
- the importance of this support;
- the choices made and to be made regarding the technical and informatics infrastructure and those in the field of application management.

Purpose of the book

The purpose of this book is to provide a systematic discussion of all aspects one has to deal with in IT management and therefore to offer assistance for controlling the tasks to be carried out for supplying IT facilities. To this purpose, the book is divided in five parts. Each part consists of one or more chapters. Below we will briefly discuss the contents of the different parts.

IT management: the basis

The first part of the book deals with the basis of the field. Chapter 1 defines and demarcates the concept IT management as well as the starting points the book uses for looking at IT management. Next, the importance of the field to the various stakeholders is discussed. Carr (2003) may state that 'IT does not matter' and discard the care for IT as being no more than the care for an essential service, Ross (2002) states that decisions about IT cannot always be taken by IT-people. The interested parties in these decisions are found both within as well as outside the organization. Straub (2004) proceeds by stating that the activities of organizations operating in a network economy cannot exist without available, secure and up-to-date IT. Control of IT facilities is therefore a requirement. This control is subject to change triggered by various causes. This control is also provided from various angles.

Chapter 2 continues by giving the functional and performance requirements organizations demand from their IT facilities. The chapter clarifies that for the medium range; one can only meet these requirements providing one has a well throughout architecture for the facilities to be managed. Transparency and overview enable the controlled fitting and optimal utilizing of new technology. Lack of overview leads to ramshackle solutions, islands of computerization and a gap that is difficult to bridge between the IT support as requested by a demand-organization and the support as supplied by the supply-organizations.

IT management: processes

For the use of IT facilities organizations can set up their own IT departments. They can also employ external IT supply-organizations for this purpose. Tasks of functional management, application management and exploitation for objects of infrastructure and applications always have to be executed. Part 2 goes into the set-up of processes for executing these tasks. In Chapter 3 the possibilities are discussed for setting up these tasks in such a manner, that meeting of the customer's requirements is always at the centre stage. A more hierarchical set-up of tasks is compared to a more process-oriented approach. This results in a hybrid organizational form for supplying IT facilities: for one thing processes are set up, for another the tasks for front-office and back-office are more hierarchically structured.

Chapter 4 deals with the set-up of the demand-organization for IT facilities, in other words functional management. In Chapters 5 and 6 the organization of the supply-side, being application management and exploitation come up for discussion. When setting up the demand-organization the BiSL method is the starting point. At setting up application management, the ASL method is used.

As a basis for setting up exploitation the ITIL method is applied. The last chapter of Part 2, Chapter 7, indicates how in particular cases elements of BiSL, ASL and ITIL are combined for designing one's IT organization.

Organizing processes

Chapter 7 integrates the subject matter of Chapters 3 up to and including 6. From the angle of system approach and the set-up of processes this chapter aims to answer questions like:

- how do I organize my IT facilities in such a way that, using the same organization, I am able to realize a volume of service many times larger and at the same time a strong renewal of services?
- where do I locate IT organizations that are very labour intensive and where if these are very capital-intensive?

Control of IT processes

Part 3 goes into the control of IT facilities by the various stakeholders. Chapter 8 formulates six points of application for control of IT. These are: determining priorities, dealing with innovation of services, deciding on the IT organization, reflection on its working methods and the methods to be employed in this, taking care of the necessary knowledge and assurance of sufficient management and user support within the organisation. Each of these possibilities for control are discussed. Next, the chapter goes into the importance of this control and the information function needed for this control. In Chapter 9 attention is given to evaluation of the services and achieving improvements. The chapter's motto is 'house in order.' It starts with the necessity for reliable information as a basis for making evaluations. Next, it provides the various angles for an evaluation. The application of CobiT, CMMI, risk management and ISO 9001:2000 in IT organizations are shown. With the 'house in order,' it is possible to go flexibly into customers' and supply chain partners' wishes. Chapter 10 continues therefore, with the set-up of IT facilities for supplying new products and services. A step-by-step plan is introduced, in which building of these new services and products can take place.

Aspects

In the fourth part of the book various aspects of the field are discussed. The aspect finance is taken care of in Chapter 11, the aspect personnel in Chapter 12 and the aspect procurement in Chapter 13. These chapters go into, amongst other things, the groundwork to control IT costs; the competencies as needed in an IT organization and at procuring IT facilities the Information Systems Procurement Library (ISPL) method.

The last two aspects up for discussion are contract management and security of services. At contract management the concluding and safeguarding of service level agreements are gone into, whilst the chapter on security discusses the ISO 17799 standard.

The part ends with a chapter on standardization of context data, products and processes. It will be clear that at expanding services, a certain degree of standardization is advisable for enabling a service provider to live up to the expectations, with regard to the required availability and flexibility.

The future

The last chapter of the book discusses IT management in 2027. Many of the patterns that can already be recognized will by then be realized. Using experiences in other sectors, such as the sector for physical transport of people and goods, the telecommunications sector and the energy sector, parallels are drawn with the IT sector. These are used for predicting the development of the IT management field.

Manage *IT*! Organizing *IT* Supply and *IT* Demand

In the network economy almost every organization depends on perfect *IT* facilities. Every organization is forced to reflect on its *IT* demand. Realizing the organization of supply and demand is the subject of this book.

The book consists of five parts. These are *the basis, traditional IT management, controlling IT facilities, aspects of IT management and IT management in future.*

In the first part, *IT* management tasks and the objects involved are discussed. The execution of these tasks has to meet with functional and performance demands. These requirements are more easily met when an organization has a transparent *IT* architecture at its disposal.

The second part outlines traditional *IT* management. The starting point is a process-oriented functioning of the *IT* organization. This goes for both the *IT* demand organization as well as the *IT* supply organization. In this part, methods like *BISL*, *ASL*, *ITIL*, *MOF*, *MSF*, *TMN* and *eTOM* are discussed.

The third part deals with controlling *IT*. The aim of this control is diverse. Control is different when striving for efficiency and complying with accountant's requirements, compared to the control as used when *IT* is a means to comply with customer's and/or chain partners' wishes. In the latter case, innovation of *IT* processes is an issue.

Part four tackles aspects of *IT* management. Amongst other things, the financial, personnel, purchasing, legal and security aspect in *IT* are discussed. Besides this, entering service agreements and achieving standardization are gone into. The book ends with a look into the future. The effects of striving for "utility computing" and better control of *IT* by means of "*IT* portfolio management" are explained.

The book is supported by the website www.ict-management.com. On this site every chapter can be found in the form of a presentation. Lecturers using the book have access to suggestions with solutions for all of the 17 smaller and 8 larger cases, as included in this book.

Curriculum author

 Theo Thiadens teaches information management and *IT* (service) management at, amongst other places, the universities of Amsterdam, Tilburg and Groningen, the Open University, the Erasmus University, the Avans University and the University of Twente.

Theo Thiadens worked for the Royal Dutch Navy, Foxboro, IBM, and the ministry of the Interior and Kingdom relations, the Land register, the IB Group and the police force. In these organizations he held functions at all levels in an *IT* organization. He was director *IT* at the IB Group and director Governance at the Dutch Land register.

Part 1

IT management: The basis

What is IT management?
What is managed?
Why is IT management important?
Who should manage and why?
Views on ICT management.
The field of IT management and external
  · influences

Chapter 1

The basis of the field

Our bank is in actual fact an information factory. Without the use of IT, our services would come to a dead halt. This really goes for all our services but in particular for Direct Banking. It is therefore not surprising that the status of our three most import product innovations and the status of the exploitation of IT are high on our weekly management agenda.

We started by realizing the importance of IT being 100% available. Next, we set up our IT organization process-focused, using the methods available to us. The following step was to determine the IT priorities and to control the IT organization accordingly. That was a success and this transparency actually led to more. We asked ourselves whether we shouldn't organize service level management, the service desk and the back office separately. Labour intensive tasks should either be computerized or moved to low-wage countries, capital-intensives ones could be undertaken in Canada for example.

'Consolidation, sourcing, standardization and competence centres' are the buzzwords of today. It all really boils down to us cleaning up the mess we created over the last thirty years. Once this is done, we can start all over again with a transparent architecture and supply the services of tomorrow. Making use of an architecture for supplying these services, it becomes clear these evolve easily in line with the requirements of the company.

3

IT management

IT management is all about controlling IT supply. Organizations like banks, insurance companies, travel agents or social services would grind to a halt if the IT facilities that support their operational processes weren't operational. These IT facilities are supplied by an IT organization. In the structure of this IT organization front-office and back-office processes can be recognized. The front-office is equipped to deal with customer queries every hour of the day or night. The back-office focuses more on systematically to be executed tasks. Customer queries are considered to trigger a chain of processes within an organization. These processes can be carried out in one single organization. It is also possible to split these up and have them executed at the best possible location. This way, an IT organization structure emerges, aimed at developing in pace with the customer's wishes. This IT organization provides a practically 100% available standard workstation, has clearly structured IT facilities for storage and processing, carries out certain activities from competence centres and rationally determines which tasks are carried out by the organization itself and which services and products it will purchase from others.

Content of this chapter

IT management 2004 is the subject of this book. In this chapter we will examine the tasks as carried out in the field of IT management and the subjects it deals with. The field is defined and it becomes clear where management of information function ends and where IT management starts. The basic principles of the field are formulated and its importance explained.

Within the network economy, available, secure and up-to-date IT facilities are of great importance. This economy is based upon transporting data in digital form. In order to make this a simple process, it makes use of standards to a high degree and is able to supply strongly personalized information services at any time, anywhere and to everybody. Organizations' products and services often cannot exist without IT. Decisions to do with IT are therefore more than just decisions about management of the IT department. General and business management control this department's services. They determine the demand; an IT department offers the required services. Amongst other things, points of control by general and business management are setting of priorities and organization of services. So the application of IT within an organization increases and development takes place.

The chapter ends by giving an overview of the field and the external influences on the domain. Over the years one sees how the discipline IT management comes into existence. Within this discipline service and optimum price/performance relations are increasingly becoming determining factors as application of IT is a must. 'IT does not matter,' it must be there, as Nick Carr says for good reason (Carr, 2003).

WHAT IS IT MANAGEMENT ALL ABOUT?

Tasks and objects

IT management is the controlling of IT facilities within an organization. This control takes place at operational, tactical and strategic level and by all parties involved. These parties are in general a combination of the management of an organization, the management of the business functions and IT management. The purpose of this control is to achieve an application of IT facilities complying with the demanded functional and performance requirements.

At controlling IT facilities two questions are asked. The first question concerns what this control actually entails. The second question concerns the objects that are controlled. Control is exercised on the development and maintenance of applications and infrastructures and their exploitation. Control concerns objects of infrastructures, their applications and organization (see Figure 1.1). Infrastructure objects can be divided into objects of the technical infrastructure and of the informatics infrastructure. The technical infrastructure comprises of hardware and software for storing data, processing data, transporting data and input and output of data. The informatics infrastructure includes the tools for developing and maintaining applications and tools for supporting the IT (service) management tasks. This can be software for calculating costs, security software, tuning software, service desk tools and so on and so forth.

The application objects can be divided into objects for applications that support business processes, applications like spreadsheets and word processing that support individual work and intranet and extranet applications (Applegate and others, 2003).

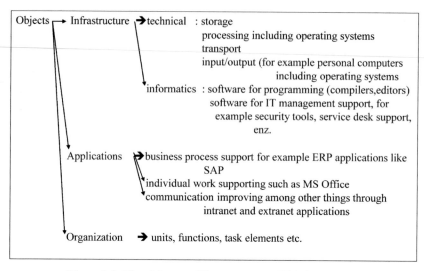

Figure 1.1. The objects at IT management (Thiadens, 2001)

Through this breakdown in objects, the IT manager is capable of distinguishing organization objects, infrastructure objects and application objects. This distinction is important. In principle, one likes to be able to change applications without having to allow for the different versions of objects present in the technical and informatics infrastructure. Even more so, if changing these versions, it should not have any effect on the functionality of an application.

Example

An organization is in the middle of changing from a client-server version of a CRM-package to a browser-based version. The client server version requires the presence of certain releases of the supporting database management software and operating systems. The browser version requires different releases of both the data base management system as well as the operating system. In that case, upgrading the CRM-package is no isolated matter. This leads at the same time to upgrading the software for the technical and informatics infrastructure. The last upgrade may have impact on other applications using the same server. If application and infrastructure do not function independently this creates extra work for the IT organization.

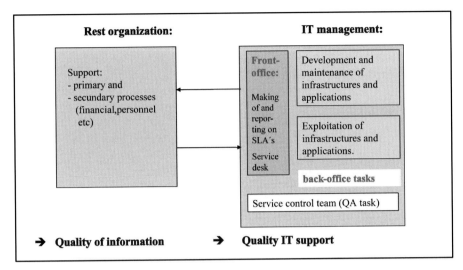

Figure 1.2. The IT management domain

Definition of the domain

IT management concerns management of IT facilities. These are supplied by an organization offering IT services. The organization units demanding services of this IT organization, bear the responsibility for the quality of the information that is processed, transported and reproduced using these IT facilities. This information is necessary in their primary processes. Those requiring IT services use the provided IT facilities in performing their business tasks.

They enter the 'content.' The IT organization supplies up-to-date infrastructures and applications. The general and business management of the organization is responsible for the data being up-to-date and reliable and providing sufficient organizational and physical security measures. Availability and response of support provided by IT infrastructures and applications as well as taking logical security measures (like providing passwords, back-up recovery of data collections, security, encryption and so on) is the responsibility of the IT organization.

In this book IT management concerns the controlling of IT facilities being in production and their adjustments or extensions. IT management starts when the first version of an IT facility becomes operational.

Starting points

In this book, the following three starting points are employed when looking at managing IT facilities:

1. IT products and services attune to the organization's strategy. IT services have to comply with certain requirements with regard to functionality and performance. The IT organization supplies these services and therefore has an IT products and services architecture.
2. The controlling of IT facilities is based on logistics and operations management principles. There are distinguished control targets and based upon these targets processes are set-up. These processes are measured and in this way adjustment takes place. In order to control using the right information, the administrative organization of an IT department has to be in order.
3. At supplying IT services and products one distinguishes between customers and providers. Providers may procure products and services from others and this can lead to an entire chain of service providers, reflection on more concentration or centralization of tasks and recognition of roles and functions in the field of IT management.

THE IMPORTANCE OF IT MANAGEMENT

The service environment

The environment in which IT services are supplied changes. In the industrial economy, IT services were never the focal point in an organization. Organizations then extended their production capacity by investing in new factories or new means of transport. Every time one wanted to sell more or somewhere else, the sales organization was extended or a new sales organization set up. IT was proprietary and the own IT organization tailor-made solutions. In the network economy this is different. When extending the production capacity in the network economy, one looks at the possibility of cooperating with partners. Expansion of sales possibilities is realized by making use of non-proprietary

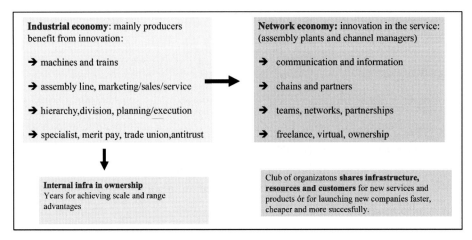

Figure 1.3. Differences between working within the industrial economy and the network economy

technology. In Figure 1.3 the differences between working within the industrial and the network economy are shown.

Today, many organizations are in a transitional phase; from being organizations working predominantly along the lines of the industrial economy they are turning into organizations using the principles of the network economy. Drivers for changing to the network economy are:

- increasing information digitalisation. Data in digital form flows through the organization;
- use of standards for places of work and networks simplifies development alongside products and services;
- an increasing pressure on costs and profit margins of organizations leading to different ways of organizing and shorter elapsed time at supplying services and products;
- the development of increasingly more 'intelligent' products and services like the Personal Digital Assistant, that uses the Global Positioning System for drawing someone's attention to something;
- the arrival on the market of products adjusted to the customer. An example of this is equipment with built-in microprocessors for carrying out preventive maintenance enabling advise to the customer on how to use his installation optimally.

Decision on IT:	Role demand-organization	Why?
How much budget? **What do we spend it on?** **What skill and organization do I need?**	determine role IT with regard to strategy and matching budget indicate clearly what is done and what not. determine what is done centrally and what in the business units.	no **platform** to support strategy but high expenses IT unit lacks **focus** and does not get projects introduced. excessive standardization costs **flexibility**, too much exception increases $ and limits synergy
How good do the IT services have to be? **What security and privacy risks are acceptable?** **Who do we blame when an IT project fails?**	determine **service levels** (example: higher availability) based on price performance lead the discussion about assessment **security/privacy** compared to convenience business executive project leader measure result in business terms.	paying for options that are not worth the money. too much emphasis on security results in inconvenience and too little results in vulnerability data. otherwise you never realize the **business value** of IT.

Figure 1.4. Questions IT management should not decide (Ross, 2004)

In this economy IT management is important. Availability, security and keeping IT facilities up-to-date are a must. Aiming for quickly dealing with incidents and problems is necessary. Decisions about IT facilities are not just left to the supplying organization anymore. The customers, general and business management, demand to play their part. They want to determine the IT strategy and demand a say in the execution of this (see Figure 1.4).

Why a part for general and business management

Active controlling from the side of the customer is required for various reasons. In the longer run an optimal fit develops between what the organization wants and how the IT organization supports this. The IT organization knows focus and supplies products and services one can implement. IT-input means an optimal standardization, without the standards being unnecessarily restrictive or rendering the organization inflexible. In the short term in daily IT support active controlling by the customer insures the right level of service. Too little or too much effort in the area of security is out of the question. Finally, a close eye is kept on whether the planned advantages of the use of technology are indeed achieved. The business itself is responsible for this.

Points of application for controlling

There are six points of application with regard to controlling IT. The points are the innovation of product and service, determining the organization of IT service, decision on the in-house knowledge and skills and the knowledge and skills that are to be obtained from outside the company, reflection on the methods to be used at the application of IT and the creation of support for IT application at the side of customer and supplier.

The customers are to fill in the functional and performance requirements with regard to services to be supplied. They take care of functional management. Functional management specifies the demand, indicates the organization of services and at the customer-side one takes care of implementation of the facilities. Functional management at a strategic level determines the priorities, the innovations and the suppliers that are to be worked with. Functional management at a tactical level controls the execution. It determines the service level and adjusts it if necessary. Functional management at operational level takes care of the daily handholding, mans the service desk and takes care of testing and the implementation of changes in the administrative organization.

The supplier's side takes care of development and maintenance of IT facilities. This is called application management. It also takes care of the exploitation of IT facilities. Based upon the demand at strategic, tactical and operational level, these application management tasks and exploitation tasks are filled in. Suppliers and the technology are determined at a strategic level. At a tactical level the daily exploitation and the daily application management are controlled. In addition the change tasks are controlled.

In following chapters the processes in functional management, application management and exploitation will be further specified. The recognition of these three tasks is known as **the triple management model** for managing IT facilities.

Shifts in the IT management-field

Over the years, the field IT management has changed. Figure 1.5 shows these changes. In the eighties, Van Schaick (1985) and Looijen (1998) recognized the tasks in this field. The triple management model was recognized and it became clear that IT management includes tasks at different levels. In the nineties,

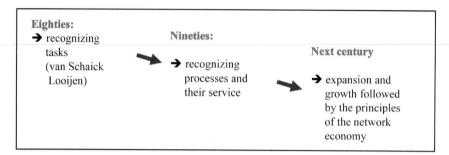

Figure 1.5. Shifts in emphasis during the years in IT management

these tasks were converted into in processes to be designed and services to be supplied. The IT organization was equipped with front-offices and back-offices. The customers of the IT facilities negotiated service level agreements with the suppliers. The agreements were a basis for achieving an improvement of the services quality. In the twenty-first century we see the use of IT growing enormously. The guarantee for optimal services by IT organizations requires for them to think about their working methods. Innovation of their services leads to:

1. IT organizations replacing physical processes by other means of data transmission. Users are informed by means of a broadcast, instead of being called personally. Automatic download of versions means that in situ installing is no longer necessary, and so on and so forth;

2. installed products and services informing the IT organization. This means it is possible to proactively replace parts, keep abreast of the customers' use of these, advise them about these and to reckon with the gained experiences within the purchasing policy;

3. use of standards in the IT management field. Whilst the nineties showed the advent of methods, it was recently announced that also in the exchange of communication in the area of IT management standards are formulated. *EDS* and partners issue so the Data Center Mark-up Language (www.dcml.com);

4. IT organizations considering to detach front-office and back office processes. In this the relative advantages are weighed up against each other. One poses questions like:
   – is this a labour-intensive or a capital-intensive task?
   – what is the optimal location for every type of task?
   – what is the optimal size of an organization for a specific task etc.

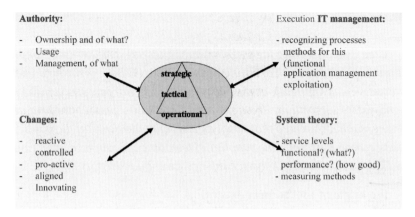

Figure 1.6. Views on IT management

VIEWS ON IT MANAGEMENT AND THE EXTERNAL INFLUENCES INVOLVED

The field IT management

IT management can be approached from a number of different angles. Some four angles are distinguished here because that way the various methods and models of this field can be positioned. These angles are (see also Figure 1.6):

(a) **the angle of authority.** This concerns the authority of those involved. A distinction is made between:
   – owners of the objects or those owning the right to use the objects;
   – users of the objects;
   – managers of or service providers for the objects or possibly of
   – derived *interested parties* like organizations acting on behalf of the owners towards users and management organizations and the advisors that advise all or some players about the measures to be taken.

   In this view on IT management, the question is asked who determines what should be done with regard to IT management, where it will be done, how it is done and when it is done.

Example

Clearly recognizing the stakeholders is, amongst other things, important when thinking about the risk of wrong investment in IT. Both in the field of infrastructures as well as applications this plays a part. An IT organization in the public order and safety sector that, amongst others, works for police, fire brigade and ambulance, soon discovered that when extending the network in the public order and safety sector, especially the supplier of telecommunications connections and not the IT organization, that service the network, increased its takings.

(b) **the angle of methodical execution.** Methods indicate which processes are set up and how these processes cohere. IT management methods are partly formulated on the basis of knowledge and partly based on 'best practices.' They concentrate mostly on indicating the demand and on organizing and controlling of the supply.

This book discusses three methods more extensively:

–ITIL (IT Infrastructure Library) for the exploitation of IT;
–BiSL (Business Information Systems Management Library) for functional management;
–ASL (Application Services Library) for application management.

ITIL is an often-applied best practice method. BiSL and ASL are methods developed by the Getronics company that have been made available to everyone. Most applications of these methods can be found in the Netherlands and at a relatively limited scale.

The reason for choosing these methods is the fact these provide a further elaboration of Looijen's often-applied triple management model (1999). The tasks this model recognizes are executed in processes that are indicated in the ITIL, BiSL and ASL methods. For setting up exploitation environments ITIL is the most widely used method. BiSL and ASL are attuned to ITIL.

(c) **the angle of change in the objects to be managed and in the quality of work.**

During IT management, changes may occur in: the type of object, the quality of an object and the quality in which the processes are carried out. This book discusses two models in this field in more detail. One is the Nolan model that examines the controlling of implementation of facilities. The second model is an application of the EFQM model that makes it possible to identify at which levels one executes an IT services process.

The Nolan model distinguishes between a phase in which a technology is discovered, a phase in which it is tried out, a phase in which indicators are composed in order to arrive at a more factory made management and a phase in which the objects are managed routinely. Recognizing these phases leads to insight in the risks that one runs at implementing a service. Often it is wise to first try out an innovation in services on a small scale. A service that one has a lot of experience with, can on the other hand, be rolled-out more routinely and according to plan.

An application in IT management of the European Foundation of Quality Management (EFQM) distinguishes a number of levels on which IT management can be carried out. This application discerns a level of reactive working; a level of being able to perform tasks repetitively; a more proactive IT management; an IT management directly attuned to the customers' priorities; and an itself constantly renewing IT management. The application of EFQM indicates the demands for working at a certain level. It prescribes amongst other things what service processes have to be set up, the organization and procedures involved, staff skills, their training and the available documentation (Giesberts (2002), see Appendix F).

(d) **that of system's theory.** At the system angle the 'demarcation of services' plays the dominant role. One distinguishes a demarcated entirety of products and services that have an interface with other services and products. Making clear demarcations in the management of IT facilities is important at, for instance:

   – The start of new infrastructures and applications. These can work entirely separately from existing ones. This may also involve interfaces with other facilities or entirely integrating a new service within the existing IT infrastructure, the existing IT organization or the existing applications.
   – Making IT facilities available. The IT facilities may be provided as a service, whereby every service has an obvious customer. The

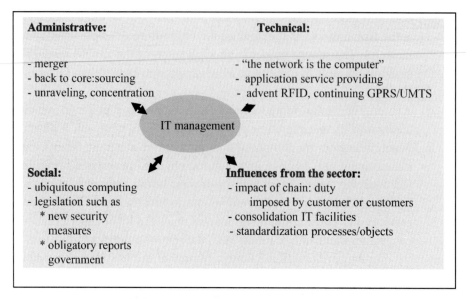

Figure 1.7. Impact of external developments

organization itself can supply this services but this can also be sourced elsewhere. In both cases the functional and performance requirements to the service have to be clear.

External influences

Changes in IT management are actuated by a number of factors. In Figure 1.7 the four major motives for change are indicated.

The motives for changing are:

(a) **the administrative developments in and around an organization**. Mergers or sales of company divisions may result in having to cope with the management of other objects or less objects. This may lead to a change in the way IT is control-led in the organization. One may decide to concentrate computing centres and control more centrally, one may subdivide these and concentrate front-offices etc. One may also decide to outsource tasks.

Example

Because of the merging of different police organizations in the Nether-
lands into one single region in 1994, many regions disposed of different
applications for supporting the normal police tasks. This complicated the gen-
erating of management information at regional level. It led to extra costs for
training people for the IT organization. A development was started for achieving
standardization of applications to be used, at first at regional, later at national
level.

(b) **developments in technology.** The introduction of new possibilities in
the area of infrastructures and applications often leads to the need for
managing new applications and/or multi vendor IT architectures. At the
moment these include the rise of Radio Frequency Identification (RFID)
and the exploitation of the possibilities of new mobile technologies like
GPRS (General Packet Radio Service) and UMTS (Universal Mobile
Telecommunications System).

Example

In the nineties many organizations proceeded to implement the CRM
application of manufacturer Siebel. This application in those years assumed a
client server architecture. Because of the arrival of internet technology, the cur-
rent release of the same application is based on calling for functionality in the
workplace by means of a browser. Implementation of the new release provides
possibilities for a more centrally and concentrated management of the applica-
tion. This leads to reflection on the IT organization.

(c) **the social developments**. Legislations fix demands. With digital data
processsing being available everywhere these demands change. The
customers demand change. The government also asks different things.
Organizations are for example told to make sure products can be
identified or, within the framework of a better financial account, to have
their own processes in order. That way, new legislation leads to new
versions of applications.

Social developments are at this rate of significant influence on the services of organizations. The rise of the 24-hour economy for example leads to a different way of looking at the availability of IT facilities. Banks having internet services is considered normal. Internet services furthermore must be open 24 hours a day. Operation of these services leads to checking 24 hours a day whether the infrastructure and the application are functioning.

Example

Charles Schwab, an advisor for asset formation in the USA, started in 1996 as well as a possibility for seeking asset advice through a network of offices, also a separate sales channel for providing advice on the internet. Until 2001 customers got different services if they worked through the internet. In order to get the same services as an office customer, people had to pay extra. This organizational layout was chosen, in order to prevent the cheaper way of working on the internet from cannibalising the sales through the network of offices.

At the start of 2001 this set-up led to many customer complaints and it is decided to offer internet and office customers the same services and rates. The decision to offer full Internet trading at a low price leads to heavy demands on the IT facilities. Charles Schwab finds his computers have to deal with around 4000 transactions per second. His large IBM mainframes appear to be close to overload and Charles Schwab is forced to spend 20% of his annual turnover on IT development, maintenance and exploitation.

The trade on the Internet also appears to have more highs than the normal online trade and therefore more sensitive to failure and possibly insufficient capacity. One should build in more security provisions as well as dedicating more capacity to transport, processing and archive capacity than was calculated for the old models. Instead of having a capacity of three times the average daily trading volume, one should aim for a capacity of a size of three times the average trading volume per hour.

Furthermore, an availability of 99.2% of IT facilities is insufficient. The effects of down time are greater and bad publicity in the press and the media takes care of the rest. Charles Schwab is forced to lower the performance requirements to non-planned and non-availability of his services from 0.8% diminishing to hardly 0.02%. This process took two years (Applegate et al., 2003).

(d) **the pressure for going along with the developments in the sector, in which one operates.** If the primary process of an organization is processing information and the product is information, innovations in IT will often enable other services.

Example

Looking at a number of techniques that appeared over the last five years, one might ascertain the technologies that became available over the last five years, encouraged many organizations to set up e-commerce services and a front-office supported by a call centre. The Land register has opened the possibility for both the professional as well as the private customer to obtain online information until 10.00 at night. It won't be long before this government window will be open 24 hours a day.

The dynamics in the field of IT management are in the network economy larger than in the industrial economy. In the industrial economy progress in production and transport technology is the basis for being able to compete in a market. In the network economy one applies the possibilities, that digital technology offers an organization.

The evolution in IT management

In about thirty years the field IT management developed. At the start of the eighties Van Schaick (1985) described the outlines of the field and distinguished between operational, tactical and strategic tasks on the supply-side. Working for IBM, he aimed at structurally designing the computing centre organization. Looijen (2000) indicated in 1988, that the tasks to be performed for IT management were different in nature (Figure 1.8). There are not just tasks on the side of the supplier but also on the side of the demand. He introduced the triple model that distinguishes functional management, application management and technical management. In this book technical management is referred to as exploitation. In practice organizations namely speak of the exploitation of IT facilities. The triple model because of its simplicity makes organizations aware how responsibilities for the various tasks are determined.

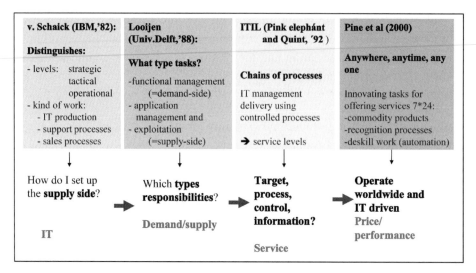

Figure 1.8. From art to professional service

The interpretation of the triple model was then done mainly by businesses. These applied methods like ITIL and recorded their daily practice using methods like ASL and BiSL. This meant the entry of process approach in the field of IT management. Goals of processes are formulated, the process is set up, control information is determined and agreements about the process are recorded in service agreements. From now on, one speaks of IT services and professional supply of IT facilities. In this industry that supplies IT services, businesslike considerations will catch on increasingly. The network economy, where every object is available everywhere and at any time, will also have its impact on this field. In worldwide operating organizations that have been set up process like, businesslike answers will be given to demands for the optimal location of a process and the optimum size of IT organizations.

DEFINITION OF THE BASIC CONCEPTS AS USED IN THIS BOOK

Now that we have charted the subject IT management, we can define the basis concepts of the subject in more detail. These basic concepts are:

- Organization (Bosman 1996): a system of production factors, including people and procedures, that collectively pursues the achieving of one or more goals.
- *Data*: a formalized representation of 'something.'
- *Information*: data that enhances the knowledge of the recipient of this data (Shannon, 1948).
- *Information management*: making sure organizations have the data available they need to be able to execute processes. This data has to be present conform requirements stated in advance. These requirements are called functional and performance requirements.
- *Infrastructure*: the unit of technical and informatics facilities required for supplying the demanded information maintenance.
- *Applications:* (in the restricted or 'management' sense because in a broader sense this could also include parts of the infrastructure, see Looijen (2000)) the programmes and procedures operating within an infrastructure.
- *Decide or conclude*: indicating what tasks have to be carried out and in what manner, starting from a given responsibility, current insights and experiences from the past.
- *Control:* indicate in what manner a task has to be carried out and checking up on this. This realizes the Deming cycle: plan, do, act and check.

QUESTIONS

1. What is IT management about? What tasks have to be carried out and what types of objects are involved in this? How do we demarcate the field? Why?
2. What are the objects of the technical infrastructure? What are those of the informatics infrastructure? And what are those of the organization? Illustrate your answer with three examples.
3. Why is the transition to the network economy crucial when we speak of the field IT management? Why are the demands made by the network economy different from the ones the industrial economy makes? From what is this evident for example? Illustrate your answer with three examples.
4. What are the drivers for organizations to change from an organization that operates as usual in the industrial economy, to an organization operating

using the possibilities of the network economy? What is the impact on the subject IT management?

5. Why do general and business management have to control the efforts of an organization in the field of IT? What happens if one does not do this? Illustrate your answer with three examples.

6. What are the pretexts for control by the management? And how is this translated into the triple model of management?

7. In the field IT management the emphasis changed over the years. What were the emphases of the eighties and nineties? What are the accents these days? And what does this extension and increase mean to the IT organization? Illustrate your answer with four examples.

8. What perspectives exist in the field IT management? Illustrate every perspective with an example.

9. What external influences change the field of IT management and why? Illustrate your answer with three examples.

10. How did that IT organization change into a professional organization, that can be judged on the price/performance relation of its services?

What do IT services include?
Functional and performance requirements at
    different levels
Functional requirements from various
    perspectives
Performance requirements, such as ISO 9126
An IT architecture along the lines of the
    standard IEE1471
Realizing the IT architecture
Testing the IT architecture

Chapter 2

Supplying IT products and services within an architecture

Functional and performance requirements can be made at different levels in an organization. Functional requirements are often made because we cannot process large quantities manually if we want to achieve certain elapsed times or because we are never able to get information that quickly. This is one of the reasons why we invest in IT support. This requires choosing infrastructures and applications. That is how we came to work with personal productivity tools. That is how our business processes happen to be supported by SAP these days and also how we got an internet channel. We demand our IT to be adaptable, we need it 24 hours a day/7 days a week and the costs have to be calculable.

There were gaps between our expectations as a customer, the picture the supplier had of the agreements and the way in which he and his employees outlined the entered agreements. The latter thought: 'Oh well, these service agreements, they are all the same and there is no reason for us to divert from our normal services.' The supplier's management never checked up on the compliance and we seldom looked at the monthly reports. All that was changed, as soon as our sales and purchases became truly dependent on e-business. We had to be really available 24 hours a day/7 days a week, we checked the reports and arranged regular contact with the supplier. Within a year, we filled in all the gaps.

Control, processes in order and architecture: according to Gartner those are the ingredients when optimally supplying IT services. That prevents an organization from wanting to do e-business and discovering the ERP application does not really allow this and one has to apply a separate e-business application with an interface to the ERP system. An architecture indicates how to get from the old situation, via a transitional stage to the new situation.

Contents of this chapter

In this chapter we specify that in order to be able to comply quickly with changes in functional and performance requirements with regard to IT support, organizations have to have an architecture for their IT facilities. This architecture consists of agreements with regard to IT objects and the recipes used for applying IT. These recipes may concern application of methods, they can be models for plans, they may be instructions for administrative organization etc. By having an architecture it becomes possible to react quickly to new demands. One fits in with choices that have been already made or notices immediately where new choices are needed.

The chapter starts with a service lemniscate. This lemniscate indicates that the customer and his supplier first determine the need for IT services and set up agreements about this. Thereupon, the supplier realizes these agreements. The first process is called service level management. The second service process management. The IT services to be delivered consist of the service and/or the product, 'the service pit'; the accompanying services are called the 'service shell.' The latter may include for example the service desk staff. Both product and service have to comply with functional and performance requirements, in order to reduce the gaps between what the customer expects and what he gets, to an absolute minimum. Functional requirements are about 'the what.' Performance requirements are about 'how well' and are always expressed in quantities. In general one can find clues for the performance requirements in the ISO standard 9126.

The demands on IT services can be recorded at various levels. This may be at the same level as all IT facilities of an organization, it may also be at the same level as a part of an organization, it may also concern an individually supported process. In all cases, it is convenient if the demand organization controls the supply organization and has a clear view of the recipes it uses. This supply organization becomes really transparent if it can indicate within which architecture it supplies the required services. The second part of this chapter deals with this architecture in IT management. What is this architecture, how can it be realized and how is the architecture concept tested.

WHAT REQUIREMENTS DO IT–SERVICES AND PRODUCTS HAVE TO MEET?

Requirements concerning IT products, services and processes

Looking from the point of view of the demand organization we see the supply organization supplying IT services and products. These may be supplied by an internal supply organization but also by one or more external providers. Together with the supply organization the demand organization determines what IT services and products are to be supplied. This process is called service level management. After determination, the services are supplied. This process is known as service process management. Agreements with the demand organization concern the product or IT service to be supplied and the services that support the product and/or the IT service (see Figure 2.1).

The first, 'the service pit', is the product or the IT service. This is the facility that supports the business process of the organization. This may be an e-business service for enabling customers to order on line, it could be the support of the financial administration with an ERP-package, it could be the supplying of monthly pay-slips. This IT product has a functionality and complies with a number of performance requirements, such as 'the ERP application is 99.99% available during the planned hours, the application can support at least 50 workstations with an average response of less than 1 second measured at the workstation in 99% of all cases, and so on.' 'Service shell' is the term used for services that support the IT product or the IT service. This may be a 24-hour service desk, it can be the agreement to solve incidents within 24 hours, it could be the guarantee for a certain degree of data assurance etc.

Ruijs et al. (2003) once gave an example of this, looking through the eyes of a demand organization at functional and performance requirements for an email service. Figure 2.2 shows the application of the service pit and shell concept for this service.

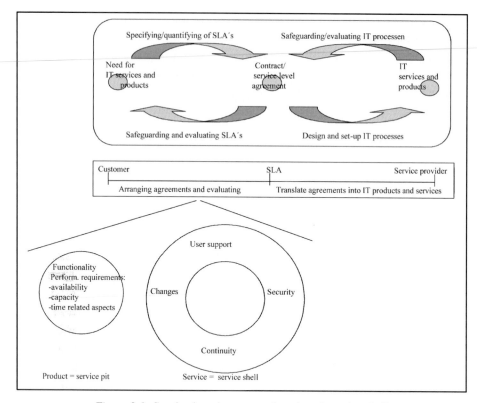

Figure 2.1. Service lemniscate: service pit and service shell

Functional requirements

Functional requirements to IT facilities are supplied at chain level, organization level, department level or otherwise. These concern what a service or product should do. Functional requirements can be made from different angles. These angles may be:

–the *user*: his requirements are made on the basis of the service and/or the products needed to support his operating process;
–the *chain coordinator, the general management of an organization or the business management of a department* determines the value of an IT product or service for his organization or part of his organization. Based on this the investments and the budgets for the product and/or the service are freed;

E-mail:	Functional requirements:	Performance requirements: Availability:	Time aspects:	Capacity:
MS-Outlook	-diary and mail	- 7x 24 hours - max. 2x a month interruption of max. 2 hours	- e-mails have to be sent within 2 seconds	- maximaal 2000 e-mails per dag
Users support	- just technical problems	- on working days from 07.00-18.00 hrs	- problems have to be solved within 2 hours	- per week average 5 contacts per day
Changes:	n.a.	-reporting changes on working days from 08.00-17.00 hrs.	-within 2 days after submitting request	- max. 5 small changes each time
Security:	- against all known virusses - encryption of data traffic	- 7x 24 hours	- n.a.	- n.a.
Disasters:	- just e-mail no diary	- within 24 hours after occurance disaster	- e mails sent in 2 minutes	- minimum of 500 e mails p day

Figure 2.2. An application of the service pit/service shell concept (Ruys et al., 2003)

–the ICT *service manager*: the product and/or the service must be usable day in, day out and adaptable to changing circumstances. For this purpose functionality has to be built in, so information needed for enabling control of the ICT service, ICT product and ICT service processes is generated.

–the *one who realizes the product or the service*. He wants insight in the construction of the service and the importance of the various functions to those, that decide on the functions being in place or not. This information influences his consideration when setting priorities at delivery and the inclusion of possibilities for degradation of certain functions.

Performance requirements

Performance requirements indicate what qualities a delivered product or service should have. Performance requirements are always expressed in numbers. One may speak of the quality of a unit of IT facilities or also of a single IT facility. Boeters et al. (1997) indicated that the ISO 9126 standard supplemented with the findings of the Quint 2-report, offers a starting point for formulating these requirements. Boeters et al. distinguishes between requirements with regard to (see Figure 2.3):

	Effectiveness	Reliability	Serviceability	Efficiency	Maintaine-ability	Portability
ISO 9126	Suitability Accuracy Connective Compliance Securable	Oper.reliab. Fault tolerance Repairability	Understandable Learnable Operable	Time req. Resource require-ments	Analysable Changeable Stability Testable	Adjustable Installability Conformity Replaceable
Quint 2	Traceable	Available Degradable	Installable Equipment level		Controllable Reusable	

Figure 2.3. Performance requirements to IT facilities (Boeters, 1997)

- −*effectiveness* of a product or service. Below they indicate for instance that a product has to fit in with the whole of IT facilities, that is, can be linked to existing facilities etc.;
- −*reliability* of a product or service. This includes properties like the operational safety of the facility, the fault tolerance, the degradability and the availability;
- −*practicability*: this means, amongst other things, the product is easy to operate, the training for use can be accomplished quickly and efficiently and there is a clear equipment level;
- −*efficiency*: the time needed for processing and the amount of means that are used;
- −*maintainability*: this includes the swiftness with which one is able to trace faults in the IT facilities; the testability of the facility and it's reusability;
- −*portability*: this is about, amongst other things, the installability of the facility in other infrastructures, the replaceability in the current facility and the way the facility fits in with the architecture of the IT facilities as a whole.

These performance requirements for IT facilities fit in with the demands generally made to services. Slack (2004) states that performance requirements with regard to services include aspects of quality, flexibility, delivery rate, delivery assurance and costs. IT performance requirements conforming to ISO 9126 are no different from the demands as made generally to products and services in an organization. These general requirements are shown in Figure 2.4.

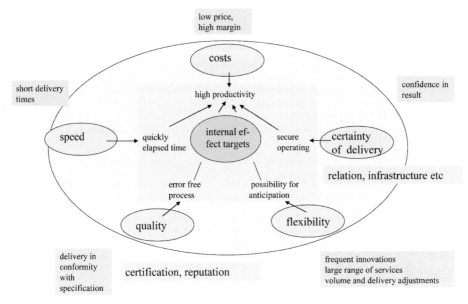

Figure 2.4. Performance requirements as given by the general theory of operations management in the service industry (Slack, 2004)

In IT management performance requirements are strongly determined by the number of platforms in volume and diversity that have to be managed and the matching services, such as a 24 hours a day/7 days a week staffed service, increased requirements with regard to availability, security and recovery time and the method for introducing improvements.

Gaps in the services

By specifying functional and performance requirements to IT products, IT services and the services supplied with these, the demand organization tries to indicate the desired services. This way, they try to prevent differences in expected and supplied performances. These differences or gaps may result from Ruijs et al., 2000 (Figure 2.5):

1. the fact the customer has different expectations from a product and/or service than the supplier;
2. the fact the sold service and/or the product is a different one than the service that was developed and implemented;

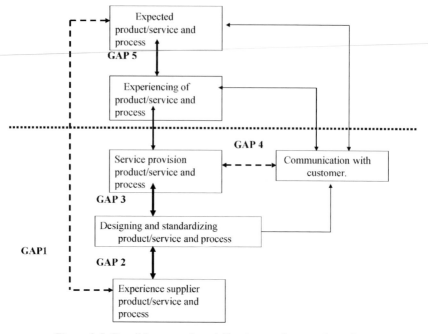

Figure 2.5. Possible gaps when delivering products and services

3. the fact employees of the organization do not utilize the product and/or service as it was designed and implemented;
4. the fact that reports on the products and/or services deviate from the reality;
5. the fact the customer's expectations with regard to the product and/or service are different from his experiences with the product and/or service.

WHY OPERATE UNDER AN ARCHITECTURE?

The IT supply organization(s) deliver the services. They have to makes sure there are no gaps. They have to ensure their products and services comply with the demanded functional and performance requirements. Mingay (2003) states that, in order to be able to controllably comply with the requirements, a process-oriented set-up of the IT organization and within this organization keeping to an agreed architecture for IT facilities is a requirement.

In this IT organization front and back-office processes are designed. The front-office processes are in direct contact with the customers. The back office processes operate more in a ex ante planned way. With such a set-up one can quickly and transparently deliver high quality services that are adjustable within margins and of which the certainty of supply is high.

WHAT IS AN ARCHITECTURE FOR IT FACILITIES?

An architecture can be described as, amongst other things, a description of the current organization. One may also see this as a blueprint of the desired organization. A third opinion is that architecture is about the guidelines for realizing new developments. Rosser (1999) calls this respectively the today-architecture, the tomorrow-architecture and the next-minute-architecture.

Architecture

In this book the notion architecture is defined as a combination of the three above definitions of architecture. The resulting definition complies with the recommendation IEEE standard 1471. In this book an IT architecture is:

(a) a framework for providing IT, in which the available IT objects and the matching services fit, while at the same time the IT architecture

(b) indicates along which lines, extensions or adjustments are realized and which parties decide and which parties are involved in its definition.

Within this definition one can come to agreements on the objects of the organization. The recipes for realizing and utilizing these objects within IT demand and the IT supply organization as a whole is also part of this. This deals with the lines of policy, the models, the instructions, the plans and the best practices (see Figure 2.6). The point of departure for the definition of architecture is that every organization has its own architecture of IT facilities; that this is the basis for control and that coming from this situation one arrives at systematic changes.

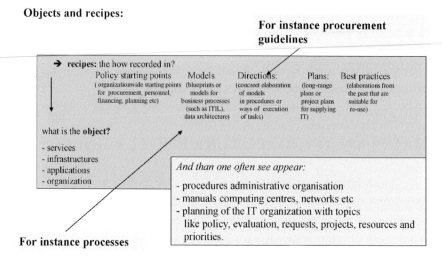

Figure 2.6. An architecture for IT facilities

The convenience of an architecture

When the architecture of IT facilities has been agreed, the organization has a language at its disposal in which demand and supply organization may communicate. Having an architecture brings order and coherence in the IT products and services, which enables an organization to determine quickly if and how new products and services are realized. An architecture supplies overview, if one wants to integrate applications and infrastructures or wishes to link these with interfaces. Finally, an architecture provides guidelines for achieving an efficient and effective implementation of new facilities.

Architecture for IT facilities

An architecture consists of recipes and objects. In the recipes for developing, maintaining and utilizing IT facilities we distinguish between:

–*policy starting points:* organization wide agreements that are used when purchasing goods and services, personnel management, financing objects, outsourcing of tasks, internal planning and budgeting etc.;

–*models:* blueprints of operating procedures the be used when setting up new processes or applications, infrastructure or organization parts;

- *regulations:* concrete elaborations of principles or models in procedures or methods in which tasks are carried out;
- *plans:* long-range plans or project plans for the execution of management tasks;
- *best practices*: elaborations of management tasks, application architectures etc from the past, that may be eligible for reuse.

As far as objects are concerned, we distinguish between:

- the *services or products* to be provided: this may be the support of a work-station with internet access, it may also be a workstation with access to an application that supports operational processes, it could be a combination of IT services. It always concerns the support of a business process by IT in one form or another. The services or products demand usually an input of objects of infrastructures, as well as of applications, as well as of the organization;
- the *infrastructures*: these include the objects of the technical and the in-formatics infrastructures;
- the *applications*: these include business processes supporting applications, personal productivity tools and applications like intranet that boost com-munications etc.;
- the *organization of the management*: this describes the processes that have to be executed enabling delivery of the products and services, and the organization of the services.

In the architecture objects are fitted using recipes. The architecture is usually recorded in the internal procedures of IT organizations, in manuals and in the IT organization's plans.

Architecture must grow proportionately

The experience shows that changes in the strategy of organizations quickly evoke changes in the information function and this may lead to changes in the set-up of IT. The enneahedron model illustrates this: a different organi-zation policy leads to adjustment of the set-up of the information function and often also to a different set-up of IT facilities. This enneahadron model finds a general connection between the policy ('setting'), the 'set-up' and the execution

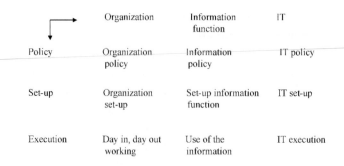

	Organization	Information function	IT
Policy	Organization policy	Information policy	IT policy
Set-up	Organization set-up	Set-up information function	IT set-up
Execution	Day in, day out working	Use of the information	IT execution

"enneahedron model information management" (Truijens c.s.)

Figure 2.7. The enneahadron model for information management (Truyens et al., 2003)

of tasks ('perform') in the field of the organization, its information function and its support by IT (see Figure 2.7, Truijens et al. (2003)).

Example

> *Kwik Fit ascertains that having all possible types of tyres in the shop is costing a lot of money. It decides therefore to limit the stocks to the 20% popular tyres and stocking the other tyres regionally. This change in organization policy leads to adjustment of the information function and a possibility for checking and entering the regional stocks up on the computer monitor. The IT set-up also changes as a result of this.*

Flexible and quickly adjustable IT facilities are based on an architecture. A basic architecture is often incorporated organization wide. Autonomous units in the organization this way obtain the same level of possibilities. The organization in its entirety can realize transparent purchases. It can also step by step work more broadly and adjust its sales channels quickly. This demands a settled IT organization; where IT facilities are controllable and controlled and that has agreed on the methods of realization and delivery. One can't have to invent everything anew all the time.

Realizing an IT architecture

Mintzberg (1991) states that, broadly speaking there are three ways of coming to a strategy. The same counts for coming to an architecture. Mintzberg distinguishes a top down approach, an approach, whereby the vision of one or more people is guiding; and a bottom-up approach. Van der Aart (2001) evaluates the top-down and the bottom-up implementation of an IT architecture. He establishes that the top down achievement of an architecture demands thorough support of the management of an organization. This management must understand which role IT plays and must realize that having an IT architecture speeds up implementation of projects and innovations. The challenge of the top down approach of an IT architecture consists of incorporating an architecture that is implemented organization wide, something that often needs a lot of time in a more bottom-up approach. The maximum achievable is then often no more than collecting the best practices and leaving its management with a central contact. The implementation of the architecture and its use often gets stuck in this approach at one or more departmental levels.

From today towards tomorrow

Gartner (2003) states that one can look at IT organizations in three different ways. One may look upon it as a cost centre, as a service centre and as a business partner. Every form has its own characteristics. These have been shown in Figure 2.8. In the first form one knows structure in the IT and processes are

Phase 1: basis	**Phase 2:** transformation to organization that listens to the customer	**Phase 3:** partners with the business
Growth phase 1 and 2: **= cost centre**	Growth phase 3 and 4: **= internal services supplier**	Growth phase 5: **= work as owner**
Requirement:	Requirement:	Requirement:
1. IT strategy and organization strategy attuned	1. Services portfolio present and providing insight	1. Control of IT by the demand = control by general and business management
2. Primary processes set up in IT organization	2. Management of resources and competence management of people set up and functioning	2. There is an organization wide IT architecture.
3. IT organization has structure	3. Costs and investments per product and service clear and charging in order	
4. Work in IT organization is supported by tools	4. Clear procurement strategy and transparent execution of this	

Figure 2.8. Various ways: an IT organization as a cost, a service or a profit centre

set up and supported by tools. The IT strategy is geared to the business strategy. The next form is the IT organization that operates as a service centre. This form has all its processes aligned and its goals clearly marked out and controls on these. This organization is run like a company. There is a purchasing strategy, an investment strategy, there are resources and human resource management and every project and task has its financial justification. Cost structures are clear at this type of service provider. The third type is partner in business. This involves a true control from within the demand. The demand organization and supply organization both operate from a clear IT architecture.

Assessing the level of architectural thinking

Both the Gartner organization as well as Nolan Norton, both trend watchers in the field of IT management, present models that show how the architectural thinking in an organization at a given moment got its shape. Gartner (2003) states that the IT organization can operate on five levels and every level has its own typology. In a more reactively set-up organization one strives for reliable services. In an organization that wants to provide reproducible services, one strives for providing a consistent performance and sets up processes. In a more proactively operating IT organization one records agreements and controls on the meeting of these commitments. If demand and supply are clearly defined, portfolio analyses will take place. Then agreements and compliance with architectures come within view. Portfolio management can only then take place for real, when one is considered a partner of the business.

The Nolan Norton group (2000) presents an instrument for assessing the level of architectural thinking in an organization. Their model (see Figure 2.9) distinguishes the following levels of architectural thinking:

1. *Level 1:* at this level individuals in an organization develop initiatives for achieving an architecture. There is only a global idea of what this might be. The results of the work could be seen as a first attempt.
2. *Level 2:* the management has appointed several employees for achieving an architecture in a certain part of the organization. There is still ongoing discussion about the set model. Per part of the organization a process has been globally started and architects have been appointed.

	Control:	Models etc	Role architect	Process	Product
Level 1: ad hoc activities for arriving at an architecture	none	first attempt	n.a.	n.a.	rough idea
Level 2:employees have a role but activities per department, domain or project	control on people	determined but still discussion	assigned	roughly per domain	uniform described per domain
Level 3: Attunement of activities,terms the same, total repeatable.	Control on process	determined and accepted	responsible for process	attuned between domainss	uniform described& standard over domains
Level 4: Architecture comes from view on organization.Architect is responsible.	Control on alignment and results	ditto	responsible for results	Integrated Process	central coordination
Level 5: Continuous improvement and renewal.	Control on continuous improvement	ditto	initiates innovations and improvements	optimized process	continuously adjusted.

Figure 2.9. Architectural thinking on different levels (Nolan Norton, 2000)

3. *Level 3:* the management controls at this stage, the process for arriving at an architecture. An architect is responsible for the process. The products have been described uniformly. There are recipes and standards for objectives applicable to the entire organization.
4. *Level 4*: the management now controls an architecture that directly connects with the operational processes and is attuned to these. The architect is held responsible for the results of the process for achieving an architecture. This process is centrally coordinated.
5. *Level 5*: there is control on continuous improvement and innovation of the IT architecture. The architect takes care of innovation and improvement. This leads to continuous, step-by-step adjustment of the architecture.

And now testing!

If an organization has an architecture at its disposal it is a good idea to test this for its comprehensiveness. A suitable framework is The Open Group Architure Framework (www.opengroup.org, TOGAF).

This framework was made by the Open Group. The Open Group is a private organization of purchasers and sellers that operates on standards in the area of IT. The TOGAF-framework is an instrument that may be used for testing

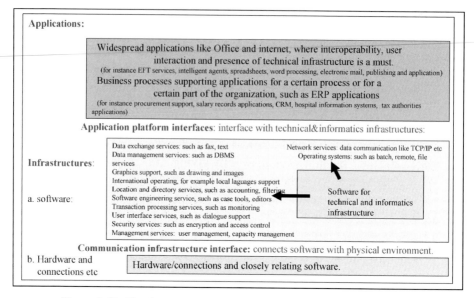

Figure 2.10. The Open Group Architecture Framework (TOGAF, 2001)

an IT architecture for an organization. TOGAF consist of a reference model and a method for achieving an architecture for an organization. The framework has a list of building blocks. These building blocks are shown in Figure 2.10. Basically, there are three main building blocks: applications, software that may be considered infrastructure, and the hardware and connections of the infrastructure with closely related software. The infrastructure software is the heart of the TOGAF-architecture. It includes parts as software

- for network and operating system services and for transaction processing;
- for data(base)management and data-exchange;
- for location and directory services;
- for building and maintaining applications;
- for security services;
- for users interfaces and for international operating;

The TOGAF-framework can be used for checking whether one has included all objects in the area of applications and infrastructure in one's management architecture. The TOGAF-framework can't be used for evaluating the IT architecture in its full width. For this, it lacks the objects and the entire management recipes-side.

QUESTIONS

1. What does the IT service lemniscate do? What is the service pit? What is the service shell? Give two examples.
2. What are functional and what are performance requirements? What angles do we know on the functions of a product or a service? Why is it important to recognize these? Illustrate your answer with an example.
3. How can one check the performance requirements of a product or a service systematically? Explain your answer by giving an example.
4. What is the link between the general performance requirements on products and services from the domains logistics and operations management and the performance requirements on IT products and services as follows from ISO 9126 supplemented with Quint-2?
5. What do you want to achieve with these functional and performance requirements with regard to IT facilities? Explain your answer by giving an example.
6. Gartner states that in order to control IT one has to have designed one's organization and should have an IT-architecture at one's disposal. What is the definition of the IT architecture? And why is it useful to have this architecture? Explain your answer by giving and example.
7. Explain what is meant by IT architecture and how this is translated into the daily working methods of organizations. How does such architecture grow along with the IT requirements of an organization and why is this necessary? Explain your answer by giving an example.
8. How does one realize IT architecture? Explain your answer by giving an example.
9. Gartner recognizes three types of IT organizations. What should one have in order, being a true business partner and what characterizes organizations that are true business partners?
10. How is the position of an organization with regard to having an IT architecture determined? What is the position of an IT architect, if the organization respectively operates on level 1, level 2, level 3, level 4 or level 5?
11. What is useful about testing one's own IT architecture against the TOGAF framework? What is impossible to test in TOGAF?

Part 2

Traditional IT management: organizing demand and supply

Chapter 3

Task focussed and simultaneous process-focussed supply of facilities

Recognizing supply and demand-side results in the supply focusing on the demand and therefore a more customer-oriented operation. Customers demand transparency. This requires a logical chain of activities that are carried out to fulfil the demand. This means the rise of process-focussed operating. This is how attention to workflow control comes about and is the start of the application of general logistics models for providing IT services.

The opportunity to measure and compare presents itself at setting up processes. Every process has its purpose, its set-up, its control and the information needed for those. We know that voluminous processes at the same time are often hardly diverse. With this type of process the IT input is of great importance. The Daimler Chrysler service desk also realizes that. The simple processes at the desk are first standardized and than computerized. If one wants to keep people employed, there is an option to develop into a service desk, with processes aimed at providing customers with handholding using tools for generating management information.

Calculations with key performance indicators for the average time needed for answering a question provide insight into the capacity we need in our front-offices. The necessary queuing theory will fit on a spreadsheet. The calculation shows how the handling time of a service organization depends on the number of staff. This can be a revelation for the customer. Knowing this he might be only too glad to pay for extra employees. His waiting period can be strongly reduced.

Grouping processes in degrees of customer contact made Atos Origin think. The front-office includes labour intensive work at the service desk and in account management. The back-office is a more capital-intensive task with regard to operating. Atos knows two types of labour intensive work: work that, at all times, has to be done close to the customer and work that could, if necessary, be done elsewhere. Back-office tasks can be situated anywhere in the world using these modern networks. Process-focussed thinking thus provides handles for finding ways to achieve more efficient services.

Contents of this chapter

This chapter goes into the organizing of IT tasks. A distinction is made between a task-focussed way of organizing and a more process-focussed one. Every way of organizing the advantages and disadvantages is explained. Introduction of the more process-focussed approach happens planned. The logistics theory gives indications for this. This is applied at the designing of processes for exploiting, developing and maintaining IT facilities.

In a process-focussed operating IT organization one can subsequently check and improve the efficiency of the various processes. The theory of constraints has its own interpretation in IT service processes. Control of set-up processes has both qualitative as well as quantitative aspects. Qualitatively one uses the conditions for effective control. This leads to observations about certain conditions being in place or not. Quantitative control provides clues on measures to be taken. The queuing theory could for example assist at providing insight into capacity problems and subsequently solving these.

ORGANIZING WORK
Task or function-focussed approach

For exploiting, developing and maintaining IT facilities, tasks at strategic, tactical and operational level need to be carried out. These tasks work with

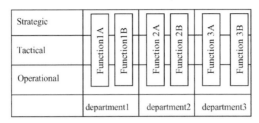

Figure 3.1. Task-focussed organization (Ruijs, 2003)

objects. Employees of the organization are authorized to perform a task and may be responsible for the performance of the task.

An example of task-focussed looking at IT organizations is the triple management model. This model makes a distinction between tasks of functional management, application management and exploitation. Another example of this angle is given by Looijen (2002) when distinguishing according to task areas, task fields and tasks in the domain of IT management. He distinguishes for instance as task areas, the task area management, the task area technical service, the task area general company support etc. Within every task area, task fields are distinguished. In the task area management one makes distinction between strategic, tactical and operational management. Per task area certain tasks are known.

The task-focussed approach is shown in Figure 3.1. In this figure we see the advantages and disadvantages of this approach. At approaching an organization task-focussed, one mainly establishes responsibilities and roles. Achieving coherence in a chain of tasks is then more difficult.

A more process-focussed approach of the organizing of IT efforts (Figure 3.2) may change this. At this approach the emphasis is on connecting activities that logically succeed each other. Processes change into tasks and connect activities that may be executed in different locations. By operating more

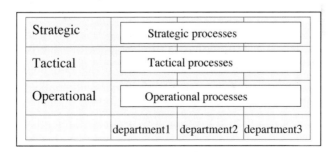

Figure 3.2. Process-focussed organization (Ruijs, 2003)

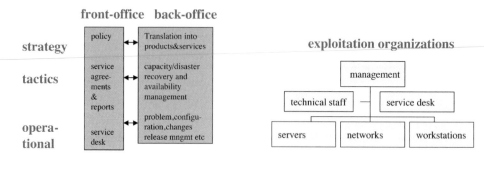

Figure 3.3. Organization of IT facilities, two examples

process-focussed, one can recognize structure in the execution of activities; the performance of a task becomes transparent and therefore can be monitored. Workflow control is introduced and at a tactical level capacity control. Processes are compared to the same processes elsewhere and one arrives at standardization. The execution of processes can be planned and throughput of processes can be calculated. This way, theories and ideas can be imported from the disciplines logistics and operations management. As disadvantage of the more process-focussed approach for setting up an organization, the fact is mentioned that it is not always clear who performs what part of the process and who may be held responsible.

Figure 3.3 shows the application of the task-focussed angle and the process-focussed angle on the organization of the IT facilities. The recognized processes are the processes in conformity with the ITIL method, which is discussed in Chapter 6. One sees a task-focussed approach creating a concentration of knowledge in one department alone. This can be very efficient. From a customer's point of view, the more process-focussed approach leads to the possibility to come to understandings with an organization across the separate tasks. This approach, leaves less space for individual departments for establishing their own priorities. The process is in sight, leading towards the desired solution for a customer. The organization, this way establishes priorities that take their departure from the customer's interests. Process-focussed organizations have more structured operations. This may lead to 20 or 30% profit with regard to effectiveness and efficiency. Every employee has namely a view of the broader picture, which leads to fewer mistakes and less costs for modifications. It also often means

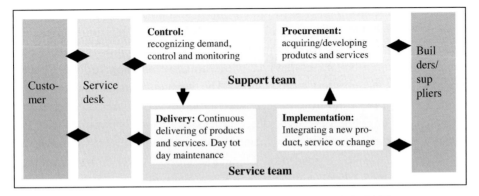

Figure 3.4. The end-to-end service organization (Alofs, 2002)

better service. Splitting up of the organization into processes is usually decided in consultation with the management and through participation and simulation introduced in the organization. People have to be trained and shown the ropes to be part of a more process-oriented operating organization.

Example

> *The end-to-end service organization (Alofs, 2002) is an application of the process focussed way of organzing. Alofs indicates that from the customer's point of view it should be a matter of 'one stop shopping.' He therefore constructs an IT organization with a front and a back-office. The front-office is demand controlled. The back-office systematically handles four tasks: two primary and two supporting ones. The primary tasks are supplying and implementing IT services. The supporting ones are controlling the organization and purchasing IT facilities. He calls this the end-to-end organization. In Figure 3.4 this organization is indicated.*

HOW TO INTRODUCE PROCESS-FOCUSSED OPERATING?

Introduction of a process-focussed approach

The process-focussed approach has processes at various levels. One distinguishes operational, tactical and strategic processes. At the tactical level, for instance, service level determination and the controlling of the service performance take place. At strategic level it is decided which products and services are going to be supplied. The process-focussed approach also includes processes that are strongly controlled by the demand, which are therefore more difficult to plan, and processes that progress more planned. The demand-controlled processes are to be found in the front-office. Here, individual customers are recognized and questions are answered. The back-office-processes are mostly detached from the processes in the front-office. In the back-office one operates more systematically in order to realize the agreed products and services. One is doing this for all customers or for a certain section. If one likes to talk of a customer uncoupling point, this uncoupling point is situated between the processes in the front and those in the back-office.

The processes are part of a chain. Let us go through such a chain. A customer's problem may for instance induce further investigation. This investigation may lead to a solution. This solution is implemented through change management, whereby the introduction of the change may result in a change in the configuration.

Design of processes

Davenport (1993) shows in a diagram what stages the design of processes passes through. He starts with a perception on the set-up of the organization. Of the processes that occur in there, the characteristics are established. This results in performance goals for every process. These performance goals indicate what should at least go well when executing a process. Finally, one establishes what the risks are when realizing the design, so these can be taken into account. In Figure 3.5 this way of designing is indicated. When setting up an IT organization such a design cycle is gone through. In this cycle one can go by the best practices in the field of setting up processes in IT organizations and look at comparable organizations.

Some processes in an IT organization are different because these have a lot of volume and at the same time little diversity. At designing this type of processes, attention is paid to:

–the process design;
–standardization of the product and the supply process;

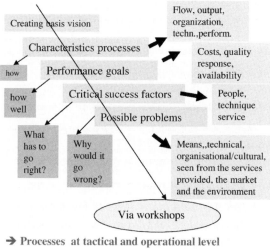

Figure 3.5. How to design processes?

–the work locations. When there is a lot of volume and little diversity, this often means work is carried out in one geographical location;
–the way in which the processes are supported. When combining high volume and little diversity, dedicated IT support can be very efficient;
–the mode of operation of the employee. When combining high volume and little diversity, the employee is often employed strongly system-focussed.

That changes as soon as there is a lot of diversity in provided services and a much smaller demand. In such a process one focuses on designing the service itself, hardly any attention is paid to standardization, one is often close to the customer or at the customers' premises and does not supply the service continuously. There is often no special IT application for supporting the service and people operate very task-focussed.

These points of particular interest teach us that a large service desk benefits from totally computerizing simple demands. A top ten on the internet and automatic downloads of solutions result in a significant reduction of work pressure at the processes in such a service desk.

Apart from points of interest related to the design, there are also points of interest concerning the control of processes. The controls used and the way of measuring differ between a process that is typified by a lot of volume and little diversity in products, and a process with a lot of diversity in products that are at the same time supplied in small numbers. In the first case it is a matter of:

- the necessity of a quick response to a customer;
- being able to keep going and (having to) planning of the capacity;
- the fact, that the critical success factor concentrates on handling the volume, and collects data about this in order to ensure that if high volumes are needed
- the response time does not increase;
- the concern, the service is limited and vulnerable to incidents.

The second situation is the reverse of the first. There is no need for a quick response, one controls on a more detailed level and is more vulnerable in one's services. From the above, it follows that service desks that are typified by a lot of demand and little diversity mainly use measures as rate of response, the frequency with which the customer has to call back, etc.

Processes in an IT organization

There are various methods in place matching processes with the triple management model. We know for instance a method that indicates the processes on the demand-side (see Chapter 4, functional management) and methods that do the same for the processes on the supply-side for application management and exploitation (Chapter 5/6). Furthermore there are methods that indicate processes in the field of purchasing of IT facilities. The methods for purchasing are discussed in Chapter 13.

On two levels performance requirements are made to the processes that are set up. This is on process level and at the level of a chain of processes. These requirements are with regard to:

- the *quality* of a process or the measure in which an organization complies with the specifications given for the output of the process or for the process itself. Being able to comply with the specifications demands clear norms and the employee's familiarity with these;
- the *speed* of a process or the elapsed time between question and answer per process and also the delivery time of the product;
- the *reliability* of delivery. Is the supplier able to deliver the demanded service in the required time and within the required timeframe? For a

service desk in India the latter for instance would be opening hours during Dutch office hours;
- the *flexibility* with which the supplier can handle changes in volume and diversity. It is possible that there is a sudden increase in demand;
- the *costs* of a process or a service. In this field IT organizations always dealt with processes and product, that are more capital-intensive and processes and products that are more labour-intensive. A service desk may be labour-intensive; keeping infrastructures in production is often very capital-intensive.

Assessing processes

A process-focussed organization can be analyzed using these performance requirements (Wijngaard (2003)). It is examined what the processes should achieve and how these processes perform if measured for these performance requirements. When checking processes one should have the descriptions of the process at one's disposal. Apart from this, an analysis of the functioning of the processes measured on the demanded performance requirements is a must. Furthermore, one has to know in which manner the performance of the process is accomplished. When carrying out such an analysis one will often find that one doesn't have norms at one disposal when the quality is too poor and therefore will never be able to improve. The fact that a slow service often results in stacks of work that is waiting means one has to find a reason for this. A low reliability could be caused by the way in which an organization takes on orders and commits to delivery times. The same reasons also play a part when ascertaining a lack of capacity or a costs problem.

Theory of constraints

Goldrath (1993, see Slack (2004)) poses the fact that in a chain of processes one first has to identify the process that causes problems. This process is often easily recognizable. There is usually a large amount of work waiting, people work under a lot of pressure and more often than not information about the bottleneck is lacking. The theory of constraints consists of checking how this problem can be solved. Hereby one does not take into account possible problems, that can arise with the other processes. When the solution is implemented, one starts with the next process, where now problems arise.

CONTROLLING PROCESSES

Qualitative aspects of controlling

The recognizing of processes in setting up the IT organization leads to queries about its control. In order to be able to control processes effectively, one must know how the process and its environment are put together; one should know what one wants (norms); should have sufficient control possibilities and should process the information for being able to control the process. In Figure 3.6 this is shown.

From this figure it becomes clear that it is not only possible to control the process itself but one can also influence its environment. In an IT organization this may mean that one takes care of telling the environment in advance that maintenance is taking place, even though one does control optimally. So the customers don't notice the effects of the maintenance.

In order to be able to control one might need various types of information. The balanced score card (Kaplan c.s., 1996) indicates that when controlling processes one might need financial information, process information, innovation information and/or customer information. In Figure 3.7 the areas of attention with regard to control information are shown. In Chapter 11 the use of the balanced score card in controlling IT organizations is further discussed.

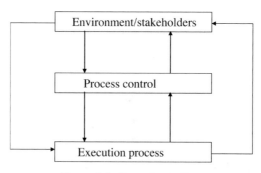

Figure 3.6. Control paradigm

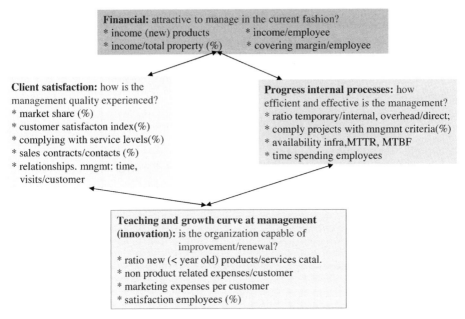

Figure 3.7. Four areas where information might be needed for enabling optimal control

Quantitative aspects in controlling

Apart from qualitative aspects, controlling processes also has quantitative aspects. An example of this is the planning of capacity at a process. By recognizing processes it is possible to measure at the processes and dimension these. An example of this is a service desk with many staff. In case the:

- incoming reports arrive statistically with a Poisson-distribution or law of small numbers;
- the processing of these takes place at a transaction rate that statistically also happens in conformity with the Poisson-distribution;
- the number of employees is equal to 'm' and an occupancy rate of b (this is the number on average to be dealt with;
- reports per unit of time divided by the average incoming reports per unit of time);
- and also the average transaction rate of a request is equal to 'a',

than the average waiting time for a customer is equal to:

$$\text{Average waiting time} = [(b \uparrow (\sqrt{2} \times (m + 1)) - 1))/m \times (1 - b)] \times a$$

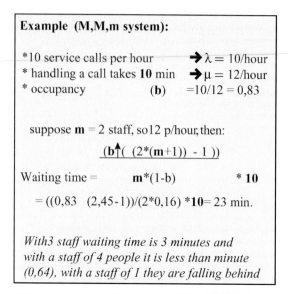

Figure 3.8. Example of application queuing theory at a service desk

The length of time a customer spends in the system, is equal to the waiting time plus '*a*'. In Figure 3.8 an example of the application of this formula is given. From the given example it follows that an increase in the number of employees from two to three shortens the average queuing time by a factor 10. It will be clear that customers confronted with this approach in figures in a number of cases might be prepared to pay the extra costs for a higher degree of service.

Consequences for the IT organization

The trend towards a more process-focussed organization of IT facilities results in many IT organizations, currently designed more task-focussed, include process-focussed elements in their organization structure. They set up front and back-offices and in those, design various tasks more process-oriented. That way they are able to come to agreements with their customers about the service performances and how to control achieving these.

Simultaneously with the realization of a more process-focussed set-up one should clearly define tasks and responsibilities. The trend towards a more hybrid organization of IT facilities, that is designed partly task and partly process-focussed, is in that case set. Figure 3.9 shows both a more task-focussed design

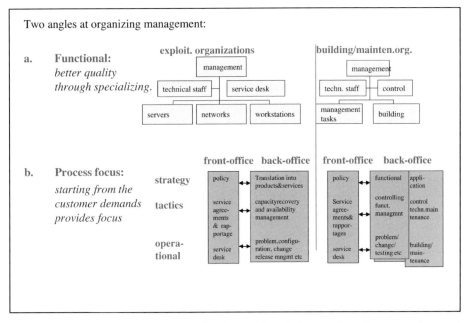

Two angles at organizing management:

Figure 3.9. Often there is a hybrid organization: partly task-focussed, partly process-focussed (concerning the processes, the supply-side with regard to exploitation is shown)

of a (part of the) IT organization, as well as a more process-focussed designed one. The hybrid type is in between these.

QUESTIONS

1. What is a task-focussed set up of an organization? What is a more process-focussed set-up? Which are the advantages and disadvantages of each type of set-up?
2. Give an example of a task-focussed type of setting up of an organization.
3. What does an IT organization that is set-up more task-focussed look like? What does it look like when it is set-up more process-focussed?
4. What is the 'end-to-end' service organization? When could one choose for this type of organizing? Explain your answer.
5. How could one design, according to Davenport a more task-focussed operating organization? Which aspects have to be taken into account? How do these aspects affect the set-up of the organization?

6. Having a process set-up at one disposal immediately leads to the testing of that process organization on five performance norms. Indicate what these norms are and how the test is carried out. What does the theory of constraints say with regard to this?

7. The process organization can be controlled. What is the control paradigm? And what do we learn from this when looking at the set-up of processes in the IT organization?

8. What are the relations between the theory of constraints and the conditions for effective control? What do both angles on processes teach us?

9. What is the position of the balanced score card, when speaking of goal-process-control and the necessary information. Illustrate your answer with an example.

10. What is the importance of the quantitative aspects of processes? Give an example in the field of the capacity calculation for processing reports at a service desk.

Chapter 4

The demand-side: functional management (using the method BiSL)

Over the last few years, our organization has entered into partnerships with companies in China and Poland. They want insight into our sales and we want the same into the status of our orders with them. That results in functional demands on the information function, which may only be filled in step by step. In a chain, companies that cooperate for a number of years should really exchange data openly and transparently. With our information function and its IT support that is not always as easy as all that.

We do happen to have rather a lot of back-office facilities that are crucial to our organization. The market demands a multi-channel approach. That is why functions for internet banking, internet-asset management and internet-insurance are opened up. Analytically seen, the old back-office applications do still exist. Using a whole new front-office in internet technology the back-office is connected with the customer. Of course we didn't put the current functionality at the disposal of our customers in one go. We did that step by step. First, we supplied general information; then the customer was able to obtain specific information and finally we developed the possibility to do transactions.

Without organizing the demand, the supply-side would have problems. Suppliers would bombard all the different parts of the business organization separately. This would, apart from the unclear focus of the demand, also result in blurring of the supply-side. An example of this is the police-information function in the Netherlands. After a period in which the police forces themselves looked after the demand for and the supply of their information and the accompanying IT facilities, from the mid nineties onwards the supply-side with regard to IT was combined. A central application management organization, the ITO, was set up. This didn't happen overnight. Police regions also continued to develop applications. Whenever a supplier of IT facilities didn't have a chance with the ITO, he went to the regions. That way, a number of regions created a second ITO and various applications remained available for roughly the same business process. This method of working costs extra money, makes it more difficult to exchange data between regions and their chain partners and makes it virtually impossible to manage applications for the Dutch police force as a whole in a truly professional manner.

Contents of this chapter

Supply chain computerization, multi-channel approaches, organizing of the demand: these are all subjects in the field of functional management. Functional management indicates the demand for information. It controls the application management and the exploitation. Virtually every change in the tasks or execution of the tasks of an organization has impact on the set up of the organization and its information function. Changes in strategy may result in outsourcing of tasks, may result in new, long-lasting partnerships and make it possible to comply with different demands of the market. These changes lead towards different goals, different processes and a different information function. Introduction of new technology may help to realize the desired changes. Organizations therefore make demands on their information function. Functional management collects these, functions internally and externally as spokesperson for the demand and realizes the desired information support of operational processes.

This chapter is about this functional management. First, it is indicated how the tasks in this field are often distributed within an organization. Next, the reasons for functional management are discussed and the set-up of functional management in larger and smaller organizations is gone into.

Next, we give an outline of all tasks that have to be carried out within the framework of functional management and the objects that are managed. As method for functional management, BiSL was chosen. This method indicates what tasks on a strategic, tactical and operational level have to be executed for functional management. When discussing functional management we go into dealing with the legacy in information function and IT, as known by many organizations.

THE DEMAND FOR IT FACILITIES

The situation in organizations

Organizations often have a policy. From this policy, actions are started in order to realize this policy. In the area of information function these actions result in various architectures and implementations of these. An organization often has an information architecture, an application architecture, an architecture for the informatics infrastructure and an exploitation architecture. The latter three architectures are part of the architecture as defined in Chapter 2. These architectures and their definition are shown in Figure 4.1.

These architectures are often realized under the guidance of an information manager at an organization's general management level. Next, functional managers in the various business units take care of the implementation of these. An information manager and a functional manager carry out the functional management tasks together and have contacts with the organization(s) for application

> → **policy model**:   how does one want to realize one's policy: processes and requirements with regard to customers, products, suppliers, raw materials, organization and infrastructure.
> → **information architecture:** logical information model, being data, processes worked out in functions and data groups and possibly used applications.
> → **application architecture:** information function of an organization in terms of applications and parts of these. Distribution over applications with databases, tables, functions and programmes
> → **informatics infrastructure:** development and management tools, a.o. for making and adjusting applications.
> → **exploitation architecture:** the infrastructure, on which and with which the applications run in production and the production application themselves.

Figure 4.1. Framework for the information function

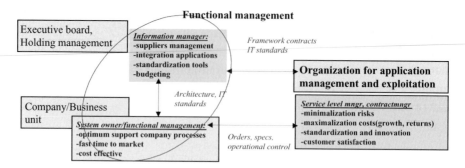

Figure 4.2. Connections between functional management, application management and exploitation

management and exploitation. The information manager concludes framework contracts and sets standards for the organization as a whole. Within these frameworks, the functional managers give orders to the suppliers of application management and exploitation services. Figure 4.2 shows this.

Why functional management?

The organization has set up functional management for various reasons. In the first place, it needs a communication channel between the organization itself and the IT service organization. Its general and business unit management often lacks knowledge and usually also lacks interest for dealing with IT demands adequately. This may result in isolation of IT service providers and make it difficult for them to follow the developments in the business. A second reason is the wish to agree on desired IT facilities in only one place. There is often insufficient knowledge to agree on desired IT facilities in more places than one and to trace whether these agreements are honoured. In that case, an organizational facility is set up, that is able to translate the demands of the organization and is a true conversation partner to the IT service organization(s). Finally it is convenient to have a point of support somewhere in the organization that one can call in case of any intrinsic queries with regard to the information function and the IT. This support point knows what consequences possible actions of the IT service providers might have to the business. One knows, for example, what the impact is of reversing changes in the data files and one knows the advantages and disadvantages of the use of certain technology.

Functional management is situated at the demand-side. It is no part of the IT supply-side. The reason is, that joint management of demand and supply may result in influencing the way in which functional management serves the interests of the owners and users. It may also lead to accessibility by users being harder and less feeling with what makes them tick. And finally, having functional management, application management and exploitation under one management may lead to functional management focusing on technology in stead of functionality of information support.

What are the objects of functional management?

Functional management is about the functionality of the IT facilities. These IT facilities consist of objects. These are objects in the domain of the technical infrastructure, the informatics infrastructure and the applications. At functional management one will often choose from a series of products and services available on the market from one or more suppliers. In that case one uses standard products and services. In smaller and less specialized organizations this will almost always be the case. Larger or highly specialized organizations will, apart from standard IT products also use tailor-made products. These are products that have been made especially for this organization using specifications supplied by their functional management. In this type of organization the relation with external suppliers often passes through the organization for application management and exploitation itself. In Figure 4.3 this situation is shown for larger and smaller organizations.

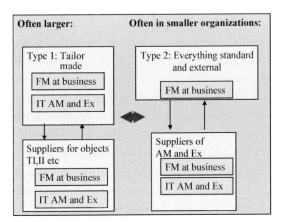

Figure 4.3. Positioning of functional management, application management and exploitation at large and small organizations

The method for functional management Business Information Systems Library (BiSL) is discussed in this book as a method for functional management of all IT facilities. Organizations have to have the processes in place somewhere as indicated by this method.

LOOKING AT THE DEMAND-SIDE SYSTEMATICALLY: BiSL

Functional management tasks

The tasks to be performed in the area of functional management are systematically lined up in the BiSL method. This method knows tasks on strategic level with regard to the set-up of the information function and its contents; at tactical level with regard to planning, costs, quality and service level management; and at operational level with regard to usage and functionality management. The task areas at strategic level know a task for mutual attunement. At operational level the link between usage and functionality is given by tasks in the area of change management and release transfer (Figure 4.4.1).

Queries at strategic level concern the attribution of tasks in the field of information policy and the execution of these. In addition, at this level the contents of the information function is determined as well as its IT support. Renewal of the IT facilities portfolio and thinking about the life cycle of separate facilities are part of this. At operational level the organization must be able to rely upon the execution of its operational processes not being hindered by IT facilities being unavailable. Here, is also where it is made sure that new facilities are implemented in such a way, not just the IT facilities but also the embedding of the facility in the organization, the so-called administrative organization of a business process, is taken care of.

The BiSL-framework is shown in Figure 4.4.1. In Figure 4.4.1 the method is shown as a collection of operational processes. In Figure 4.4.2 the same method is shown. In this case a distinction is made between the tasks that are carried out in a front-office setting of functional management and tasks performed in a back-office setting. In direct relation with the user organization and the suppliers, various information exchange processes take place between those involved. More planned, other tasks in the field of planning, preparation of the execution and performance may take place. This happens in the back-office.

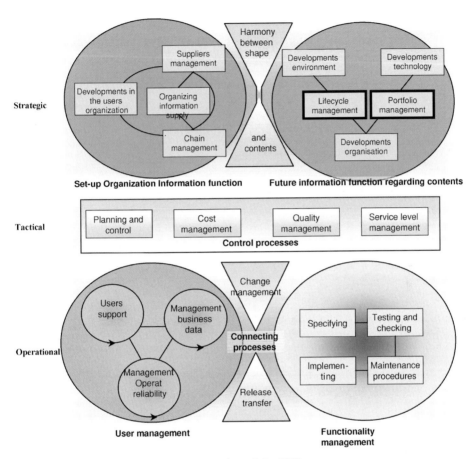

Figure 4.4.1. Overview of the BiSL processes

Four types of objects to manage

The BiSL-processes manage four types of objects. These are objects of the organization, the documents concerning content and process documents of the application, the objects of the informatics infrastructure and that of the technical infrastructure. In Figure 4.5 this is shown. This figure proves there is a difference between objects to be managed. If an organization has to deal with a tailor-made product, one partly knows different objects as compared to a standard product. In managing standard products there are always requests for proposals present and often also objects needed for managing the interface

Front -office tasks		Back -office tasks	
Information interchange with regard to		Planning, preparation and execution	
Strategic Organization	chain supplier users organization	Organization	chain supplier users organization
Contents	environment technology applications/portfolio organization	Contents	environement technology applications/portfolio organization
Tactical Information with regard to evaluations portfolio, planning; costs, service, quality		Execution of evaluation of the portfolio, planning and check; costing; tasks for service level management and quality monitoring.	
Operational Daily support	questions, incidents control of supply organization at incidents etc user communication training, notices user consultation	User management tasks: Functionality mngmnt:	availability capacity management continuity management problem management drawing up of specifications and requirements testing and checking, making AO omplementation tasks.

Figure 4.4.2. BiSL in a front and back-office setting

between existing objects and the new objects. In tailor made by contrast there are definition studies that reflect exactly the consequences of an IT facility and acceptance tests that investigate whether one can operate with the delivered tailor made products.

All objects may be present within an organization in various releases and versions. In this case a release is a certain collection of objects of an IT product that is implemented as if it was one and operates in a certain setting of the informatics and technical infrastructure. Every release succeeding the first includes significant changes in functionality with regard to the previous release of the product. A version is an edition of a product within a release. A version of a release includes some changes in functional or technical sense with regard to the release or compared to the previous version in a release.

Versions or releases have within the functional management organization often different statuses. A version may, for instance, be in development, in functional test-stage, in users test, in exploitation test and in production. With

The objects to be managed can be divided into four categories:

1. **Organization of management**:   - set-up functional management organization
                                          - administrative organization management processes
2. **Applications with regard to contents and process documents:**

Procured packages, for example ERP:	Tailor made applications:

- prep.studies, requests for proposal
- functional design interfaces
  (possibly for other applications as well
- test files and test sets: functional test
  and exploitation test
- functional management manuals.
- user manuals
- manuals administrative organization
	- prep.studies, definition studies, functional
	  designs,
	  (plus same for interfaces and conversions)
	- test files and test sets: system test, functional
	  test, acceptance and exploitation test
	- functional management manual
	- user manuals
	- manuals administrative organization

3. **Informatics infrastructure:**   -functional information on building tools
                                          such as Java;
                                          -functional information on management
                                          tools, such as end to end measurements
4. **Technical infrastructure:**   -functional information on operating system,
                                          application monitoring and network software

Figure 4.5. Objects at functional management

every status belong objects in the form of software and/or hardware and in the form of documents.

Through application of different technology, the objects managed by an organization also change (Figure 4.6). Fitting in object-oriented working leads to objects that within the information function supply certain functionality. It is a matter of 'granulation.' Functionality of an application is divided into the smallest particles with the same function, where before a programme included various functions. The advantage for a user is that the same function is done everywhere in the same way and there is only one version of this function present. Functional and application management at this function therefore results in one set of documents and to changes in one location in the IT facility as a whole.

If a tool is used for managing one's versions of IT objects, it becomes apparent that it is possible to use fairly generic tools for version management of programmes. For object-oriented operating for version management often a tool as provided by the supplier of the building product (an object of the informatics infrastructure) in question has to be used. A tool ensures that versions are always marked with a time stamp, so one knows which version is operational in the IT facility that is in production.

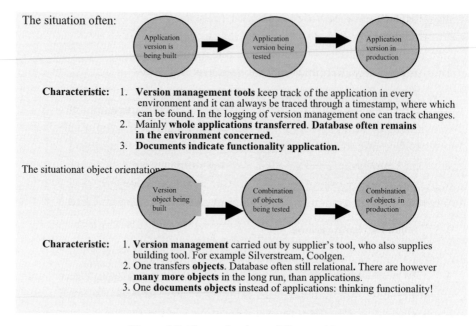

Figure 4.6. New technology, different objects

THE PROCESSES AT THE DEMAND-SIDE IN MORE DETAIL: VARIOUS BISL-TASKS

Explanation of each BiSL-task

Next, each of the five BiSL task areas will be discussed in more detail. The connecting tasks between the various task areas will also come up for discussion.

Organization of the information function

At strategic level in BiSL, reflecting on the future organization of the information function is positioned. This task breaks up into four child tasks. These tasks are firstly the following of the developments in the user organization. Through mergers, (de)centralization, (de)concentration, (out)sourcing, organizations change as regards their form of administration. Functional management ensures these changes have their repercussion in the direction of the responsibilities with regard to the information function. Functional management maintains communication channels with users and management of the demand-side. Every business process may have its own process owner and a need for support by IT.

Secondly, functional management follows the developments in the chains the organization is part of. The functional management continually has to deal with integration of processes between organizations. This integration may lead to weaker or stronger connections in the domain of the information function. Successful operating of the organization is determined by its opportunities for operating within the chain. Functional management can play a large part in this. Agreements between supply chain partners are in first instance often about improving the mutual information function. These agreements can become quite detailed and far-reaching if the relationship is a long-standing one.

Because of the increasing importance of an optimum information function and the increasing dependency on products and services that are supplied by external parties, the attention for choosing of and the relation with suppliers of IT products and services is also on the up. This is therefore the third child task. In this child task the relation with mostly application management and the exploitation organizations is shaped. Framework contracts and/or service level agreements are often used for controlling this relation. These are concluded and secured at this level. Setting up and carrying out tender procedures, the determination of core expertise, decisions about strategic cooperation etc. are tasks that come under this child task.

In conclusion, at this level ideas are developed about the organization of the information function. Hereby the situation may arise where functional management reports at more levels within the organization. In that case broad guidelines are set at central level. Other levels set the limiting conditions in this.

The future of information function concerning content

The second task at strategic level is determining the future with regard to content of the information function. This task breaks down into five child tasks. It is linked to the previous task by means of a process, whereby attunement takes place between the set-up (the shape) and the content of the information function.

If someone is for instance responsible for supplying certain data within a chain, this should be made possible by the applications.

The first child task in this domain is translating the developments in the environments into the consequences for the information function in the organization. The internal information function must fit in with the information function needed for working within the chain. It should also meet the customer's requirements optimally. This may result in different operating methods with direct consequences for the information function.

Application of new technology might also give organizations different possibilities. Internet has giving banking once and for all a home dimension. Functional management also translates the possibilities the new technology gives towards new products and services. It sets standards, stimulates try-outs and encourages exchange of experiences. This is the second child task.

The third consists of positioning adjustments in the IT facilities portfolio. Application of IT is often closely linked to one or more operational processes. A change in IT facilities rather soon concerns a lot of organization and users. For this reason control at portfolio level is needed. This is about indicating which steps we acknowledge and which changes we are going to make geared to the change capacity of users and IT organization.

The fourth child task is controlling the life cycle of an IT facility. This comes down to outlining its functionality and the possibilities for maintaining and exploiting these in the future. The last child task is the optimum support of the organization by facilitating changes within the organization from the point of view of the information function. Functional management is in charge of making sure the IT facilities develop alongside the demands of the organization.

Dealing with legacy

When looking at the portfolio of IT facilities one could come across the legacy of IT facilities. This occurs when the used IT is out-of-date and the organization depends on the IT facility in question. Legacy may occur as:

- an application that no longer suffices with regard to functionality or presentation;
- infrastructure that can no longer be maintained and/or is difficult to supply;
- certain knowledge in the domain of management is not (or no longer) available etc.

Organizations are namely not just working on new developments. They also have to deal with the need to phase out objects that are in production. These could be objects of the technical infrastructures, the informatics infrastructures, the organization and the applications. Organizations are then able to choose. They may choose to continue as usual and isolate the facility. They may replace the facility by a tailor made one or by an application of a standard solution. They may develop the entire facility anew, whereby components of the existing facility could be used, if so desired.

Example of the different approaches to solve a legacy problem

- *isolation of a facility. Many banks have back-office applications that cannot be rebuilt overnight. They are confronted with the need for online banking using the internet. In doing this they use a front-office, which through a standard interface product—usually IBM's MS-queue—is connected with their back-office application.*
- *replacement by a standard solution was frequently used for solving the millennium problem. Organizations replaced applications with standard ERP-solutions.*
- *developing a facility anew is done when there is no fitting standard solution available and the old facility cannot be maintained. Prudential Life for example, had a large part of its applications programmed in a Cobol-version it developed itself. It didn't want to maintain this version and had to partially rebuild the applications.*

Evolution or revolution

When setting up a portfolio planning for an innovation the theory of 'result-focussed implementation' is often applied. This theory consists of implementing new IT facilities step by step. Organizations then evolve to a next phase; they do no arrive there through a revolution. At result-focussed implementation (see Figure 4.7) one divides the implementation in mutually independent parts, whereby each part has its own benefits. At every implementation the necessary changes are simultaneously made to the organization structure, the work

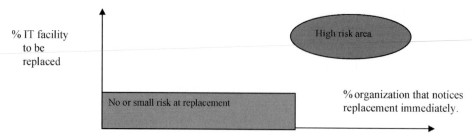

Figure 4.7. Result-oriented implementation (Fichman, 1999)

processes and information for controlling these. The change is therefore complete. Subsequently, within a limited time span (maximum of nine months) the results of an implementation are visible. Future versions are obvious supplements or improvements.

Condition for result-focussed implementation is that the size of the functions in the new or changed information function or the number of involved organization parts can be limited; that the number of users is not the limiting factor and one can split the implementation into various parts and these parts can be implemented separately and independently.

Controlling functionalities and user management

After the BiSL processes at strategic level, the processes at tactical level are discussed. At tactical level the processes for user management and functionalities management are controlled. At this level four child tasks take place. These are planning and control, looking after cost management, quality management and service level management.

At the first child task, planning and control, based upon the strategy and the annual plan, the annual plan functional management is drawn up. In this annual plan the priorities concerning the information function and the functional management are recorded. Besides, this includes the planning of the activities and the budget available for realizing these activities. After the plan is drawn up, its execution is secured, whereby if necessary the activities are adjusted or the plan is readjusted.

The child task cost management deals with the budget and monitors the costs for the information function and the functional management. This is where the rates are set; costs are attributed and on this basis if necessary invoicing takes place. This concerns amongst other things the costs for execution of functional management, application management and exploitation tasks.

The child task quality management periodically checks the technical and functional quality of the IT facilities from a more operational perspective. A quality plan is made and maintained for the services and products in the domain of functional management, application management and exploitation. Hereby attention is given to the process and product quality, customer satisfaction and employee satisfaction.

The last child task at this level is service level management. Within this framework the functional and performance requirements to the information function and IT services are determined. Based upon these requirements, agreements are made, guarded and if necessary revised with the ones that pay for the services and products on the one side and the organizations for performing application management and exploitation on the other side. These agreements set the norms for the products and services to be supplied. These also record the way in which cooperation takes place. This includes procedures, reports and the shape in which the cooperation will be moulded.

Functionalities management

At operational level we find the tasks user management and functionalities management. The first deals with keeping the IT facility in production day in day out, the second with the planned changing of these facilities. The two tasks are connected by the process changes management and the process release transfer. The first process also dictates the contents of a new version or a new release of an IT facility. The second involves the transfer from building to production of a new version or a new release.

The functionalities management process includes four child tasks. The first is the drawing up of specifications and demands to the information function and the necessary IT facilities. In a following phase this also includes safeguarding the realization of these specifications and demands. The child task leads to determination of the need for information of the user organization and indications (changes in) of requested functionality, making performance requirements to these and safeguarding the realization. Finally, this child task includes the indication, safeguarding and organization of relations with the other IT facilities.

The second child task is the checking and testing of the supplied facilities. This includes the performance of a functional test, a user acceptance test and an exploitation test. The first type of test checks whether the IT facility is made in conformity with the specifications. The second type of test investigates whether one can work with the application, whilst the third type determines the consequences for the exploitation. This child task therefore includes the functional testing out of the own specifications to those of the application manager. This also includes preparing, executing and/or supervising functional tests, acceptance tests, exploitation tests and the reports on these. This all finally leads to acceptance of the IT facility.

The third child task includes maintenance of procedures. Management and distribution of documents in which procedures, work instructions and user manuals are described, are all part of this third child task. This also includes control of the distribution of IT facilities and data at distributing these over various locations.

Finally, functionalities management has to take care of and assist at the implementation of IT facilities. This could be the implementation of the solution for a showstopper. This is a fault in a facility that has to be resolved immediately because vital processes are at a standstill. This may also concern the implementation of an entirely new release and everything in between. This child task also includes the drawing up of change requests and the order for a change. This also includes checking of the elaboration of change proposals as given by application management and safeguarding of the progress at realization of the proposals at application management and exploitation. This child task takes care of coordination in the handling of showstoppers and change proposals.

Arriving at a new release or a new version

Showstoppers immediately demand a solution. Change proposals often can wait longer, before the change has been made to the facility. Change proposals are usually included in a next version or next release together with the facilities necessary for a new project. In that case, this release is built from the functionality as developed in a new project, the answer to the change requests that came from the users and did not immediately require a solution (they could live with these (COLW)) and the answer to change requests from other sources. Figure 4.8 shows the progress of such a release or version.

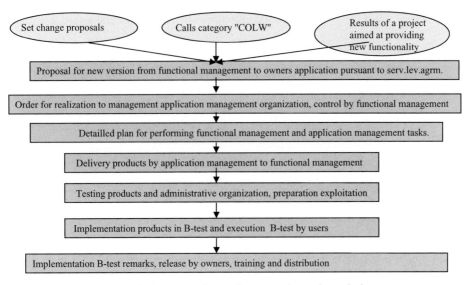

Figure 4.8. Progress of a version or a release through time

Users management, daily management

The second task within BiSL at operational level is user management. This task is split into three parts, being daily support, tasks at a coordinating level and management of business data. The child task daily support includes two tasks, being:

1. taking care of:
   - the calls (incidents/problems) registration, handling and ensuring this is done;
   - handling of complaints;
   - execution of single tasks, for example for application of data;
   - control of application management and exploitation at execution of extra tasks, or resolution of incidents;
   - advise and answering questions;
   - entering authorizations
2. communication with owners and users. This means:
   - taking care of training, additional instruction and/or handholding;
   - publishing mails, newsletters or general announcements;
   - consultation and chairing of users meetings.

The second child task 'coordinating management' includes:

- availability management: activities that take care of present and future information function. This also includes providing authorization possibilities.
- capacity management: this maps the expectations for the use of the facilities. This also drives the activities that ensure optimal use and one performs activities in order to safeguard this optimal use.
- calamities management: this activity implies looking after and maintaining a system of measures for recovery of the entire or part of the services.
- problem management: arriving at a structural solution for incidents and determining the direction of this solution. This means an incident may be qualified as a showstopper but it may also be a problem one could live with. In the latter case it becomes a change proposal that enters the procedure for being assessed for inclusion into a next version or next release.

The third child task, management business data has two subtasks, being:

- data definition management: this is the managing and safeguarding of the definitions of and the relations between data elements. This makes it easier to determine the impact of changes.
- data management with regard to content: this is the managing of the contents of system tables and parameters, that control the functioning of the facility, and the determination of preservation periods for data.

QUESTIONS

1. Why do organizations set up functional management? Illustrate your answer by giving two examples.
2. Where is functional management positioned within an organization? What are the reasons for this?
3. Which objects have to be managed functionally? Why?
4. What is the difference between small and large organizations in the field of functional management? Why?
5. Which tasks in the field of functional management are parts of BiSL? Explain every task and illustrate your explanation by giving an example.

6. Which types of objects are managed in functional management? Give an example of every type.
7. What impact does the progress of technology have on the objectives of management?
8. Why do organizations use tools for performing version management?
9. What is legacy and how does it come into being? How is legacy resolved? Illustrate your answer by giving an example.
10. What is result-focussed implementing? How and when is this applied? When is application of result-focussed implementing not possible? Illustrate your answer with two examples.
11. What is the difference between showstoppers and change proposals?
12. How does a new version or a new release of an IT facility find its way from the drawing board to implementation?

Why application management?
Who controls application management?
What are the objects of management?
ASL as collection of processes
ASL: front and back-office processes
Objects at application management
ASL unravelled in processes

Chapter 5

The supply-side: application management (using the method ASL)

As Siebel application managers over the last five years we had to deal with the switch from client server technology to more browser-based applications. And at the same time we experienced the consequences of the trend for changing from paying for licences per user of an IT facility to arrive at paying for use of the application alone, the so-called utility computing. These changes both led to a different life cycle for many of our products and to considering the furnished management tools. Configuration management, security management, availability management and cost management are all subjects we'll have to address explicitly in future.

The domain application management deals with change of IT facilities. Quality of application management does not just have a product component but also a service component. A proactive service desk for application management can truly improve the image of the services provided. Customers request to know what is done with their remarks. Customers want to be able to see to what extent settlement of their complaints is followed up. Customers demand a proactive front-office.

With this trend towards standard applications, the nature of our job changes. Our supply organization changed from a supplier of tailor made applications to an implementations organization for other supplier's packages. That simply

77

demanded a different focus and often also different people. By methodically thinking about our organization and about the technology to be used we were able to 'get into lane' and this change over went well. Looking back: we now work with 50% less people than before and 50% of the people in the current organization joined us in the last five years.

Contents of this chapter

Handling application management in a structured manner, one of the two tasks at the supply-side at the production of IT facilities is the subject of this chapter. The task application management is divided into front-office and back-office processes. Hereby the method Application Systems Library (ASL) is used by means of a stepping stone. The main subject of this chapter is the discussion of this method.

The chapter starts by positioning application management. Application management is a task at the supply-side. The activities of the supply-side are controlled by the functional management task at the demand-side. This functional management task is accommodated in the users organization. It controls application management. The application management deals with the development and maintenance of IT facilities. Even though one speaks of application management, in this entire chapter the object of management is an IT facility. This may be both an infrastructure, an application as well as the accompanying services. It can also be a combination of them all. There are several reasons for this approach. One of them is the fact that, what is an application for one company, like the product Oracle database management systems is for the software manufacturer Oracle, is part of the informatics infrastructure for another. Another is, that often the same kind of activities have to be organized for maintaining of an IT facility.

THE SUPPLY-SIDE: APPLICATION MANAGEMENT AND EXPLOITATION OF IT FACILITIES

The supply-side

Functional management controls tasks in the field of application management and exploitation. Each of these tasks has activities at operational, tactical and strategic level. The functional management team has connections at each of

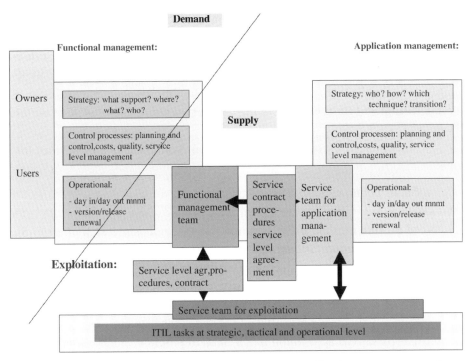

Figure 5.1. The relation between functional management, application management and
exploitation

these levels with exploitation and application management. In Figure 5.1 this is
shown.

Functional management is situated in the users organization, so on the demand side. Application management deals with IT development and maintenance
and is with exploitation part of the IT supply side. Both tasks can be assigned to
one organization. They can also be executed by separate organizations. Independent software houses increasingly perform application management these days.
These produce for instance ERP or CRM applications or personal productivity
tools. Examples of these software companies are SAP, Siebel, JD Edwards, Oracle, Peoplesoft and SAP. Another example is the application management for
personal productivity tools, as done by Microsoft.

Reasons for organizing application management

There are a number of reasons for organizing application management.
The first is the fact that an IT facility—and certainly an application—often gives

years of maintenance. Furthermore experience teaches us that 80% of the money spent on an application, is in fact spent on maintenance. Finally, it is important to be careful to a certain extent when entering innovations into the application in production because the application could have many users and a tiny error might cause many problems. In actual practice an IT facility has an average lifespan of between eight and thirty years. During that period maintenance is done on this IT-facility.

Advantages of organizing application management are the fact that one:

- obtains better control of the costs;
- obtains better insight into the supplied products and services;
- can be sure of, that, if the acquired knowledge is structurally passed on, continuous support is guaranteed;
- can make continuous adjustments within a framework aimed at working in future with an up-to-date facility;
- obtains a reliable business process, among other things because there is structural attention for testing and change management;
- by applying the application into a chain of processes and/or organizations a high degree of uniformity in the management can be realized.

METHOD FOR APPLICATION MANAGEMENT: ASL

Application systems library (ASL)

ASL is a method for looking at application management in a structural manner. ASL was developed by Getronics and made available to the public domain. It shows the *best practices* in the field of application management, as experienced by the Getronics company. ASL consists of six clusters of processes (see Figure 5.2). These processes take place at operational level, at tactical level and at strategic level. At strategic level processes have been set up for looking at the long-term organization of the management and the technology needed for this.

At tactical level one controls the daily management and the maintenance and renewal processes. Daily management and innovation are connected through the processes change management and programme management and distribution.

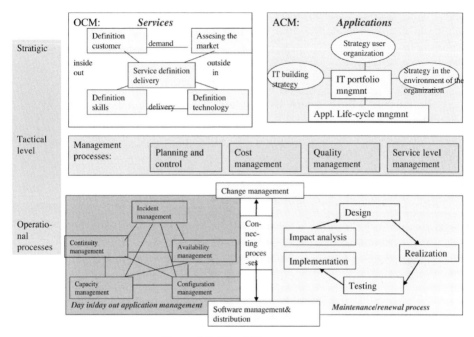

Figure 5.2. The ASL processes

The ASL method, as propagated by the ASL foundation (www. aslfoundation.org) consists of generic descriptions of the ASL processes, templates for making annual plans, management plans per facility, SLA's and dossiers administrative organization (DAP-dossiers), in which the administrative organization about the working method is recorded, checklists, scans etc.

Front-office and back-office tasks

The ASL tasks can be divided into front-office and back-office tasks. Front-office tasks deal with tasks in direct contact with suppliers and customers. These tasks take place at various levels. At strategic level the market is informed of one's products and the services surrounding these. At tactical level one informs the market of planning and quality aspects, speaks about costs, concludes service level agreements and reports on the compliance with these. At operational level the daily support takes place in the shape of a physical and/or virtual service desk, collects data about compliance with functional and performance requirements and proactively informs customers about the service and the product. In the

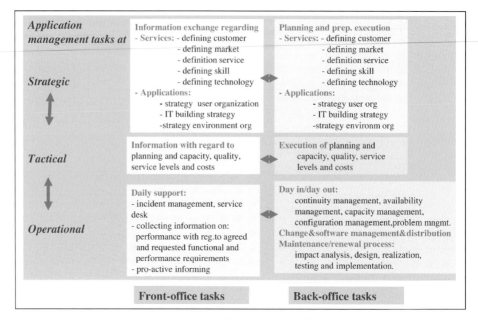

Figure 5.3. Front-office and back-office tasks

back-office all the tasks that have to be carried out more methodically take place. Figure 5.3 indicates the front and back-office tasks of ASL.

Objects of management

Application management has to do with four types of objects. These are objects of the organization; the process documents and documents concerning contents of the applications; the objects of the informatics infrastructure and the technical infrastructure. These objects always concern a certain release or a specific version of an IT facility and the status, this release or this version has. These statuses may for example indicate whether a facility is in the phase of idea development, the planning phase, the design phase, the implementation phase or in production.

In Figure 5.4 the objects of management are shown. From this figure it emerges that at application management of IT facilities a distinction can be made at the object applications between tailor made and standard applications also called application packages. At tailor made applications in house management develops the entire application and its interface with other applications and

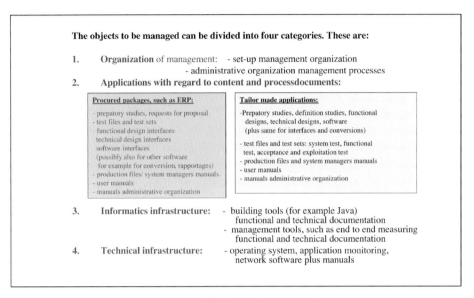

Figure 5.4. Objects to be managed

therefore all programmes and their documentation are available at the application management organization. When application management has procured a standard application, this is not the case. In that case the code of the application programmes are often lacking, just like the database layout of the application. The supplier considers these his own property.

When an organization uses standard applications one therefore often sees the task application management changes size. An organization only performs the full application management for the interfaces with the package needed; for the software for converting from the old situation to the standard package and possibly for the extra applications built to meet the extra management information demands.

These objects are managed within the six clusters of ASL processes. Smaller organizations will often not have set up these six clusters to their full extent. It is however a good idea to compare the inhouse organization briefly with ASL and ask oneself which processes occurring in ASL are not available in the organization and why this is the case. It is for these reasons we will indicate the ASL processes in some detail. Each organization will fit the ASL method in with its own organization in its own way. Let us have a closer look at the six clusters of ASL processes one by one.

THE ASL PROCESSES LOOKED AT

Organizing application management long-term (OCM)

There are three reasons why an application manager should pay attention to his field in the long-term. In the first place there are reasons to do with competition. Users increasingly shop around and discover the products and services other suppliers have to offer. They look at the market and compare. The supply organization cannot stop this, just as well as it cannot take this task away from the demand organization. The fact is that the demand organization is differently positioned 'in' this process than the supply organization. The demand wants optimum support and is sometimes prepared to take risks in this process. This is however not in a supply organization's best interest, this supply organization is much more conservative. The supply organization often starts from the paradigm 'do not change a winning team.' Besides, once stated functional and performance requirements may change step by step with time.

In the cluster 'organization of application management in the longer run' or OCM (organisation cycle management) ASL knows five detailed processes. These are determining the market; determination of the way in which the relation with the users organization can be shaped; determination of skills one needs now and in the future; determination of technology needed in future; and the process service delivery determination.

The process market determination, researches which developments are playing in the market and what these mean to the application management organization. The result of this will lead to a clear positioning of the organization in the field of (internal or external) IT providers, inclusive of possible partnerships or alliances. At determining the way in which the relation with the user organization(s) is shaped with regard to the provision of services, among other things the following issues play a part:

- the image of the application management organization with the user organization;
- having access to people that decide within the user organization;
- the design of the own 'accounts'-system;
- and the service that is delivered or may be delivered. Here one will have to weigh up whether this is what it should be and one will have to take measures in order to arrive at the desired situation.

The process 'determining skills' investigates which expertise is needed for the future and to which extent. The achieving and effectuating of a desired situation takes as a rule several years because of measures like training or attracting these skills. Besides the process 'technology determination' plays a part. This process deals with the tools with which the application management organization realizes its services. This is where one will have to choose. One cannot support all types of IT facilities and it often does take several years before certain IT facilities, like for instance building environments, building lines and other tools or methods are well controlled. Besides the costs for procurement are often high.

All previous considerations have to meet in an univocal proposition, an univocal service provision that matches the market, the customers, the skills of the in house organization and the tools. Service delivery determination is the process, where all of this comes together. In this process the service as desired in two to three years time is designed and the mission of the organization is determined. This is also where the strategy is determined in order to arrive at this service. This strategy is elaborated in the other OCM processes.

Many of these processes don't seem that advisable for internal IT organizations. This may be right for the smaller supply organization; for the larger one it is certainly not right. Demand organizations are often not that attached to the internal IT organization. An supply organization may be outsourced, be privatized or outsource parts. Exactly that is why guarding the inhouse proposition and services are possibly even more essential to internal application management organizations.

Applications cycle management (ACM)

Apart from thinking about the organization of application management, the application manager also has to consider the portfolio of IT facilities he manages and the individual facility within this portfolio. This helps to prevent making changes in a manner that is in conflict with the directions in which the business process develops in the next three to five years. Furthermore introduction of ACM often results in people realizing that facilities often last for years and one should see substantial improvements in productivity and quality (like restructuring bad software) as a true investment one could benefit from for years.

Application cycle management knows three processes. These processes are targeted at making the IT facility fit in optimally with developments in the user organization, its environment and technology. The three processes are:

1. determination of the development strategy in the field of IT facilities. This is the process, in which new technological developments are monitored and tested;
2. the process of keeping track of the developments in the environment in which the customer operates in relation with the used or to be used IT facilities;
3. the mapping of developments within the user organization(s).

The established developments could have an effect on the IT facility. The internal state of the IT facility (quality and costs) could also lead to the need for radical changes. This demands a policy at two levels.

(a) the level of the individual IT facility or application life-cycle management. This entails defining a strategy for the future of an IT facility, elaborated in actions.
(b) the level of the IT facilities portfolio or portfolio management.

ACM often starts with a bottom-up approach: structured voicing on the technical, functional and exploitation quality of the IT facility in relation with the requirements from the business process towards the future. The advantage of mapping the strengths and weaknesses structured in the current situation is that one gets a

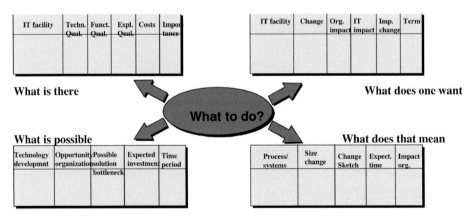

Figure 5.5. Bottom-up passing through of a portfolio of IT facilities

good picture of the feasibility of changes and the proposed strategy. In principle the questions of Figure 5.5 are in that case applicable.

Control of the operational processes

The day in day out keeping in production of IT facilities is controlled from four angles: time and capacity, costs, service levels and matching agreements about this, plus the quality of process and product.

This is why ASL has four controlling processes. These are planning and control, cost management, quality management and service level management.

Planning and control

The process planning and control operates on meeting deadlines. IT facilities in maintenance often have very rigid deadlines. For example: the new legislation comes into effect on 1 January, the insurance product is launched 1 May, and the new invoicing starts from 1 July. That means that delivery of new versions on time is critically important. In maintenance situation there is no fallback. It therefore has to be done. The process 'planning and control' has for an objective to make sure that scheduled time and possible delivery time are realized by using the right input of (human) capacity at the right moments in time. The process boils down to management of time and human capacity in the broadest sense. Together with the client it is determined which services have to be supplied at which moments. The process is therefore closely related to the process 'change management.' Planning and control secures both the 'project-oriented' activities (the processes within the maintenance/renewal cluster) as 'continuous' activities (the day in, day out application management cluster). The simultaneous controlling of these, often executed by the same department and the same people, is the big challenge of application management. This task is complex namely because regularly supplementing not immediately eye-catching operational activities have to be carried out as well. Examples are improvement projects as result of quality management or service level management and activities for the benefit of the strategic processes within ACM and OCM. All these activities demand human capacity. Planning and control is the process that has to organize it all.

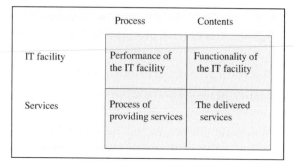

Figure 5.6. Four different subjects for agreement about service levels

Cost management

The second process is cost management. At cost management it is about providing insight into the costs and making these controllable. Cost management includes the processes around managing and charging on the costs of the IT services. Based upon this matters pertaining to business economics by the functional management are possible. Purely financial subjects like: what are depreciation periods, how is the cost price of an hourly rate built up exactly and what is included in that and what isn't, don't come under application management and therefore not under cost management within ASL. These are issues for the staff department finances in an IT organization.

Service level management

Service level management is the third process. In this the agreements with the customer are made and safeguarded. Central point is the 'quality perception' of the customer: that what the customer perceives as quality. This as opposed to the process 'quality management,' whereby the internal quality of application and application management organization are the central point. The agreements with the customers are usually connected with four areas, that is to say (see Figure 5.6):

  − the performance of the IT facilities: these are about the availability, the performance, the reliability and the security of the IT facilities.

- the functionality of the IT facility and the changes to the functionality. 'Service levels' in this domain are specified and checked by means of, amongst other things, acceptance tests.
- the process of service providing, that is to say the functioning of the service and the application management organization. This includes entering into agreements about the accessibility and availability of the organization itself, the rate of operating in case of incidents, the manner in which software is delivered, the timelines along which the processes elapse, etc.;
- the provided service: this concerns the services that are provided and the additional services that are available under matching conditions. In other words, the service catalogue of the organization.

Service level management therefore does know the activities definition, safeguarding and evaluation. Application management makes agreements with functional management. The results of these agreements, like a contract and an SLA (service level agreement) are important products of service level management.

Quality management

The last process at tactical level is quality management. The goal of quality management is taking care of maintaining the internal quality of process and product. In order to achieve this it aims at four subjects:

1. The quality of the product: by this is meant the (technical and functional) quality of the IT facility and its functioning.
2. The quality of the process: the way in which the process of maintenance is set up. At professionalization and increase of the level of services the attention is mainly fixed on this subject.
3. The quality of the IT facilities, used for making the products and along which this process elapses. This is also called the quality system. It includes among other things the methods used and techniques and tools for system building.
4. The quality of the organization. This subject aims at matters like quality of people and expertise, explicitness, its coherence and the position of the application management in the organization and the environment.

Maintenance and renewal

The first process at operational level is maintenance and renewal. This process differs from the process of introducing entirely new applications or building new applications because it takes place in a situation of an existing organization, an existing infrastructure and an existing application. It therefore includes less measures of freedom. Furthermore, the introduction of changes follows the 'bottom-up' principle. In this situation one would sooner see a change to be just a small change. If that is not possible, a wider view is taken by looking at, for instance, a group of IT facilities. Apart from this the process takes place in a line setting. And finally, the deadlines for maintenance are usually rigid. Different from an entirely new facility, not yet in production, the alternative of keeping the existing IT facility on line a little longer is not possible: that is the facility that is being adjusted.

Within the cluster maintenance and renewal five processes can be distinguished. These are:

1. *impact analysis*: the activities being performed within the framework of conditioning and mapping of the consequences of a proposal for change;
2. *design*: the analysis of the situation and the design of the IT facility. The activities that deal with determining and recording of the desired functionality;
3. *realization*: the modifying, realizing and assembly of the IT facility;
4. *testing*: the testing of the modified components as well as the whole equipment, with for an end result acceptance and release of by the client delivered products;
5. *implementation*: the definitive introduction of the changed software and other service providing components, including attention for things like conversion, acceptance (tests), training, instruction and migration, followed by release.

Day-in/day out management

The cluster of daily management activities within ASL distinguishes five processes that are closely related. These five management processes are:

1. *incident management*: this takes care of the primary dealing with queries, requests and incidents, including the communication from and towards functional management;
2. *configuration management*: the process surrounding the recording and keeping up to date of information on the use of the (versions of) objects;
3. *availability management*: takes care of, secures and safeguards the availability of IT facilities;
4. *capacity management*: looks after the optimum application of means, that is to say in the right place, at the right time, in the right quantities and at justified costs;
5. *continuity management*: in this process measures are taken for ensuring the continuity of the execution and the support in the long run.

Target group of incident management is the functional management or those that, within the user organization(s) carry out functional management tasks. One could distinguish between reactive communication and proactive communication between application management and its customers. When communicating reactively, one waits. One deals with 'calls' or 'incidents.' And only at the moment these come in. An incident is in this case a query, request, and complaint or problem report, mostly coming from users or end users. In application management these are not just originating from functional management but could also come into being within the processes of application management itself (one establishes for instance that an IT facility operates much slower than one could possibly expect) or from exploitation (one reports for example that an IT facility does not function any more).

The second form of communication is proactive. This means that customers are approached in order to prevent queries. If for example a new release goes into production, detailed information is given in advance about the new functionality and about the use of this new functionality. Through this last type of communication one may prevent 'reactive' reactions.

The process configuration management ensures insight into what it is all about. The process configuration management aims to register this information and supply information on this. This information consists of two parts:

– The IT facility: what runs where? And when deciding to archive data about this, one should always take decisions on the measure of detail and the

	Availability	Reliability
Central: availability: offering requested functionality at a given moment and reliability: extent to which IT object supplies the requested functions		
IT facility	Up time	Operating according specifications
IT service that comes with it:	Opening hours service desk	Correctness of acting

Figure 5.7. Subjects availability management

status of the data. Concerning the latter, it may be a facility that is planned, in development, being tested or in production.
– The agreed services: which agreements where?

In organizations that deliver packages or organizations that deal with applications that run in various places this process is very important. One should know which versions of a package have been delivered where exactly, of what these consist and on which infrastructure they run. This information is necessary for being able to react adequately in case of, for instance, incidents or questions.

At the third process, availability management, two quality characteristics are central: the availability and the reliability of the IT facility. The availability indicates the measure in which an IT facility is able to offer the desired functionality at a certain moment in time or for a certain length of time. The reliability is the measure in which this offers the agreed or expected functionality, during an indicated length of time. Both quality aspects concern both the contents and the process of service provision. This means that the process of availability management controls the four objects indicated in Figure 5.7.

The fourth process is capacity management. In application management capacity and performance also play an important part and this also needs attention during management. The reasons being:

(a) an adequate set-up and an adequate data approach to a high extent determine the performance of the IT facility;
(b) many IT facilities were procured at an initially assessed workload;
(c) the amounts to be processed may vary greatly sometimes. The knowledge or how this finally results in processing lies with application

management. They provide the translation between business process and the IT facility.

In order to keep the performance up to standard or optimize it, several measures are possible like revising of data (removal of no longer used data), changing of the access paths to the data, the increasing of rows or the optimising of the set-up of the software. Dealing with this is the task of capacity management.

The last process in day-in/day-out management is continuity management. This process deals with the continuity of the IT facility. Continuity is the measure in which the IT facility in the long run, without incident or with an acceptable risk, can keep functioning in future. This subject is discussed in Chapter 15, security of IT facilities.

QUESTIONS

1. Who controls application management? Why should application management be organized? Or is this not always necessary? Explain your answer using two examples: a case in which this should be done and an example of a case where this is less opportune.
2. What are the advantages of organizing application management? Illustrate at least five advantages with an example.
3. How is ASL put together?
4. What is OCM? Of which processes does it consist? And why are these needed?
5. What is ACM? Of which processes does it consist? And why are these needed?
6. What is the difference in objects in application management for tailor made and application management for standard applications? Illustrate your answer with an example.
7. To what do we control the operational processes of the day in/ day out keeping in production of IT facilities? Which processes can be distinguished?
8. To which four domains do the agreements in service level agreements often apply? Illustrate your answer with an example.
9. Which processes come under the ASL processes maintenance and renewal?
10. What comes under the ASL process day-in/day-out management? Illustrate your answer with three examples.

Chapter 6

The supply-side: exploitation (using methods like ITIL, MOF-MSF/eTOM)

Introduction of ITIL led to structuring of exploitation tasks. This enables measuring at processes, which after a while can result in actions to improve of the quality of these processes. Next, it became possible to take the customer's priorities more into account. For instance within the Imtech company introduction of ITIL provided structure and overview. So it was possible to process more calls and one was able to work more in conformity with the priorities as set by the customer. The customer satisfaction improved because the supply-side met the agreements to such an extent that it really fitted in with the organization's strategy.

There are many methods for lining up the processes at the supply-side. ITIL is in The Netherlands clearly the most frequently used method for exploitation of IT facilities. Apart from this, TMN is also widely used in the telecommunications business, whilst Microsoft also offers its customers some support in this field with MSF and MOF. What are actually the differences between all these methods? Is there a framework available?

Such a floor plan of a computer centre explains a lot. It clearly shows the evolution that took place in the centre through the years. Zoning became a necessity. Networks for speech and data were set up. Massive print facilities

95

were introduced and lately servers with their demilitarised zones for internet. This computer floor has been witness to a lot of history over the past thirty years.

ITIL structures the tasks in the field of exploitation. This can be looked upon with the eye of efficiency. You may also look upon this with the eye of the quality of labour, if this still exists after a while. ITIL clearly results in a more balanced division of tasks, to more sight on the results. Introduction of ITIL however also allows less freedom of action and provides a stronger sense of control. Some organizations counteract the negative effects as much as possible by involving people at the introduction and communicating the reasons for introducing ITIL.

Contents of this chapter

Structured handling of the exploitation of IT facilities is the subject of this chapter. For structuring the processes at exploitation the Information Technology Infrastructure Library (ITIL) method is chosen. Discussion of this method is the core of this chapter. Apart from this, other methods in the domain of structuring of exploitation processes like the Microsoft Operations Framework (MOF), the Microsoft Service delivery Framework (MSF), the Telecommunication Management Network (TMN) and the enhanced Telecom Operations Map (eTOM), TMN and eTOM being recommendations of the International Telecommunications Union, are explained in this chapter.

The chapter starts with positioning the exploitation task at the supply-side. This supply-side is controlled by functional management at the demand-side. Functional management is housed with the demand organization. The exploitation deals with the keeping in production of IT facilities. In this chapter first the layout of a computer centre is discussed and the points of action available to control such a centre. Next, the ITIL, MOF/MSF, TMN and eTOM methods come up for discussion.

THE PLACE OF EXPLOITATION
The supply-side

Functional management controls tasks in the field of application management and exploitation. Each of these tasks includes activities at operational,

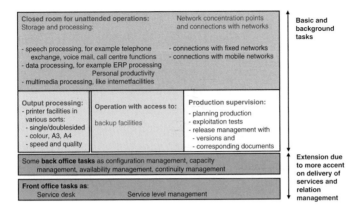

Figure 6.1. Floor plan of a computer centre

tactical and strategic level. The functional management team has connections at each of these levels with exploitation and application management.

Functional management is situated in the user organization. Application management is at an IT development and maintenance organization. Exploitation is located at a computer centre organization. This organization keeps computer centres in production. In these centres storage, processing and transport hardware and software have been installed. In Figure 6.1 the floor plan of such a computer centre is given.

COMPUTER CENTRES AND CONTROL OF COMPUTER CENTRES

Computer centres

Exploiting IT facilities means that the objects in production operate in conformity with the agreed functional and performance requirements and in the managed objects changes are made according to plan. The exploitation environment recognizes three types of objects: organization objects, infrastructure objects and application objects.

In a computer centre (see Figure 6.1) four rooms are distinguished for basic and background tasks, each intended for a different task. These rooms are designated for:

–operating the hardware, which often includes running the service desk. This room is often connected with a room which the employees use for their break;
–functioning of processing, storage and transport hardware and software;
–providing space for printer and converting facilities;
–preparing the implementation of new applications and infrastructures, as well as controlling the day-to-day operation. Amongst other things this is where change management is taken care of and batchwork prepared.

Set-up computer centre

Hardware is placed in each of these rooms. In the computer room you can see processing, storage and transport hardware and software, printers in the printer room, back-up units with off line storage capacity on cartridges and tapes plus control consoles in the operating room and personal computers in the production room. In the equipping of these rooms attention is paid to things like:

–the requirements of hardware with regard to energy and cooling;
–the performance standard of availability, what can be translated in uninterrupted facilities such as air conditioning, maintaining the right degree of humidity and electricity supply;
–the necessity for providing extra security for certain rooms;
–installation of mock-ups and stands for consoles and modems;
–the placing of transport facilities for local area networks, wide area networks and telephony inside and outside the organization;
–location of processing, storage and network facilities;
–the need for simply posting hardcopy.

Performance requirements

The exploitation of IT facilities has to meet with performance requirements. These requirements mainly figure in the field of availability, response time and security. For meeting these requirements one can take measures. In general one increases the availability of technical infrastructures by means of:

–Executing parts of the infrastructure in duplicate, like the one for printing, storage and processing. After all, if the chances of a machine breaking down are 0.01, the chance two identical machines fail at the same time is

0.01 times 0.01 or 0.0001 (if the chances of failure are independent). It is also possible to carry out the entire transaction centre in duplicate. One then has an escape route.

–Proactive reacting to reports as given in the error logs of hardware and in the output when using system software.
–Having insight into the functioning of the fixed and mobile network by using network monitors that often graphically reproduce the network and its usage.
–Having remote support facilities at one's disposal for repairing software and hardware at distance or being able to download programme technical fixes (PTF's).
–Having the facilities for checking the transaction units day and night for errors and taking action when errors occur, so users can continue working because the necessary repair has been taken care of (even before they arrive at work).

The guarantee of a general good response time is directly linked to the presence of sufficient capacity. When assessing this mainly the occupation of the servers and storage units is taken into consideration. Securing of infrastructures has many sides. Measures such as logging transactions and encrypting data at transport and archive are examples of this.

Precautionary measures

When looking at the availability of applications it is also possible to take precautionary measures. One could for instance implement facilities to:

–Record what data was stored, before processing the transaction and then record the transactions. Combined with a back-up of the data it is then always possible to reconstruct the data collection.
–Regularly making a back-up of data collections and of the applications. This back-up is often made according to the grandfather–father–son system. It is possible to realize the situation of a few days back, providing a back-up was made every day. Transactions processed after the back-up are not available.
–Having the procedure of the most common action available online, which means that fast and controlled assistance according to a predetermined script can take place. This promotes a standard procedure. Mostly this procedure is recorded in the administrative organization handbook.

Possible problems at the response time of applications can be prevented by checking during the test for taking an application in exploitation, in which areas there could be possible problems in response time. The security of applications can be increased by limiting the number of persons authorized per part of the application or by making sure that it is always clear who used the application at a given time and therefore to take care of guarantees of authentication.

Controlling computer centres

Exploitation environments are controlled in a number of different ways. Firstly this is the control based upon qualitative and quantative data of components and service processes. A second method is the use of standards for objects to be implemented and for implementing these objects in projects using project management methods. The latter method of control is control on the basis of agreements as recorded in manuals.

Standards

Using standards is important, when realizing that organizations get the bulk of objects to be exploited delivered from third parties. Suppliers deliver for instance servers or processing units, applications and network components. Suppliers also deliver operating systems, database management systems and network software. New applications and hardware have to be supported by higher versions of the current infrastructure software. In these later versions the programmes are found to control these new objects. The system management and network software for infrastructures therefore recognizes releases and versions within releases.

An organization mostly has a policy with regard to the versions of the various types of infrastructure software it installs. The policy dictates under which versions it provides its products and services. This policy is called version policy. By outlining a version policy concerning all versions for infrastructure software, the diversity in versions can be lessened. Version management concentrates mainly on management of versions of operating systems, network management software, data management software and support software.

In version management one should preferably have the version to be installed in future at one's disposal, as well as the currently installed version and the version that was replaced at the last install. These versions of every product are supplied with manuals or documents. When these manuals are supplied on paper, a central library where all these manuals can be found is certainly no luxury.

Administrative organization

The administrative organization of an exploitation environment consists usually of a description of three subjects. These are: a general handbook describing the organization and its modus operandi. This handbook includes a description of the working methods in a number of departments and for executing certain processes. Furthermore it records the configuration concerning objects to be managed and indicates the existence of manuals that provide a detailed description of the processes of document- and version management. Besides these manuals there are production dossiers per application, in which is recorded how an application can be taken in production, which errors could occur in the production and how to remedy these. The manuals, that are present in a computer centre, so often include:

- An operations manual, which includes: the actions at starting up in the morning (checks); the organization within the building: who should be notified and when; the procedure at disasters: which and what next; the use of registrations; the manner of back-up and how this is done; the manner in which the most frequently used hardware is operated; warnings which actions definitely should not be carried out, etc.
- A production supervision manual including amongst other things the tasks of the production supervision; the organization of production supervision including the necessary forms; the procedure for implementing system changes; applying for and realizing of system environments for building, testing and production and the procedure for applying for storage media.
- A description of the working of the service desk. This is the department of the front-office the customers of exploitation call, when they require help.
- A description of the processes change management and release management. These are the processes that are in charge of the implementing of new versions methodically. Often this also includes how to deal with emergencies in this field, such as the implementation of showstoppers. These are incidents that have to be fixed immediately. Showstoppers are implemented directly in the production environment after having been tested in an exploitation test environment.

– A security manual, in which the organization has indicated in which manner security is organized, who is responsible for what, what the policy is in various situations and which measures have been taken.

– A description of the way in which service level management, capacity and availability management and reporting on management are dealt with. This includes financial management.

Apart form the above manuals there are manuals describing the process of version and document management in detail. These manuals are:

– A version management manual that deals mainly with the versions of application software. It indicates how one gets versions from the stage of building to functional testing, user test, exploitation test and from thereon towards production. It also reports which and how many versions are kept for enabling return to a previous production environment and who is responsible for which task. It also includes chapters on taking in production of hardware using change management. This indicates when and how hardware to be taken into production is tested and also what hardware is tested and which measures one should take, if implementation fails.

– A document management manual, which describes how all documents made during the building and implementation of applications are archived. These documents could be for instance definition studies, functional designs, technical designs, test files and administrative organization manuals. Usually there are a design version, a test version and a production version of a document.

Finally within the computer centre documents have to be present for the hardware that is going to be used and for the infrastructure software that was procured from third parties. For each of these objects there are generally spoken available a general introduction, a users manual and an installation manual.

THE IT INFRASTRUCTURE LIBRARY (ITIL): A METHOD OUTLINING THE PROCESSES IN IT EXPLOITATION

ITIL

For arriving at transparent work processes in the exploitation these processes are often set up in conformity with the ITIL (Information Technology Infrastructure Library) method. The seven books in which ITIL is described,

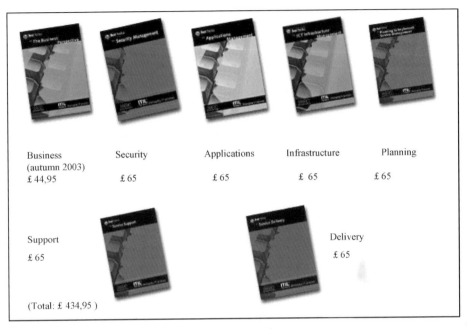

| Business (autumn 2003) £ 44,95 | Security £ 65 | Applications £ 65 | Infrastructure £ 65 | Planning £ 65 |

| Support £ 65 | | Delivery £ 65 |

(Total: £ 434,95)

Figure 6.2. The ITIL books

are shown in Figure 6.2. The ITIL method recognizes a number of processes at strategic, tactical and operational level. An exploitation organization should include each of these in some form. ITIL is based on 'best practices' of British government organizations. ITIL then, in cooperation with many other organizations, was extended further. The method in practice developed at the privatization of the (mainframe) computer centres of the British government. The customers of these centres started to ask themselves next, how they could make demands on the services provided by privatized computer centres.

They realized that for doing this they had to have insight into the processes that take place in these computer centres. This resulted in ITIL, a method providing insight into the processes of computer centres, their proceedings and their coherence. Based upon this insight into the processes one was able to agree on quantitative criteria for the quality of the delivery of services and the quality of products. These became the later service level agreements.

Angles

ITIL distinguished five closely connected angles on ITIL management of IT facilities (see Figure 6.3). These five angles are:

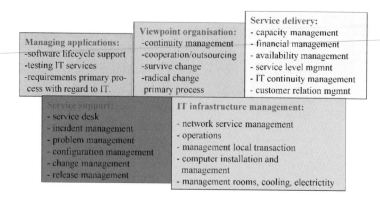

Figure 6.3. Cohering angles on the exploitation of IT

−the organization of the facilities. This goes into continuity management, cooperating with third organizations, dealing with an evolutionary change of the IT organizations, and realizing of radical changes in service processes;

−managing of applications. This includes supporting the life cycle of software, testing of new services and the care for making these services mesh with the customers' wishes. In this book the ASL approach to application management is used. The reason for this choice is that ASL is more complete and less aimed at sheer exploitation of IT facilities. The person who performs application management, also recognizes his tasks in ASL;

−the service delivery processes. This is where the more tactical tasks at exploitation come into play. These are the tasks capacity management, financial management, availability management, service level management, IT continuity management and dealing with customers;

−the service support processes. This discusses the tasks needed for running a service desk, for executing incident management, for problem management, for configuration management, change management and release management;

−the IT infrastructure management. This includes network service management, operations of IT facilities, management of local processing, installation of computers and maintenance on these and management of rooms with subjects like cooling, electricity supply etc.

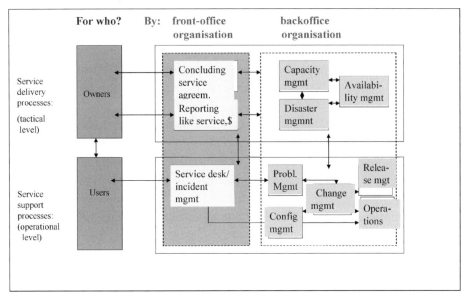

Figure 6.4. ITIL tasks in service delivery and service support plus the operations task

Concentrating on service delivery and support

In the United Kingdom and the Netherlands, IT organizations often apply service support and service delivery tasks in conformity with ITIL. The service support set contains tasks at operational level. The service delivery set contains the tasks at tactical level. In Figure 6.4 these tasks are shown and in Appendix E these are explained in more detail.

Application of ITIL in IT exploitation provides insight into the coherence of the tasks to be performed. These tasks are often performed by various departments, whereby every department takes care of part of the task. Attuning of tasks between departments is usually combined with measures at organizational level and measures to provide the information needed to perform the task.

In Figure 6.4 the ITIL tasks are shown in such a way it is possible to distinguish front-office and back-office tasks. It becomes clear which processes are used by people that own or pay for IT facilities, for controlling the exploitation organization and come to agreements about services to be delivered and the level of these services. It also becomes transparent, where the questions from customers enter the exploitation organization.

Agreements with the owners of, or the people that pay for IT facilities are translated in the back-office. Customers use these facilities and have then contact with a service desk. If the service desk fails to find a solution within a given time, the query is passed on to problem management. Next, under control of problem management a solution is reached. The service desk reports this solution to the users.

Owners of or payers for IT services and products request from an IT organization services and products of a certain quality. These services are provided by the organization itself or by means of calling in suppliers. A demand for services may lead to changes in the infrastructure to be managed and in applications. These changes are implemented, tested and taken into production. The control of processes in the IT organization from the contact with users or owners is called the process approach of IT management.

The service processes in the front-office are started up by a customer query. This query may arise any moment and the moment in time when action is demanded cannot always be planned ahead. Service processes in the front-office start service processes in the back-office. These last processes are set up more systematically. One doesn't want the back-office running from incident to incident.

In Figure 6.4 is shown that owners of IT facilities and managers enter into agreements with each other about the services to be provided. These agreements are often in the shape of service agreements. Staff members of capacity management, availability management, disaster management and financial management participate in the realization of these agreements in order to see what the impact of the owners' query is for the IT configuration, its use and the costs involved in this. After conclusion of a service agreement the provided service is periodically reported on.

Example

The immigration and naturalization service demanded a 7 × 24-hours availability of the central register aliens (part of Dutch immigration services), with the normal response times and security. Any incident within the application also had to be fixed within fifteen minutes. At translating these demands into IT facilities two aspects are involved. Firstly, getting the functional and performance requirements clear and also their translation into action to be carried out and the responsibilities for the front and back-office. Secondly, the set-up of the organization in order to substantiate the agreed functional and performance requirements. These actions could mean two people having to work in five shifts and charging at the appropriate expense level.

Change in the exploitation environment is carried out under coordination of change management. These changes could be different in nature. These could be implemented systematically; these could also have more of an ad hoc character. Changes of a more ad hoc character are showstoppers. These are calls that come in at the service desk and have to result in immediate action of the back-office. In that case, there are incidents of such a nature; the supporting primary process had ground to a halt. When this happens, the service desk reports the show-stopper to problem management; they immediately start an investigation into the problem and find a solution. Implementing of the solution takes place under coordination of change management. Through change management release management is brought into action, the production environment adjusted, the change implemented and the configuration updated. In order to get an approving audit certificate this process may be provided with extra guarantees. An example of this is the requirement that application of the change in the production environment by the IT department is only done in the presence of at least one member of staff of the internal control department.

Example

If a customer reports a function of an application can not be used and it is clear that the other 10,000 customers of this application also have this problem and this function is used by each and everyone of them at least 100 times a day in their work, action has to be undertaken. This is called a showstopper.

Furthermore it is possible to arrive more systematically at change in the configuration. In this case, this is called implementing a new version or a new release. Other more systematically carried out tasks are keeping the IT environment in production day-in day-out.

ADVANTAGES AND DISADVANTAGES OF INTRODUCING ITIL

The organization that manages the ITIL method has indicated what the advantages for an organization could be, when implementing ITIL. In Figure 6.5

Process:	Goal:	Example costs/benefits:
Configuration management:	Control of the IT objects Ensure only authorized hw+sw is present,	After CMDB implementation there is better insight at the service desk. Number of staff can decrease by 35%.
Incident management	Deliver service continuously at the right level.	Incident management has lowered the downtime/user by 1 minute per person per day.
Problem management	Minimizing incidents	Through problem management 10% less repeating calls occur.
Change management	Dealing with changes efficiently	Two changes implemented at same time. This causes problems.
Release management	Ensuring the right modules are used.	Application over and 50 customers lost.Application has to be installed again, wrong version=>shut down 67% staff doing nothing for 3 hours
Service level management	Agreeing on and controlling of service levels. Understanding needs of customer.	Good SLA´s so less calls about matters not included in SLA. Service desk of 4 people is 5% more efficient.
Availability management	Ensuring high availability of the services.	Physical error makes server crash, supporting 100 people. It takes 3 hours before being online.
Capacity-management	Ensuring optimal use of the IT facilities	There is an over capacity of 20% at a 5 million infrastructure.
Continuity management	Guarantee a fast recovery after a disaster.	Watermains burst. Restoring computer room takes 2 days. Average user can't work for 10 hours
Financial management	Ensuring insight into, control of and charging of IT services.	A 10% cost reduction for new services➔ 10% less IT costs

Figure 6.5. Advantages of the implementation of ITIL according to the OGC

these advantages are listed. Studying this figure, it is obvious these advantages are caused by improved structuring of work processes. At the same amount of work this results mainly in savings on labour.

Schreuder (2001) has also researched the effects of ITIL. He examined the service desk processes because these processes are often the starting point at introducing ITIL. By means of in-depth interviews with heads of the service desk and by means of a written survey of employees of service desks he carried out his research. In Figure 6.6 the views of the employees on the use of the method are shown. Schreuder concluded that, when striving for better quality of labour, introducing ITIL may result in better functional contacts, a more evenly balanced distribution of work, a clear view of the results of the work and a clear

Plus points and minuses ITIL according to employees

Positive points:	Negative points:
* registration of all calls provides overview	* bureaucracy: leads to delays during incidents
* procedures provide insight into the course of a call	* strict procedures limit freedom of movement
* structured approach works easy.	* rules sometimes petty
* more structure provides more clarity	* ITIL only functions if everybody sticks to rules
* creates more uniformity	* sometimes it is more time consuming

Figure 6.6. Advantages and disadvantages of ITIL according to the employees

and transparent work structure. At the same time, introducing ITIL may mean that employees experience their work as less varied, less challenging and get less opportunities for fleshing out their job. The structuralization may also cause decreasing possibilities for social contacts and make it easier for the management to control the work.

A FEW ITIL PROCESSES IN MORE DETAIL

Next, a few ITIL processes will be discussed in more detail. These are the process service desk, the process service level management and the process availability management.

Service support

One of the processes in the ITIL service support set is the service desk process. In Figure 6.7 the flowchart of such a service desk process is shown. This flowchart shows how a call goes through four phases: registration, classification, investigation and diagnosis and finally providing a solution. During these four phases the status is guarded. Does it take too long to come to a solution; the call is transferred to a back-office-process, problem management. The solving

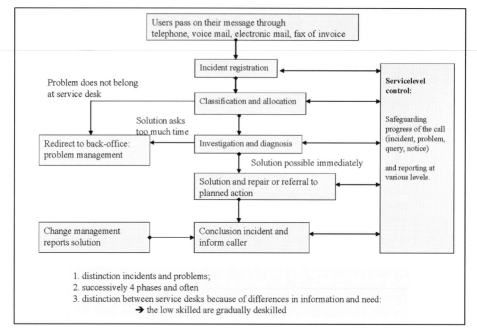

Figure 6.7. Process of a service desk

of a problem may lead to immediate action; it may also lead to a proposition for including the solution in the next version or release of the IT facility.

A service desk may be designed in many ways. If there are usually a lot of calls to be dealt with, a certain degree of standardization has to be achieved in the completion in order to enable guaranteed reasonable elapsed times. One will then often choose to put the most commonly appearing solutions on an internet site. If one usually doesn't get that many calls, one will be able to supply a larger diversity of services. This may sometimes even be tailor made. The services provided by the service desk therefore may be shaped according to the number of incoming calls.

Anyway, after the service has been in production for a while, the nature of the incoming calls usually changes. The technical problems have usually been resolved by then. By that time customers ask more often for user support and spontaneously report possibilities for improvement. In Figure 6.8 this is shown. From Figure 6.8 it also becomes clear that the incoming call is registered in every case. This way, a memory is created: that way the service provider gets a better idea of what to expect. He is able to anticipate questions, he is

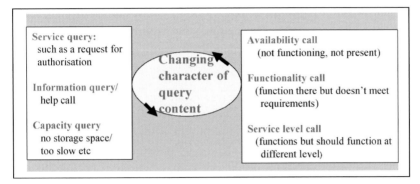

Figure 6.8. Changing types of calls at a service desk

in almost all cases able to deal with calls immediately without mobilizing the back-office and he is increasingly more able to meet the real requirements of the customers.

The service desk process is often supported by IT to a high degree. Figure 6.9 shows examples of this support. The figure also gives examples of services provided by the service desk.

The figure distinguishes between a primary and a second-line service desk. The primary is specialized in dealing with the bulk of the questions, the

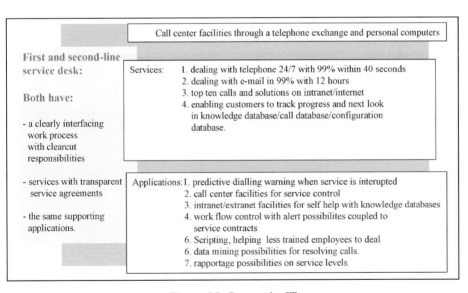

Figure 6.9. Support by IT

second-line deals with queries in a certain field and/or more in depth queries. An example of this is a primary service desk that mainly deals with authorization problems and a second-line involved in dealing with substantive questions about the usage of the ERP system.

Service delivery

Of all the processes in the ITIL service delivery set, here we would like to discuss the process service level management and the process availability management. Service level management includes the processes for planning SLA's, attuning, developing, agreeing, checking and reporting on SLA's, plus reviewing service performances. This makes it possible to ensure the required service is supplied at the right quality level and this quality is improved step by step.

Service level management

The chapter about service level management in the book ITIL service delivery is arranged as seen in Figure 6.10. The figure indicates, what the critical factors of success are for a service and how these can be made measurable. ITIL considers the following factors as critical factors of success for the set-up of service management in an organization:

  – the percentage of services, of which SLA's have been concluded;
  – the fact whether the performances as agreed are checked and measured in the SLA's and whether or not these are reported on regularly;

> Introduction: why, goal,scope, basic concept
> The process: benefits, costs, problems
> Planning the proces➜ SLA´s
> Implementing the process: concluding, setting
>   up, monitoring, review
> Ongoing process
> SLA contents and key targets
> Key performance indicators
> Annex. The service level manager
>   Example simple serv.catalogue
>   Example SLA Man. Chart
>   Framework SLA

Figure 6.10. Subjects in the chapter about service level management in conformity with the
        OGC

 −the fact whether review meetings are held and whether reports are made
  of these meetings, in which agreements are registered;
 −the fact whether there is written proof that these agreements are turned
  into actions;
 −the fact whether the SLA's and contracts are up-to-date. It is advisable to
  check the percentage SLA's that hasn't changed in two years.
 −the percentage of the set service goals that is achieved. This goes into the
  number and type of serious failures.
 −the manner in which serious failures are dealt with;
 −the gradual improvement in the view of the customer;
 −the cutback in costs for unchanged IT facilities.

Service manager tasks

   Tasks of the service manager are, according to the OGC, the organization
that manages the ITIL method, amongst other things:

 −keeping a services catalogue up to date;
 −making and maintaining an organization for service level management
  with SLA's, in which there is also room for managing contracts with external parties;
 −leading of programmes for improving the quality of the services;
 −negotiating and concluding service level agreements with internal and
  external parties;
 −analyzing and reviewing the performances with regards to the agreements
  as concluded in the SLA;
 −producing service reports and discussing these with contract partners;
 −annually performing reviews on the service level management process.

Availability management

   An example of a back-office task at tactical level is availability management. This process gains importance because of the increasing independence of
operational IT processes. The costs of not being available are the sum of:

 −the costs of using IT for solving the problem;
 −the costs of the loss of user time;
 −the costs of the impact the lack of service has to the customer and his
  organization;

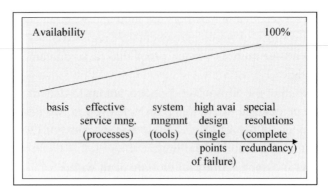

Figure 6.11. Possibilities for enhancing the availability of IT facilities

–and other costs, such as costs of overtime, the costs of temporary workers for repairs, the costs of advances, the costs of fines etc. etc.

No wonder, organizations consider achieving an increasingly higher degree of availability. Figure 6.11 shows that higher levels of availability can be accomplished by setting up service management, removing single points of failure by duplicating parts and also by multiple execution of IT facilities as a whole. In Chapter 15 the method to be used for this is systematically discussed.

Looking at availability one may conclude that availability figures are often expressed in IT terms. One speaks of percentage availability during the planned opening hours of an IT services, the number of times the service was not available etc. For users of the service these numbers have limited use. An user experiences him-self how frequent the service or a product is not available. He has to cope with the duration of the non-availability and the effect of this on his own organization. He would prefer to see non-availability indicated in his own terms, such as the number of lost user minutes or the number of transactions that weren't realized as a result.

OTHER METHODS THAT INDICATE THE PROCESSES AT IT EXPLOITATION

Other methods

Having discussed ITIL, we will go into four other methods for setting up the exploitation of IT facilities. These are Microsoft MOF/MSF and TMN/

eTOM, both recommendations of the ITU (International Telecommunications Union).

The reason for this is that every method can put its own accents on the exploitation of IT. Van Hemmen (1997) has listed these accents for a number of methods. He looked at the object of management, the focus of the method, the acceptance of the method in the market and the type of processes (functional management, application management or exploitation) the method supported. We will do the same here, having chosen four methods, that is to say MOF/MSF and TMN/eTOM. The reason for this choice is that TMN/eTOM are recommendations of the ITU and TMN as such is frequently used in the telecommunications-industry (eTOM is still too young for this) and Microsoft is the dominant player in the field of personal productivity tools in organizations. We start with the Microsoft methods.

MOF and MSF

Microsoft has two methods in the field of IT management: the Microsoft Operations Framework (MOF) and the MSF (Microsoft Service delivery Framework). The first framework focuses on the exploitation ('run IT right'), whilst the second focuses on the implementation ('build IT right').

In Figure 6.12 the Microsoft operations framework is shown. The framework has four quadrants. Each quadrant focuses on a different task of the day to day IT management. The four tasks distinguished in MOF are: exploitation, support, optimalization and change. Before an IT facility can change quadrant a review takes place. Each review has an output. This could be, amongst other things, the approval for a version to be made, the approval for an implementation and comparing exploitation with the concluded service level agreements. In these reviews the following six roles have to be considered:

- the security role: this role takes care of virus protection, protection of the intellectual property, network and system security, discovery of intrusions, auditing and looking after the compliance administration and performing contingency planning;
- the role of the partners of the management organization: this role deals with the sellers of the IT facilities, the companies for facilities maintenance and other supporters like cleaners and electricians, the suppliers of managed services, outsourcers etc.

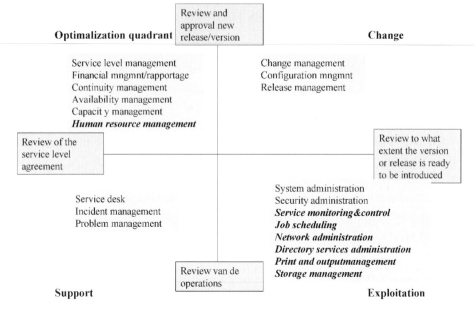

Figure 6.12. Microsoft Operations Framework

– the roles for release of new versions and releases. These take care of change management, release management, configuration management/asset management, software distribution/licences and quality assurance;
– the IT infrastructure facilities role: this role takes care of capacity management, the architecture and its realization, cost management and the means and long term planning;
– the support roles: this looks after the tasks service desk, exploitation support, problem management and service level management;
– the exploitation role: this looks after the monitoring and the key performance indicators; it performs the operations tasks for the databases and the network, availability management and network administration.

MSF

Microsoft solutions framework is about implementation of IT facilities. It distinguished in this a set of successive processes. These are executed by small, parallel working teams. The different processes are: idea development, planning,

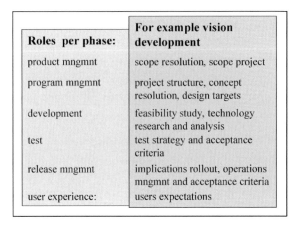

Roles per phase:	For example vision development
product mngmnt	scope resolution, scope project
program mngmnt	project structure, concept resolution, design targets
development	feasibility study, technology research and analysis
test	test strategy and acceptance criteria
release mngmnt	implications rollout, operations mngmnt and acceptance criteria
user experience:	users expectations

Figure 6.13. Roles in the idea development phase

building of the IT facility, ensuring stabilization and rollout. Per phase products are delivered and roles for teams can be discerned (see for example Figure 6.13). The teams concerned are involved in:

- programme management;
- building of the product and surrounding service;
- testing of the product and the service;
- release management: controlling SLA's, building of test environments, etc.;
- exchange of user experiences;
- product management.

Apart from the team and the process model, MSF provides advice for implementing with as little risk as possible, ensuring a basis, amongst other things by training people, and for executing projects.

TMN model

Another model for structuring IT exploitation is the TMN model. The TMN model is based on recommendation M3010 of the International Telecommunications Union. In this recommendation it is remarked that, at exploitation of IT products and services, a common basis is known for the information on security, used or to be used configuration, costs made, availability of the IT facility,

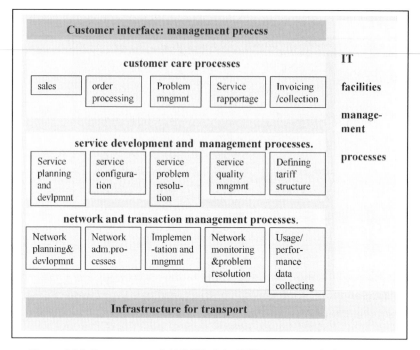

Figure 6.14. Processes model TMN of the ITU (recommendation M3010)

experienced incidents or problems and reports at the service desk. TMN remarks furthermore that this information can be used for decisions on different levels. In order to obtain the information, functions have to be included in hardware and software. These functions communicate in a standard fashion with other software and/or hardware.

In Figure 6.14 the process model for TMN (Telecommunication Management Networks) is shown. We see in this model a distinction between customer care, services building and management processes and network and transaction management processes.

eTOM-model

The TeleManagement Forum, an international consortium of service providers in the communications field, has, using TMN as a basis, brought out a new proposal for the set-up of processes at services in this sector. This proposal

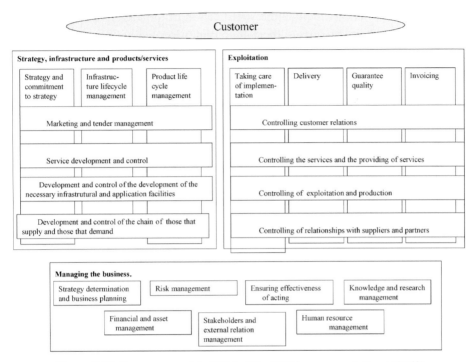

Figure 6.15. Processes model eTOM of the ITU (recommendation M3050)

was officially recognized in March 2004 as recommendation M3050 of the International Telecommunications Union in the field of telecommunication (ITU-T). In Figure 6.15 this process model, named eTOM or Enhanced Telecom Operations Map, is indicated. The ITU states the following about the relationship between TMN and eTOM in the press release in which the eTOM recommendation is announced:

> *"Network operators and equipment suppliers will be able to use eTOM alongside existing ITU-T guidelines for telecommunications management defined in its Telecommunication Management Network (TMN) specifications for internal processes re-engineering, partnership management, and product and service specification. Indeed eTOM will become an important part of TMN."*

In eTOM, the dichotomy between development and maintenance and exploitation this book started with in Chapter 1 can be seen again. Apart from that, both sections of eTOM include the stratification of the TMN M3010 standard. There are customers' processes, there are service processes, and there is technical execution.

QUESTIONS

1. Give the floor plan of a computer centre. Name four requirements, one pays attention to when setting up such a centre. Illustrate each of these requirements with an example.
2. Which performance requirements do computer centre facilities have to meet and how are these requirements met?
3. Name a number of preventive measures for improving the availability of computer centres.
4. How are computer centres controlled? Provide an example of each method of control.
5. What does the administrative organization of a computer centre entail? Explain your answer by providing three examples.
6. What does ITIL do? What angles does ITIL have?
7. Name the ITIL service delivery and service support processes. Give an example of five of these processes.
8. What are the advantages of introducing ITIL? What are the disadvantages?
9. How does the service desk process a call? How is the service desk designed? What does this design depend on? Illustrate you answer with an example.
10. How does the nature of the call for a service change with time? What does this mean for the input of people at the service desk?
11. What is service level management? What are critical factors of success for service level management in an organization?
12. What is availability management? Why is this important? What are the costs of non-availability then? Illustrate your answer by giving an example.
13. How are the Microsoft methods for management put together? How would you position these management methods using the Van Hemmen method?
14. What is TMN and what is eTOM and what are the starting points on which TMN and eTOM are built?

Chapter 7

Organizing IT Tasks and Processes

Pay per view is in this case the same as pay for use: IT organizations are organized in such a way, they are able to respond flexibly to the demand. IBM calls this on demand computing, HP speaks of the adaptive enterprise, Microsoft talks about the dynamic systems initiative and Gartners' term is the real time infrastructure. It all boils down to the deliberate structuring of the IT tasks in organizations in such a manner that it is possible to change capacity flexibly in IT facilities; one runs relatively little risk of the facilities being too expensive or that they do not work. The predicted result: in 2006 there will be 30% less money to be spent on facilities as comparable to 2004.

Philips Semiconductors and computer supplier HP work at realizing shared service centres. The aim is to be able to control eighty IT-shops that currently cost over one hundred million euro a year, from five locations. At the moment all eighty still have their own IT organization. Philips Semiconductors will this way arrive at the remote controlling of the eighty centres and each control centre controls at least fourteen physical locations. This is probably a first step: because why wouldn't one be able to use two or three physical centres worldwide in the long term, that are remote controlled and operate almost without staff?]

Where would the staff of the back-office be located? With an hourly wage of 50 eurocents per hour in Asia compared to 17 euro per hour in Western Europe, an organization has to consider the positioning of the tasks to be performed. Labour intensive work that needs 500 people, costs per hour ceteris paribus at 50 working weeks per year and 40 hours per week 5,000,000 euro in Asia, compared to 180,000,000 euro in Western Europe. The question is however, how long this labour-intensive character will persist. Should one not immediately deskill work that can simply be replaced by IT ?

Contents of this chapter

Utility computing, reflection on shared service centres and consciously dealing with outsourcing, are currently subjects of the day in organizations thinking about organizing IT facilities. In the previous chapters, the tasks needed in an IT organization were discussed. This chapter shows how these tasks can be set up within an organization. Organization of IT tasks is thereby considered an application of the principles of organization. The developments in the principles of organization since 1985 are outlined and their impact on organizing IT tasks is made clear.

The chapter next presents four points of particular interest when organizing tasks. These four points of interest are the care for coordination of tasks; organizing it so that everyone has the information needed for performing their task at their disposal; reckoning with impact of new technology on the set-up of the organization and the awareness one can practice tasks at different skill levels.

The theory is then applied to larger and to smaller organizations and tries to provide insight into what an organization looks like when one has recognized IT tasks according to ASL or ITIL and these are designed within one's own IT function. This leads directly to the question whether one should include all these tasks in the in-house organization or whether one also could outsource some tasks. Criteria that come up for discussion in this decision-making process are discussed. Finally it is indicated what one should organize, if one wants to deal effectively and efficiently with the outsourcing of tasks.

TRENDS IN ORGANIZATION THEORY

Organizing IT Parker-Priebe (2000) looked at the way in which large organizations control their IT input. She indicated that this control of IT is

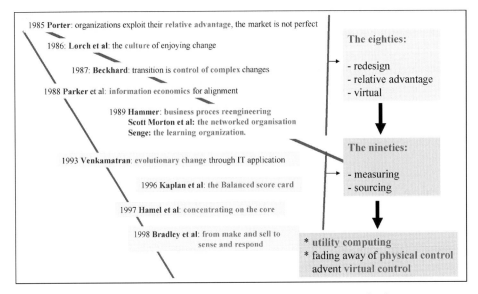

Figure 7.1. Thinkers about the theory for structuring organizations

influenced by developments in the principles of organization; and these developments saw a few milestones over the past 25 years. Parker (2000) sums them up
for us (see Figure 7.1). Application of the lessons results in one realizing that, if
the technology enables this, organizations to day strive to set up their IT facilities
as flexible as possible, want to have these at their disposal as cheaply as possible
and that the risks to be taken have to be surveyable. This is the basis for the rise
of utility computing and shared services. Utility computing means paying for IT
services on the basis of usage, shared services implies the maximum bundling
of the organization of the supply of services in the functional management area,
application management and/or exploitation area. How did one arrive at this?

The eighties

The eighties saw the vast rise of IT. The personal computer was introduced and the use of networks grew. Organizations starting to realize the
technology enabled them to organize their tasks differently and that whoever
went about this in the smartest way, at least had a temporary advantage over his
competitors. Redesigning of tasks occurred and that could lead to a virtual way
of organizing. In virtual organizations there is no need to sit in the same office

building, as long as one can contact each other through the network. Porter stated this could result in competitive advantage. Parker with his information economics figured out what the costs/benefits were. Beckhard discussed the change process for realizing a different set up of tasks and Lorch taught us organizations have to create a culture in which people do not mind change. The decade was closed with publications on business process redesign, the new networked organization and the permanent learning of organizations.

The nineties

In the last ten years of the 20th century these concepts expanded. The technique lent a hand because the arrival of the browser made using internet possible for everybody and made the networked organization of Scott Morton (1989) more familiar. Venkamatran et al. indicates how organizations can anticipate on the new opportunities the technique offers. He states that networks offer possibilities for dealing with customers in a different manner, configure the operational processes differently and provide an organization with faster access to the know-how needed for the working processes.

Venkamatran has a step-by-step plan to do this. He indicates that in the first instance processes should run more efficiently. A next phase looks at the added value processes may offer to organizations and whether these could not have been done by third parties. Finally, one enters into relationships in the shape of networks and the network economy arises. Consortiums of organizations cooperate in order to provide customers with an optimal offer. Bradley et al. add to this in 1998 in stating that arriving at the digital firm often implies that organizations evolve from producing in stock ('make and sell') to making products based upon customers' orders ('sense and respond'). Hamel and Prahaled (1997) remark that organizations should limit themselves to their core activities and execute these optimally. Kaplan (1996) states that one can control this optimal execution and this control should be quantitatively underpinned. He comes up with the balanced score card, a number of indicators in different fields, that indicates how an organization performs. These years can be typified in two sentences:

– knowing where and about what one talks, therefore measuring;
– and work out whether to perform the task in-house or outsource it.

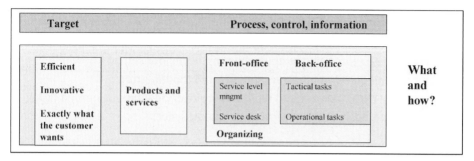

Figure 7.2. Goal, process, control and information at IT organizations

Today

From the previous text, one may draw the conclusion that technology can enable organizations to implement any operating method. By going through the points one has to consider at setting up an IT organization and assuming that based upon the goals the processes are set up and these are controlled with the aid of information, Figure 7.2 is created. This figure shows that:

– the goal is to deliver products and services in a certain manner;
– and that the IT organization to this purpose has set up front and back-office processes at various levels.

Shared services

Furthermore, organizations want to achieve efficient and effective services. This may result in setting up shared service centres. The set-up of shared services often leads to simultaneous standardization of IT facilities. It can also result in dealing more subtly with outsourcing of tasks.

To start with, let us go into shared service centres. Various types of shared service centres exist. In shared service centres for the exploitation of IT facilities, storage, processing and transport functions are consolidated. Shared services in the field of competencies—the so called competence centres—for certain applications are used to combine knowledge in a certain field. That means the knowledge and experience concerning for instance *ERP*-applications are all concentrated in one location.

Motives for arriving at shared services are (Strikwerda, 2003):

  – achieving cost reduction;
  – creating more coherence and achieving better transfer of knowledge;
  – increasing quality and professionalism in the long run;
  – enabling better control and having more overview on outsourced tasks;
  – being able to start and realize innovations faster;

Concentration of tasks in shared service centres is often accompanied by standardization of objects used in the IT architecture and organization of the purchase of these objects.

Comparative advantage

Top-down thinking about the organization of IT facilities, results in distinguishing tasks and processes within these IT organizations and may lead to consideration of other organization concepts. Organizations are increasingly able to determine rationally where each process is to be located. This means a different outlook on insourcing and outsourcing of tasks.

Where a task is performed may follow from analyses of the relative advantage that one geographical area has compared to another. Advantages of a certain area can be, for example, stable government, favourable legislation and lower labour costs. Disadvantages can be the lack of a knowledge infrastructure and obstructive legislation.

POINTS OF INTEREST IN SETTING UP ORGANIZATIONS

With these trends in the back of our minds, we look at setting up IT organizations. This can be approached from four perspectives:

1. Organizations are associations, in which coordination of tasks is achieved. Mintzberg (1988) demonstrated in this field that there is a relation between the manner in which coordination of tasks in an organization takes place and its organizational form. Every organizational form has its own design parameters and more often occurs under certain circumstances (see Figure 7.3).

	Simple structure	Machine bureaucracy	Professional bureaucracy	Divisionalized form	Adhocracy	Mission organization
Attuned especially by:	direct supervision	standardization of processes	standardization of knowledge	standardization of products/ services	mutual attunement	standardization of norms
Most important part of the organization	the boss	the technicians on the staff	the supervisors	middle mngmnt	the support staff	the ideology
Design parameters:						
- job specialisation	little	much	much	little	much	little
- training	little	little	much	little	much	little
- indoctrination	little	little	little	some	some	much
- formalization	little formaliz. organic	much formalization bureaucratic	little formalization bureaucratic	much formaliz. bureaucratic	little formalizat. organic	little formaliza. bureaucratic
- grouping	functionally	functional	funct&to market	market	funct.&to market	market
- size group	wide	wide at bottom narrow elsewhere	wide at bottom narrow elsewhere	wide (at top)	narrow throughou	wide(in enclaves of limited size)
- planning&control	little	action planning	little	much perf.cntrol	limited action plan.	little
- liason devices	few	few liaison devices	in administration	few	many throughout	few
- decentralization	centralisation	limited horizont. decentralization	horizontal dec.	limited vertical decentralization	selective decentr.	decentralization
Situational factors:						
-age & size	young and small	old and large	varies	old and very large	often young	both
-technical system	simple	regulating	not regulating	divisible	very 'sophisticated'	simple
-environment	simple&dynam.	simple&stable	complex&stable	relativily simple	complex&dynam.	simple&stable
-power	chief executive	technocrates	profess.manager	middle management	experts	ideology

Figure 7.3. Coordination of tasks within an organization and matching organizational forms

2. Organizations want to be able to control their tasks and this requires the necessary information to be available. An organization may take ex ante measures in order to ensure date becomes available in a reliable way. Ex post it has to be checked whether this data is indeed correct and complete.

3. Technological progress provides an organization with a chance to rethink its set-up. The network economy leads to reduction of the costs for information and communication and therefore offers possibilities for controlling organization parts differently or executing tasks differently. Shared service centres, already technically possible, become affordable and can be realized without any unjustified risk. The fact is that the reliability of networks has strongly increased.

4. Organizations choose the level, on which tasks are executed. Five levels can be distinguished: reactive, process-oriented, system-oriented, supply chain-oriented and transform and excel. These levels have been derived from the model of the European Foundation for Quality Management (EFQM-model).

All four perspectives will be explained below, each time finding a connection with the organizing of IT tasks.

Coordination of tasks

Organizations exist through application of distribution of work. IT tasks are executed by organizations. Distribution of work means that specialization takes place on the execution of a certain task. A task includes one or more activities. Distributions of work are constantly in development, resulting in possible changes in many activities within a task. The existence of distribution of work in practice leads to the work carried out by certain individuals or parts of the organization having to be geared to each other. Mintzberg (1988) demonstrated that the dominant manner of coordination of tasks in an organization coheres with the way in which an organization is structured. The organization structure doesn't just come out of the blue, according to him. Mintzberg recognized six organizational forms: the simple structure, the machine bureaucracy, the professional bureaucracy, the division form, the adhocracy and the mission organization. Each of these organizational forms has its own way of coordination of tasks. In each organizational form the emphasis lies on a certain part of the organization. Each form has its own interpretation of the design parameters for an organization. Finally, certain organizational forms are found more often than others in certain situations. Figure 7.3 shows per organizational form the way of coordinating tasks—the most important part of these organizational forms—its design parameters and the situations in which these organizational forms are mainly found.

For the execution of IT tasks, functional management tasks, application management tasks and exploitation tasks have to be recognized. For each of the six structures as recognized by Mintzberg, one can indicate who decides on these three. Let us go through these six organizational forms in more detail.

The six organizational forms and the triple IT-management model

In the simple structure, the company boss decides on each of the three tasks. The tasks for application management and exploitation will often be outsourced. Decision-making with regard to the functionality in a simple structure usually means choosing between the functionality of various standard solutions.

In the machine bureaucracy the technicians in staff functions decide on the three tasks of management. This type of organization moreover uses predominantly standard packages. Functional management then amounts to choosing for the functionality of a certain solution. The remaining functional management is carried out at the suppliers'. In this type of organization, exploitation will more often than not take place in-house.

In the professional organization, the situation with regard to the standard solutions for maintaining the financial and personnel administration (the secondary processes) is comparable to that of the machine bureaucracy. With regard to the primary processes, the trend also goes in this direction but for the time being it is still the professionals that determine the IT facilities that support their primary process. In this situation the allocation of tasks for this last mentioned type of provisions is comparable to that of the simple structure.

In the divisionalized form the situation is less clear. With regard to the secondary provisions the Executive board has the casting vote. Regarding the primary processes the divisions have the casting vote.

This way it is possible to interpret the responsibilities for the tasks of the triple model for each of Mintzberg's organization structures. These tasks may be executed in-house, these may also be outsourced.

Information function

When setting up the organization it is also important to reckon with the information needed for controlling the processes to be set up. Starreveld et al. (2003) perceives that a reliable information function in organizations makes demands on the structure of an organization. He also states that the actual information has to be periodically checked for its accuracy with regard to contents. This prevents organizations discovering too late that the required information is not present and/or the information that is present is not optimal as regards to content. Starreveld et al. (2003) states that:

1. organizations have to structure themselves in such a way that reliability of information is an integral part of the manner in which data is collected. Organizations have to consider which data they need for controlling

their processes. Next they have to allocate responsibilities internally for collecting this data, reckoning with the necessary separation of responsibilities. Determination what data is needed; saving the required data; performing data collection and checking of the data have to be preferably carried out by individuals with incompatible interests. In functional and application management organizations, with often labour intensive work, this means that time registrations are signed by managers. In exploitation organizations, that are strongly capital-intensive, this means that orders are placed by someone other than the person that receives the orders.

2. organizations must, apart from this, periodically check the correctness of the information. These checks include running through whether:
   - a supplier was actually allowed to supply the data supplied by him. This is called the authorization check. The authority of the signatory is looked at.
   - the supplied data tallies with the physical reality. Are the items on the packing note actually present in the computer room?
   - the data is actually reliable. One asks oneself for instance, whether the data definitions correspond? Was the data collected at the right time and does this justify the conclusions? Is corroboration between data in fact possible? Can one have the data at one's disposal on time and is this data sufficiently accurate? Apart from all this the data is checked for obvious measuring errors.

Impact of the advent of other technology

A third perspective on the set-up of organizations is the one that verifies the impact of the use of technology. The Galbraith theory provides leads. Galbraith (1973) investigated the influence of improvement of the information function concerning the structure of an organization. Galbraith ascertained that the structure of an organization is determined to a high degree by the possibilities the organization has for processing the necessary information. He discerned two situations (see Figure 7.4):

(a) through organizational measures, organizations endeavour to seek to avoid the release of too many coordination problems through the hierarchy and clogging the hierarchy with the vast number of problems one

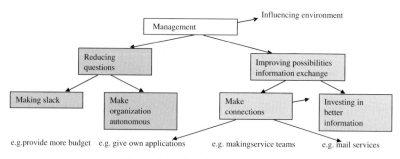

Figure 7.4. The Galbraith theory

has to deal with. The management of an organization does leave some elbowroom, allowing more time to mull over a decision or one makes organizations autonomous, so the base can decide for themselves;

(b) one improves the information flow between divisions of the organization and that way prevents the hierarchy getting obstructed with requests for decisions. There are two ways of doing this: one can improve the circulation of information through the organization, or one can make connections between the various departments. These departments will then exchange information, without forwarding their questions to the higher management.

The Galbraith theory teaches us that this improved information function makes it possible to quickly set up organizations, with less elbowroom and it is also possible to adjust business units faster. This way the input of technology may not immediately result in centralization and concentration of tasks. It does however lead to the awareness that the technology as available in the network economy calls for recalibrating of existing organizational forms. The Philips Semiconductors example at the beginning of this chapter makes it clear that an improved information function is the basis for achieving shared services.

Choosing an operating level

A last point of particular interest at setting-up organizations is realizing that an organization has a choice with regard to the level on which they execute its tasks. This level of task execution can be indicated in the shape of a model.

There is for instance the CMMI (Computer Maturity Model Integrated), the model as supplied by the European Foundation for Quality Management, the service management *CMM* and the world class IT management model. Using a model may help if one wishes to optimise a process in an organization. It provides an impression of the current quality of the services provided and where to find room for improvement. At a study into the level of execution of IT tasks for an e-portal Giesberts (2002) investigated said models. He ascertained that an IT organization could operate at five different levels (see Appendix F). He typified these levels as:

1. *an IT-organization working in a reactive way:* At this level skill is highly valued and supported by training. In case of complaints the IT organization tries to remedy these. One is product-focussed. The organization has function descriptions but no process descriptions. Serious events are reported. Knowledge is not structurally recorded or transferred. Training is aimed at increasing skills. The customer is not part of the picture;

2. *a process-focussed IT organization:* the organization has grouped and described cohering activities in processes. Individual steps in the process are identified; tasks and responsibilities are fixed. Performance indicators act as means of control. Processes are improved on the basis of established problems. Costs and planning are safeguarded using methods and aids. Process owners are responsible for progress of the processes. Staff skills are trained and proposals for improvements are stimulated. Reproducibility is the norm;

3. *a proactive, system-focussed operating IT organization:* works on improvement of the IT organization as a whole. The feedback loop is applied. Customers' focus dominates the policy, which is aimed at preventing problems. The responsibilities and the mutual coherence between processes and the departments involved are in view and recognized. Policy for the IT organization is assessed together with the employees on desirability and feasibility and translated into measurable objectives. Progress is measured and evaluated. Audits and trend analyses are used for introducing improvements pro-actively. An integral training plan is in place and the IT organization knows its needs for personnel in the long run;

4. an IT organization aimed at cooperation with partners within the chain. The IT organization strives for maximum added value. It is determined per partner who is most suitable for performing a certain task. Control systems are connected with each other. Innovation is paramount. Exchange of information takes place structurally with clients, users, customers and suppliers. This and evaluations of the organization's performances, form a means of control for the IT organization. One matches oneself to the best organizations in the branch. Personnel policy is an integral part of the organizational policy;

5. an IT organization capable of continuous transformation of the service chain: The process of continual improvement is embedded in the structure and culture of the organization. Based upon a long-term outlook the sails are trimmed with the wind in time and new activities started. The organization anticipates future developments and adjusts its processes accordingly by collecting information actively and structured. At outlining a policy one looks further than the own organization. The employees are able to direct their own training and careers.

An IT organization or a part of the IT organization can be positioned at a certain level. Reaching a higher level is only then possible, when the requirements of the previous level are met. Most IT organizations function with regard to their operating level at level 1 or 2. This is because descriptions are not present for all processes or because one does not have a policy explicitly translated into measurable standards or because insight into the need for personnel in the long run is lacking.

THE THEORY, THE IT ORGANIZATION AND THE ITIL, ASL AND BiSL PROCESSES

The result

We have discussed the various perspectives on setting up organizations. In previous chapters we got to know a multitude of processes in the fields of functional management, application management and exploitation. Furthermore, there is a trend towards utility computing and shared services. Finally we have

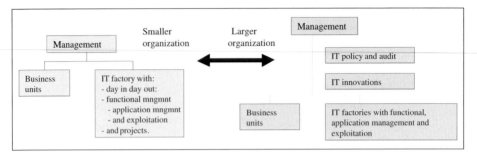

Figure 7.5. Set-up of IT functions in conformity with Uijlenbroek (1999)

research as done by Uijlenbroek et al. (1999) at our disposal about the set-up of the IT function in organizations. This research states that IT organizations as they have to deliver more diverse products and services will split off certain tasks. The policy for the IT architecture, IT contracts and the check on the execution of this policy and the compliance with these contracts, will than for example rest with management units or competence centres. The functional management can become a demand organization in the business units and IT houses execute the application management and exploitation tasks. Figure 7.5 shows the result of the research by Uijlenbroek et al. (1999).

Using knowledge of ASL, BiSL and ITIL, trends and research results for a background, we are able to indicate the possible set-up of IT organizations in the year 2007. This can be seen in Figures 7.6 and 7.7.

Figure 7.6 shows that functional management in smaller organizations is often designed as a separate information management unit. This unit, as dictated by BiSL, executes the tasks, entirely or partly. The organization usually procures standard IT facilities. The application management of these IT facilities is located with the supplier of these. This supplier carries out the tasks indicated by ASL. Concerning exploitation the organization may have decided to outsource the exploitation in its entirety, partly or not at all.

In larger organizations the set-up of IT function has a more complex character. Functional management is carried out at different levels in the organization. It is often determined centrally and in one location what the organization of the information function and the side with regard to content of the information function have to look like. In the business unit the more operational BiSL tasks are carried out. Application management is sometimes carried out by the organization itself. Sometime standard IT facilities are used. The business units are

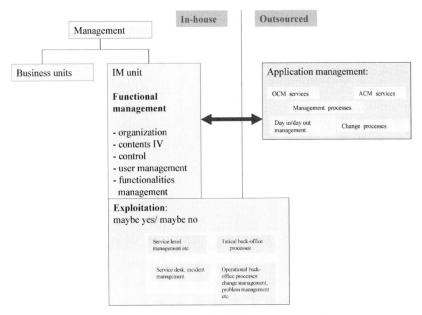

Figure 7.6. The structure of the IT function in smaller organizations

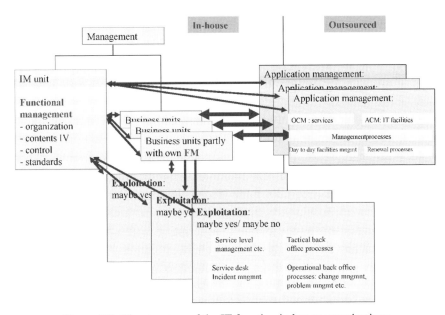

Figure 7.7. The structure of the IT function in larger organizations

in daily contact with the suppliers of these IT facilities. The central functional management organization sets the frames for contractual agreements to be made, concludes the contracts and evaluates these. Application management tasks as described by ASL are found in one's own application management organization and at the suppliers of standard IT facilities. The same situation occurs both in the field of application management as well as in the field regarding exploitation tasks. The processes as named by ITIL can be regained in the in-house exploitation organization and in that of suppliers of exploitation services. Control regarding contracts is dealt with centrally; the every day contacts may lie at a lower lever in the organization.

WHO PERFORMS THE PROCESSES: INSOURCING AND OUTSOURCING

Do-it-yourself or outsourcing

The preceding already indicates that organizations have to decide whether to perform IT tasks themselves or have these performed by others. In practice, organizations operate very differently in this field. They seldom outsource their entire IT facilities all at once. They more often than not decide to outsource part of the tasks. This has everything to do with the way these facilities are looked at. This view is increasingly more businesslike. Part of the tasks can so be outsourced for a number of reasons. These reasons can be that:

- an organization does not have to acquire and maintain IT knowledge;
- one can be operational quicker;
- one wants to prevent having to set-up an exploitation environment that is 7×24 hours operational and guarantees 99.99% availability;
- one runs less risk of taking the wrong decision. Outsourcing can as it happens work like a subscription. One pays an amount of money per period and is able to cancel one's subscription after a given time;
- one can achieve costs reduction in a chain of partners. This is because the necessary management tasks are executed in one single location.

There is so a shift in the reasons organizations use when deciding about outsourcing. Figure 7.8 demonstrates this. In this figure the shift of reasons for

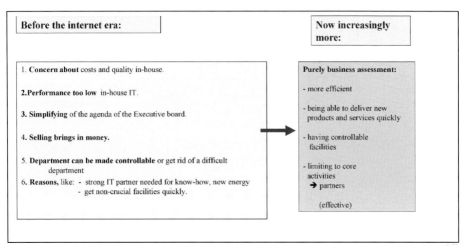

Figure 7.8. Shifting of the reasons for outsourcing IT tasks since 1995

outsourcing is shown. The current reasons for choosing for outsourcing are of an out-and-out businesslike fashion. One just wants to see the needed services delivered more cheaply. One wants to be able to launch new products and services quickly on the market. One wants to have the IT facilities at one's disposal flexibly and controllable. Furthermore, the organization wants to be able to limit itself to its core activities.

Technical possibilities

The decision for arriving at outsourcing is so increasingly a decision of businesslike nature, in which the importance of IT and the knowledge and skills the organization wants to acquire and maintain also play a part. Apart from this, the possible forms in which IT services are delivered change technically. Internet technology enables different forms of outsourcing, such as for example through webservices. This shift with regard to possibilities is shown in Figure 7.9. The first two possibilities as indicated in this figure, have already been known for some years. The third possibility became feasible because of the advent of internet technology. It is called application service providing (ASP). This means one supplier enables a number of users to use an application at a set price per month. To this purpose, the users have a browser at their place of work. Let us have a closer look at the three possibilities as outlined and their advantages. The

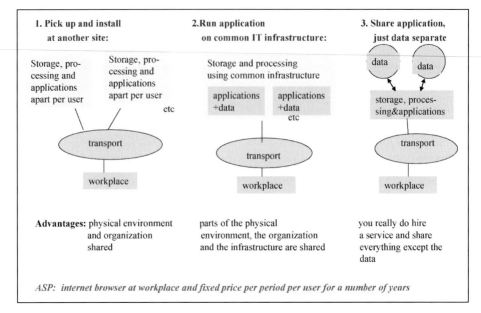

Figure 7.9. Different technology, different possibilities for sourcing

first possibility is hosting of facilities for transport, storage and processing. An example is placing the hosting of processing and storage facilities for internet sites at a supply organization.

Example

> *Altavista's site in Palo Alto accommodated in 1998 IBM, Dunlop, Nike and other internet sites. The basement houses in closed rooms per company the necessary storage and processing equipment. Getronics does in its computer centre in Apeldoorn (Netherlands) the same for a number of banking customers in the Netherlands. Through concentration of the exploitation organization efficiency profits are made.*

The second possibility is the use of the same infrastructure by all customers. The used applications and data are specific to each customer. This method of working adds to the advantages of the first model also the advantage that one as supply organization can optimise one's IT infrastructure facilities. Exploitation of all applications is done on the same storage and processing facilities.

Example

> *On the same mainframe in the Getronics computer centre the housing benefit application, the system for funding of education organizations and other government applications, are operated.*

The third form of outsourcing is application service providing (ASP). At the ASP-form all participating organizations use the same application. Just the data is customer specific. The application is used at a fixed rate per user. The supply organization has to be able to guarantee continuation of the working of the application. It has to know the process, for which an application is supplied. It has to be able to expand its product portfolio with different applications. It has to take care of optimum quality with regards to availability and response. Finally, guarantees have to be provided on the measure of guarantee that is offered regarding safeguarding of the customer's data. This type of outsourcing has for the supply organization the advantage that it can determine its way of service provision all by itself. The customer hires the use of a product with a service around it.

Example

> *Exodus supplies Lycos with the possibility to use the functions of an ERP package. Lycos can thus expand without immediately having to invest in the financial application necessary for a large company.*

Organizing sourcing

Once an organization has decided to outsource tasks, it will concentrate on drawing up the outsourcing contract. In the conclusion of this contract it is recommendable to pay attention to:

1. *The flexibility in products and the services included in the contract.* In general the environment and technology undergo changes over a ten-year period. Kodak experienced that the possibility to expand its contract as far as outside the USA was necessary. It also had to reckon with a change in IT architecture and the wish for better services. General Dynamics for this reason has a contract in which for each of its eight divisions different

conditions have been put in with regard to including changes in insight into the technology and in the strategic direction of investing in IT.

2. *The standards for IT performance and the way the contract is managed.* Although one also leaves water and electricity supply to third parties, when using IT it is recommended to agree in advance on quantitative standards for response times, percentage availability of the facility, response of the contract partner to changes in infrastructures and applications, and so on.

3. *Dealing with extra activities that (on top of what was already done) are outsourced.* When the first contract is successful, one will want to outsource more and questions arise like: is it easy to split this part from the rest? Are there special skills involved, for which the organization has neither the time nor the energy? Is this IT activity less of a core activity for us compared to other IT activities? This is how the partner will be approached with the request to include these extras in the contract as well. It is a good thing if this has already been provided for in the first contract.

4. *The fact whether there is a cost reduction.* In practice this can often only then be determined when making a study of which results are reported directly to the top management of the organization. Rapportage to the IT supply organization may lead to a distortion of the facts because this is the party concerned. These studies should take place on the demand-side.

5. *Assessing whether the supply organization aims for continuity and delivering quality.* One asks oneself whether the supply organization is set up for continuous innovation of products and services; and whether it is financially sound. Once outsourced it is rather difficult to insource a task. When going for total outsourcing the supply organization makes its money by concluding long-term contracts. In the course of this term the costs are reduced. If extra services are delivered, this is done at higher tariffs.

Contract management

After concluding the contract, which in the case of a contract over several years must be considered a strategic cooperation, the contract has to be managed. In the case of long-term contracts, attention certainly has to be paid to (see e.g. Applegate, 2002):

1. *The clear embedding of the responsibility for control of the contracts at the right level in an organization.* Sometimes the function functional management has to be positioned high in the organization. This then results in setting up a function such as Chief Information Officer (CIO). This CIO is part of the management of the organization. The CIO manages the sourcing contracts and is the link between the demand organization and the supply organization. This high-level functional management function especially targets the execution of the strategic BiSL tasks.

2. *The managing of the outsourcing agreement.* To this purpose, one has to be able to measure the performances of the supply and demand organization in this field. This entails setting standards, measuring and next interpreting. When transferring IT facilities to an external supply organization one often will reorganize these first and then transfer them. While reorganizing it usually becomes clear what the needs for application of IT are and how these should be measured.

3. *The allocation of new projects.* This way, one can arrive in the long run at a combination of tasks in a contract. There are then tasks that focus on cost reduction and tasks focussed on innovations. Initially the application management of legacy applications will often be the object for outsourcing. In these legacy applications one will focus on maintaining these as cheaply as possible. The supply organization will in case of success only too gladly participate in projects that yield new applications. In a real partnership they are given this opportunity.

4. *The interface between the demand and the supply organization.* In outsourcing it is often a matter of the transferring of crucial tasks. Certainly in the case of large contracts, an organization has to maintain relations at many levels. To this purpose, functional management should be set up at the demand-side and service level management, amongst other things, should be set up at the supply-side.

Large, long-term outsourcing contracts should be seen as a strategic alliance between the demand and the supply organization and controlled accordingly. In smaller contracts one can focus on execution of the actual contract. Outsourcing of tasks is possible in many ways and in many forms. In large, long-term contracts, the party that outsources the tasks runs the risk of losing critical knowledge; the risk of losing knowledge across the various company functions (two thirds of all innovations are after all connected with the customer/supplier

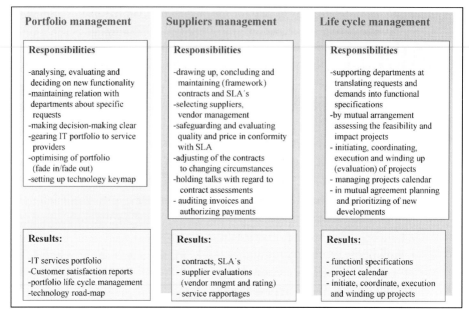

Figure 7.10. Key processes on tactical level (Heuschen, 2004)

interface) and the loss of control over a supplier. Nike and C&A, working in a different sector to IT, try to secure this control by doing the rounds on their suppliers work floor. In IT facilities, one could position an office of the functional management organization with the partner.

Key processes at tactical level

Heuschen et al. (2004) has listed which three processes are crucial to the supply organization, when this changes over to outsourcing. These are portfolio management, suppliers management and life-cycle management. These tasks are part of the strategic BiSL tasks. Heuschen et al. defines of each task what the result should be (see Figure 7.10).

QUESTIONS

1. Which developments in the eighties and nineties in organization theory have led to the current trend towards utility computing and shared service centres? Illustrate your answer with an example.

2. What are the advantages of setting up shared service centres? What does cost effective operating and being able to innovate IT facilities quickly often demand?

3. The technology of the network economy results in organizations being able to fairly rationally determine where they can execute certain IT processes. What are the boundaries that limit this rational decision? Illustrate your answer with an example.

4. From which perspectives can one approach the setting up of IT organizations? Illustrate each perspective by giving an example.

5. What is useful about the Mintzberg model, when speaking of responsibilities within organizations for functional management, application management and exploitation? Illustrate your answer by giving an example.

6. Information is an important component in the goal/process/control/information model. Starreveld recommends two measures for ensuring one can dispose of reliable information in decision-making. Which are these and what is the reason for each of them?

7. Give the Galbraith model. What is the importance of Galbraith when speaking of the design of IT organizations? Illustrate your answer by giving an example.

8. Organizations may make choices with regard to the level on which they operate. Provide an example of a reactive and a pro-active way of operating an IT service desk.

9. What does the IT organization of a small organization look like? What does one of a large IT organization look like? What are the differences? Illustrate your answer with an example.

10. What are reasons for outsourcing tasks? Illustrate your answer with an example.

11. Why does the technical range of possibilities organizations have at their disposal for outsourcing tasks increase? What is the impact of these new technical possibilities? Why should an organization want to use these?

12. What points deserve attention in an outsourcing contract? Illustrate your answer by giving a few examples.

13. How is an outsourcing contract managed? Why is this done in this way? What type of measures does this require?

Part 3

Controlling IT facilities

Control of IT services: by whom, how and
  why?
The possibilities:
    – setting priorities
    – dealing with innovations
    – reflecting on the organization
    – working methodically
    – control on knowledge and competence
    – ensuring basis
Information needed for controlling
Plans as an instrument for controlling

Chapter 8

Controlling IT facilities (IT governance)

At our company Oracle, without IT the glue would be missing from our organiza-
tion. Without this glue there would be no more exchange of information. Nobody
would have access to stock, customer or order data. Failing IT services are
disastrous. We therefore control IT on the quality of the operational processes
and the number of successful implementations. Our boss Larry Ellison performs
this control (Ghoshal, 2002).

Since 1999, together with the concentration of country specific applications
towards corporate-wide applications and the standardization of five e-mail
systems into one, the cooperation between the international organizations
strongly increased. Innovations are introduced more quickly and customer
data becomes available to every-one at every level. Furthermore, this led to a
reduction in costs of $2 billion per annum (Ghoshal, 2002).

If a private individual buys a car, he does not buy the chassis from General
Motors, the engine from BMW and the interior from Ikea and asks Mitsubishi
to assemble all the parts. That would be considered strange, just like buying
an entire car from one make is considered normal. Along the same lines, could

147

one not argue that selecting 'best of breed' applications and infrastructures in IT has it limitations? (Ghoshal, 2002).

As a rule, AKZO has housed standard facilities with its strategic partner Atos Origin. In our organization we have made arrangements for this. At every level, connections have been put in place between both organizations, each with their own reports and moments for reporting. We have had to shape contract management structurally (Geertsema, 2002).

Our IT also could not get round the question, who they were actually working for. Over the past eight years the IT organization made a 90° turn. The IT organization structure became process-oriented. These days, everybody knows who they work for and on what they are judged. This turning over of IT happened in phases: first we distinguished groups of customers and from that idea we set up the IT supply organization. This led to the set-up of a front-office with customer teams and the appointing of service managers. These service managers were made responsible for the contact with the customer and the internal settlement of customer calls. They have dealings with a back-office, where teams have been set up as well. They are dealing with special tasks for certain groups of customers.

Contents of this chapter

Every day we hear about business IT alignment, reduction of the elapsed time from idea to implementation, outsourcing, customer focus of IT departments and the change towards a more process oriented way of working of the IT organization. All these subjects directly link to the control of IT facilities by general and business unit management of an organization and the consequences of this control for the IT organization itself. Control or governance of IT facilities is a subject involving various stakeholders. Nowadays we see groups of stakeholders emerging. There is a demand organization. There is a supply organization. Both can be supported by third parties.

This chapter starts with a summary of the stakeholders. Having made clear who is controlling and who influences this control, the manner of control is discussed and the impact of this control on IT products and services. In the second part of this chapter we go into the information necessary for enabling control measures and planning of ensuing actions.

WHO CONTROLS AND HOW DOES HE/SHE DO IT?

Parties involved in control of IT facilities

Control of IT facilities can take place in a number of ways. Applegate et al. (2003) distinguishes six ways of controlling. The general management of an organization, the management of the business units and the management of the functional management organization (together they make up the IT demand organization) have all their own targets.

The control by general management is aimed at achieving the most optimal support for the strategy of the organization using IT in the short, medium and long term. Business unit management controls directly from the demand for IT facilities. It strives for an optimal support of its operational processes. The functional IT management organization combines the demands. It tries to react optimally to the demand from general and business unit management and organizes support by IT facilities accordingly. The demanded IT facilities are provided by IT supply organizations. Figure 8.1 shows this process.

The force field

IT facilities cost of old strongly a lot of money. This means that organizations traditionally procure large parts of their facilities from third parties. In the eighties these were usually the infrastructure facilities. Organizations themselves

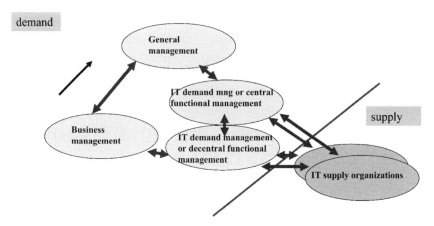

Figure 8.1. Relation between demand and supply organizations

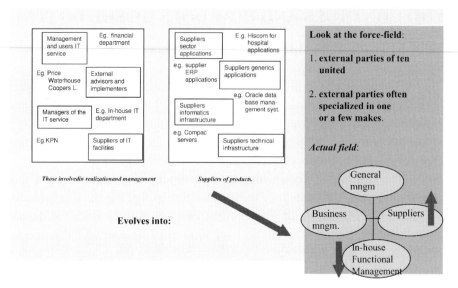

Figure 8.2. The force field at controlling IT facilities

built and maintained applications. In the nineties the idea gradually occurred that many organizations have comparable support needs regarding IT. Organizations procure standard applications on the market. During the same period the advent of suppliers of personal productivity tools and enterprise requirements planning (ERP) packages started. This created a whole landscape of supply organizations. This landscape is increasingly shaped through mergers and take-overs. In the years 2002 and 2003 applications of some suppliers appear to be used on a large scale. Large monopolies are created more or less de facto. At the same time, the number of consultancies, able to support large and medium organizations with thorough experience in implementation of standard solutions, has become less numerous. A situation has arisen, in which the demand organization encounters a strongly developed external force field. Set-up of functional management within the demand organization becomes inevitable. This is shown in Figure 8.2.

WHAT ARE THE CONTROL POSSIBILITIES FOR THOSE THAT DEMAND IT FACILITIES?

Subjects for control

Figure 8.3 indicates which subjects should receive attention when IT facilities are controlled by general management, business management and IT

Control by: Objective of control:	General management	Business unit management	Functional management, combining the demand
1. Establishing prioities	Are the managed investments in line with the strategy?	How should I design our release Policy for achieving a better return on investment?	What are the priorities in the field of infra-structure and applications?
2. Attention for innovation	Which innovations were there with regard to service management and what was their impact?	Why is the competition more adaptive in the adjustment of their IT support and what can we do about this?	Which technologies are important to our organization and how is this translated in projects and management?
3. Reflection on organization and sourcing	What external partners do we have? Who is internally responsible for our strategic IT projects?	How have I organized functional management and who manages my most important applications?	How are application management and exploitation organized and why?
4. Attention for methodical operating	How does the IT procurement process progress? How is our project management structured?	How do the functional management processes progress and which are invested?	At what level are the service management tasks executed? Do I have to raise this level and how?
5. Control on knowledge and competency	How do we maintain our knowledge of IT and where are our strong points and weaknesses?	Do I have the skill to perform optimal functional management and if I don't, which actions Should I undertake?	Which knowledge should the IT organization maintain itself and which is procured?
6. Foundation	How do we organize foundation? Who are the key players?	As business unit management Do we show ourselves a real partner of IT demand management	How do I organize perma-nent cooperation with my customers?

Figure 8.3. Examples of possible controls in the different management areas. Examples of control measures in each of the six areas

demand management, if they want to control application and use of IT facilities. For each of these subjects an example is given of what control could possibly entail. The six different areas, to be elaborated below, are:

1. **Establishing priorities** for IT tasks. IT tasks should be geared to the goals of the organization. New projects should fit in with the organization's strategy. IT line tasks support organizational processes.

Example

At its annual conference Gartner (2001) indicates that the cost ratio for IT in organizations is shifting (see Figure 8.4). Relatively more funds are invested in e-commerce and e-business applications. This results in having to reduce the relative costs for infrastructure and basis applications. This can be achieved by concentrating computer centres, standardizing workstation facilities

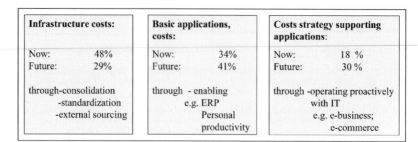

Infrastructure costs:		Basic applications, costs:		Costs strategy supporting applications:	
Now:	48%	Now:	34%	Now:	18 %
Future:	29%	Future:	41%	Future:	30 %
through-consolidation -standardization -external sourcing		through - enabling e.g. ERP Personal productivity		through -operating proactively with IT e.g. e-business; e-commerce	

Figure 8.4. Shift in cost patterns at IT facilities (Gartner, 2001)

and by procuring parts of the facilities from outside. These actions necessitate implementation of functional management.

2. **Innovation** of IT products and services. This means checking whether the product package should not be changed and whether the way of providing service does not need adjustment. In innovations one differs between radical innovations that result in entirely new services and incremental innovations, in which existing services can be supported by different facilities.

Example

Xerox (Brown, 2002) has included a service module in its new printer range for large organizations. This module detects incidents and predicts the consequences. This information is sent to the Xerox services department. They determine the seriousness of the incident and next decide when the incident will be repaired. Next, the information obtained will be used in developing new printers and the module provides information on printer use, the latter is used in consultancy about printing.

IBM is in the middle of developing the Eliza. This is a server that is capable of detecting incidents and also able to remedy these in 95% of all cases without the intervention of an engineer.

3. **Organizing** of the IT service and sourcing of the necessary facilities. This covers a variety of subjects such as:
   – standardization of IT facilities;

- considering centralization and concentration of IT responsibilities and the execution of IT tasks;
- arriving at more customer-oriented operating. This may result in the introduction of a more process-oriented approach and the subdividing of tasks in front-office and back-office tasks;
- distinction between commodity services and non-commodity services. Commodity services are IT services, an organization may procure directly from the market and where the execution in in-house management of these services cannot provide it with a competition advantage. For many organizations these consist for example of network and workstation facilities. Non-commodity services are relatively hard to procure from a third party and/or in-house execution of theses services provides an organization with a competition advantage. For many banks this could be for example the execution of treasury services. When taking care of commodity services efficiency comes first and the procurement of IT services from third parties may be considered;
- limitation to the core activities of the organization and for support of the operational processes by IT choosing for an alliance with a strategic partner.

Example

ABN AMRO in 2002 changed over to outsourcing part of its IT services with EDS. It wanted to concentrate on core processes and for IT support it sought cooperation with a worldwide operating partner.

4. **Take care to work methodically** at supplying IT products and services. Since the eighties there is the ITIL method for setting up an IT exploitation organization. In the nineties the tasks functional management and application management were distinguished and worked out in more detail. A certain consensus was reached on the application of PRINCE2 as a method for managing projects, whilst the increase in outsourcing of tasks by the IT organization resulted in a need for designing the procurement process of IT facilities more methodically. This produced, amongst other things, the Integrated Service Procurement Library (ISPL) method. This method phases the procurement process in steps, indicates which

tasks have to be introduced in each step and who should be involved in these tasks. Controlling of IT facilities means amongst other things the control of processes in an IT organization. Methods indicate which processes can be set up. The execution of the set-up processes can be linked to a performance standard and this can be used for the purpose of control.

Example

At concluding service level agreements organizations agree on the contents and performance level of services to be supplied. Take for example the delivery of network services by KPN to the IB Group. The IB Group hired data communication facilities from KPN. When incidents occurred, the IB Group compared its incident information to KPN's information. It turned out that KPN, operating with a front-office and a back-office, was able to generate all data from the registry of its call centre. This included for every single incident data about the call, checkout, contact, cause, resolution process and solution. It was simple to find out where—both at the customer as well as at the supply organization side—there were possibilities for optimising the service.

5. **take care of knowledge and competencies**. With the increasing application of devices, replacing manual processes and the rapid rise in new services learning becomes important to the IT organization. Being able to get to existing knowledge quickly and being able to quickly transfer this knowledge accompany this. This care of the right knowledge leads to:
   – competency management for IT staff;
   – knowledge management within the IT organization;
   – IT human resource policy and its execution.

Example

A consultancy organization has a policy, that for consultant functions only people from higher and university education are recruited. In a job interview it is also determined whether the employee will fit in with the organization as far as personality is concerned. After commencement of employment, the employee is if necessary provided with extra knowledge and the social skills as needed for doing the desired job. Provided he has been authorized to do so, the employee uses the in-house intranet, where all quotes, all advices, all courses etc. can be found.

Example

In an IT organization in the solution of calls the service desk, the second-line support and possibly a supplier may be involved. This usually results in a change in the IT infrastructure, the organization or the application. The customer perceives this change, even though it has not necessarily been implemented by an employee that has been in contact with this customer. The originator of the change is often not directly confronted with the result of his actions. This can be prevented in various ways. It can be done internally by means of control, communication and reportage. It can however also be done by regularly employing specialists at the service desk, using problem managers as specialists etc by means of work placements or job rotation. This way of working enhances the learning ability of the employees involved. It demands a management that is aware of the diffusion of knowledge within an organization and active involvement of this management.

6. Relation between the IT demand and supply organization. This relation is designed in many different ways. It can be done by:
    – control by means of setting targets and recording these in plans, esti-mates, budgets, service agreements and reportages;
    – designing relationships by means of steering committees, project com-mittees, working groups and task forces;
    – the way in which decisions are made as recorded in procedures and standards;
    – appointment and rotation of employees;
    – and by setting up an organization structure with clear responsibilities;

Example

Transavia has an IT board that annually grants budgets for executing IT projects. These projects fit in with the company policy. Owner of the project is the person that submits the project proposal. This person is free to set up his or her own project organization, reports as prescribed and is judged on the result (Zomer, 2001).

On the following pages, these six ways to control or govern IT services will be discussed in more detail.

Establishing priorities

The priorities at controlling IT facilities have to be geared to the strategy and the current position of the organization with regards to the support by IT. Applegate et al. (2003) discerns in this field the following four situations: (see Figure 8.5):

(a) The application of IT is not of great importance and this situation does not change. The use of IT does not distinguish the organization from other organizations. In this case, cost reduction is strived for and one will want to see evidence of an increase in the quality of the services at the same time. In the agenda of the IT manager there are projects aimed at standardization, managing of outsourcing contracts and centralization of facilities. What is left of the IT department, will concentrate on

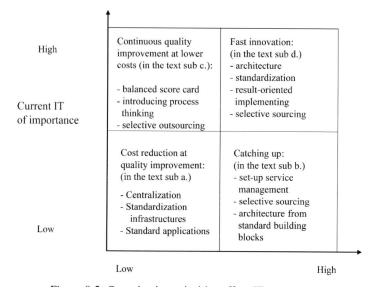

Figure 8.5. Organization priorities affect IT management

procurement of IT services, support implementation of IT services and contract management.

(b) Another case is the situation in which the application of IT at present is of minor importance but could become vitally important. Concerning IT, one is as it were busy catching up. IT demand management is set up. The necessary tasks for application management are defined. For innovative IT applications one does not want to procure immediately. The same counts for applications in which one wants to be different. Selective outsourcing is considered and one is building an IT architecture step by step. The architecture consists as much as possible of standard building blocks. In the year 2004 this will often be expansion through implementation of ERP facilities towards application of e-commerce and e-business applications.

(c) A third situation is the one where application of IT is currently vitally important. The company would come to a standstill without IT. There is however not much development needed to supply new products and services. The current strategy is perfectly supported. IT management concentrates on increasing the management quality at lower costs. Actual topics are standardisation of workstations, introduction of a process oriented way of thinking and selective sourcing. Controlling processes using bench marking is the 'in' thing to do and use of a balanced score card becomes a priority.

(d) In the last situation the current applications are vitally important and it is impossible to continue without IT innovation. For quickly anticipating users wishes, one will now focus on operating within an architecture, implement new services under this architecture very result-focussed and always look for partners that might also like to share the load of more standard IT facilities. In this case, one should think of network facilities, workstation facilities, support by ERP packages, etc. Tasks are outsourced selectively in this case. The organization has done or is doing business with a process-focussed IT supply organization.

The Applegate et al. (2003) quadrant of Figure 8.6 indicates how it is possible to see that organizations consider control of IT facilities important. This importance is obvious from the actions of general management, the location where IT demand and support management reports and the way in which IT efforts are planned.

Control IT involves:	IT not important	IT important:
Direct influence from general and line management	Bilateral agreements between IT and the manager in question	Managers and IT control the necessary IT facilities together
Good planning of IT efforts in place and clear sourcing policy	Value planning not clear, projects are started ad hoc. Management often outsourced.	Qualitatively good plan in line with strategy
At the IT renewal there are risky projects	Prefers to stay slightly behind.	The projects always include a few more risky projects.
The competency of the IT people	Are not controlled rigidly. Knowledge often outsourced.	Competency of IT employees is an important issue.
IT reports directly to:	(A) head of the financial department	Usually directly to the general management.
Innovation of workprocesses through use of IT	Is simply two years behind state of the art.	Keeping up-to-date is a must.
When economizing:	Save costs by putting off innovation	No area where one can economize immediately.
When the IT management does not perform	Enough time for rectifying mistakes.	Replace non-performing managers quickly.

Figure 8.6. Effect on aspects of IT management of the importance of IT for the organization

Organizing IT facilities

A second point of application for control is paying attention to the organization of IT facilities. This involves allocating tasks to the IT demand and the IT supply organization and determining its organizational form. Organizing of IT facilities includes a number of related subjects. One may decide to standardize processes and products. One may decide on this more centrally or more locally. One may execute tasks concentrated or less concentrated. One may execute tasks in-house. One may also procure the services and products from third parties. All these decisions concern the organization of IT facilities. The basis of all decisions is recognizing products and services and the tasks necessary for producing these. These tasks may be linked together in processes and chains of processes. Each process and every chain of processes is executed by order of a customer and each process may be more or less standardized and/or deliver a more or less standardized product. An organization can indicate for every task who executes this task and where the task should be executed. Arguments for

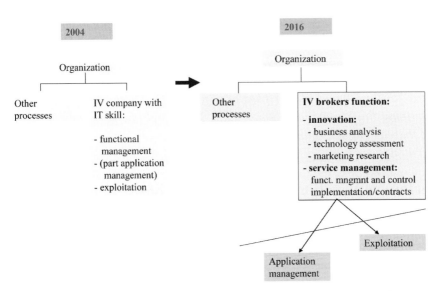

Figure 8.7. From set-up of the IT function in 2004 tot the one in 2016

this are to be found especially in the core tasks of an organization. These are the tasks, the organization exists for and which make it stand out. Organizations execute core tasks in-house. Non-core tasks are the first tasks to be outsourced.

Set-up of tasks

In the Chapters 3 to 7 (inclusive), the tasks and possible considerations at organization of the tasks in the field of IT management are discussed. The demand management determines which products are delivered and which IT services surround these products. Demand management decides at what quality level the supply organization operates. The supply organization delivers the IT products and the services that are demanded with these. The models discussed in the previous chapters provide an indication of processes that could possibly be set up and form a basis for a discussion on the need in a certain organization for setting up certain processes or not doing so. Figure 8.7 shows that choices in this field may change over the years.

Example

A bank established that in the field of IT support of the mortgage ap-proval, various parts executed comparable tasks. The bank then decided to concentrate the functional management, the application management and the exploitation of the applications in one single organization. This organization determines the functionality of applications that support mortgage approval. It takes care of their maintenance and utilizes these. Units hire the services of this centre for the support of mortgage approval by IT. These could be services for describing the applications functionally, these could be programming services and these could be exploitation services.

Certain suppositions that choices are based upon

A choice for IT products and the set-up of IT processes is often based upon the suppositions of an organization, about what is possible at a certain moment both organizationally and technically. This choice is usually not reconsidered periodically. This could mean that, after a certain period of time, the set-up of an IT supply organization is less fixed on the customer's demands. This is the reason for the rise of the process-oriented approach to IT service providing. This process-oriented approach leads to service processes that in a structured manner and in conformity with protocols deliver products and services to a specific market or customer. Because of the structure there is a visible demand organization and also a visible supply organization.

The IT processes that have been set up each run a specific course. These are carried out by parts of the organization explicitly set-up for this purpose. These processes are permanently measured on criteria of quality and performance. If necessary these processes are adjusted. The division of the effort over the various tasks to be carried out in a process or chain of processes is clear. This makes it also possible to recognize in which way technology for arriving at an improvement of the level of service provision can be applied. In Figure 8.8 this has been done for a front-office (service desk/incident management) and a back-office exploitation process (problem management/changes management).

Attention for innovation using IT

A third point of particular interest in controlling IT facilities is the innovation of products and services. Innovation enables new and different products and services. In Figure 8.9 examples are given. This figure shows that two types

Process: Technology:	service desk/incident management	problem management/change management
Application of techno- logy for achieving cost reduction and at the same time service improvement:	call center technology and workflow control for providing access to certain knowledge intranet technology for disclosing information on previous solutions, a top ten, and progress	broadcasting technology (e mail) for making customers anticipate change in infrastructure and applications measures in the infrastructure as duplicating and using in the applications facilities as logging, by which less incidents occur or these are resolved more quickly.
Application of technology for achieving faster repair and shorter mean time for arriving at repair:		
- detection process . - repair process - implementation solution	including detection of possible problems in objects and based on these plan on site repairs call centers take over the customers screens using web services for checking versions when logging on and if necessary download the latest version.	graphical reproduction of the infrastructure and applications working on these, making incidents visible at a single glance. application of location services, through which location can be detected and solutions implemented immediately. in video conference with local engineers deciding, which solution is implemented and how this will be implemented.

Figure 8.8. Impact of technology on IT processes

Type of management Type innovation:	Detecting/ trying out	Making indicators/ introducing routine
Radical innovations Incremental:	e.g. self repair facility	e.g. automatic update applications

- planned evolutionary
  fitting in of new services
  and/or products
	e.g. enabling
	customers to track
	online service
	level
		e.g. centralization and
		concentration front-
		office service
		providing.

- daily/small improvements in services and/or products	e.g. other types service contracts	e.g. support front- office with tools such as taking over screen user or top ten questions on intranet.

Figure 8.9. Examples of types of innovations and the way of introduction

of innovation can be recognized. These are radical as well as gradual changes in the way of operating or products of the IT demand and supply organization (Fitzsimmons, 2004). The more incremental changes can next be subdivided into changes that happen more or less gradually and small and numerous daily adjustments in the services of a service company.

The distinction between these types of innovations is of importance when looking at the way in which innovations are implemented. Implementation of innovations happens in roughly four phases. These four phases are: discovering, trying, assembling experiences to realize a managed roll-out and finally routinely implementing the innovation.

An implementation of an innovation in the first phases of discovery and trying out characterizes itself by the way in which the innovation is dealt with and by the people involved in the innovation. In the first phases this is usually a limited number of people. These people are strongly user-oriented and a lot of feedback takes place between the users of the innovations and its developers. There is not much attention to the more budgetary side. At the customer-side people are thinking along, about the way in which the innovation will be optimally paying for them as well.

During the following phases this is different. The first experiences with the innovation are gained and the innovation is systematically introduced in the organization. The further implementation is carried out in the form of a project using clear control and a budget. Indicators are available or are especially formulated for the implementation. There is a rollout plan that is clearly based on these indicators and in conformity with this planning an implementation is controlled. The state of affairs is regularly discussed with all those involved.

Control of innovations means that the demand organization is looking permanently at opportunities for innovations in processes and services. Radical innovations might result in a different IT organization. In these types of innovation one often breaks with the current way of operating. This type of innovation does not build on the experience of an organization. Customers do not always ask for this either (Christensen, 2002). This type of innovation requires thought for the form of the innovation process and those involved in the implementations. In the later phases of introduction this may also require an organization that is detached from the current demand organization. Incremental innovations often build on customer's requests or IT organizations' in-house ideas for improvements. This type of innovation often takes an IT supply or demand organization to a higher level of operating and will be implemented by the organization itself either by means of a project or in line.

If IT is strategic (quadrant d of Figure 8.5), this means that in the field of IT management apart from the usual improvements as made by any organization, there will be more innovative improvements implemented. The organization will have to consider in advance, under which category improvement in IT management comes and what the appropriate approach is.

Ensuring knowledge and competencies

The fourth subject of control is the care for knowledge and competencies. The demand management chooses for set-up and organization of its IT services. If it uses an in-house organization for this, processes, tasks and functions have to be set up. The description of functions to be set up for IT services, is determined by the activities that have to be carried out and the skills needed for these. Factors that have impact on the function performance are the environment in which one operates; the level at which a functionary is tasked; and the role a functionary has. In many cases organizations will use their own staff for functional management (see Figure 8.10).

For determining the knowledge necessary for filling a function, an organization will often use knowledge clusters. These clusters indicate the necessary knowledge at every level of function performance. Recognizing the necessary functions and the for these functions essential knowledge clusters, is important because this way it is possible to secure the necessary knowledge within the organization. Management can control using the correct competencies being present within the organization at all times and these competencies being extended in the right direction. This makes the organization less dependent on the skill and knowledge of a single individual. Or, if this is the case, the organization is fully aware of this.

Example

Knowledge management was configured in the IT supply organization of the Dutch tax authorities in the years 1997–2002. It is, amongst other things, used for determination of the content and level of functions. It works as follows. In this service, the knowledge clusters as indicated in Figure 8.11 are defined. In developing and procuring knowledge, these knowledge clusters are the point of departure. Knowledge can be acquired in a number of ways. It is possible

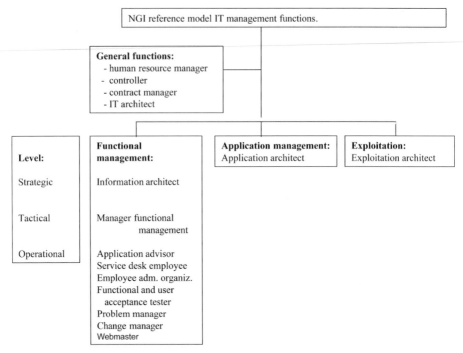

Figure 8.10. The accent is usually on interpretation of functional management tasks and some knowledge of application management and exploitation

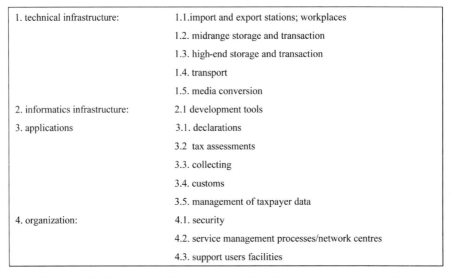

Figure 8.11. Knowledge clusters as recognized by the Dutch tax authorities

to procure licences; one may procure the right to use patents and manuals; one may start research programmes with third parties, one can recruit people; one can use benchmarking and competition analysis; one can utilize universities and other knowledge institutes, one can visit suppliers; attend training and seminars, examine external databases; carry out literature studies, talk to customers, etc. etc.

Working with methods

A fourth type of control is ensuring a methodical approach of tasks in the field of IT management. This book indicates many methods for structuring these tasks. In Figure 8.12 these are summarized. The book supplies methods such as BiSL, ITIL and ASL. To the demand and supply organization, these may be the point of departure when designing tasks in the field of service providing. To external advisors, methods supply frameworks for enabling comparisons between organizations and these provide a thought model, in case one wants to arrive at a more quantitative measuring of performances. Clearly specified processes can be measured, measurements can be compared and discussed and that way the organization can step by step work on upgrading.

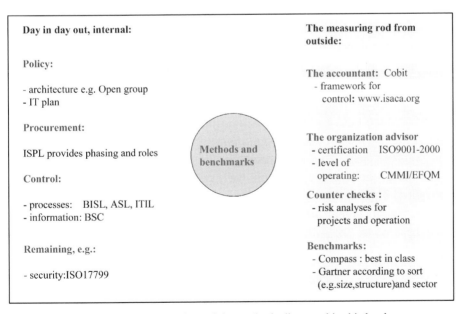

Figure 8.12. An overview of the methods discussed in this book

Example

> *The Gartner group, Compass and the Nolan Norton Institute provide benchmarking indicators for various items of IT organizations. Organizations wanting to put their own experiences to the test can use these. This usually demands a first effort for making the in-house situation comparable to the benchmarking points of departure, the indicators of the advice organizations are based upon. With regards to this, it is important to know which is included in the indicators for which processes.*

Ensuring organizational support

General, business unit and IT demand and supply management look at IT service management each from their own responsibility. It may be useful to have a concrete look at this way of looking and investigate how these stakeholders together arrive at controlling IT facilities. Innovations in IT facilities are investments for an organization. The stake-holders together substantiate the expectations with regards to an investment. Investments once done are marked down, the procured investment goods, possibilities or rights are further utilized and at a given moment disposed of.

Figure 8.13 shows the responsibilities of the stakeholders in an organization. From this figure it transpires that IT demand and supply management aim at a long term IT service architecture, at transparent renewal of the service provision and at taking measures aimed at the continuation of the services within a given architecture. Business unit managements' responsibility in the IT management field focusses on delivering the right knowledge for enabling support by IT. General management mainly deals with gearing business needs to IT support, seen from the perspective of the organization in it's entirety. It looks after the strategy, monitors the execution and if necessary facilitates innovation. This control of general, business unit and IT demand management organizationally comes forward in five different ways. Parker-Priebe (2002) has listed these ways. She distinguishes:

(a) Setting targets and recording these targets in plans. IT plans essentially consist of five parts. One discusses the policy, the current situation, the requests and possible projects and determines on the basis of these the priorities for a certain period (Ministry of Internal Affairs, 1980).

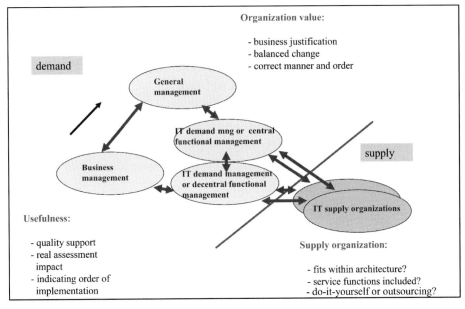

Figure 8.13. Contents of responsibilities

(b) The translation of the policy into control measures. These result in the prescription of the contents of estimates, allocation of budgets and setting rules for the reportage about budget depletion. In this situation, general management may ask business and IT management to report periodically on the services and products as supplied within the budgets. Availability of IT facilities and the timely completion of projects may be a reason, why set targets are or are not made.

Example

If e-Bay or Yahoo is not available for one whole day, this costs the organization many millions of dollars. None or limited availability of the necessary facilities will then immediately show up in the quarterly figures.

The same applies to new projects, www.Boo.com for example, an internet site aimed at what yuppies in society buy, was online six months too late. The IT services were not in place on time and furthermore the necessary facilities for telecommunication were not present. This resulted in a loss of six months income and any purchases made in fashionable clothing were immediately ready for some depreciation (Laudon, 2004).

(c) Setting up of connections by using the setting up of steering committees, project groups, working groups and task forces. These organizational associations may be set up for the implementation of new services, for realizing infrastructures, etc.

Example

At organization XYZ general management, business management and IT management are members of a steering committee for IT. This steering committee advises the Executive Board about project to be undertaken with regards to innovation and the measures for IT management to go with these.

(d) Setting up rules for decision-making at applying for investments in new projects and for the in-house internal processes on the basis of standards, often set for enabling comparisons with other organizations or parts of the organization itself.

Example

The costs for a workstation at a bank can vary per division, as well as their functionality. These prices are compared and the goal is to arrive at a basic workstation that has the same price tag for every division. In this comparison, the data with regards to costs for a workstation are used as collected by the Gartner group and the British organization Compass. Additional facilities are only possible in certain situations in the long run.

(e) Actively managing knowledge and competencies within an organization. One may consider in this instance rotation of employees, deliberate allocation of functions and otherwise organizing of transfer of know how by means of meetings, trainings, investing in tools like internet etc. For actively managing knowledge and competencies an IT set-up with clear tasks and responsibilities is a requirement.

By applying these methods organizations can ensure sufficient basis for innovation of business products, services and processes. It is then possible to appeal to the possibly in-house available IT organization; it is also possible to procure the necessary facilities via this organization from third parties.

CONTROL USING INFORMATION

Information necessary for control

At the control of IT facilities data is needed. This data is obtained through official and unofficial channels. Officially the information often comes in through:

(a) Overall plans, such as information plans in which the policy with regard to IT is often formulated, the current situation is recorded, requests concerning IT application are voiced, the resources enabling realization of these plans are indicated and in which a list of actions and priorities is formulated. On the basis of these plans, plans for projects are drawn up and tasks are configured and controlled. The overall plans lead to project plans for infrastructure and application projects and to management plans (per division) of the infrastructure and (per group of) application(s). These plans often spread across several years and are periodically updated.

Example

Each information plan includes the managed infrastructures and applications. It defines which change projects for infrastructures are realized in the plan period, which actions are undertaken to that effect and what the estimated costs will be. It also states the effort necessary for keeping the facilities in production. The applications furthermore include which releases/versions per application are implemented and managed, what effort is necessary and what the costs are. The plan also contains the standards and procedures for providing management and compares this with the current situation. From thereon possible lifecycles of change are started.

(b) Estimates and budget allocated to these, reportages about the performances carried out on the basis of concluded service level agreements and progress reports of projects in progress. This information often emphasizes on complying with agreements and staying within the budget. This is information of a more short-term character.

Example

A service report is delivered monthly indicating per business unit as well as for the organization as a whole what the availability of the network is, the increase of the number of users and transactions, the total number of users and transactions, the number of changes in the configuration as a result of planned and unplanned actions, the number of service desk calls, the security violations and their location, etc.

(c) Audits to do with IT support and the effectiveness and efficiency of the IT part. The in-house internal audit department may carry out these audits but these may also be done by external organizations. The latter audits often concern the management method, the satisfaction of the users, the staff turnover and its reasons, quality trends in the supplied management, managing planning and the underlying reasons, and so on.

Example

An audit takes place on the quality of an application and the level of the employees managing the application. It may become obvious that chiefly functional managers are used to manage and the application management side does not have any project leaders and information analysts.

What is available, what is not available?

The official information function for supporting management decisions in general, reckons with the phase of development of the technique, the level of the users of the information—one should understand the influence of what is reported on one's own situation—and the relation between IT management, business management and general management. Reports on IT application and management may provide useful insight into the effectiveness of the execution of the task in the lines of business. The question is however, whether everybody should have access to this information.

Examples

If the network traffic in a certain information-intensive organization on a certain day permanently is at a low level, whilst at other moments this much higher, questions should be asked.

If one for instance discovers through the reports that every tenth transaction is a transaction for logging into the application and this seems to be caused by the fact that the used notebooks in the vehicles have a limited battery capacity, which makes these stop every time the vehicle stops, one might ask questions about the lifecycle of implementation of this innovation.

Unofficial sources

Apart from information from official sources that checks the actual situation with planning, reports and points out exceptions, in decision-making one often also includes the information from unofficial channels and impressions gained by walking around the organization. Talks to people face-to-face, telephone conversations and personal notes, supply better information than just that from official sources. Using unofficial sources one often gets, amongst other things, views on IT investments and on the day-in day-out IT management.

ISO 9126 and ITIL

ISO 9126 lists qualities that are important when building and utilizing IT facilities. There is a link between these qualities of IT facilities and the information needed for controlling IT exploitation processes. De Best (2000) and Van Boxel (2003) have made this link. They indicate which information from ISO 9126 is of importance for IT exploitation processes. Figure 8.14 shows this link.

ISO 9126			ITIL help desk	problem/change/conf.	Service lvl,availability
Functional	use-	comprehensibility	Concept appl.simple		
requirem.	ful-	learnability	Learning to work with		
	ness	operability	Simplicity operation		
		adjustability	Ease to adjust		
		equipment level			
	functio-	suitability	Mapping on tasks		
	nality	correctness	Degree deliver.right serv		Degree right results.
		connectivity		Need for comunication	
		compliance		Standard compliant?	
		securability			Degree occur. br. in
		traceability		Right transact to be determ	Ease detect. errors
Technical	main-	analyzability		Simple to change?	
requirem.	tain-	changeability		No unexpct.behaviour	No unexpct. behaviour
	abi-	stability		Ease validation	
	lity	testability		Ease keeping operational	
		manageability		Ease ports	
	porta-	adjustability		Ease installation	
	bili-	installability		Keeping to standards?	
	ty	traceability		Ease replacem other?	
		replaceability	Down when error		Degree incidents
Infrastruc-	re-	operational reliabilit	Perform. when part down		Degree maint. level
ture	lia-	fault tolerance	Ease of rebooting		Ease of rebooting
quality	bili-	repairability	Degree of plann.avail.		Really avail. if?
	ty	availability	Ease function repair		Ease function repair
		degradeability			
Exploita-	Efficient	time requirements			Response to transact
tion quality		resource requiremen			Use of resources

Figure 8.14. ISO 9126 and the information needed at various processes recognized by ITIL

BSC and the level of operations

Delen et al. (2000) furthermore makes a connection between the level of operating in an IT demand and/or supply organization and the four operations areas, in which according to the balanced score card (BSC) method an IT organization information should be collected structurally. The fields of attention of the balanced score card are:

- financial information: revenues, expenses, audit reports, losses and profits etc.
- operational information: elapsed times, calls, absentee rates etc.
- information on innovations: projects, education, knowledge building etc.
- customer information: their contracts, their importance and their opinion on products, services and processes.

Delen et al. (2000) ascertains that in practice this data is not always available. For explaining this, they link this to the level on which the organization operates. They recognize IT organizations that always work from a technical angle; organizations, where the basic control data is present; organizations, where one controls structurally and based on figures and supplies services; organizations, where one in controlling activities takes the remarks made by customers and suppliers into account and IT organizations, where one adjusts constantly to the demand and sets the trend in IT service provision. Each level of operating has its own emphasis with regard to its information function.

When controlling more from the technique, there is often hardly any or no data at all on innovation and customer aspects available. When IT and other management cooperate, all four aspects are filled in. The nature of the data is different at every operating level. This different nature is reflected in the information function that enables the in-house management to control work processes. Living organizations and their information function will resemble the ideal and typical examples more or less. Delen et al. (2000) make it thus clear that IT organizations use other information depending upon their level of operating. This is shown in Figure 8.15.

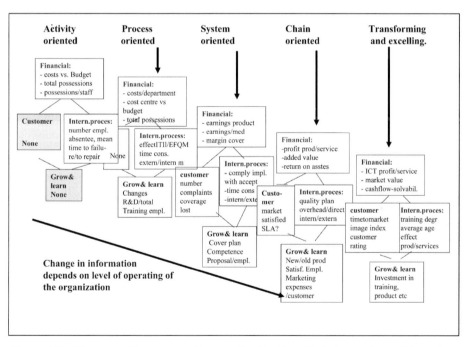

Figure 8.15. The connection between the operating level and the interpretation of the various task areas of the balanced score card (Delen, 2000)

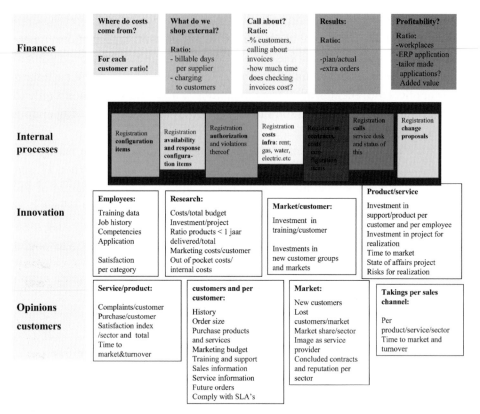

	Where do costs come from?	What do we shop external?	Call about?	Results:	Profitability?
Finances	For each customer ratio!	Ratio: - billable days per supplier - charging to customers	Ratio: -% customers, calling about invoices -how much time does checking invoices cost?	Ratio: -plan/actual -extra orders	Ratio: -workplaces -ERP application -tailor made applications? Added value

| **Internal processes** | Registration configuration items | Registration availability and response configuration items | Registration authorization and violations thereof | Registration costs infra: rent; gas, water, electric.etc | Registration contracts, costs configuration items | Registration calls service desk and status of this | Registration change proposals |

Innovation

Employees:	**Research:**	**Market/customer:**	**Product/service**
Training data Job history Competencies Application Satisfaction per category	Costs/total budget Investment/project Ratio products < 1 jaar delivered/total Marketing costs/customer Out of pocket costs/ internal costs	Investment in training/customer Investments in new customer groups and markets	Investment in support/product per customer and per employee Investment in project for realization Time to market State of affairs project Risks for realization

Opinions customers

Service/product:	**customers and per customer:**	**Market:**	**Takings per sales channel:**
Complaints/customer Purchase/customer Satisfaction index /sector and total Time to market&turnover	History Order size Purchase products and services Marketing budget Training and support Sales information Service information Future orders Comply with SLA's	New customers Lost customers/market Market share/sector Image as service provider Concluded contracts and reputation per sector	Per product/service/sector Time to market and turnover

Figure 8.16. The balanced score card and an IT organization

Data and the BSC

The information part concludes with Figure 8.16. This figure shows per area of the BSC what information could be found within IT organizations. This overview acts as a checklist. However, one should always ask oneself which data one should have at controlling towards a specific target. A surplus of data is costly.

PLANNING IT FACILITIES

What precedes shows that control of IT facilities departs from operating systematically and that this operating is based upon using data about facts and objects. An information plan, in whatever shape or form, is a requirement for this way of operating. In such a plan, choices are fixed and based on this plan control is provided to the IT organization. And organizations have to choose! They cannot do everything at once. The rapid changes in society and technology force them to apply new applications and infrastructures all the time. They have to set up their IT organization accordingly. They are in actual fact constantly changing and this change demands control.

Example

AKZO introduced standard workstations between 1995 and 2001, the use of an ERP application and the application of an intranet and an extranet. The introduction of new technology was coupled with a reconsideration of the IT organization. Atos Origin became their partner that took over the IT organization set-up for, amongst other things, management of the workstations as well as the ERP application.

The contents of an information plan consist of six parts. Such a plan is annually adjusted. The first year the plan is fairly detailed. In the next two or three years this becomes increasingly more broad. The six parts of the plan are:

1. **An evaluation** of the current situation. Here the products and services in relation with the customer satisfaction are discussed. This is measured in users surveys. This also transpires from service management reports. At the organization of IT facilities the size, functional requirements and performance requirements, the geographical dispersal and skill level are looked into.
2. **The policy** with regard to procurement, development and maintenance of IT facilities and the services provided with these. The following matters are raised:
   – the methods to be used and the supporting tools;
   – the organization of management;
   – the standardization of objects and processes.
3. **The current IT facilities**. In larger organizations a clustering can be seen here. There is often distinction made according to generally used applications and applications that support specific organization units. Per cluster is indicated:

–the objects to be managed in numbers and year of procurement;

–the number of changes per type object per annum, the average effort per release, the number of service desk calls and the backlog with regard to changes and projects still present for this object;

–the expansion plans in the next three years;

–the used technology;

–the organization and knowledge necessary for execution the management task;

–the costs for management, if possible per object.

4. **The requests with regards to (new) IT facilities**. Per cluster of part 3 is discussed:

–the (new) objects concerned in numbers;

–the objects to be replaced in numbers and year of procurement and the activities still to be carried out for these;

–the reason for replacement and the possible lifecycle of replacement;

–the number of changes to be expected per cluster per year, the average effort to be expected per release/version, the number of service desk calls;

–the plans for expansion in the next three years;

–the used technology;

–the organization and skill necessary for executing the requested tasks;

–the estimated costs for service management.

5. **A summary of current and requested IT facilities with regard to expenses**. Now the current expenses and the possible expenses for realizing requests are listed. The expenses are divided into investments and costs. For new request also further details of a 'Total cost of ownership' can be included. The expenses are subdivided in:

–expenses per cost centre and type of costs;

–the expenses per cluster and per object in the cluster;

–expenses per cluster, often being a part of the organization, after allocation.

6. **An approved establishing of priorities for IT activities in the next four years**. The choices made are indicated in this part. This is where the projects for setting up a new IT organization or renewal of the organization come up for discussion.

Implementation

Implementation of the information plan in a current organization means both partial as well as entire continuation of the running operation, as well as starting of projects for implementation of requested IT facilities. The process for arriving at an information plan demands: knowing what one wants, a clear step-by-step plan for execution of the planning process and indication of who is to be involved in the planning process and in what role.

The contents of an information plan may differ. In general an organization starting plans, does not arrive at an optimal plan in one go. The plans as delivered in the first years will therefore be more of a 'just good enough' character (the basis minimum). After some time has passed, the plan process will start to yield more matured plans. These more matured plans are not just of sufficient quality but the foundation of finished activities is also strong with regards to quantity. This also applies to activities that still have to be carried out. Use of quantities enables a clearer evaluation of the past year and makes planning for the coming year more credible.

Choices in the planning process

The planning process is set up in such a manner that this provides sufficient basis within the organization for execution of the plan. At the same time the process should take no longer than three months and be fully transparent to all participants. With regard to the planning process one has, dependent on the organization, in principle three choices. These are:

- top-down planning of IT facilities, using a scenario approach. Demand management is offered the possibility of choosing one of the possible choices.
- middle-out planning. On the basis of an indicated framework one asks the organization parts each to set up plans for its own cluster. These are then centrally incorporated into the final information plan;
- bottom-up planning: allowing ideas to bubble up from below. Afterwards in a next stage general management, users management and the IT management set up the final plan together.

Dependent on the importance of IT, the culture of the organization and the phase in which the organization is concerning IT, one will decide how one plans and who is going to be involved in the planning process.

QUESTIONS

1. Under what influence are decisions about the control of IT facilities made? Explain your answer.
2. In which fields can the demand organization provide control to IT facilities?
3. Explain your answer using four examples.
4. Give the four possible positions in which organizations may find themselves with regard to control of IT facilities and the type of projects one may expect in the various positions.
5. Indicate how the organization of IT facilities will probably shift in the period between 2004 up to and including 2016.
6. What is a radical innovation? What is an incremental innovation? Why does one have to differentiate in innovation between radical and incremental innovations?
7. Which knowledge should the IT organization definitely have in-house? Why?
8. Which five organizational possibilities does an organization have, according to Parker-Priebe in order to control IT clearly? Give an example of each possibility.
9. In controlling IT facilities we need information. What is the difference between data sourced from unofficial and data from official channels? Which data originates from official sources?
10. Why is it handy to make a link between ISO 9126 and ITIL?
11. What do Delen et al. (2000) state with regard to the information function in IT-organizations?
12. Give the contents of an information plan. Indicate how one may arrive at such a plan. Illustrate your answer by giving an example.

Looking at the product, looking at the
    process
Methods
    of change and by whom: via the line/or
    via a project insourcing/outsourcing, etc.
Process perspective:
    −minimum
        requirements: ISO 9001-2000:
    −level of operating
    −project risk and operational risk
    −auditing by EDP auditors: CobiT
Products and their performance requirements.

Chapter 9

House in order: evaluating and improving

Functional and performance requirements relate to the product to be delivered and the services to be furnished with it. Service level agreements deal with both. These also indicate which process one can go through, in case one has queries about a product or service.

A product or service can be improved. Charles Schwab improved his availability from 99.9% in the planned hours to 99.999%. The project to do this went in stages and took three years. The reason for the project was an external one. The company made the news as soon as it was off line for fifteen minutes. This media attention acted as negative publicity.

The process for obtaining an ISO 9000-2000 certificate provided the Dutch ITO computing centre with a chance to describe its processes clearly. The concluded service agreements then made use of this. Step by step, using different technology the performance requirements were accentuated.

From the development department one wanted to get a grip on the exploitation of the e-business channel at the Dutch tax supply centre for IT, BCICT. Giesberts

179

(2002) looked at various models that go into the level of operating in IT organizations. He examined the world-class IT management model, the CMMI model and the EFQM model. With the aid of these models he defined a model for an IT organization and decided that the BCICT with regard to the exploitation of internet solutions operates somewhere between the levels 1 and 2 as defined in this model. His research then opened the way for starting projects that aim to raise the operating level.

Managers want to change organizations with as little risk as possible. Changes are often implemented by executing a project. It is in that case useful to be able to determine in advance what the risks of such a project are and how one may minimize these risks. McFarlane defined a method for this purpose, indicating when, what measures have to be taken for keeping the risks of a project as minimal as possible.

Isaca provides a framework with the CobiT model, which may be used to determine which EDP audits can be performed in organizations and what their results could be. These Control Objectives for Information and related Technology (CobiT) make use of international standard methods such as ITIL.

Contents of this chapter

This chapter focusses on the evaluating and improving of IT organizations. On the pretext of 'house in order,' methods for improving services and products of organizations are discussed. The chapter starts by indicating the functional and performance requirements with regard to the products and services of an IT organization. The services and products are effected by executing processes. The execution of those can be looked at from various perspectives and one may methodically arrive at improvement of these products and services.

After positioning the methods, these are discussed. These may be specifically aimed at improvement of processes or more aimed at laying down standards for products and services. With regard to the processses, the ISO 9001-2000 set of methods and their relation with the ITIL method and the EFMQ model are discussed, amongst others. Regarding products and services, the translation of agreements as laid down in service level agreements into products and services to be supplied is discussed.

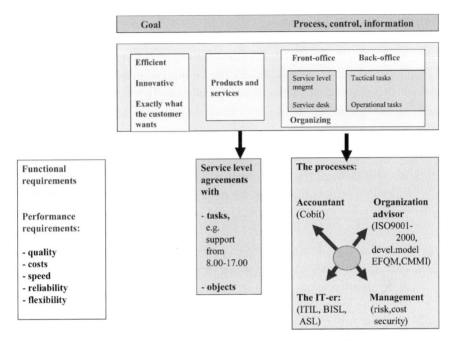

Figure 9.1. Evaluation and improvement: an overview

EVALUATION AND IMPROVEMENT
Perspectives and reasons

Figure 9.1 gives and overview of this chapter. The IT organization operates on a basis of targets and delivers products and services. To this purpose
processes are executed in a front and a back-office. These processes concern
objects. The execution of processes can be regarded from different perspectives.
These are the perspective of:

- the person working with IT, looking at the work processes to be performed;
- the accountant, who ensures the processes in question are carried out
  controllably;
- the organization adviser, who tries to improve the processes;
- the management that aims to deliver the products and services with as
  little as possible risk, at costs as minimal as possible and with the largest
  possible degree of reliability.

Methods for improving the organization

Customers make functional demands and performance requirements to the products and services delivered by the IT organization. In order to be able to deliver these, processes have to be carried out. The management of the IT organization has to make choices, if it wants to improve the organization. It can choose:

(a) to carry through the improvement in the line organization or especially start up a project for achieving an improvement;

(b) to apply the improvement in-house or (partly) hiring another organization for this;

(c) beforehand and/or during the implementation of the improvement, to have a risk analysis or a countercheck carried out. This helps to look at an improvement from a distance and changes possibly one's ideas about the improvement.

There is a difference between having a countercheck done and making a risk analysis. A risk analysis can be done in-house by an organization. It involves focussing on checking the risk and advising on measures for reducing this risk. A countercheck however is always performed by a third party. Moreover a countercheck can be performed for various reasons, for example because:

−one want an external confirmation whether the right approach was chosen;

−one wants an external check of one's own actions;

−one wants arbitration about issues raised;

−one wants to see whether there are any blind spots;

−one wants to cover oneself;

−one flounders and asks oneself, what next?

−there are failures and the plans have gaps. One wants to point these out.

(d) about the approach to improvement. One may design this first and next introduce it. One could also check first together with those involved which improvements are needed, design these together with them and next implement these;

(e) About the control of the lifecycle of improvement. This can be controlled top down, thus forcing change. A second strategy is the management relying on the rational behaviour of people and introducing the change using communication and training. A third strategy is stimulating employees to be as largely as possible involved in the change. Finally, the management can limit itself to facilitating the process and have the employees implement the change.

THE PROCESSES: PERSPECTIVE ON PROCESS IMPROVEMENT

Concentration on processes

Various methods concentrate on the processes of an organization. One asks oneself questions like: is the process possible? Is the process affordable and what are the risks for executing the process like this? Next we discuss the process improvement using the way as described in the quality system ISO 9001-2000; via looking at execution of projects involving as little risk as possible and via checking processes through the eyes of an accountant. This last mentioned perspective is the one used in the CobiT method.

ISO 9000-2000

The series of standards ISO 9000-2000 describes a systematic approach for realizing a certain quality level of processes within an organization. The *ISO* standards pay a lot of attention to the customer. Besides taking the customers' needs as a starting point, it is also ensured that the organization is aware of the customers' requirements and it checks customer satisfaction regularly. The position of the management of the organization is central in this case. A second remarkable point of the *ISO* standard is that this puts emphasis on the evolutionary improvement of the processes. Below in this context, a connection will be made between the ISO 9001-2000 standards and a development model derived from the EFQM model and the CMMI model.

The ISO 9000-2000 standards include the ISO 9000 standard that provides the basic principles and a glossary; the ISO 9001-2000 standard that provides the requirements for certification; the ISO 9004-2000 standard with guidelines for improvement of performances and the ISO 10011 standard that provides guidelines for audits of quality management systems. Points of departure for the *ISO* standard are customer orientation, leadership, involvement of the employees, the process and the system approach, continuous improvement, decision making based upon facts and realization of a win-win relationship with the suppliers.

Parts ISO 9001-2000

The ISO 9001-2000 standard describes the requirements to a quality system. These requirements are:

(a) The organization has to set up and manage a quality system. This quality system includes a description of all processes. Next it records the standards, on which are checked at execution of the processes. Based on this, measurements to the processes are carried out and the execution is controlled.

(b) The management of the organization is demonstrably involved in the control and ensures that the organization works customer oriented. It is aware of the benefit of quality management, allots the necessary resources in order to guarantee quality of execution and regulates the management of the quality system.

(c) Controlling the organization, attention is paid to sufficient training of the employees; the environment where the processes are executed and the facilities one provides for execution of the processes.

(d) The organization's products are made by processes that are set up from the customer's requests. Frequently the customer satisfaction is measured.

(e) The performances of the organization are measured permanently, these measures are analyzed and improvements are implemented on the basis of these findings. Amongst other things the process execution is audited, the control of special processes, the preventive measures that were taken, customer satisfaction etc.

In Figure 9.2 is indicated roughly which requirements an organization has to meet according to the ISO 9001-2000 standard. A combination of ISO

Obligatory assessments:	Obligatory validation		product not comply requir. reg.corrections identificat.
Documents on suitability	Validation w.r.t. realization	results assessment suppliers and the advanced measures identification product for tracing possessions of customers, that go missing, get damaged etc calibrations	reg.non-conformity reg.preventive measure identifcation non-conform. and the causes of that
Assessment by management	process. All stages of design		
Effectivity provided training	and develop process		
Assessment product requirements	Validation design and devel.		
Each stage design/development	process, as soon as product		
process	complies with all requirements	results audits and verifications	**Obligatory documents.**
Input design/development	Changes in design and/or	results measuring and monitoring	
Output document	development	conformity and release product	some six req. procedures
Design and develop process	With the processes the	results correcting measure	plus documents for the
Changes to design/develop.	planned results can be	results preventive measure	organization
Periodical assessment procur.	achieved	some obligatory procedures, e.g	procedures
Requirements laid down in	Of previous results, if the	- management documents	quality manual
purchase documents	measuring results are outside	- management quality registrations	planning realization proc.
Validity previous assessments	the tolerances.	- responsibility&requir.internal	input reg. product requir.
Customer satisfaction		audit	output
Internal audit results	**According to ISO 9001:2000**	-control non-conformity	assessment changes to
Meas. and monitoring processes	**obligatory registrations:**	-correcting measures	design and development
Meas, and monitoring product		-preventive measures	purchase documents
Suitability and effectiveness	quality registration		proof of conformity
quality management system	results of assessments	**Obligatory identification**	
Continuous improvement of	training, experience, training and		**Obligatory mngmt meas.**
quality management system	qualifications personnel	processes quality mngmtsyst.	
Measures for preventing	assessment advanced measures	identification product	e.g. production and
non-conformity	assessment of the output	property customer in use	service facilities
Correcting measures taken	of all stages of the design and	care, product keeps complying with	**Obligatory to determine**
Preventive measures taken	develop process plus validation	requir. during transact.and delivery	etc etc

Figure 9.2. Overview of some requirements to a quality system according to ISO 9001-2000

9001-2000 standards with models that represent the level of operating in an organization, results in a plan for arriving gradually, in a structured manner, to a higher level of operating.

Level of operating

Since 1991 CMM's (Capability Maturity Modellen) have been developed, aimed at various disciplines. The CMM's came into being with the development of Software CMM, after which amongst others Software Acquisition CMM, Systems Engineering CMM and People CMM were developed. Although the developed CMM's are regarded separately as useful, combining several of these models proved problematic for organizations. The Software Engineering Institute (*SEI*) was therefore given the task of integrating various CMM's. This *SEI* is a research and development centre, sponsored by the Ministry of Defence of the United States. The *SEI* is part of the Carnegie Mellon University. The order to the *SEI* resulted in the integration being reality in August 2000 and version 1.0 of the Capability Maturity Model Integration, CMMI, was released.

This new framework relies on the success of Software CMM whilst offering a larger supply of activities and process domains and also is in conformity with international standards.

CMMI

The CMMI includes 24 process domains. A process domain describes what organizations that make use of an effective process do and why they do this in this manner. The process domains as distinguished by the model are:

- Requirements Management
- Project Planning
- Project Monitoring and Control
- Supplier Agreement Management
- Measurement and Analysis
- Process and Product Quality Assurance
- Configuration Management
- Requirements Development
- Technical Solution
- Product Integration
- Verification
- Validation
- Organizational Process Focus
- Organizational Process Definition
- Organizational Training
- Integrated Project Management (adjusted in product development)
- Risk Management
- Decision Analysis and Resolution
- Organizational Process Performance
- Quantitative Project Management
- Organizational Innovation and Deployment
- Causal Analysis and Resolution
- Integrated Teaming (just for product development)
- Organizational Environment for Integration (just for product development)

Each process domain is composed of targets and activities. Through execution of prescribed activities, described targets may be achieved. CMMI aims at a level of operating of the organization as a whole. Organizations may vary

Level:	Process areas: SW-CMM version 1.1	CMMI
Repeatable: (2)	control requirements planning software mngmnt tracking software project subcontract control quality assurance management appl. configuration mngmt	control requirements planning projects track and control project contract control process&product qual.ass. configurattion mng. data management measuring and analyzing
Defined (3)	process focus organization determining processes organ. training programm integrated appl.mngmt application product engineer.	process focus organization defining processes org training organization integrated project mngm risk management customer and product req. technical solution product integration&verifi- cation, validation
	attunement between groups reviews by colleagues	*integrated project mngm* product *verification* analysis deciding&resolv.
Controlled (4)	quantitative control applicatie quality mngmt	*process improv. organ.* *quant.mngm.qual&process* *org. process performance* *quant.mngm.qual&process*
Optimised (5)	preventing errors change mngmt IT change mgmnt proces	check cause&resolve org. process techn.innovat. process innovation *org. process innovation* *process innovation*

Figure 9.3. Operating level, as distinguished in CMM and CMMI

with regard to their level of operating. These levels have been defined in advance within CMM and CMMI. The levels are attained by complying with all targets of the process domains. In Figure 9.3 these targets are given for the software CMM and for the CMMI. One can notice that operating at level 1 is considered a given.

EFQM Model

In 1991 the Steering Committee Dutch Quality was established, with the goal (also) to pay more attention in future to quality in the Netherlands. The steering committee chose to use the European quality model of the European Foundation for Quality Management (EFQM) as point of departure for quality management in the Netherlands. The choice for the EFQM model was made because of the self-assessments, the matrices for positioning an organization and

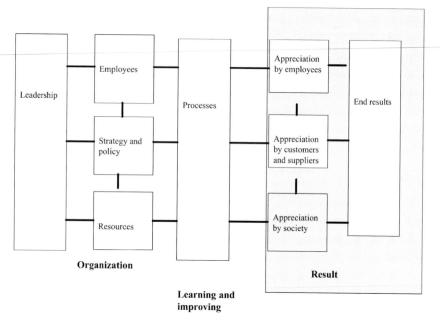

Figure 9.4. The EFQM management model

the graphic representations the model offers. The EFQM model was extended by distinguishing some five development phases in each organization. These development phases bring into vision which development an organization goes through in its views on quality.

This Dutch version of the EFQM model is called in this book the EFQM management model. The model is composed of nine practically oriented areas of attention. The areas of attention are composed of five organization areas and four result areas. The five organization areas concern the set-up and control of the organization. The other four areas of attention related to the achieved results, or in other words, what the taken measures actually yielded. In the result areas measures are taken using direct (external) and indirect (company internal) benchmarks (see Figure 9.4).

The model should be read from right to left: ultimately the achieved company results, based upon customer satisfaction, staff satisfaction and the position in society are of importance. These three aspects are the result of the processes in the organization. These are in turn influenced by policy and strategy, personnel management and resources management. These organizational aspects are in turn entirely dependent on the contents and control of the leadership.

Phase	Description
Phase 1: Activity oriented	Everyone strives to do the job as best one can in his/her own work situation. Expertise is highly valued and supported by training. If there are complaints, the organization tries to remedy these. This phase is characterized by being product oriented.
Phase 2: Process oriented	The production process or primary process is controlled. The dependency comes into the picture. The individual steps in the process are identified; tasks and responsibilities have been laid down. Performance indicators act as a means of control. Processes are improved on the basis of established problems.
Phase 3: System oriented	Improvement of the organization as a whole is worked at systematically on all levels. The feedback loop is applied in primary, supporting and controlling processes. Customer focus is dominant for the policy that is aimed at preventing problems instead of repairing these.
Phase 4: Chain oriented	With partners in the maximum added value is strived for. Per partner it is determined who is most suitable for executing a certain task. Control systems are interconnected. Innovation is the main thing.
Phase 5: Excel and transform (Total Quality)	The organization is at the top of its market segment. The process of continuous improvement is embedded in the structure and culture of the organization. On the basis of a long-term outlook the sails are trimmed to the wind in time for starting up new activities setting up the organization for these.

Figure 9.5. Levels of operating in the EFQM model

Apart from attention areas, the EFQM model recognizes the development phases as mentioned above. The five development phases describe the different phases an organization will go through, when progressing from an ad hoc oriented organization to an organization with total quality care. The development phases are defined in Figure 9.5.

Choosing a model

Giesberts (2002) compared the stages an organization can operate at as recognized by the CMM/CMMI models and the EFQM model. Next, he investigated the IT service CMM. He ascertained in this comparison of models that the level on which is prescribed how an organization should set up its processes differs considerably. Both the CMMI as well as the EFQM management model provide concrete targets that have to be made. Each model indicates five levels, where the IT service CMM only has three levels of operating. The CMM models furthermore progress further than the EFQM model by describing activities to be executed providing extensive explanations for these. The approach to these is however mainly aimed at use in a software and product development environment. The process areas of the CMM models are aimed less at the upkeep of IT products, services and processes. This makes these models in his opinion less suitable for offering support at measuring the operating level of an IT organization.

The line of approach of the EFQM model is more befitting. This model does not target a specific area. The targets set per area of attention, are general in set-up and may be used at the level of organizations, departments or projects. The general terms are meant to be applied on a certain situation after translation. The layout of the areas of attention guarantees moreover a wide covering across the entire (IT) organization.

ISO 9001-2000 and ASL

Apart from the distinction between levels, there are checklists available that enable an organization to determine its position regarding application of ITIL or ASL. The checklists for ITIL can be found on the *ITSMF* website (http://www.itsmf.com/news/news.asp?NewsID=71). The checklist for ASL can be found in a manual.

Furthermore, Meijer-Veltman (2003) has tested the ASL method against the requirements as included in ISO 9001-2000, when talking about quality

Subject:	Requirement from ISO 9001:2000 norm:	ASL process:	ASL best practices solution:
General requirements:	organization with a quality management system devel.,implementing &improving.	Quality management	
Documenta-tion requirmt:	quality manual required, targets and policy. 6 processes+registrations.	Quality management	product is quality manual, in which internal working methods &procedures. Besides DAP files and SLA's.
Responsibility and involve-ment mngmt	management lays down policy and makes resources available	Quality management	recording is explicitly arranged in Quality management. Propagation not explicitly subject of ASL.
Customer oriented	needs and expectations customers have to be defined. Management takes care of this.	SLM,incident mg,ACM,CM	requir. etc. stated in SLA. Temporarily recorded in incident mngm, later implementation in CM,future in OCM.
Quality policy:	quality policy aimed at organisation and on improvement. Mngmnt propagates this.	OCM, quality Management	OCM records future. QM take care of cont. improv.The communication about this is not arranged for in ASL.
Planning:	targets policy and measurable	Plan&control	through planning and control control on achieving strategy of OCM
Responsibi-lity, authori-rity and com-munication	must be clear how these are divided and how one communicates internally.	Quality management	responsibilities and way of communicating within team is laid down in mngmntplan. For organ. in manual ASL.
Management assessment: etc .	operation quality mngmnt system must be assessed regularly.	Quality mng. SLM	Standard ASL provides series review moments. Norms & standards for management team are laid down and if needed adjusted. This might be as result of experienced service levels

Figure 9.6. ASL and the requirements to a quality system as demanded by ISO 9001-2000

of application management processes. Figure 9.6 shows where in ASL the requirements as stated by ISO 9001-2000 are discussed. In general she arrived at the conclusion that ASL tested against the *ISO* quality system does have certain flaws, concerning:

- communicating quality policies to the employees;
- explaining that making facilities available is necessary when working in conformity with ASL;
- the aspect procurement of people and resources;
- clear indication of the responsibility of the management when working in conformity with ASL and the execution of management reviews.

ASL does cover the responsibilities within the application management teams and the quality measurements at the level of application management teams.

THE PROCESSES, RISK PERSPECTIVE

Dealing with risk

Apart from the perspectives evaluation and improvement, it is also possible to look at the processes in an organization from the perspective of risk evasion. In doing this, a distinction is made between the risk involved in executing projects and the risk one runs when the tasks that have to be carried out daily stop. The first is called project risk; the second is called operational risk.

Project risk

Project risk is the risk that innovations of IT facilities are not implemented at the time and within the budget agreed in advance. It is a risk that remains, even if the best tools are used and one has all the resources one asked for at one's disposal. The result of occurrence of project risk is that:

- planned profits are not achieved or not entirely achieved;
- the project overruns, which makes the project more expensive than expected;

–the project does not turn out very well from a technical point of view;
–the application at closer inspection is not as optimal as expected or does not work on the existing technical infrastructure.

Project risk has in general three reasons. The first being that the size of the project is relatively large compared to other projects within the organization. More departments are affected than is normally the case. The project involves a larger budget etc. The second reason is often that the organization has not or not sufficiently mastered the used technology. One comes across surprises and is not sure how to deal with these. The last reason is the fact that one does not know what one wants. During the course of the project one constantly changes the scope and the requirements the end result has to meet. The project team is more or less driven to distraction and increasingly loses its motivation.

Definition project risk

The project risk may be discovered by means of interviews or by organizing Delphi meetings. Various levels in demand and supply management are asked for their opinion on the progress of the project, the results already achieved, their expectations and possible measures for adjustment. If the risk is considered too big, one may decide to take measures. These could include reinforcing the team, changing the scope of the or/and pursuing an adjusted lifecycle of implementation.

Figure 9.7 shows what the project risk is, if the aforementioned causes for risk apply to a project. All the same, organizations will not always be able to avoid risky projects, especially when application of IT is of great importance

		not knowing what you want	knowing what you want
Technique known,	size large	low risk	low risk
	size small	very low risk	very low risk
Technique unknown,	size large	very high risk	medium-sized risk
	size small	high risk	medium-sized risk

Figure 9.7. Assessing the risk of a project (Applegate c.s., 2003)

to them. The reasons why an organization decides to press ahead with projects could depend on the fact that on the demand-side:

- one has built a reputation, with regard to the number of successful projects that have been carried out over the past few years and one works strongly result oriented;
- one is able to provide good project managers and experienced users;
- one is financially healthy.

On the supply-side the following factors help to decide to continue a slightly more risky project after all:

- the supply organization has a good reputation with regard to the exploitation of facilities;
- it is a matter of continuous improvement in quality and innovation of services;
- the planning often comes true;
- the test avenues work well;
- and one stands by one's agreements!

Measures for limiting the risk

Depending on the type of risk one may take measures for limiting the risk. In case one has to deal with the risk, one does not know exactly what one wants, measures to do with integration are of importance. In dealing with large projects, in which the technique is less familiar, correct planning and use of experienced IT employees will have to get attention. In Figure 9.8 gives an overview of measures that could possibly be taken. Projects are often part of project programmes. Each project is in that case result-oriented implemented and yields return on investment within a maximum of nine months. Furthermore, each project has its own justification. In the previous text the result-oriented implementation of changes was discussed.

Operational risk

Apart from project risk an organization is open to operational risk. De Wijs (1995) investigated this operational risk. He indicates when it is opportune

external integration	internal integration
user project manager setting up steering committee users control change all information spread selection of users as team members formal approval process with user user responsible for training and implementation, etc	experienced IT-man leads team many team meetings minutes spread over key decisions regular technical status included many experieneed team members members take part in objective meetings etc
formal planning	**formal control methods**
formal planning methods choice of milestones standards for reports etc project approval process evaluations per phase and of total.	periodical actual vs. budget formal change procedures regular milestone presentations deviations of plan observed

Figure 9.8. Overview of risk limiting measures (Applegate c.s., 2003)

to take measures for limiting this risk. His method for dealing with operational risk consists of three steps. These are:

1. Defining the complexity of the IT facility. In this step one works out which tasks are supported and to what extent this support is strongly integrated or whether one uses various facilities that are linked to each other. Based on the findings the operational risk is determined. One takes into account:
   - the seriousness of the occurring disaster;
   - the measure in which the consequences of this are immediately experienced;
   - the irreversibility of these consequences in the long run;
   - the controllability of the disaster given the measures taken;
   - the extent to which everyone fears the occurrence of the disaster;
   - the relative news value of the disaster for the media;
   - the familiarity of the experts with the disaster and its consequences;
   - and the willingness of user management for accepting the possibly occurrence of the disaster.
2. Determine the possibilities one has to prevent the occurrence of the disaster. One could think of extra facilities for increasing availability,

a fallback computer centre for being able to continue working after disasters such as a fire and an extra, separate cable link for keeping the connection, even when one cable is broken. In general one checks one's IT facilities and tries to find out which is the weakest link.
3. And finally, the necessity for taking measures, given the reliability of the facility and the specific requirements of the situation.

De Wijs (1995) determines this way after thorough analysis the possible facilities. In order to realize these he demands that the risk is quantifiable and directly influences the demanded performance requirements. This way they may be justifiable in a business economics context.

THE PROCESSES: AUDIT PERSPECTIVE

EDP audit

The third perspective on improving and evaluation of processes, discussed in this book, is the one of the EDP audit as seen from the accountants point of view. Accountants often use the CobiT method for audit of the IT organization (www.isaca.org). CobiT makes a direct connection between the operational processes and their support by IT. CobiT uses international standards. CobiT consists of a number of parts. These are (see Figure 9.9):

- a framework of targets and requirements to do with 34 processes in an IT organization;
- specification of 302 audit targets for these 34 processes;
- audit guidelines in step-by-step plans for the various audits;
- management guidelines included in defined critical success factors, indicators and benchmarks;
- tools for implementing CobiT, such as case studies, presentations, frequently asked questions, diagnostic tools, etc.

Figure 9.9 shows the 34 CobiT processes. These 34 processes cover the domains planning and control, procurement and implementation, management of IT facilities and monitoring of these facilities.

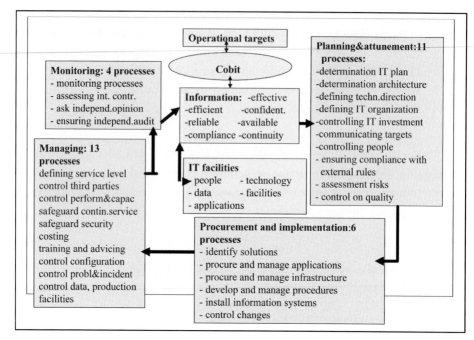

Figure 9.9. The 34 processes in an IT organization as recognized by CobiT

PERFORMANCE REQUIREMENTS REGARDING PRODUCTS

Performance requirements regarding products

The products of the IT organization have to comply with functional and performance requirements. These functional and performance requirements are laid down in service level agreements. In Chapter 2 we indicated that functional requirements depend on the perspective one uses for looking at an IT facility. The management for instance looks at targets; the user has to be able to work with it; the IT supply organization poses requirements from application management and exploitation considerations and the project manager would like insight into the importance of a function to each of those concerned. Functional requirements are often not so quick to improve for one single organization. The evaluation also does not often have immediate results because these requirements often concern the outcome of applications. In case one deals with tailor made applications it is possible to reduce this gap between requirement and reality gradually. In a standard application this is often more difficult to achieve because the application is shared with many users outside the in-house organization. In general it is not advisable now to build a facility for bridging the gap between wish and reality but to wait until the manufacturer of the standard package meets the functional requirements. Thinking up one's own solution may turn the implementation of next versions and/or releases problematic quite quickly.

Actions as a result of performance requirements

When speaking about performance requirements, the situation is a different one. An organization can often choose between alternatives for reducing the gap between wish and reality. It is therefore useful to indicate per performance requirement, where the excuse for possible action can be found and what the result of this action might be. The performance requirements:

1. **Speed of delivery** is influenced by the presence or lack of architecture. Are there any agreements about the objects to be applied and the way in which this application is designed—shortly, is there architecture, then speed of delivery is favourably influenced. This speed can be increased if within the architecture it was decided to go for drastic standardization.
2. **Flexibility of the supplied product.** The desired flexibility has to do with fluctuations in the volume of demand. The measure in which one is able to deal with changes in volume depends on the chosen objects and their organization. Some technical infrastructures can be scaled to a high degree. Some ways of setting up the organization make it possible to quickly bring in extra capacity.

Example

The IBM mainframe model zSeries890, in full the 2086A04, has four processors and seven capacity settings per processor. This enables the user to bring in extra processing capacity as desired during the time he needs it. The customer only pays for the actually used capacity. This is the start of on-demand or utility computing.

3. **Quality of the product.** This involves characteristic qualities of the delivered product, including reliability of delivery, the confidentiality

of the data and the continuation of the IT facilities. With regard to the continuation requirements in conformity with the *ISO* standard 17799 have to be met. Availability of objects is discussed below.

4. **Costs of the product.** In Chapter 11 the costs of a product are discussed. In this chapter notions such as investment versus costs, the total cost of ownership (TCO) etc. are discussed.

5. **The certainty of delivery.** This requirement is about the certainty that a supplier of IT facilities will stick to agreements. In Chapter 13 the procurement process for IT facilities is discussed. In Chapter 14, in discussing the subject contract management the agreements made about products in service level agreements will also come up for discussion.

The five performance requirements examine the question how an IT facility is delivered and what guarantee one has. These questions are answered in a service level agreement for a service or product. It is therefore an interesting exercise to check concluded SLA's for the five aspects mentioned above.

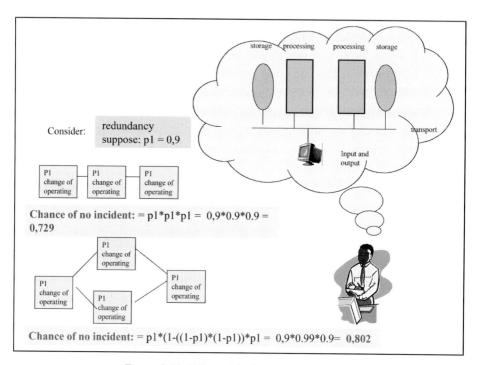

Figure 9.10. Effect of doubling on availability

Availability

For indicating there are different methods for realizing a specific performance requirement, we would like to examine the improvement of the availability of an IT facility. This availability is laid down in the requirement that the average planned downtime of a facility should be less than 0.1%, daily from 07.00 a.m. until 19.00 p.m. measured over a three month period. In Figure 9.10 is shown that by doubling parts of the hardware facility this downtime can be reduced considerably. Besides one can reduce this downtime by limiting the time needed for getting the facility back on line. The latter may require better training of the employees or using more employees. An organization has therefore various alternatives for increasing the availability of IT facilities.

QUESTIONS

1. Indicate which possibilities one has for improving the products and processes of an IT organization. Illustrate your answer with two examples.
2. Give at least four possibilities, from which an IT organization has to choose when it wants to improve its processes or products. Illustrate your answer with two examples.
3. What does the quality system ISO 9000-2000 consist of? What requirements does an organization have to meet to comply with this quality system?
4. Why is it useful to employ a model besides ISO 9000-2001 that indicates the level on which an organization operates? What do the CMM models do with regard to this? What does the EFQM model do?
5. What does the EFQM model look like? Which levels of operating are included in the EFQM model? Give four requirements an IT organization has to meet, when operating on the 'system-oriented' level.
6. List some four points on which the ASL method fails, when checking this against the requirements of the ISO 9000-2000 quality system.
7. What is useful about the checklist for ASL and ITIL? What is missing when using these checklists? Illustrate your answer with an example.
8. What is project risk? How is this defined? Why is a project sometimes still pursued in spite of a larger risk? Illustrate your answer with an example.
9. What type of measures is taken for limiting the risk in a project, in which there is no sufficient sight of the functional requirements and one does

not really have control over the technique? Illustrate your answer with an example.

10. Which type of measures is taken for limiting the risk in a project, in which one has a proper view of the functional requirements and really has control over the technique? Illustrate your answer by giving an example.

11. What is operational risk? What are the steps to be taken in the method for checking whether measures have to be taken to limit operational risks?

12. What does the CobiT method consist of? What four areas do the 34 processes distinguished by CobiT cover? What is the importance of CobiT?

13. Why is there a difference in actions to be undertaken with regard to 'house in order' measures if one ascertains gaps between wish and reality between gaps concerning functional and gaps concerning performance requirements? Illustrate your answer with an example.

14. Check the five performance requirements and define how one could arrive at reduction of the gap between wish and reality in each of the five areas? Illustrate your answer by giving an example per requirement.

15. Which possibilities does one have for increasing the availability of IT facilities? Illustrate your answer with an example of each of the possibilities.

Chapter 10

Innovation from the customer and the chain perspective

Ordina uses offshore sourcing for developing and maintaining software. To this purpose, it went into partnership with a company from India. For labour-intensive services that are not tied to one location, there is free choice with regard to location. Criteria are in that case knowledge and skill, the cost of labour etc.

Companies increasingly bring in partners for specialized tasks and enter into long-term deals with them. If an entire company process is taken over from an organization, this is called business process outsourcing. Taking over the administrative transaction from an insurer by a third party is an example of this.

With network suppliers, customers have direct access to the status of the network and real-time projects for improvement of the network are monitored. In this way the ITO can show its customers, the traffic on each of the lines it has in exploitation at all times, including highs and lows in the traffic and in the average traffic. Furthermore, the customer is able to see online, in which stage of execution the changes are.

In the case of services with a high volume and little diversity, one does have to pay lots of attention to the design of the service, the extent of standardization and the employees' focus. In network services on the fixed network of Dutch telecom provider KPN a lot of attention was given to the design of the management tools and the information function. There is information per incident per customer; there is also overall information per period about the quality of the service and the service provision.

When organizations increasingly procure IT facilities from third parties and their support is increasingly supplied in the form of standard packages, it follows that in implementation of innovations use is made of different organizational possibilities. There is hardly any project organization left, that is only made up of internal employees. As a demand organization, one has often only indirect influence on the functional specifications either by partaking in user boards or by having contact with the management of the supplier of the packages.

Contents of this chapter

Offshore sourcing, business process outsourcing, real time tracking, being a member of user boards etc. are all subjects that could come up for discussion at the innovation of product and process of service provision in the IT field. This chapter goes into this innovation of the product and the additional process of service provision. The chapter starts by defining the trend in the service industry and the impact of this on the IT demand and supply organization. Next, the principles of the IT industry are explained. It becomes clear that in innovation one can both develop a new product as well as the matching service and that these products and services may differ with regard to their qualities. It is for example possible to choose for a more capital or a more labour-intensive implementation of a service process. One may also choose for a more or less radical innovation of the product to be delivered or of the delivery process. The demands the demand organization makes on a product and on the process of service provision, furthermore have impact on the type of product and the control of the process of service provision.

The chapter also discusses the phases that can be distinguished when arriving at a new product and the process possibly delivered with it. The front-office of the IT organization is used as an example for illustrating the importance of vision development. Various elements that can be involved in the designing of the IT organization are explained, such as cooperating with partners, determining of the location and searching for employees. We also discuss the steps one has to take for being able to exploit IT facilities reliably and also the way in which the rollout of such facilities is planned. Finally, the way in which innovations in organizations are organized comes up for discussion. It is noticed that one comes across increasingly multiform ways of organizing. One sees interorganizational control, project and working groups, one comes across user boards alongside the old internal project organizations etc.

TRENDS IN THE SERVICE INDUSTRY, INCLUDING THE IT SERVICE INDUSTRY

Trends in services

Figure 10.1 shows the trends in the service industry. These trends have impact on the IT demand and supply organization. In general, the package of services gets more and more focus in this industry. This package is aimed at a certain market segment or at a specific customer. This customer moreover shops with increasingly more awareness. He or she wants information about the delivery

Aspect:	Previously:	To morrow:
Structure sales	Processes per product	All products per segment or customer
Position customer	Passive	Cooperates in process
Channel integration	Entire channel in in-house mngmnt	Possibly bringing in partners
Way of delivery	Waiting for the customer	Only active when there is a customer
Information	Often later	Direct access to the most up-to-date
Management info.	Little knowledge of use resources	Real time tracking
Demand control	Limited to reservation and making of appointments	Customer actively involved in plans for giving optimum

Figure 10.1. Trends in the service industry

process and wants to cooperate with the supplier in an open relationship. The customer also quite often wishes to contribute to the implementation and delivery process. The supplier is also often unable to provide the requested products and/of services all by themselves and therefore has to cooperate with partners.

Impact on the demand and supply organization

These trends in the service industry are of influence on the IT demand and supply organization. The demand organization combines the customer's wishes for IT facilities. Because of its knowledge of the customer organization, it is a valued partner for the supply organization, with regard to implementation of new services and the daily contact about products and services. It knows what experiences the organization has had with the provided products and services. It wants insight into the delivery process and the product at the supply organization. It prefers to get this insight on line because this enables real-time warning and early warning in case of problems. As a spokesperson for the demand, it aims at payment of services according to usage, up to a clearly defined ceiling.

The supply organization sets up a front-office, in order to have a contact point for the question. This front-office is aimed at a certain customer segment or a specific group of customers. In standard services this will increasingly make use of IT. The customers are than able to see the answer to their question on the internet and may, if necessary, download and install the solution to a problem. If a front-office is set up, then each location will be evaluated on advantages and disadvantages. This is because, with the modern network front-office work or back-office work as well as individual processes of front and back-office may take place anywhere in the world. The supply organization next sets itself up in such a way that subcontractors can be controlled.

POINTS OF DEPARTURE IN DEVELOPING IT PRODUCTS AND SERVICES

Principles

Within these trends, one arrives at innovation of products and the services to be supplied with these. When designing a product, one designs the IT facility as well as the organization for keeping this up-to-date and in production. The

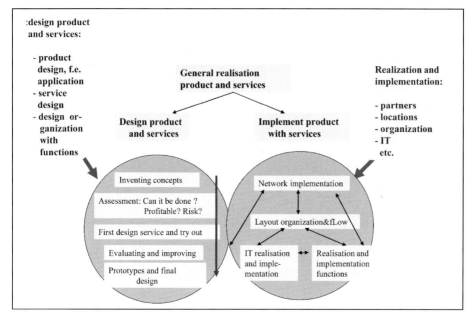

Figure 10.2. Innovation of product and service

product can be delivered in combination with a provision of services around it. One will have to ask oneself which services these are, also how these services in the field of functional management, application management and exploitation are provided and what these choices mean to the work in a front and back-office. Figure 10.2 shows in a diagram what designing a product and the matching service implies.

Qualities of services

Services distinguish themselves in four areas. These are the degree of interaction between the supplier of the service and its customer and the work this brings to the supplier. Furthermore not every product and every service can be delivered just like that. In order to supply certain services, one first has to have a number of basic facilities at one's disposal. Besides, the supplying of products and services results in a certain relationship with a customer. Finally, services

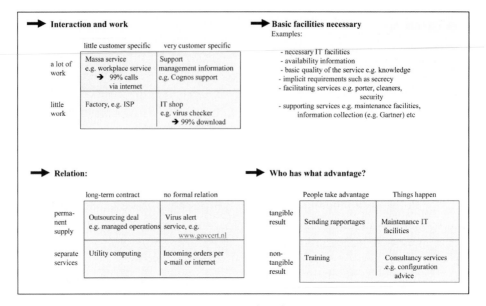

Figure 10.3. Qualities of services

distinguish themselves with regard to result. We will examine these four areas (see Figure 10.3).

Interaction and work

Products are often delivered with a specific package of services around them. This package may lead to a lot or a little work. The package may not be tailored to the customer but on the other hand may also be entirely tailor-made for the customer. If the product 'Office workstation' is supplied, one will often have a work package that involves the most work in installations and migrations. The dealing with calls will be computerized more and more.

This computerization goes as follows. The customer looks on intranet and notices his problem in the top ten of problems. He downloads the solution and installs this. The effort the IT supply organization has to make is an effort in advance, when designing the service. Once this service is up and running, the work will take place automatically in 99% of the cases. This might change, if the front-office starts to supply advice, development and handholding skills. This could be the case, if a demand organization wants to set up a facility for business intelligence information. The company has for example procured a product, such as Business Objects or Cognos and wants to open up the databases for its management. Depending on the type of service, implementation of the product leads therefore to a more or less labour-intensive support process.

Basic facilities

Delivery of some products and services is impossible without having certain basic facilities at one's disposal. A supplier of *ASP* services should for example have the necessary IT facilities at his disposal, as well as information on deliveries that were made, the expertise for exploiting the service up-to-date, ensuring that the necessary security measures are in place etc. A supplier of consultancy services on the contrary, does not always have to have basic facilities for being able to advise. Each product and every service surrounding a product has its own requirements regarding the necessary basic facilities.

Start of relationships

Supply of products with surrounding services may result in a certain relationship between customer and supplier. This relation may have a permanent character, such as with a large sourcing deal. It may also be a more one-off procurement of a facility. Apart from this, the relationship may involve permanent supply of products and services, as well as each time on demand supply of individual services.

Result

The fourth and last quality in which services may differ, is its results. Some services provide people with a tangible result. Other services cause tangible things to happen, such as the proactive care for maintaining the technical and informatics infrastructure. Apart from this, services may also lead to a less

New type of service	Description:	Example:
	Radical innovation:	
Important innovation	New service in market not yet existing	ASP service for MS Office for ,medium & small bus.customers
New company	Delivering new services in an existing market	Virus alert service
Suppy new service in the already suplied market	Delivering new services to existing customers	Utility computing as implemented on IBM mainframes
	Incremental innovation:	
Extension package of services	Extension with quick dial, new training etc.	Gradation of services supplying to Customers e.g. 7*24, 5*14, 5*8 h/d
Improvement of the services	Change in characteristics of the current service	Instead of teleph. calls and faxes just dealing with e-mails
Change in style service	Modest adjustments that have impact on perception customer	Front-office rings back, asking whether customer was well served.

Figure 10.4. Innovation of services and producten

tangible result. An example of this is training people or providing advice on a possible configuration of facilities.

Risks at innovation

The implementation of new products and services can be seen as the introduction of innovations in organizations. Christensen (1999) teaches us that there are types of innovations. He makes a distinction between more radical innovation and more incremental innovation (see Figure 10.4). The most radical innovation leads to an entirely new product and an entirely new service for a yet unknown market. Examples of this were internet services in the year 1994. Less radical but radical all the same is a new company that supplies a new service in an existing market. Besides, the new service can be supplied in an existing market to existing customers. Apart from a radical innovation of a product and/or service, an organization may also decide on a more incremental innovation. The least drastic here is a change in the style of the product or the service. The most drastic concerns a straightforward extension of the package of services.

As the innovation is more radical, questions about the risk involved in implementing this innovation emerges. One asks oneself whether the innovation is technically possible, one asks oneself whether there are sufficient customers for it and one asks what the implementation risks are. As we know from the above mentioned, these risks are relative. Each organization has its limits.

Functional requirements to product/service and their effect

Functional requirements to a product and its service may result in the service being very large in size, not being very diverse, that it has to cope with vast changes with regard to demand and is at the same time very visible. Examples of this are the check-in applications of airlines. These have to deal with a few hundred thousand transactions a day. The application is fairly straightforward. The use of the application varies. For British Airways at Heatrow airport in London, the daily peaks are between 7 and 9 a.m., 12 and 14.00 p.m. and between 17.00 and 19.00 p.m. If the application does not work, this presents a big problem. This problem becomes quickly visible for all and sundry because of the resulting queues.

The effect of volume, diversity, variation in demand and visibility, expresses itself in the design of a product and its surrounding services and in the planning and control of the supply of products and services. Figure 10.5 shows how a high volume with little variation in demand results in:

– a design of the service provision process that was given a lot of attention, that is standardized to a high degree and is mostly supported by especially targeted IT facilities;

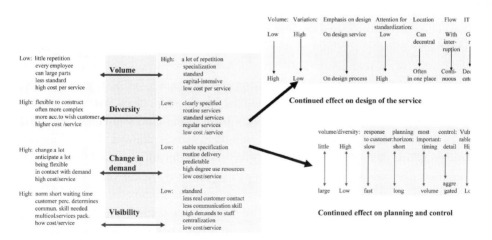

Figure 10.5. Relation between functional requirements and design, planning and control

–making sure in planning and control of the services to deal with the customer call quickly, that sufficient resources are planned in and controlling takes place at authorized level.

DISCOVERING, DEVELOPING AND IMPLEMENTING A NEW PRODUCT OR A NEW SERVICE

Designing products and services

The process for realizing a product including matching services goes through four phases. These phases are: vision development, closer analysis, development of the product with the surrounding service provision and the introduction of the product inclusive of services. In the first two phases, mainly the demand organization is at work. In the development and the implementation phase the supply organization usually plays the largest part.

In the first phase, that of vision development, the target and target group of the product and its services is defined. Ideas are generated and screened on contents and on form and way of working. From this a first conceptual idea originates. This idea of product and service is internally checked against the business management and put to the users. Next the concept is adjusted.

Thereupon, a business case is made up of the created product/service combinations. The way in which these are to be realized is also given consideration. This may be through a top-down design approach; it may also be in dialogue with the people that at a later stage will have to deliver the products and services. Next, control of realization and introduction are of importance. This may be described as directive control but other types of control are also possible. As soon as the business case is arranged and the go-ahead for development has been given—in other words the order has been given to the supply organization—we go to the next phase. In this phase the implementation is planned, the operational processes are designed, the marketing is started, the supporting IT and other functions are realized and the employees trained. In these last mentioned tasks, the supply organization plays a part.

The development is followed by the implementation. This implementation may take place possibly at replacement of an existing product and service, whilst the old product and the surrounding service are still being supplied. In that case we speak of a dummy run. There might also be a first introduction on a small scale. In that case we call this a test run. The supply organization can, if necessary, assist in this or/and apply extra service teams. In time full-scale introduction takes place. This is when the regular checks are running, product and service are periodically evaluated and all management reporting is in place.

Example of a choice

An example of a choice in the phase of close analysis may be demonstrated using a workplace service. In the exploitation of 5000 workplaces, one has to have a facility at one's disposal for installing these workplaces and also a facility for being able to migrate these. Apart from that, the minimal requirements are a service desk and a planning/control function. When designing the product there are therefore choices to be made. These are:

- a purely standard workplace;
- a workplace in which the customer has a standard configuration per type of work;
- a workplace in which the customer chooses from a number of options;
- a workplace made entirely according to the customers' wishes.

There are also options when designing the **service**. The customer may for instance take care of the installation and also download updates later on. The workplace may also be installed by the organization that supplies the workplace service. Choices also have to be made at setting up the service desk. One of the choices might be that the service desk only solves technical problems. Another might be that the customer can look online, diagnoses the problem and subsequently installs the solution. Finally, one may choose to run a full service desk that does not only solve problems but also provides advice and handholding services. Besides, this desk registers what the customer is doing so one may arrive at a proactive management.

The more the workplace service is tailor-made, the more information a front-office needs about the installed product, the work process of the organization that supplies the workplace services and about the customer. If this information is lacking, it becomes more difficult to specify the customer's problem and act pro-actively and a call is often referred to the back-office too quickly.

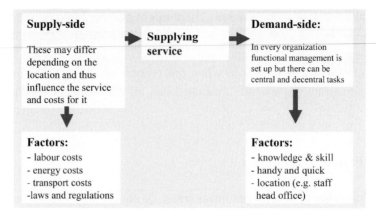

Figure 10.6. Factors involved in determining a location for the demand and supply organization

Elements to be included in design

In the designing of a product and its services, questions might arise about the location from where the products and services are supplied, the parties involved in the delivery and the manning of the organization that supplies the product and the services.

Figure 10.6 shows that an organization could ask itself questions with regard to the location of the demand and the supply organization. These are always cost-related. In the supply organization labour costs will play a part, in the demand organization these will mainly concern the positioning close to those that decide the demand.

Apart from looking at the location, the insight into the chain of service providers that is created is also of importance. By drawing the chain of service providers and the checking of every one of the service providers, insight is provided into the dependency of the product and the service on a particular partner. One sees to what extent this partner is dependent on this contract and what possibilities there are for bringing in extra resources in case of problems. This way, the importance of the contract becomes clear, as well as the risk one runs in granting this contract. In Figure 10.7 a drawing of such a chain is made.

The way the organization is fleshed out with functions and the fulfilment of these functions also demand attention. This subject is discussed in Chapter 12.

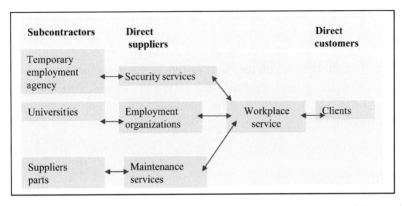

Figure 10.7. The chain of suppliers involved in delivering the product and the service

Points of particular interest concerning the design of the IT facilities

After establishing vision and set-up of the business case we arrive at designing the IT organization. Looijen (2000) did once indicate in which steps one could arrive at the necessary facilities on the supply and the demand-side. This step-by-step plan by Looijen is adjusted below to the situation of today. There is often already an explicit organization of the demand and one or more supply organizations.

Designing of the IT organization as necessary for the new product and the services needed with this, proceeds using the following steps:

1. The demand organization draws up functional and performance requirements for a product and its services that are to be supplied.
2. The supply organization(s) describe the objects needed for supplying the product and the service.
3. The demand organization defines the tasks to be carried out in order to comply with the requirements.
4. Demand and supply organization(s) translate the task into processes and indicate, what the processes for this situation look like. The processes are divided into processes for functional management, application management and exploitation.
5. The IT organization is described: who is responsible for what?

6. One designs the IT organization by allocating tasks to organization units.
7. One describes functions and roles of functionaries.
8. One lays down the functional and performance requirements in SLA's and executes tasks on the basis of this in the implementation phase.
9. One evaluates and simulates the set-up IT organization. On this basis changes are made (e.g. using role-play with people in simulations of procedures).

The rollout of IT facilities

The design is followed by the rollout phase. This phase goes according to plan. In a rollout plan attention is given to the following subjects:

(a) The **IT organization** for exploitation, application management and functional management that is constructed further during the rollout.
(b) **The tasks to be executed in the domain of rollout.** These include:
   –more concentrated tasks such as planning/manning, setting-up of the infrastructure and applications, extra service desk, extra release management and extra change management;
   –more deconcentrated organized tasks such as configuring of the authorization of employees, setting-up and training of departments and implementing the IT facilities in areas reckoning with conversions, testing and handholding and dummy running.
(c) **Measures that promote organizational support** (depending on choices in a further analysis made) such as:
   –personnel measures: like working with a permanent team, changing employees less often, encouraging people of the demand and the supply organization to work on the teams etc.;
   –communication measures, such as publishing a magazine, producing and showing videos, organizing conferences etc.;
   –evaluations of actions, such as organizing Delphi sessions for defining the risk to be taken and discussing how to deal with these, the collection of experiences and including these in future implementations.

THE IMPACT ON THE ORGANIZATION OF WORKING WITHIN CHAINS

Organizing change

The previous text shows that result-focussed implementing takes place on the basis of a rollout plan and that a client from the demand organization sponsors this implementation. This client chooses whether he introduces the innovation as a change within the line or to start with as a project beside the line, of which the results in the long run will be assimilated within the line. Both types of introduction of innovations have their advantages and disadvantages.

Furnishing a project and especially a large project holds the risk that the innovation at a certain moment cannot be transferred to the line organization fast enough. The line looks at the case, has it's own ideas and leaves the project to lead it's own life. The project can then become that large and take that long, a shadow organization comes about. The sponsor of the project might then be tempted to communicate changes throughout the project and in fact passes the line left and right.

Furnishing a project beside the line does however also have advantages. The programme management of such projects can be clearly managed. That is to say, employees can be made available more easily and multidisciplinary teams are possible. It is also possible to work faster.

Projects with partners and projects within chains

In these years the form of projects for designing and implementing new IT facilities changes more and more. This is shown in Figure 10.8. Until way into the nineties, it was predominantly the organization that took care of projects and in large projects one knew the construction steering committee, project groups and working groups attached to these, which were mainly manned with employees of the organization itself. These days, one may find that this situation has changed. With the distinction between demand and supply organizations and the arrival of chain wide information function one sees:

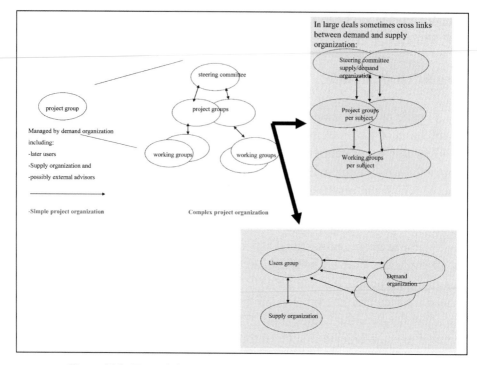

Figure 10.8. Towards increasingly more multiform types of organizing

(a) the old steering committees, project and working group constructions are back. These are now manned by members of the demand and supply organization. The majority of these members of organizations are however no longer just members of one single organization;

(b) more often than not, situations occur in which organizations can no longer exercise direct influence on their own information function. One uses standard IT solutions, for which the functional management is performed at a different organization. Only through the external user boards of the package, one has influence on the functional specifications of the facility and the way in which this may change.

This way many more forms for organizing projects have evolved, in which innovations in IT facilities are designed by more organizations or in which organizations have to participate in order to realize at least some of their preferences in this field.

QUESTIONS

1. Give three trends in the service industry and how these affect the set-up of demand and supply organizations for IT facilities.
2. What does the design of a new IT facility consist of? Illustrate your answer with an example.
3. What are the four qualities of services? What is their impact on the consideration of a new IT product with matching service? Illustrate your answer by giving two examples.
4. Which type of innovations do we know? What is the difference between the two types of innovations? Illustrate your answer by giving two examples.
5. How do functional requirements to a product and the matching service affect the design of the service and the planning and control of service? Illustrate your answer with an example.
6. Which four phases does the realization of a product and matching service go through? What does each phase entail? Illustrate each phase with an example.
7. How does one include elements such as location, set-up of the chain of service provision and the choice of functions and employees for these functions in the realization of a new product and the matching service? Illustrate your answer with three examples.
8. Which nine steps does Looijen discern in the realization of an IT facility?
9. What does a rollout plan look like?
10. Why would one want to realize an innovation by means of a project? Why not? Explain your answer with an example.
11. The sharper contrast between demand and supply organizations has resulted in the emersion of a more pluriform image of the ways in which implementations of innovations take place. Why is this? What is this pluriformity?

Part 4

Aspects of IT management

Demand and supply each have their own
    perspective on the financial aspects of IT
Trends with regard to IT benefits and costs.
Value IT from demand and supply
    perspective.
The groundwork: organizing.
Use of financial data, for instance when:
    – charging;
    – benchmarking;
    – the strategy and the value of IT
Assessments, time aspects, arbitrary
    assignment etc.

Chapter 11

The financial aspects

Microsoft Windows '95 did cost Microsoft hundreds of millions of dollars on development. These costs are mainly made up of labour costs. On top of this Microsoft was granted one billion in subsidy for developing the product. This subsidy was given in the shape of free testing. 400,000 beta versions were distributed. The test results of 300,000 users were received. Each of these users tested over several months. What did the customers get in return for this? No money but a product that was much more stable (Schrage, 2004).

The ING bank had Gartner and Compass benchmark the cost for their office workplace against the world best on their database. On the basis of these results, the programme for arriving at a Common European Desk Top was started. This programme should take the costs for a standard workplace with standard personal productivity tools to less than 1800 euro per annum (Van der Burg, 2004).

The IB Group takes care of, amongst other things, the implementation of the Act on Student Grants. Its services cannot be introduced without IT support. The costs for IT facilities are included in the costs for its services. In 1994, the IB Group was praised by the minister because of its utterly strong performance in keeping the IT costs and benefits balanced. In 2001 HERO, its most important project was discontinued for reasons of permanent overspending and overrunning of the planning. The lesson: IT is a means of production and should therefore be controlled like one. In 1994 prudent policy was the done thing, in 2001 customers are apparently not willing to pay for IT projects that lack control (Thiadens, 2004).

Contents of the chapter

In this chapter three examples are given in which the financial aspect plays a part. This chapter discusses these financial aspects of IT management. It starts by giving a rough outline of the interests of the IT demand and the IT supply organization. Demand and supply each have different interests. The demand organization wants both a controllable as well as a transparent price. The supply organization has to recover its costs through its tariffs, often increased by some profit. Money is however not the only issue: the application of IT must add value to the organization and having insight into the expenses for IT is a necessity.

When the importance of the financial perspective is demonstrated clearly, it is indicated which concepts one comes across in the financial field at the demand- and the supply-side and what is required to obtain insight into one's IT efforts from a financial perspective.

Next, it is defined when the financial aspect plays a part in controlling IT. Three specific domains are discussed: benchmarking, charging of costs and the added value that application of IT might have for execution of the strategy of the organization.

The chapter concludes by giving some comments in this field. Definition of the expenditure on IT includes arbitrary elements. These creep in because expenditure on IT facilities is spread over a certain period and one divides certain common costs pro ratio. Furthermore, in comparing expenditure between organizations, choices as made earlier in the field of infrastructure, applications and structure of the organization have their effect.

THE FINANCIAL PERSPECTIVE AND IT PRODUCTS AND SERVICES
The field costs/benefits

Expenditure for IT is made from the perspective of the demand organization and from the perspective of the supply organization. The demand organization wants to be able to control the expenditure for IT. One wishes to understand, what the money is spent on. A tariff structure as suggested by the supply organization must be transparent to this organization. This could be a fixed tariff or a tariff based on purchase of services and products or a combination of both.

This is different for the supply-side. The provider must recover the costs made for delivering the products and services. The provider sets the tariff for the efforts using this cost price. This is often a combination of a fixed and a variable tariff. The fixed tariff provides a base for the takings and the aim is to recover the fixed costs entirely or largely.

Products in the network economy

This situation is in fact no different from any other situation in society. What is different however, is the fact that typical IT products such as applications (e.g. MS Office) are usually characterized by the fact that these are expensive to produce. After the first version, copies are however cheap and distribution and maintenance can usually be realized by means of a download. Besides, the use of these products often results in a long-term relationship with the supplier. A demand organization does after all train people so they can use the product; one gears one's working method to the possibilities of the product, gets volume discounts etc. etc. As a demand organization one is also often committed to a long-term agreement.

These qualities of IT products result in supply organizations considering the way in which they sell their product and their services. Larger organizations are often offered site-licences. One often aims to get as many customers as possible for proprietary products. Demand organizations are increasingly aware of this and reflect on which products and services are currently produced in an in-house supply organization and which are procured from other supply organizations.

Trends

Facing these facts, it is no surprise having to conclude that ideas about the cost–benefit-side of IT application changes. Until recently saving costs came first; there was attention for application of extensive cost accounting techniques; one concentrated on the costs/benefits of stand-alone projects and determined these once-only, whilst at the assessment of investment costs and elapsed time of a project were at the forefront (see Figure 11.1).

In the nineties:	Towards 2010:
Working towards costcutting through - benchmarking - activity based costing	*What is the contribution* at: - house in order - serving the customer better - functioning within the chain
Attention for cost accounting techn., such as internal rate of return, payback period etc	Attention for cost accounting and process of decision-making: ➔ *IT is production factor*
Looking at technical *risk*	Also *organizational and financial*
Nature project often *stand alone*	Mostly *infrastructural and organi- zation wide* rolled out applications.
Optimization return: *desirability* IT facility central	Avoidance uncertain adventures : *feasibility* central
Assessment IT facility *in advance*	Assessment *in advance, during* development and use *afterwards*
Project management: *costs and elapsed time central*	Project management:*quality and* benefits

Figure 11.1. Changes in the use of IT and the implications regarding costs/benefits (Renkema, 2004)

Gradually one establishes that attention for costs and benefits is important in every phase of a project as well as in the day in, day out exploitation of IT facilities. In every investment proposal, a financial justification is included. In the realization of projects, budgets are awarded. During the realization of the project, apart from the planning, the depletion of the project budget is a permanent point of interest. When a project enters the exploitation phase, tariffs for the services and products should already be set. During the life of the project, the entire portfolio of projects is permanently evaluated and subjected to life-cycle management (see Chapter 17 about portfolio management). This includes weighing up the costs and benefits of every IT facility. In the evaluation of the IT facility financial indicators are used. The financial aspect has become an integral part of IT management.

It is therefore not surprising that the fact that IT facilities are increasingly looked at from a financial perspective, results in more emphasis on other aspects. One looks more and more at the contribution of IT in realizing the strategy; one wants organizational support when deciding on an IT project, all this so that somebody feels responsible in case the project fails; one does not just take care of the technical but also of the organizational and financial risks of a project.

Insurer:	life	house	cars	other
turnover:	400	450	800	900
Costs IT department:				
- expl:	4	2	5	8
- application management	1,5	3.3	1,2	4
Number of work places:	350	300	300	250
IT workplece/yr	15714	17666	20666	21818

Figure 11.2. Turnover and IT: expenditure in line with strategy?

Furthermore, during the entire project one also controls on working in conformity with the budget (see Figure 11.1). Within the realization, quality and achievement of benefits take first place.

Value of IT application

The value of the application of IT can be perceived from the perspective of the general management and from the perspective of the business units. General management asks itself whether a project fits in with the strategy and whether the set benefits are achieved. Business unit management makes a comparative assessment with regard to priority and makes a direct connection between IT application and the resulting profits. In exploitation it wants controllability and transparency of expenses. Figure 11.2 shows the IT expenditure of an insurer per year, in relation to the turnover. The insurer may then well ask whether these costs have the right ratio with respect to the desired strategy.

Method to value IT

Wiggers et al. (2004) have developed a method for conveying the place of an IT facility for the demand-side and what the costs of this facility are for the supply-side. Figure 11.3 is based on the ideas of this method. This figure shows the expenditure for an IT facility, divided over a number of categories. The data can be reported on the level of a project and/or line task and also on the level of the IT facility as a whole. It becomes immediately clear, for which purpose what expenditure is made every year.

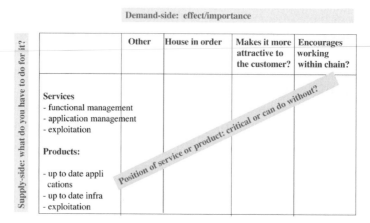

Figure 11.3. Value of *ICT* application

The groundwork

In order to be able to calculate with IT costs and benefits, insight into a number of concepts is necessary. In Figure 11.4 these concepts are represented. These are placed, sometimes arbitrary, on the side where these are used the most.

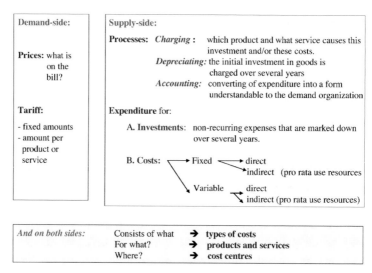

Figure 11.4. Concepts regarding defining IT expenditure

That could be the demand-side, that could also be the supply-side. Some occur equally as much on both sides. In this case, no choice was made.

Concepts on the demand-side

On the demand-side one has to deal with the price one pays for the IT facilities. This price is based on tariffs for services and products. These tariffs may be fixed. These may also depend on the purchase of a product or service. In the first case, this is called a subscription. In the second case, the multiplication of number of items purchased and tariff results in the price to be charged.

Concepts on the supply-side

On the supply-side, investments in objects are made for realizing IT facilities. These investments are often written off over several years. The yearly write off is included in the cost price of a product or a service. These are recurring expenses. This cost price is the basis for arriving at a tariff. The cost price is made up of part overheads and part variable costs. Each of these costs may in turn be direct or indirect. Direct costs are costs that are demonstrably made for just producing a service or product. Indirect costs are costs that are also needed for realizing the product and services but were not made specifically for this product or this service. Indirect costs are ascribed to a product or service pro ratio of use using a formula.

In order to arrive at tariffs, costs have to be ascribed to products and services; markdowns on investments have to be defined and the final cost price should be translated providing insight into a price that is clear to the demand organization.

Concepts on demand and supply-side

Both on the demand as well as the supply-side there are types of costs, cost centres and cost units. Types of costs are the costs made for applications, infrastructures and organization. Cost centres indicate where these costs were made, with the focus on department or task.

Cost units indicate for which product or which service the expenditure is made. By knowing types of costs in sufficient detail, insight is created into what the money for an IT facility is exactly spent on. At the same time, it becomes clear whether this expenditure is more or less controllable. By knowing the cost centres it becomes clear where the expenditure is made. One concludes immediately what the overhead of a service could be. At a single glance one sees whether the organization works on the products and services of tomorrow. The cost units are the products and services that are supplied. This is what the customer pays for. The prices, as seen, are a first point of particular attention when one benchmarks one's own facilities with those of third parties.

KNOWING COST PRICES DEMANDS

The knowing of the cost prices for IT products and services by the demand and supply organization demands the permanent commitment of an organization. For defining the costs an organization must a priori get clear:

- what the objective and the position of the IT organization is. If one supplies IT services and products to the internal organization, one of-ten does not need more than just an impression of the costs. In case one wants to be able to compare oneself with others, one has to standardize one's concepts according to the concepts, as used in the comparison. If one is the supplier of services to third parties, one will have to arrive quite quickly at a professional organization for determining costs, tariffs and prices. Each objective has its own demands with regard to the degree of detail, in which one has to be familiar with one's expenditure;
- whether the culture of the organization does allow the desired determination of expenditure. Having to determine expenditure exactly requires a measuring culture. In exploitation one has to deal mainly with costs to do with capital. In functional and application management these are mainly labour costs and labour costs have to be differentiated into working processes (Figure 11.5 gives an example of an arrangement into working processes). The registration and processing of this data costs time. Moreover, formulas have to be defined. The service desk for example, works for more than one customer. The costs for storage and processing have to be spread over several applications etc. etc.

Tactical processes Exploitation				Tactical processes Application management			Tactical processes Functional management		
change management	testing of software	computer instal-lation and accep tance	incident management	continui ty management	design	user support	change management	testing and checking
software management and distribution	problem management	service desk	availability management	change management	realization	management company data	release transfer	maintenance procedures
computer operation	unattended operations	network management	capacity management	program management and distribution	testing	management operational reliability	specifying	implementing
management of local processing	environmental measures etc	configuration management	configuration management	impact analysis	implementation			

User costs infrastructure	User costs applications

Figure 11.5. Example of working processes in the Pink Roccade (2002) cost scan

Organizing charging

Once one has decided one really wants to charge, one has to furnish an organization that ensures that the registered hours are processed; that write offs are determined and prices set. In short this organization has the task:

- to determine, set and communicate the price policy: e.g. on amount per service or product or on subscription;
- to take care of collection and transaction of data. This requires the application of division of functions. For example, when timekeeping the immediate supervisor signs for the correctness of the hours. Furthermore, one has to take care of the logging in and out of users and authorize them to keep time on certain tasks. One has to take care of the detail of data necessary for writing off etc.;
- to determine the use of a facility per customer. This could be the registration of use per customer or the allocation of costs based on distributive codes set in advance etc.;
- to provide an explanation on invoices and collect payments. This also includes the approachability of the supply organization, if the demand organization asks for an audit on the correctness of the amounts as charged.

WHAT DO WE USE OUR KNOWLEDGE ABOUT THE COSTS OF PRODUCTS AND SERVICES FOR?

Use of the data

In the previous text, it already transpired that financial data is used in an IT organization in many ways. Next, we want do discuss three of these applications in more detail. These are the use of financial data in benchmarking, the use in charging and the use in considering the value of IT application.

Use in benchmarking

Let us start with benchmarking. The reason for benchmarking is that the management of organizations occasionally wants to get confirmation whether the organization is on the right track. One wishes to know how the in-house organization compares with other organizations in certain aspects and under comparable circumstances. Benchmarking is done in many fields by organizations and this also includes the expenditure for IT. Well-known organizations that have statistics in the IT field of many organizations at their disposal are for example Gartner and Compass. For being able to perform benchmarking one has to make sure one standardizes the concepts to be used and agrees on the timing and the frequency of the measurements. Figure 11.6 suggests agreements regarding the framework of concepts. With regard to timing, it can be stated that one preferably measures in a normal period and that the frequency of measuring should enable the showing of trends. It is furthermore often useful in benchmarking, to use the regular

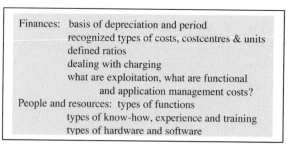

Figure 11.6. Concepts to be standardized at benchmarking

data collection and reporting of an organization. The results of a benchmark are preferably reported by an independent rapporteur.

Common concepts

When benchmarking one often comes across the concept total cost of ownership (TCO). This concerns all the costs for an IT facility over its entire lifecycle. The definition of the facility can be chosen freely. Using TCO organizations can be compared on the basis of their TCO. That TCO could include corrections with regard to the sector in which is operated, the structure and the size of the organization. Having a relatively high TCO does not necessarily mean that the organization performs poorly. The IT facility possibly has to meet extra requirements, resulting in a higher TCO. TCO's therefore cannot always provide sufficient points of action for achieving cost reduction. These are often determined per sector and do not take specific factors into account.

Example

At the ING bank, the TCO for the costs of a place of work is set. A specific part of the organization was expensive with regard to printers. It did however employ many fieldworkers that have to be able to provide an on the spot quote to a customer. This meant that every pc was connected to its own printer.

Another concept that is often used in comparing IT expenditure is activity based costing. In this, the costs and the structure of these costs for IT facilities are defined per activity. After this definition it is examined to what extent these costs are really necessary with regard to the requirements of the demand organization. Point of departure in activity based costing is that the organization knows its products and services and how these are constructed and that data is available for determining the activity based cost price.

However, organizations often want to know more than the expenditure with regard to IT. They also want to know what the revenues are. Furthermore, one wants to control on more than just financial data. This is how the use of multi criteria methods at the evaluation of projects started. This is also how the use of the balanced score card arose in controlling (parts of) an organization.

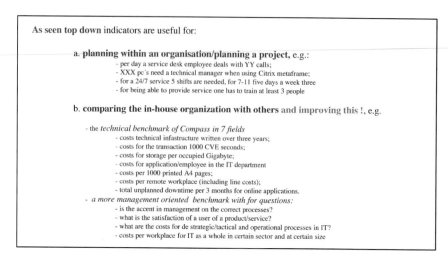

As seen **top down** indicators are useful for:

   a. **planning within an organisation/planning a project,** e.g.:
- per day a service desk employee deals with YY calls;
- XXX pc´s need a technical manager when using Citrix metaframe;
- for a 24/7 service 5 shifts are needed, for 7-11 five days a week three
- for being able to provide service one has to train at least 3 people

   b. **comparing the in-house organization with others** and improving this !, e.g.

- the *technical benchmark of Compass in 7 fields*
  - costs technical infastructure written over three years;
  - costs for the transaction 1000 CVE seconds;
  - costs for storage per occupied Gigabyte;
  - costs for application/employee in the IT department
  - costs per 1000 printed A4 pages;
  - costs per remote workplace (including line costs);
  - total unplanned downtime per 3 months for online applications.
- *a more management oriented benchmark with for questions:*
  - is the accent in management on the correct processes?
  - what is the satisfaction of a user of a product/service?
  - what are the costs for de strategic/tactical and operational processes in IT?
  - costs per workplace for IT as a whole in certain sector and at certain size

Figure 11.7. Use of indicators and benchmarks

The convenience of indicators

Benchmarks result in an average for IT expenditure when examining a number of organizations. The case study that goes with this chapter gives an example of this concerning the sector house building corporations. These standards for certain IT expenditure may than develop into indicators.

Indicators are useful in two ways. These help when planning activities. These also support the comparison of organizations. Based on these, one may achieve improvements. Benchmarks employ various types of indicators. Organizations can be compared on the basis of costs, on the basis of use of technique, on the basis of the control that is given etc. etc. Figure 11.7 gives some examples of the use of indicators and the questions and answers that arise in benchmarking.

When using indicators, there may be some misrepresentation possible because organizations may differ with regard to their quality requirements, the necessity of extra security and their history. Installing personal computers in a prison for instance, will take a lot more time than installing these elsewhere. This because, one has to work under supervision. An operation that is manned 24 hours/7 days a week is really more expensive than an operation of 5 times 12 hours etc.

Charge

A second use of financial data is the use in charging IT expenditure. Brandt Allen (1987) indicates that an organization can finance IT expenditure in various different ways. These ways are:

(a) Financing application of IT from the general resources of an organization. Dealing with the payment of expenditure for IT application in this way is called *overhead costing*. One operates as a cost centre. Application of IT facilities is controlled on delivery of products and services as part of an agreement. The advantages of operating like a cost *centre* are that innovation of task execution and innovation of services and products are encouraged. Experiments are carried out as part of general expenditure. Apart from this, one does not have to keep any administration for expenditure and appropriation of expenditure. Disadvantage of this method of working is however that one will soon see internal conflict for getting more priority for IT application. In order to be able to make the right appraisals, one should have more insight into the expenditure. This view on charging of IT application occurs a lot in centrally managed organizations, where the management of the demand organization defines the IT priorities and sets the IT budget periodically.

(b) Application of IT *direct costing*. IT products and services require expenditure. This expenditure can be passed on in two ways. The first method implies that organizational targets determine the prices for services and products. Using the second model one makes a direct connection between the expenses as made and the price of services. This model is called the *service centre* model. Direct costing directly provides insight into cost prices and results in cost-conscious users and cost-conscious management. This is an efficient mode of operation.

Some elements of the charging are arbitrary. When comparing with the prices on the market without having insight into this, the wrong decisions might be taken. A supplier can as a matter of fact charge bulk-purchase prices for getting an order in. In the long run, these prices cannot be realized. Direct costing often occurs in bureaucratically managed organizations, where the staff departments of the demand organization decide on the application of IT.

(c) Charging the application of IT with a profit margin on top of the cost price. IT products and services are provided with a margin. The internal supply organization is viewed as an internal service supplier and is allowed to make a profit. This is called the profit centre approach. Because the IT budget originates entirely from the user, there is no budget round and no limit for the application of IT. After all, the user pays. This mode of operation is seen a lot in strongly decentralized organizations, where users make decisions on the application of IT. In this mode of operation the IT budget is variable and dependent on the services provided.

Emphasis at the different models

The three models, service centre, cost centre and profit centre, each have their own emphasis regarding expenditure. In a cost centre, efficient working is pursued. One shows one's costs to the demand organization, possibly split up according to use. Expenditure for IT is regarded as costs for overheads. That changes, as soon as one behaves as a service centre. This involves charging and means that every investment has its own analysis of proceeds and costs. The cost price includes a mark up for financing innovation of products and services. Operating effectively is the first matter of importance. In the third model, the profit centre approach, the emphasis is on profitability of products and services. Each charging model has a different strategic starting point. Knowing these model(s) for charging is important when managing IT. A demand organization should choose the provider that fits in best with its own strategy.

Example

There are four reasons for sourcing: improved control, cost management, risk management and being able to innovate faster. An organization that aims for cost management, often aims for realization of one or more of the following goals: lower costs, focussing on its core task; achieving predictable IT expenditure; a better looking balance sheet, a better price/performance and/or sharing the expenses for necessary investments with third parties. If an organization aims to limit risks, one will want access to new knowledge and/or upgrade one's own

IT shop without having to shell out on large investments. Finally, if one wants to introduce new services or products faster to the market, one tries to cooperate with third parties and aims one's focus on one (or more) of the following targets: change of business, increasing the flexibility of operating, better quality of service providing and/or if necessary a merger or take-over. In every strategy certain choices are made. In cost management efficiency is the main thing, in new skills effectiveness is important and profitability is often important in faster innovation.

Relation between the value of IT and the strategy of organizations

There is a relationship between the strategy of an organization and the way it deals with expenditure for IT. Treacy et al. (1995) listed the various strategies of organizations and states that organizations can choose between three different strategies. Organizations can choose to work with the utmost lowest total costs (operational excellence). They can aim for delivering the best products and/or services and finally they can strive at finding the best solution for a particular customer. Kersten et al. (2004) has translated these strategies into the way in which these choices affect organizations. A strategy aimed at operational excellence strives for efficiency. The organization recognizes standards for IT objects and works with a catalogue of services and products. In an organization that aims for product leadership, the chosen IT solutions are usually aimed at leading edge innovation and one finds state of the art services and products, whilst an organization that arrives at an optimal choice for the customer, often focusses on effective operating (Figure 11.8).

Translation of strategy into tools

Each of these three strategies has its own selected methods that are used for dealing with costs/benefits considerations of IT facilities. In a strategy aimed at efficiency methods fit that calculate the TCO, the net present value and the internal rate of return of IT facilities. In product-leadership methods arise that target the elucidation of the real options, enlarging 'customer wallet share' and market share, whilst in an organization that aims for customer intimacy, customer satisfaction is measured and application of methods such as activity based costing are found.

Focus:	Category:	Reasons:	Used method:
Business as usual	Operational excellence (cost reduction)	→ minimise costs → basis for creating value → standard functions for personal productivity& bus.proc. applications	→ ROI → TCO → Net present value → Internal rate of return → Pay back periode
Application of IT that adds value	Growth and seize opport. (e.g. customer intimacy)	→ Elapsed time and output business processes better → cost reduction across all functions → optimising in chain → basis for chances	→ economic value added → activity based costing → customer satisfaction → limitation links
	Innovation with aim strategic advantage (e.g. product leadership)	→ Giving lasting advantage through innovative prod → making hard to copy strategy → high switching costs	→ real options → customer wallet share. → market share → what does the sector do?

Figure 11.8. Dealing with financial aspects in relationship with the strategy of an organization (Kersten et al., 2004)

AND WITH REGARD TO THE FACTS THERE ARE......

Epilogue

This chapter discussed the financial aspect of IT management. Expenses for IT facilities are in this ascribed to products and services. After encryption these appear in tariffs on which prices are often based. It will have become clear in this chapter that at determining costs and tariffs, arbitrary elements creep in. A financial figure is not necessarily 'written in stone.' Let us once again list the possibilities for misrepresentations:

(a) Applications are implemented in the existing infrastructure. The life of applications differs from that of the infrastructure. This results in:
    - choices regarding the use of the infrastructure by an application. This choice concerns the determination of the percentage of the total costs that is charged to the users of the application and on the length of time over which the infrastructure is written off;
    - choices regarding the writing-off period of the application;

(b) IT facilities consist of infrastructures, applications and the organization needed for these. These facilities are aimed at complying with functional and performance requirements. This has resulted in choices:
   - concerning standards of processes and products;
   - concerning the organization of IT facilities;
   - with regard to the tasks that are outsourced or performed in-house.

These choices can sometimes only be changed in the long-term. These do however affect cost prices and tariffs. The lesson may well be: when looking at a cost price and a tariff always look 'under the bonnet.' In the definition of the tariff and the cost price, starting points have been used that are important to a demand organization.

QUESTIONS

1. What is the difference between supply and demand organizations, when considering the financial aspect of IT facilities? What does this lead to when considering applications?
2. Name four trends in the field of financial aspects of IT facilities that have changed over the last few years. Where do these changes lead to? Illustrate your answer with two examples.
3. Indicate how the value of IT facilities from the demand and from the supply-side can be graphically represented in one go.
4. Explain the concepts of prices, tariffs, investments, types of costs, cost centres, cost units, overheads, variable costs, indirect costs and direct costs. Illustrate each concept by giving an example.
5. What conclusions may be the results of clarifying types of costs? And clarifying of cost centres? And of cost units? Illustrate your answer with an example.
6. Which ex ante measures require the charging of expenses for IT facilities? Which are the tasks of an organization that has to be able to realize charging expenditure for IT in detail?
7. What is benchmarking? What does benchmarking demand of an organization? Illustrate your answer with an example.
8. What is the TCO concept? What can one do with a TCO? What is not possible with a TCO?

9. What does activity based costing do? Why is activity based costing useful? What does activity based costing demand of an organization? Illustrate your answer with an example.

10. What are the methods for charging expenditure for IT facilities? What are the advantages and disadvantages of each method? What is their focus?

11. What is the relationship between the various strategic options of an organization and its thoughts on possible ways of charging?

12. Which financial methods do we see appear in organizations that aim for operational excellence? Which in organizations that target product-leadership? And which in organizations that aim at customer intimacy?

13. Give three reasons, why statistics on IT expenditure for certain products and services are not 'written in stone.' Illustrate your answer by giving two examples.

Chapter 12

The personnel aspects

Functional managers work on the functional side of the application of IT. They target what application of IT offers. They often started their career as an employee at a service desk or as a functional tester. Next, they progressed through functional designer into information analyst. For an organization to enable such progress it requires, amongst other things, to have career management in place and having a clear idea of the competencies of the employee within the organization.

Managing IT organizations requires employees that have a vision on a specific field; that dare to take responsibilities; that are capable of controlling processes and keeping these moving. Spirit, vigour and decisiveness are essential for success. The employee often starts at implementation level, and then becomes team leader, next project leader or service manager. These functions can be executed at various levels. The organization can influence and control this career path. This demands sight of the necessary function profiles, of the competency profile of the employee and the possibilities for changing competencies in the desired direction.

We do need functions but these functions should not be rigid. We have to cluster tasks. However this is not enough. The harsh reality does not just demand certain technical skills but also calls for certain behaviour and personality characteristics. This changed the way IT functions were looked at from a description of functions and tasks into a description of functions with requirements to both the technical competencies as well as the personal competencies.

Looking at competencies in IT originated at, amongst others, Career Space, www.career-space.com, a cooperation of IT companies. They wrote down, which competencies the IT employee of the future should have. This was the basis for many training programs that are aimed at teaching IT employees certain competencies.

Contents of this chapter

This chapter discusses the staffing of the IT organization. This involves for instance the progress of employees to a different job function, career management, competency management and training management. This chapter touches on all these subjects. The chapter starts by defining functions in the demand and the supply organization. It next indicates how the way in which these functions are interpreted using people has changed over the past 25 years. In an organization this concerns less the function itself but more about interpreting the right competencies now and in the long-term. This chapter discusses this interpretation with regard to the managerial informatics. The managerial informatics deals with the management information systems science. The field of IT management, the subject of this book, is found within this discipline.

After this positioning, the chapter discusses the subjects that play a part when one wants to come to IT functions. These subjects come up for discussion step by step. One sees how context and role, influence a function profile and how one can arrive at a function profile. The last part shows how one works with functions and competencies in IT organizations. The application of task clusters and competencies for functions are used at human resource management, for competency management and when making plans for training.

STAFFING THE IT ORGANIZATION

Staffing the demand and the supply organzation

In order to meet the demand for IT facilities, one has to deal with IT demand organizations and IT supply organizations. These organizations carry out tasks of functional management, application management and exploitation. Functional management is a task that a demand organization has to set up. Functional management combines the demand for IT and explores how this demand can be met. IT supply organizations meet the demand. Within these organizations, we find at the very least application management and exploitation tasks. This is shown in Figure 12.1. Figure 12.1 could be a simplification of the reality. The reasons for this simplification are:

(a) If one procures an application package, such as the personal productivity tool MS office, the supply organization also has to have set up a
functional management task. Before one is able to develop and maintain
the application one should know after all what it should do functionally.
(b) Within the supply organization one might have invested tasks of application management and/or exploitation with third party organizations.

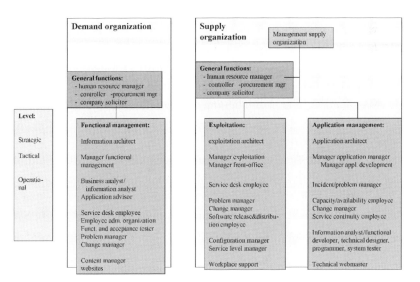

Figure 12.1. Set-up of the IT organization

In that case we speak of a supply chain, in which the first supply organization is interlocutor for the demand organizations. This is for example the case in the Exodus company that offers application service providing services to customers with the ERP package Peoplesoft. Peoplesoft here takes care of a large part of the functional and application management.

From Figure 12.1 it emerges that an IT organization includes tasks at strategic, tactical and operational level. These functions are in a more general field, such as the functions human resource manager, controller, company solicitor and buyer and in a more specific field such as functions in functional management, application management and exploitation. Next, these functions will be discussed in more detail and also the way in which one arrives at description of these functions.

Functions in an IT organization

The Dutch Society for Informatics (NGI) indicates since the eighties, which functions one can distinguish within an IT organization. The NGI started this in 1982, when this society of IT professionals concluded that the function classification of an IT organization showed differences per organization and organizations were in need of some form of standardization. Next, this society came out with the report "Functions in the management information systems field." This report provided a certain structuring of functions, it tried to set a standard and provide a basis for standardization of IT functions. In the years to come many organizations based the functions in their IT organization on the function classification. The Dutch bureau for Statistics surveys used the function classification as a basis, just as well as consultancy agencies base their annual salary study on this classification.

In practice the function classification appeared somewhat rigid. An IT organization was in need of a more flexible approach. This is the reason why in 1993 a function classification was introduced based on the clustering of tasks. One was able to compose task clusters and one single functionary could possibly execute a cluster of tasks. The 1993 report is called 'Tasks and functions in Informatics.'

The years after 1993 manifested large dynamics. On the one hand because more models for classification of IT functions appeared. In the United

Kingdom the British Computer Society published the Industry Structure Model report (ISM3) that provided a number of standards for tasks, functions and roles in the management information systems profession. In the Netherlands the L-Paso model for setting up functions, competency profiles and training was published. However, the ISM3 report and the L-Paso model did not result in concrete specifications of IT tasks and functions.

On the other hand, the field itself saw some development. The rise of the internet turned the computer into a tool for the masses and there was growing awareness that the time needed for developing an application was a lot shorter than the time the application was used and also shorter than the time it had to be maintained. Management of IT facilities developed into a fully-fledged field.

These larger dynamics also affected IT organizations. These wanted some idea of the competencies needed in the IT field. They realised themselves, that these competencies had not only technical but also personality/behavioural components. This promoted attention for the 'human' element of the IT organization. The NGI book published in 2001 'Tasks, functions, roles and competencies' arrived not surprisingly at the interpretation of the various levels of IT functions from the necessary competencies. The contents of this book are the basis of this chapter (see Figure 12.2).

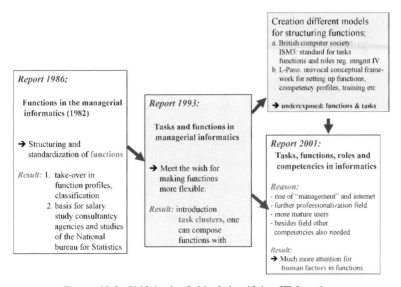

Figure 12.2. Shift in the field of classifying IT functions

Positioning the function classification

Next we define the functions in an IT organization. These functions concern functions in a certain part of information science or informatics. According to the final report of the committee Higher Education in the Informatics field of 1989 the field of informatics includes the following parts:

(a) the *fundamental informatics*, which includes the field technical informatics with its research into hardware; the core informatics that targets the logical foundations of the field, algorithms and the operating systems and finally the application focussed informatics that focusses on general applications such as developing network software, program generators and operating methods;

(b) *computer science* that aims at a field of application in which informatics play an essential and extensive part. A part of this is the management information systems field;

(c) and *the applications of informatics* in other fields, in which the fields concerned function as a main element.

The field of management information systems, which usually includes the subjects as discussed in this book, contains parts of the application-focussed informatics and parts of computer science. The field management information systems contains the activities that have in a structured manner to deal with collecting, managing, processing and provision of information that is valuable when controlling an organization, managing processes in an organization and the performing of actual acts in an organization. The model function profiles defined as follows are included in this field. These profiles may be used in creating specific functions, setting-up of competency profiles, executing tasks of human resource management, the composing of project teams and planning training.

A BOTTOM-UP APPROACH FOR ARRIVING AT FUNCTION DESCRIPTIONS

Basic concepts

For arriving at a description of functions within an IT organization the following concepts are used:

–Task cluster

a collection of cohering activities, leading to a particular result that are carried out by one person as a cohering unit of activities. The construction of a task cluster consists of the name, the description of the activities, an explanation of the field of activity, the dominant technical competencies and the dominant personal competencies.

–Context

the concept context describes the circumstances under which a task cluster is executed. The context includes the used resources and methods, the specific technology, the scope of the function within the organization, the level of execution and the adjoining knowledge necessary for executing the function.

–Roles

the positions of employees within an executing organization. One may function in various roles within a task cluster. One may cooperate in tasks, carry out tasks, one may cooperate with others in the execution of tasks, one may take care of the coordination of tasks, one may assist in the execution of tasks or supervise these, one may control or lead the execution, one may decide on certain tasks as well as take responsibility for the execution of tasks;

–Functions

a description of a task field, consisting of a combination of activities a person works on. A function consists primarily of an enumeration of tasks to be executed within this function. The execution of a function is often directly linked with one's profession. The construction of a function consists of the function title, an explanation of the task field and the field of activity, a collection of task clusters with the appropriate technical and personal competencies, the task clusters provided with task roles and a definition of the knowledge and experience needed for executing the function;

–Competencies

the professional skill and/or the personal skill an employee has and that is needed for performing a task at a proper level. Competencies consist of four parts, being capacities, character traits, knowledge and the styles of behaviour;

–Competency profile

a description of knowledge, experience and competencies, a specific employee has at his disposal. A profile includes: experiences in terms of task clusters, technical competencies, personal competencies, possible education and training and if necessary a personality profile.

Competencies

When defining functions, a link is made between the task to be executed, the necessary character traits and the technical skills. The size and culture of the organization, the environment in which a function is executed and the level on which one acts will often also have their impact on the function. A function is performed within a specific organizational context and has its demands on the person. This way there is a link between the task clusters and character traits.

In every function, the NGI (2001) recognizes demands on personality/behaviour and technical requirements. These together form the competency requirements. In the first field there are six categories. These six, together with the two categories in the technical field have been represented in Figure 12.3. For an organization, it is important to know whether one is dealing with a changeable competency or a non-changeable competency. Non-changeable competencies are often competencies in the sphere of capacities and personality. Competencies in the field of knowledge and behaviour can be changed through training and experience.

Example of Use of the competency model

In Figure 12.4 the competency set of the Dutch Telecom provider KPN is shown. This competency set recognizes three characteristics in a person. These

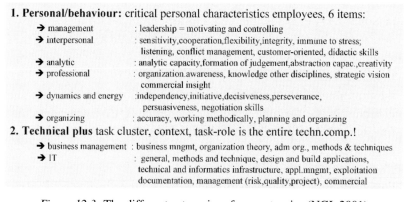

1. Personal/behaviour: critical personal characteristics employees, 6 items:
- ➔ management : leadership = motivating and controlling
- ➔ interpersonal : sensitivity,cooperation,flexibility,integrity, immune to stress; listening, conflict management, customer-oriented, didactic skills
- ➔ analytic : analytic capacity,formation of judgement,abstraction capac.,creativity
- ➔ professional : organization.awareness, knowledge other disciplines, strategic vision commercial insight
- ➔ dynamics and energy :independency,initiative,decisiveness,perseverance, persuasiveness, negotiation skills
- ➔ organizing : accuracy, working methodically, planning and organizing

2. Technical plus task cluster, context, task-role is the entire techn.comp.!
- ➔ business management : business mngmt, organization theory, adm org., methods & techniques
- ➔ IT : general, methods and technique, design and build applications, technical and informatics infrastructure, appl.mngmt, exploitation documentation, management (risk,quality,project), commercial

Figure 12.3. The different categories of competencies (NGI, 2001)

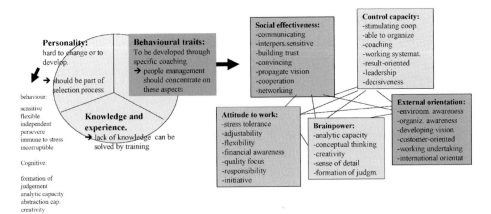

Figure 12.4. The competency set as used by the Dutch Telecom provider KPN

are character traits, behavioural characteristics and experience. The telecom provider KPN states that at a job interview it has to be established whether a person fits in with the organization. To this purpose, the character traits are checked out during the selection procedure. Should one conclude that the personality of the candidate fits in badly with the telecom provider, this person is not hired. With regard to present personnel, one only has to deal with function profiles and competency profiles of employees. Each function has its requirements with regard to knowledge and experience and has demands regarding behavioural characteristics. The first type of requirements can be remedied immediately by means of courses, the second type of requirements is often less quickly adjustable by means of training or not adjustable at all.

In Figure 12.5 competencies for functions are defined, as used by the the Dutch exam institute for informatics. These competencies originate in the Helsinki profiles for IT function, that have been drawn up by a number of IT companies with European Union subsidies. The exam institute states that there are four types of competencies, being business, branch specific, technical and behaviour competencies. These competencies may be necessary for every function at a certain level. One discerns a basic level; a level on which one can use the competency independently; a level on which one may also use the competency in complex situations and a level on which the competency can be applied flexibly and one is able to support others in using the competency. In Figure 12.5 these four competencies are illustrated with the exception of the branch specific ones. The numbers in Figure 12.5 represent the number of competencies per type.

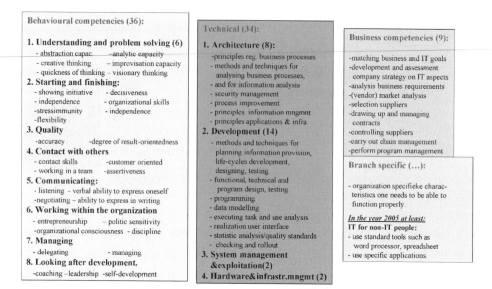

Figure 12.5. Competencies as presented by the NGI

From the examples it transpires that dealing with competencies is an integral part of dealing with the IT function classification. Below we take our departure from the competencies as defined by the NGI. Other aspects of a function such as context and role also originate from NGI:

Context

Execution of a function demands competencies. Execution is also influenced by the context in which a function is executed. This context is defined by the resources, methods and techniques used; the organizational scope within which one functions; the degree to which execution of the functions is dictated and the complexity with regard to subjects and aspects one has to deal with; and finally the adjoining knowledge one needs. In Figure 12.6 these four aspects of the context have been worked out in more detail. This figure also show the relationship between the context in which a function is executed and the necessary competencies for being able to design a function within the given context.

Roles

Apart from competency and context, the role one plays as a functionary has its impact on the function. Some six roles are distinguished, varying from

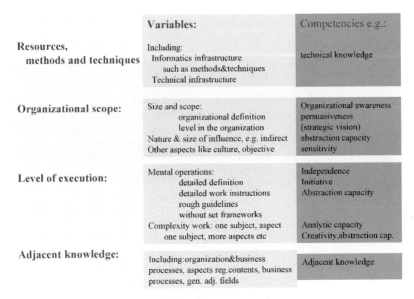

	Variables:	Competencies e.g.:
Resources, methods and techniques	Including: Informatics infrastructure such as methods&techniques Technical infrastructure	technical knowledge
Organizational scope:	Size and scope: organizational definition level in the organization Nature & size of influence, e.g. indirect Other aspects like culture, objective	Organizational awareness persuasiveness (strategic vision) abstraction capacity sensitivity
Level of execution:	Mental operations: detailed definition detailed work instructions rough guidelines without set frameworks Complexity work: one subject, aspect one subject, more aspects etc	Independence Initiative Abstraction capacity Analytic capacity Creativity.abstraction cap.
Adjacent knowledge:	Including:organization&business processes, aspects reg.contents, business processes, gen. adj. fields	Adjacent knowledge

Figure 12.6. The four aspects of context

participating in, to deciding on. In Figure 12.7 these roles have been worked out in more detail and it is indicated which competencies are needed for executing the function within the given role.

Task clusters

Now that the various roles at interpreting a function are defined and it is clear that the context also influences the importance of the function, we will distinguish clusters of tasks. A function is constructed from tasks. For the execution of every task one has to comply with specific technical competencies and personal/behaviour competencies. The NGI (2001) distinguishes eight categories of IT task clusters. These eight categories are:

– task clusters defining the framework (12 units);
– the task clusters design, development and building (36 clusters);
– the task clusters in the field of introducing and implementing (13 clusters of tasks);
– the task clusters in the field of functional management, application management and exploitation (34 task clusters);

Roles	Competencies:	
Participating	participating in a team listening	
Executing	independence formation of judgement	initiative methods and techniques for project management
Cooperating	cooperating in teams communicative capacity,	flexibility dealing with conflict
Assisting, guiding	cooperating in teams, communicative skills	didactic skills flexibility sensitivity,empathy
Advising	communicative skills,	organizational awareness didactic skills
	cooperating in teams risicomanagement	initiative, creativity methods&techniques project mngmt
Controlling, managing the execution	form.of judgm, persuasiveness, risk management independence, communicative skills	
Deciding	leadership, decisiveness, persuasiveness,initiative communicative skills,sensitivity,empathy methods and techniques for project management	

Figure 12.7. Roles and competencies

- general task clusters in the field of, amongst other things, risk analysis, setting standards and quality management (13 clusters);
- task clusters aimed at personnel management (4 clusters);
- task clusters aimed at services: the financial and commercial task clusters (12 clusters);
- basic task clusters such as planning, analysing, evaluating etc. (16 task clusters).

Within these eight categories 142 clusters of tasks are recognized. Each of the categories has a subdivision into operation-focussed, application-focussed, infrastructure focussed and more general focussed clusters of tasks. Furthermore it is indicated at each task cluster what the object of this task cluster is. These can be one of four types of objects, that is to say data, function or functionality, the process as object or the policy/the definition of the IT architecture as object.

Policy and framework:
- managing director(client)
- CIO
- information manager
- division manager (client)
- IT policy advisor
- advisor information function
- business systems analyst
- information architect
- security manager

Introducing:
- change manager
- implementation advisor
- tester

Managing applications:
- functional manager
- application manager
- data manager
- database administrator
- user manager

Managing infrastructure:
- system manager
- network manager
- server manager
- storage manager
- pc network manager
- pc manager
- empl. location management
- internet/intranet manager
- operator
- work preparator

Various management functions:
- head computerization
- head application development
- head programming
- head system and network mngmnt
- program manager
- QA manager

General:
- project manager
- project leader
- technical project leader
- team leader
- incident manager
- problem manager
- configuration manager
- content manager
- webmaster
- manager information security
- authorization manager
- advisor methods& techniques
- documentalist
- multi media manager/advisor
- teacher
- edp auditor
- advisor internal checking and security

Service-oriented:
- service manager
- employee service desk
- advisor personal computers
- application specialist

Developing applications:
- information analyst
- data architect
- system analyst
- system designer
- system architect
- application designer
- functional designer
- technical designer
- embedded software engineer
- programmer
- datawarehouse developer
- web designer
- e-business advisor
- knowledge engineer

Developing infrastructure:
- architect technical infrastructure
- network architect
- network engineer
- system programmer
- security specialist
- internet infrastructure specialist

Commercial:
- account manager
- consultant
- product manager

Personal:
e.g. resource manager

Figure 12.8. 80 functions as finally described by the NGI (2001)

Exemplary functions

Using the competencies and the task clusters, eleven categories of functions are defined (see Figure 12.8). These eleven function categories are split up into eighty functions. Function profiles have been drawn up for each of these eighty functions, in compliance with Figure 12.9. This figure provides an example of a function profile for the function of service manager. This function profile includes the description of the function as well as the competencies needed for it. It does not specifically discuss role and context. One will have to define this for each organization. In Figure 12.10 this process of function definition is represented in diagram form in conformity with the method as given here.

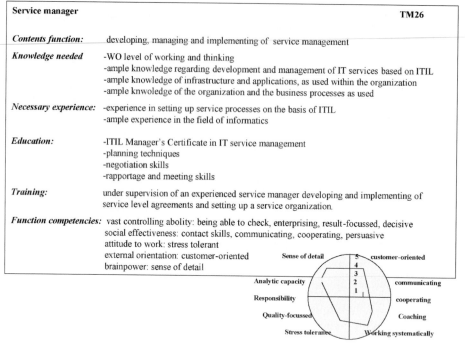

Figure 12.9. Example of a function profile in conformity with the NGI (*IB* Group, 1999)

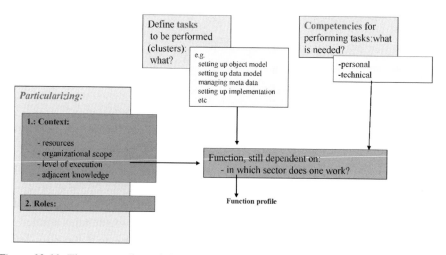

Figure 12.10. The process for arriving at function descriptions for IT functions (NGI, 2001)

APPLICATIONS OF ROLES, CONTEXT, TASK CLUSTERS AND COMPETENCIES

Application

The function profiles created this way can be used differently. We will indicate the use within the framework of human resource management (HRM), competency management and the planning of training.

Application in HRM

Execution of human resource management intends to ensure an adequate staffing of the capacity and expertise as needed by the organization, also by taking care of an optimal development of employees. The HRM function controls to this purpose a cycle of tasks that starts as soon as an employee is hired and ends with looking after the employee when leaving the organization.

The HRM cycle runs as follows. The cycle starts with the definition of the necessary functions and the capacity needed for each function. It is continued with the classification of the functions and determination of their profile. Next, the recruitment and selection process starts. This ends with the appointment of an employee. At joining, the employee gets initial training. After this, he or she starts work. During working in the organization, HRM takes care that assessing of one's functioning is done. Part of this assessment is discussing the further development of the employee and the possible adjustment of the payment in conformity with the prevailing remuneration policy. The last part of the HRM cycle is looking after the employee when leaving the organization.

At various points in this HRM cycle we have to deal with tasks, roles, task clusters and functions. Definition of the capacity all revolves around the determination of the tasks to be performed and the size of these tasks. In classifying and determining the profile, the context one functions within and the role one plays are of importance. At assessment one has to have a function profile at one's disposal, whilst remuneration is also often linked to functions. The conclusion may well be that function profiles and competency profiles come up for discussion in many phases of the HRM cycle. A function profile lays down the requirements of the function. A competency profile represents the qualities of a member of staff.

Application in competency management

Competency management is the continuous and integral coordination of skills and talents of employees to the activities to be performed and the requirements these have to meet. Competency management may be looked upon both from the perspective of the individual and from that of the organization. If competency management is seen from the perspective of this individual, one states which changeable competencies this person has and whether to change them and if so how. Seen from the perspective of the organization, one takes stock of the competencies the organization might need, to which degree and when these are needed for realizing its targets.

Competency management defines the competencies that are important and translates these into roles and functions. It determines which competencies are needed, taking into account that this also requires a translation into functions and roles. These are compared with the available competencies. Based upon this and on the basis of the competency profile of an employee, further agreements with employees are concluded about future functions and the actions that have to be undertaken for possibly being able to fulfil these. Competency management is in this way, a means for tying a member of staff to an organization. It clarifies the career path for the employee and enables the organization to assist in this.

The description of the functions with technical and individual/ behavioural competencies play a part in every phase of competency management. These are also a basis when considering training plans for employees of the organization.

Application in training plans

In an organization there are four types of training for employees. These are general training, such as a university education, function-focussed education, task-focussed training and knowledge-focussed education, such as passing on knowledge on for example the ASL or BiSL method. Each training type has learning goals. These learning goals discuss the level of learning. The learning goals determine the contents of the training. These discuss the knowledge that has to be acquired and the result. Training can include three levels of learning. These are:

−simply taking note of the subject material;
−being able to operate certain machines or using specific applications;
−and finally the acquiring of personal skills, so that position, attitude or way of thinking are changed.

With regard to the contents of the training this may be a question of passing on theory, learning concepts; of acquiring methods and techniques and of learning to handle certain resources. Because of the training one may be able to reproduce knowledge; one understands the subject material; one is able to analyse a problem to do with the subject material; from the theory one is able to make connections and is able to find solutions and finally one is able to voice an opinion using what was learned. The result of the training may be that one is able to apply the acquired knowledge and skill under supervision or entirely independently. Recognition of the competency profile of the employee and confronting this with the function profile results in recognition of the need for education and to setting learning goals.

QUESTIONS

1. Indicate roughly what an interpretation of an IT demand and supply organization with functions looks like. Do this, discussing functions at operational, tactical and strategic level.
2. How did the classification of IT functions change over the years and why? Give an example of this.
3. Why does thinking in competencies take central stage in thinking about the staffing of an IT organization with employees? What is thinking in competencies?
4. What do the outlines of the competency set of the Dutch Telecom provider KPN look like? What is useful about this competency set?
5. What does a competency profile according to the Dutch informatics exam institute look like? What is such a profile aimed at? What is therefore the difference with the competency set of the Dutch Telecom provider KPN?
6. What is the importance of context and role if we want to arrive at profiles of functions for an organization? Illustrate your answer with two examples: one regarding the impact of the concept 'context of a function' and one example of the concept 'role of a functionary.'

7. What is the importance of task clusters? How does one get from task clusters to functions with requirements regarding competencies and experience?

8. How does one arrive at the definition of functions in an IT organization? Describe this process and illustrate your answer with an example.

9. Describe the model for the structure of the demand and the supply organization as given in the book. Name at least one function at strategic, one at tactical and one at operational level. What are the two remarks with regard to the model if one puts functional management at the demand organization and application management/exploitation at the side of the supply organization?

10. What does competency management do and why would one want to introduce this? Give an example of application of this for the function service level manager.

11. Describe the career development possibility for a function in the field of management at functional and at application management. What could be the role of a training plan in this?

12. Give applications of the use of functions, tasks, task clusters and roles at Human Resources Management (HRM) for an IT supply and for an IT demand organization.

Chapter 13

Procurement of IT products and services (using the method ISPL)

The increased pressure on IT facilities with regard to usage, forces organizations to keep a record of the use of IT objects. Since the arrival of personal computers, we all know about software licences. For every pc that has a word processing programme installed on it, there should be a licence for this word processing programme. The nineties saw the rise of software licences for larger servers, which were priced according to the maximum number of users able to use the software at the same time. The year 2004 saw the advent of utility computing, a form of computing where one only pays for the use of hardware when this is actually used. Keeping a record of the use of objects prevents over-licensing, makes it possible to prove legal use and saves costs because of its transparency.

Bout a quart of all European requests in some European countries for proposals over the 1999–2002 period are tenders concerning IT facilities. This extreme representation of IT is on the one hand caused by procurements for solving the year 2000 problem and on the other hand, the IT sector is a sector in which one watches carefully whether authorities comply with the European regulations.

Internet enables organizations to provide for their IT needs in a different way. This is the dawn of application service providing. Organizations can as it were, lease computer applications. One pays for the use of certain possibilities and calls these in, by starting the application from a browser at the workplace. The supplier takes care of the transport, storage and processing facilities and of the licences for use of the application. The mode of operation changes the way of thinking about procurement: one can apparently as a service supplier provide a limited number of services. A customer can source in a so-called granular fashion.

Contents of this chapter

Organizations have to deal with different trends. They have to deal with an increasing need for being able to account for their use of IT objects. In a number of cases, they have to deal with legislation in the field of procurement of products and services. Furthermore, the internet opens up possibilities to them and enables them to obtain IT products and services in a more granular manner. These trends have put organization of IT procurement on the agenda of larger organizations. Procurement is done less and less by the IT manager alone. This chapter concentrates on the procurement of IT facilities by supply organizations. It is presumed that the demand organization combines the demand. The supply organization takes care of interpretation of the demand using IT facilities.

The chapter starts by giving a definition of the concept the purchase of IT facilities. The conclusion is that in this book, purchase of IT is equal to 'procurement.' Procurement concerns all activities aimed at managing and controlling the incoming flow of goods and services. Next, the processes with regard to procurement are listed and five reasons indicated for explicitly positioning procurement of IT facilities. After this, procurement of IT is discussed in more detail. The various types of procurement are defined as well as the difference between the procurement by private and by public organizations. It also transpires that because of the use of the internet, the procurement of IT has been given a much more important position in the supply organization.

The second part of the chapter discusses the methods to be used in procurement of IT. In this part, the point of view of the OGC and the views of users of the Information Systems Procurement Library (ISPL) method are discussed. According to the view of the OGC, procurement of IT is no different from any other procurement of goods or services by an organization. In the opinion of the users of ISPL, procurement of IT is of such importance to an organization; matters like the processes, the documents to be delivered and how to deal with risks for procurement of IT are explicitly formulated. Next, the ISPL method is discussed. The final part of the chapter discusses research into the situation of 2003 in the Netherlands, in the field of the organization of IT procurement.

DEFINITIONS OF THE CONCEPT OF PURCHASE AND MODEL OF THE PURCHASE OF GOODS AND SERVICES

Definitions of purchase

In the literature one finds a number of definitions of the concept 'purchase.' Van Weele (1993, see Harink, 2003) defines purchase of goods and services as activities that are aimed at externally obtaining goods and services that are needed for the operational management. In English one uses the concept of purchasing for this. A different definition of purchasing states that purchasing includes all activities that are aimed at managing and controlling the incoming flow of goods. In English this is called procurement. A third definition of purchasing mentions sourcing. Sourcing is the securing of the supply of goods to be purchased with emphasis on the longer term. In fact one outsources the execution of tasks. The last definition as mentioned here is the one given by Telgen (1994, see Harink, 2003). Telgen states that purchasing includes everything involving an external invoice. This last definition of the concept of purchasing is a simple one and immediately indicates what is often one of the most important source of information about purchasing, the invoices administration.

Definition as used here

In this book purchasing is defined as procurement. Procurement of IT is about the procurement of goods and services, following the procurement and ensuring that the organization after usage, disposes of the product in the correct way. This way of dealing with IT procurement ties in with 'asset management' for products and services procured elsewhere. Procurement then includes the life-cycle management of procured goods and services. Looking at procurement like this has its advantages. Heine (2003) remarks that organizations, with optimal asset management spend around 20% less on procurement of IT facilities and their implementation. They procure at the desired moment; they can implement the goods and services systematically and dispose of these at the right time and in the correct way. Procurement of goods and services for the primary process of an organization is called primary procurement. Procurement of goods and services for supporting processes is known as procurement of facilities. The procurement of facilities may be between 25 and 55% of the entire volume of procurement.

Model for procurement

In Figure 13.1 the so-called racing car model as presented by Veeke (1993, see Harink, 2003) for procurement is shown. This model distinguishes

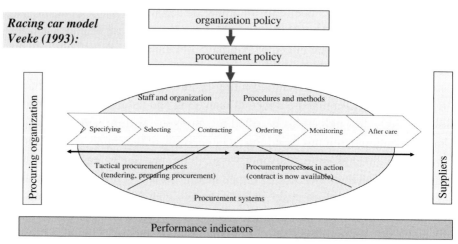

Figure 13.1. Model for procurement of goods and services (Veeke, 1993 (see Harink, 2003))

procurement of goods and services, controlling and supporting. In this model, procurement takes place within the strategy of an organization and the derived procurement policy. Procurement is a methodical process, in which the method is translated into procedures. The procurement is supported by IT facilities and performed by employees that have been trained in purchasing. The whole life-cycle of specification of goods and services to be procured up to and including the aftercare is controlled. To this purpose, performance indicators are recorded.

REASONS FOR CONSIDERING AN ORGANIZATION SPECIFICALLY FOR IT PROCUREMENT

Reasons for a systematic approach

In the year 2005, there are five reasons for organizations to consider a more explicit organization of IT procurement. These five reasons are:

1. **Organizations are able to implement changes in IT quicker.** The urge to implement new IT facilities more quickly has increased over the last ten years. In 1995 an elapsed time—from considering to realizing a request—stretching to 120 days was still the order of the day. In 1998 this time was, also because of the increased use of standard applications, brought back to 90 days. In 2004, especially because of having to adjust internet facilities fast, the elpased time is 30 days and this will be only 10 days in 2010 (Heine, 2003).

   Optimal procurement contributes to this because organizations buy the right amount of licences and over-licensing occurs less often; because organizations conclude an optimal maintenance contract and because they choose less complex solutions. Finally, organizations are quick to notice if suppliers do not perform in conformity with agreements and these can therefore be discarded sooner.

2. **Organizations save on costs.** Cost savings through optimal procurement are achieved in a number of ways. Firstly, one can save about 20% in costs by keeping sight of usage. Heine (2003) remarks that this saving is a result of the changing from 'all you can eat' contracts to 'pay as you go' contracts. Secondly, because of a clear specification of contracts and application of expertise, financial engineering can be carried out

more efficiently. An optimal form of contract and financing is the result. A life-cycle perspective on IT-procurements also results in realizing a lower total cost of ownership. An organization can as it happens, negotiate in a more relaxed manner and that way conclude better contracts. Planned replacement takes place and can be predicted. On top of that, the procurement is done within the architecture for IT facilities and an integral migration planning. This means that procurement can take place more controlled and also more just in time.

3. **Organizations are able to respond better to changes.** There are two reasons why better procurement influences this. Firstly, attention for procurement is often directly involved with attention for IT architecture. As a result of this, one procures targeted. One also turns this architecture less complex. One controls on reduction of the number of software versions per workplace. One limits the diversity of suppliers and one chooses the right level of provision of services. Secondly, by having insight into the existing IT facilities, one is able to quickly clarify the effect of the execution of requests of the demand organization. This way, one is able to respond better to the demand and if necessary supply alternatives.

4. **Organizations avert problems.** Organizations are increasingly called to account, with regard to proving their right to use IT objects. Besides, one concludes that in organizations, the use of certain IT objects, such as mobile telephones and personal digital assistants is often no longer under control, whilst at the same time, invoices for use are sent. Finally, utility computing is on the up. Payment according to use is becoming more fashionable. From the using organization this demands a user administration, even if one just wants to be able to answer queries from the accountant about invoices from the supplier.

5. **Organizations professionalize their IT procurement.** The environment forces an organization, to be able to conclude contracts in an increasingly professional way, to be able to deal with these and terminate these. Besides, configuring procurement often also results in realizing better support of the matching asset management process.

Let us first discuss the statutory regulations. Governments for example in the European Union are obliged to put out to public tender, all contracts over a certain amount. One finds that interpreting the wording of contracts correctly, more and more becomes the work of specialists. Furthermore, one has to cope with regulations regarding the environment, taxes and privacy. It is for instance possible, to avoid taxes by using certain contract construction. It is also necessary to dispose of certain objects in the environmentally correct way and licences have to be officially written off. One is not allowed to remove any objects without first making sure these do not contain any privacy sensitive data. It is therefore not surprising, that external organizations offer their services for taking care of licence administration, supervising legal recommendations etc.

Through concentration of procurement activities, one may also procure tooling that supports the work of the purchaser and also makes life easier for other managers with regard to contracts. One can support contract management, which means that one is alerted when contracts expire. One can keep an automatic record of registration of usage. One can use tools that detect when certain objects in the production environments are connected and used etc.

Configuration of a professional purchase in this way seems to bring advantages for IT organizations, when speaking of procurement. In that case 'purchasing' is combined with clear-cut asset management.

DIFFERENCES AT PROCUREMENT OF IT PRODUCTS AND SERVICES

Not every procurement process is exactly the same

Procurement of products and services and therefore also procurement of IT differs with regard to delivery risk and importance. Procurement is sometimes also surrounded by legislation. The rise of internet technology means that procurement has become more of an issue for more products and services in the field of IT. Modern IT facilities are easier to construct from parts that are supplied by different organizations. We will discuss these three procurement aspects next.

The Kraljic Matrix

Kraljic (1983) indicated that procurement differs with regard to the delivery risk and the importance for the procuring organization (see Figure 13.2). Organizations try to restrict the delivery risk as much as possible by steering well clear of legacy, by building their IT facilities from objects based on more

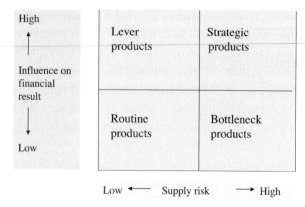

Figure 13.2. The Kraljic matrix

open architectures and by choosing partners that have proven to be reliable. Deliveries of Enterprise Relationship Planning packages, will often be part of more strategic procurements. In that case, the choice of supplier and the suppliers' package, including the implementation services that go with this is a crucial choice. By contrast, the procurement of standard work-places could be regarded as procurement of a routine product, whilst when dealing with toner cartridges, diskettes and other supplies we have to take care not to end up in the category of the lever- or bottle-neck products. Being aware of the type of procurement, results in the understanding that there is more or less choice for a company and that one may carry out the life-cycle of procurement with more or less care etc.

Legislation

A second difference between organizations concerns having to deal with statutory regulations with regard to procurement, one has to comply with. Authorities are obliged to put out a public tender in the case of procurement over a certain amount. Authorities in the European Union have to comply with the regulations as laid down in the EEC regulations. These regulations are translated to legislation of the different countries of the European Union. European tenders for IT regularly occur. In Figure 13.3 is shown that over the 1999–2000 period in for example the Netherlands, around 140 allocations to tender concerning IT took place. This is 24% of the total number of allocations for European tenders in this country. Figure 13.3 shows what the difference is to an organization, in the case of a European tender. In a European tender the requests for quotations

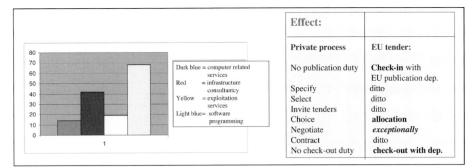

Effect:		
	Private process	**EU tender:**
	No publication duty	**Check-in** with EU publication dep.
	Specify	ditto
	Select	ditto
	Invite tenders	ditto
	Choice	**allocation**
	Negotiate	*exceptionally*
	Contract	ditto
	No check-out duty	**check-out with dep.**

Figure 13.3. Number of allocations of IT in the period between 1999–2002 based on the definitions of the common private vocabulary (CPV). Also the differences between a European (EU) tender and a tender not complying with EU rules

have to be checked in and checked out. The contract is allocated on the basis of criteria given in advance. Negotiations take place to a much lesser extent.

Possibilities created by the rise of the internet

Next we discuss the impact of the internet on the procurement of IT. In the period before the rise of the internet, organizations often had to deal with a network built with fixed lines; they concluded that exchanging data between procured applications was not always that easy and one was often was trapped in proprietary technology. This led to duplication of lines, to developing and maintaining interfaces between applications on a large-scale and because of being trapped in a proprietary architecture of IT facilities, it weakened their negotiating position.

This situation changed gradually with the rise of the internet. When using internet, organizations share the network infrastructure. They use standards such as *TCP/IP* in their network traffic. In the workplace, standard browsers appear. The market also sees the arrival of open-source products such as Linux and data is transported between applications using XML. This way the advent of the internet brings to life an entire market of suppliers of new products and services. Organizations do not build parts of applications in-house anymore but bring in the web services others provide. This way an organization is presented with the opportunity to procure services and products on a different level. One may use suppliers for just some services and the so-called 'granular sourcing' arises.

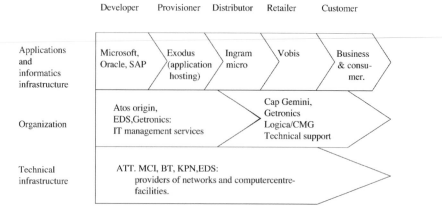

Figure 13.4. A chain of suppliers

Chains of suppliers develop, which are controlled by a customer, by means of concluding contracts. Figure 13.4 provides an example of such a chain.

THE IMPACT OF INTERNET ON IT PROCUREMENT

Impact on how sourcing is considered

This way, the advent of the internet has impact on the procurement of IT facilities. This impact emerges on the one hand, from the way sourcing is considered; on the other hand, from the changes in the way IT itself is procured.

Thinking about the outsourcing of IT facilities always meant thinking about the outsourcing of major divisions of the supply organization. One wanted to hand these divisions over for various reasons. Sometimes one was not satisfied with the quality and the costs of the in-house IT supply organization. Sometimes one simply thought IT performed badly. Sometimes one simply wanted to focus on one's core activities and not be bothered by proposals of a function that was, according to the Executive board a facility. In other situations, one simply needed the money of the sale and at the same time changed recurring expenses in a more variable cost. And so there were many reasons for obtaining large parts of the IT facilities from third party organizations. This progresses even further in the internet period. Outsourcing increasingly smaller tasks becomes cost-effective. Granular sourcing is the motto and a purely businesslike consideration takes place. Arguments for procurement are price, speed of delivery, controllability

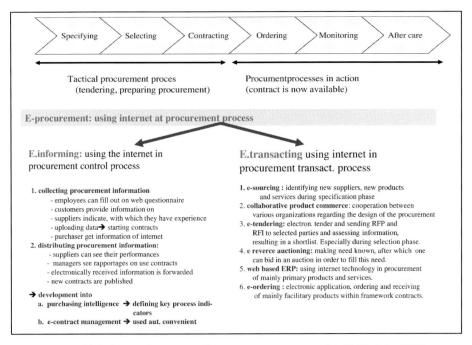

Figure 13.5. Impact internet on the procurement process itself (Harink, 2003)

and the question whether it is a matter of a core or a strategic activity. In the last mentioned case, it is also possible to consider cooperating with partners.

Impact on procurement itself

Harink (2003) stated the impact of internet on the procurement of products and services. His analysis (shown in Figure 13.5) indicates that the use of internet in the procurement process occurs in the control of the procurement and in concluding the transaction. The use of internet in procurement furthermore step by step, leads to the use of acquired information for controlling the entire process more effectively. One increasingly compares the actual situation regarding contracts and their running out with what is to be expected. This is called purchasing intelligence (Harink, 2003). Next Harink (2003) deduces that because of the use of the internet, use of concluded agreement is simplified for line management. One has online sight of the agreements and the impact of these on the operational processes one is responsible for. Harink (2003) calls this e-contract management.

CONSIDERING PROCUREMENT METHODICALLY

Perspective on procurement

Figure 13.6 shows that it is possible to get to a methodical approach to the field of IT procurement from four different perspectives. One may use the perspective of the object of procurement; one may choose the perspective of the possible method to be used; one may look at the environment in which the procurement takes place and one may examine with which technical resources one has to deal in procurement. Procurement as mentioned in this book is the procurement of all IT objects that the demand and supply organization use. Procurement takes place in environments that may strongly vary. Earlier in this chapter we discussed the difference in purchase between public and private organizations. There is however also a difference with regard to importance of procurement of IT between organizations of which the primary process is more information intensive and organizations in which that is not so much the case. The first category includes banks and insurance companies. In this category one finds oneself sooner in the quadrant of the strategic procurement as defined by Kraljic. In the second category, one will in general try more to procure routine facilities.

A third perspective is the perspective of technical developments. Internet technology has for instance impact on the products and services one procures and

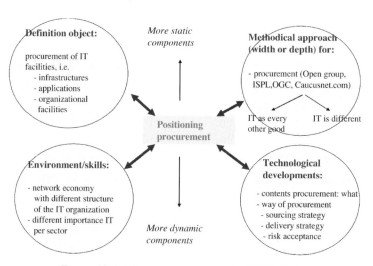

Figure 13.6. Views on procurement of IT facilities

their way of sourcing, delivering and dealing with risks. One sources worldwide, one often delivers more at a distance and one comes across risks such as supplying services and products by suppliers in different continents. This is called offshore sourcing.

The last perspective on procurement is the one of the method used at procurement. In this field, the ISPL method or Information Systems Procurement Library method will next be discussed in more detail.

View of the OGC on procurement

Before discussing ISPL we would like to remark that it should not be considered a given that one has specific methods for procurement of IT facilities. The Office of the Government (OGC) explicitly holds the opinion that procurement of IT is no different to an organization than procurement of any other service or any other goods. The OGC site, the organization that manages the ITIL heritage, refers to the subjects of Figure 13.7 with regard to procurement. There is

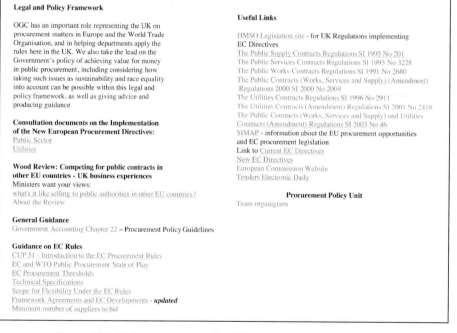

Legal and Policy Framework

OGC has an important role representing the UK on procurement matters in Europe and the World Trade Organisation, and in helping departments apply the rules here in the UK. We also take the lead on the Government's policy of achieving value for money in public procurement, including considering how taking such issues as sustainability and race equality into account can be possible within this legal and policy framework, as well as giving advice and producing guidance

Consultation documents on the Implementation of the New European Procurement Directives:
Public Sector
Utilities

Wood Review: Competing for public contracts in other EU countries - UK business experiences
Ministers want your views:
what's it like selling to public authorities in other EU countries?
About the Review

General Guidance
Government Accounting Chapter 22 – Procurement Policy Guidelines

Guidance on EC Rules
CUP 51 - Introduction to the EC Procurement Rules
EC and WTO Public Procurement State of Play
EC Procurement Thresholds
Technical Specifications
Scope for Flexibility Under the EC Rules
Framework Agreements and EC Developments - *updated*
Minimum number of suppliers to bid

Useful Links

HMSO Legislation site - for UK Regulations implementing EC Directives
The Public Supply Contracts Regulations SI 1995 No 201
The Public Services Contracts Regulations SI 1993 No 3228
The Public Works Contracts Regulations SI 1991 No 2680
The Public Contracts (Works, Services and Supply) (Amendment) Regulations 2000 SI 2000 No 2009
The Utilities Contracts Regulations SI 1996 No 2911
The Utilities Contracts (Amendment) Regulations SI 2001 No 2418
The Public Contracts (Works, Services and Supply) and Utilities Contracts (Amendment) Regulations SI 2003 No 46
SIMAP - information about the EU procurement opportunities and EC procurement legislation
Link to Current EC Directives
New EC Directives
European Commission Website
Tenders Electronic Daily

Procurement Policy Unit
Team organigram

Figure 13.7. References concerning IT procurement on the OGC site

no reference to a special IT approach. Also, the site http://www.caucusnet.com does not include a specific IT procurement method, nor that of the Open Group or that of www.buyitnet.org.

THE ISPL METHOD

Set-up of ISPL

Use of the ISPL method in a procurement process results in explaining:

(a) *the roles of and those involved* on the side of the customer and the supplier. ISPL provides the following roles and responsibilities:

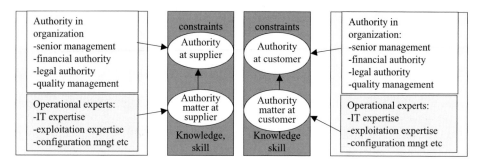

(b) *the phasing of the procurement process.* This phasing goes as follows in ISPL:

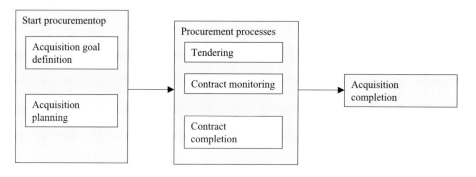

(c) *the ultimately to be delivered products and services, as well as possible intermediary products.*

These end products are often the results of projects. Such a project produces a product such as a change of infrastructure, applications and/or organization. It may also lead to an entirely new infrastructure, application and/or organization. A project may furthermore produce services. One of these services may be the execution of an ITIL process or the execution of a process as defined in the ITIL life cycle processes (ITIL-LCP). ITIL life cycle processes include:

– *primary processes* at acquisition, delivery, development, operating and maintenance of IT facilities;
– *supporting processes* such as documenting, managing configurations, performing quality assurance, verifying, reviewing together, auditing and the resolving of problems;
– *organizational processes* such as controlling, facilitating, improving and training.

The products and services and the achievement of products and services is supported by documents. ISPL describes what *contract products* such as the tender document and the data to be supplied at point of decision should contain. ISPL also describes which products and services and which documentation should be supplied with the *end products and services*. Finally, it is stated which *service products*, such as plans and rapportages, are made during the project.

(d) *What the risks at procurement are and how these risks are dealt with.* The process of risk assessment and acceptance progresses at ISPL as follows:

Documentation of ISPL

The ISPL method is documented in nine booklets: an introduction book, three basic books, three booklets with ISPL applications, a booklet with all used terminology and a booklet about ISPL in European tenders. The basic books discuss the subjects:

(a) Control of the procurement process. In this booklet the seven different procurement processes are explained. These processes are the definition of the goal and planning of the procurement; next the tendering, monitoring and concluding of the procurement contract and finally the tracking and concluding of the procurement.
(b) Specification of the documents, products and services to be supplied. This booklet discusses the contract, service and end products.
(c) Dealing with the risks and the planning of the deliveries. This booklet discusses the optimal delivery from the perspective of realizing and implementing the procurement with as little risk as possible.

The three booklets with applications discuss the application of ISPL in procurement of internet technology products, in procurement of IT services and in procurement of large migrations. We will now discuss the basis of ISPL.

Controlling the acquisition process in conformity with ISPL

The six ISPL processes all include an input, an output, a target and the activities that have to be performed for achieving this target. In Figure 13.8 these elements are shown in brief for each of these six processes.

Specification of products and services to be delivered

In Figure 13.9 the various deliverables in the life cycle of procurement are shown. This concerns the contract, service and end products. Of each of the contract products, the contents of the documents necessary for procurement and for concluding the procurement are described. It is also indicated which documents have to be drawn up during the delivery and what their contents are. With regard to the end products and services, it is indicated what is delivered and what the documents are that are part of the delivery contain. With regard to service products to be produced, possibly during the delivery to be made, plans and reports are discussed.

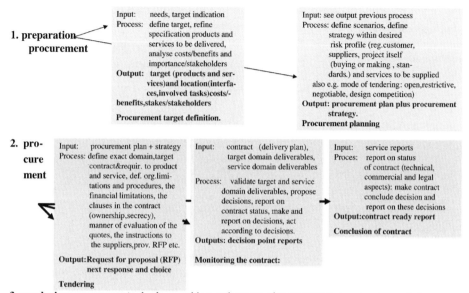

3. conclusion procurement: check everything, estimate to what extent targets are met, conclude procurement and evaluate. Draw up final report procurement.

Figure 13.8. The six ISPL processes

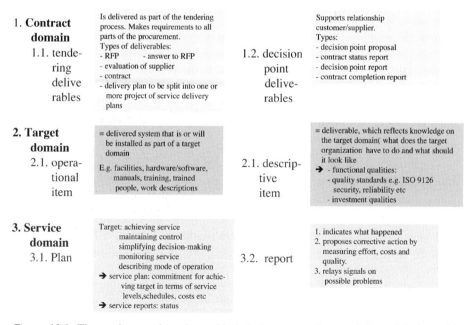

Figure 13.9. The products and services with their documents that are delivered during a life cycle of procurement

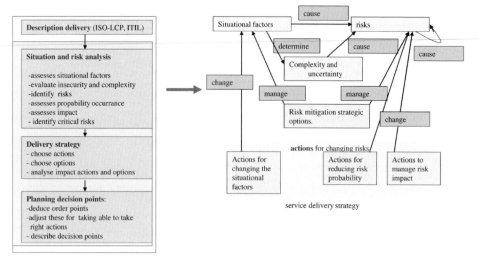

Figure 13.10. Dealing with risk at procurement of goods and services in conformity with ISPL

Dealing with risk

The way in which ISPL deals with risk, boils down to an implementation of the methods for defining project and operational risk, such as were discussed in Chapter 9. ISPL provides the life cycle for arriving at a definition of risk. This lifecycle is shown in Figure 13.10. The lifecycle of risk definition assumes a delivery. It is determined what this is, in which environment one has to deliver and what the risks involved in this are. In a next phase, the actions are defined for reducing the risk. Within this lifecycle, the options for risk reduction of Chapter 9 are applicable.

In ISPL, the complexity of IT facilities at IT procurement is mainly determined by the number of interfaces with other IT facilities, the number of operational processes to be supported and the complexity of current procedures and working methods in an organization. At assessment of the risk ISPL, just like Applegate et al. (2003) includes that requirements to IT facilities may change, the mode of operation may change and that the environment which has to be supplied to, may be dynamic to a greater or lesser degree.

The creators of the ISPL method mainly see possibilities for reducing risk in the approach of the lifecycle of delivery. To a lesser degree than this book, they discuss measures for reducing risks by giving projects more organizational attention. Concerning ISPL, it is stated that one may choose to deliver from a design or limit the risk by delivering in a more incremental way and put into production straight after delivery. ISPL furthermore states, that one can choose for arriving at a more rough solution to start with that could be finalized at a later stage, or by immediately taking all details into account and delivering a fully-fledged solution.

The practice in the year 2003

Since the reasons for organizing procurement are clear and the methods used for procurement of IT products and services have been examined, in conclusion we would like to discuss the practice in the year 2003 at procurement of IT facilities. In 2003 the Erasmus University in Rotterdam (Netherlands) carried out two studies in this field. The first study (Griffioen, 2002) examined the maturity of procurement in some four private and public organizations in the Netherlands. The second study looked at the set-up of the IT procurement in some eight organizations in the public and private sector in the same country (Braam, 2003).

Level of procurement

Griffioen (2002) researched the level of IT procurement in four large organizations. He evaluated the operating level of a customer when procuring IT and the operating level of a supplier when selling. On both sides (see Figure 13.11) he made use of a model for the procurement, respectively selling, that corresponds to the racing car model. He adjusted this model in one detail: he split the parts personnel and organization into two separate parts, organization being one and human and culture the other part. This way it was possible to make a better distinction between the set-up of the organization and the staffing of the organization with professional staff. In his study, he recognized some five different levels on which an organization performs procurement tasks. These levels are:

1. *starting*: the sub sectors as recognized in the racing car model cannot be recognized. Procurement is not an object for discussion;
2. *attention* to procurement is recognized as being necessary but the management has not yet undertaken any action in this field;

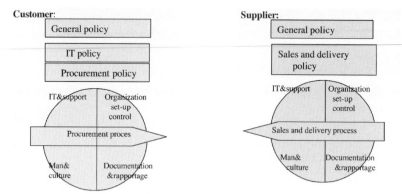

Figure 13.11. Model used in a study regarding the level of procurement of IT (Griffioen, 2003)

3. IT procurement has been *recognized* as important and is an object for (re) organization;
4. IT procurement is *structured systematically*. Procurement activities are carried out in a repeatable manner. One has experience with structured procurement and the same processes reoccur;
5. *sub sectors of the procurement of IT are set-up full-time*. It is a matter of professional customer/supplier management.

In order to find out what the model of the procurement organization and the operating level in the studied organizations are, a vast number of questions were next formulated. These questions were put to organizations in the form of interviews, which took about three hours. In Figure 13.12 the results of this study are shown. From this study, it transpires that the studied organizations have general gaps in the execution of supporting functions. There is often room for improvement in the field of the IT procurement policy and the following of the sale after concluding a contract. One may say that IT procurement in these organizations is in fact more purchasing than procurement.

Set-up of an IT procurement organizations

In a subsequent study Braam (2003) investigated how the IT procurement in the year 2003 is set up. With regard to the set-up of organizations, he used Mintzberg's theory as a starting point. This theory is discussed in Chapter 7 of

	blue service	green tele
Policy making	2.1	1.9
Human resource mngmt & culture	2.4	2.3
IT and support	2.3	2.4
Select and plan	1.9	2.6
Contract	2.8	2.8
Monitor and evaluate	1.9	1.9
Organization,set-up,control	2.0	2.2
Documentatian and rapportage	2.3	2.1

	red ZBO	yellow C
Policy making	3.6	3.2
Human resource mngmnt & culture	2.5	2.8
IT and support	3.0	2.7
Select and plan	3.0	3.4
Contract	4.0	3.5
Monitor and evaluate	2.7	3.4
Organization,set-up,control	3.6	3.2
Documentation and rapportage	2.8	3.2

Figure 13.12. Operating level at IT procurement in four researched organizations. Basis is the racing car model

this book. On the basis of this theory, he arrived at a number of hypothesises on the set-up of IT procurement organization. These are:

(a) in a centrally organized company (machine bureaucracy) central suppliers management occurs, procurement is strongly formalized, it is clear who is authorized to take decisions and the rules for procurement of goods and services are set. This mode of operation encourages attunement in procurement and improves the negotiating position of an organization.

(b) in a decentrally organized company with professional staff, help in procurement as a form of support can be offered from central departments. The central procurement sets general rules but acts in concrete cases more like a facility. There is central direction because of the setting of rules, but decentrally decisions are made about the actual transaction. The procurement knowledge is spread across the organization.

(c) in an organization that mainly carries out projects, procurement expertise is mainly hidden in projects. It is present, spread across the organization.

What does Braam (2003) establish now?

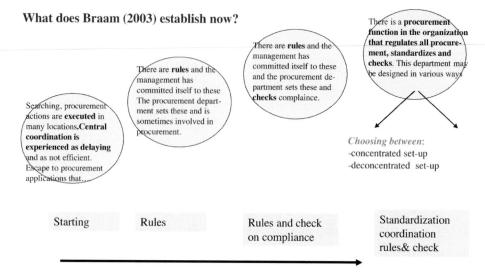

Figure 13.13. Phases to be recognized at the set-up of IT procurement (Braam, 2003)

Measures can be taken for improvement of the efficiency of the procurement. There is often hardly any sharing of knowledge between the various and often large projects. Often there is a large degree of negotiability of individual contracts.

He tested these hypothesises with a few organizations. He concluded that one could recognize phases that organizations go through in the set-up of an IT procurement organization. In the first phase, one starts an IT procurement organization. Next, one starts to set IT procurement rules for procurement of IT. In the following phase, one does not just set rules but also checks compliance with these rules. Only then does a fully-fledged IT procurement organization emerge. This is often organized according to the above-mentioned hypothesis a) or hypothesis b). Which of these is chosen, depends on the culture and the mode of operation of the organization in question (see Figure 13.13).

QUESTIONS

1. What is covered by the concepts purchasing, sourcing and procurement? Why do we speak mainly of the concept procurement of IT facilities in this chapter?

2. What is the racing car model for purchasing goods and services? Explain the model. What is in fact, the starting point of this model? Is that purchasing or is that procurement as a definition of purchasing? Explain your answer.
3. Name five reasons for setting up procurement of IT explicitly in organizations. Give an example of every reason.
4. Apply Kraljic to IT procurement. Indicate in which case, procurement could lead to development of bottleneck products. Indicate why procurement of an *ERP* package with additional implementation services is often procurement of a strategic product.
5. What is the difference between a normal tender of goods and services and a European tender?
6. What impact does the rise of the internet have on IT procurement? Illustrate your answer by giving three examples.
7. In which two ways does the procurement process itself change because of the introduction of internet technology? In which way does this induce the better use of purchasing intelligence and e-contract management?
8. From which four perspectives may one look at IT procurement? How is ISPL described?
9. What are the four pivots of the ISPL method? Which six procurement processes are included in ISPL? Which three types of documents, products and services does ISPL provide?
10. How does ISPL deal with risk? Also provide the lifecycle of risk definition.

Chapter 14

Controlling contracts using service level agreements

Our contract is worked out according to the combination of products and services in 60 Service Level Agreements (SLA's). Together with the customer, we have drawn up a quality plan per service level agreement. We have a meeting every fortnight with the employees that are involved in the realization of the SLA and quality plan. We all look at the same measuring data concerning our products and services. We know the availability, the elapsed times of changes, the response and we all aim at improving these (Boddeke, 2003).

We never realized that we spend over 500 million euro a year in keeping our current IT products online and up-to-date. This sum is spent on our technical maintenance company, that takes care of keeping certain objects on line; on generic services such as those for personal productivity, the applications that support secondary operational processes and the intranet and finally on specific IT facilities for a specific customer. In the technical maintenance company, we focus on standards; in the generic services we have a catalogue of services and for the specific IT facilities we draw up contracts, SLA's and DAP's per customer group (ABN-AMRO, De Jong, 2003).

It never became this clear, that in the telecommunication business, it is crucial to have the right configuration information at one's disposal. This data used to be the engineers' responsibility. They corrected if necessary, other people's mistakes and rarely passed that information on. That did not matter, so long as our supply of products was surveyable but when the market liberalized, we had to compete with new products and services and we did not execute every task ourselves, then the problems started. In over 30% of all installations, an engineer had to visit the customer twice because he did not come across the expected configuration. We then realized that at delivery of the IT facilities of today, many departments are involved with their own perspective, that service agreements run straight across the organization and that right and timely configuration information is a crucial factor (Lee et al., 2002).

Contents of this chapter

This chapter discusses the recording of agreements between the demand and the supply organization. Many people in the supply organization, may be involved in the realization of these agreements. There are agreements on generic and on more specific IT facilities. All these people look from their own discipline, at a part of the same data on the delivered services and products. That is the subject of this chapter: the recording of agreements and controlling on the basis of these agreements.

The chapter starts by defining what a service level agreement is. This service level agreement is positioned and it is stated that this may be part of a contract. A contract is a legal document. For this reason the legislation important when working with contracts and the resulting service level agreements, are also discussed.

Next we discuss the working with service agreements. The advantages and disadvantages of these for the demand and supply organization are indicated and it is made clear that in large organizations service level agreements cut straight across the supply organization. Controlling the observance of SLA's this way, demands considering aspects of information and organization. The solutions as found by larger organizations will be discussed.

The last parts of the chapter go into the realization of SLA's. The step-by-step realization of SLA's with functional and performance requirements for IT products and services come up for discussion. It will become clear, what the result may be of an SLA implementation. The chapter concludes by giving some tips for working with contracts, SLA's and DAP's.

SERVICE LEVEL AGREEMENTS: OFTEN THE ELABORATION OF A CONTRACT

What are SLA's?

Service level agreements (SLA's) are clear descriptions of activities, as performed by a supply organization under orders of a demand organization. An SLA describes to some degree of detail when, how and where the activities are executed. The ideal SLA's are formulated clearly and in detail. They speak a language the demand organization understands and are at the same time concise. SLA's are aimed at creating a certain level of expectation. They record the intention of organizations for cooperating in the long-run. After concluding the SLA and its introduction, safeguarding of the execution follows. This is called service level management.

Positioning

The SLA is positioned in the middle, between the contract between a demand and a supply organization and the more operationally focussed administrative procedures. A contract indicates the policy frameworks within which, the products and services are delivered. A contract is often drawn up for relatively long periods. An SLA is a further elaboration of the contract and records the agreements for a period of one or two years. The SLA includes agreements on the quality, the quantity and the costs of the IT facilities as well as agreements about the control of the delivery of these facilities. An SLA is often coupled to dossiers of administrative procedures (DAP dossiers). These hold agreements on operational level. These include concrete elaborations of the process interfaces between the demand and the supply organization. A DAP dossier is often reviewed several times a year and adjusted to the workable practice. An example of something that could be recorded in a DAP dossier, is the ordering method for procurement and installation of a workplace.

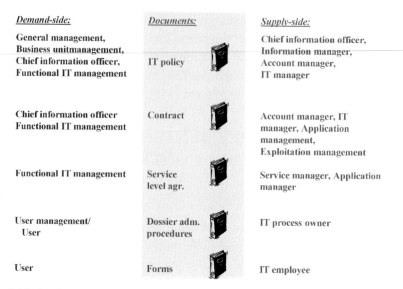

Figure 14.1. Parties concerned and their role and the documents in laying down agreements

Roles in control using SLA's

Figure 14.1 shows which functionaries on the side of the demand and which on the side of the supply organization are involved in drawing up contracts, SLA's and DAP dossiers. Depending on the size of an organization and the importance of IT facilities, differences will occur. In general those responsible for the information function, are found at the demand-side and those responsible for delivering IT facilities at the supply-side. If an organization has set-up functional management, than the head of the functional management organization will be found at the demand-side. He may be called chief information officer, manager information function or information manager. At the supply-side, account managers of IT supply organizations; IT managers and IT service managers are active.

Legal aspects of IT contracts

Agreements between demand and supply organizations are laid down in contracts. The further details are worked out in an SLA. If there are just agreements between internal parties within an organization, then the matter ends when the agreements included in the SLA are recorded. If there is a relationship between the organization and an external party, then there is always a contract. A contract is important in case something goes wrong in the delivery of the IT facilities. This may be a delivery that is too late; a delivery that does not live up to expectations or a delivery that is slightly too expensive according to the demand organization. When drawing up contracts in IT environments one observes that:

- it is not always the authorized functionary that concludes the contract;
- the contract does not always clearly specify the IT facilities to be delivered or is not sufficiently worked out in SLA's;
- sometimes the rights and duties that ensue from the contract are not really divided up proportionally;
- the contract is not sufficient with regard to the requirements or the contract is incomplete.

The legal aspects of a contract and the ensuing SLA therefore do deserve attention, even though 'sourcing of facilities' as a contract does not been explicitly provided for in the legislation of a country. However, most law systems provide explicitly for parts of such a contract. In sourcing one has to deal with the law of contracts, which speaks of purchase, sale and hire of goods and delivering services. Sourcing also involves labour law, when (part of) an in-house IT organization is passed on to third parties. Copyright is also important, if someone else is going to maintain the in-house tailor made applications. One may also encounter the Protection of Personal Data Act, when application data is worked on by a third party. An overview of applicable laws is given in Figure 14.2.

The phases in contracts

A sourcing contract is not a legally designated contract, unlike a lease, deed of purchase, sales contract and service contract, which are. Parties therefore enjoy a certain amount of freedom in determining what is recorded in the contract. In every part, it will be reviewed to what degree an agreement resembles a legally designated contract.

Arriving at a contract and safeguarding the execution of the contract has, as became clear in the previous chapter, the phase materialization, the drawing up of the agreement, the safeguarding of the arrangements in the agreement and the termination of the contract. Next, each of these phases will be discussed.

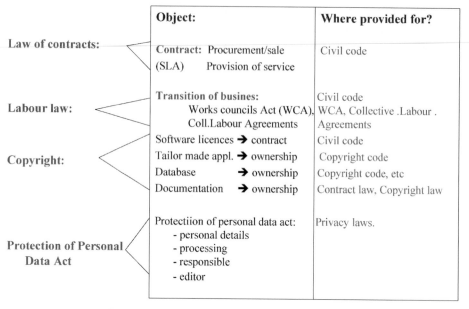

Figure 14.2. IT contracts and prevailing legislation

Materialization

In this phase the contract is prepared, quotes are received and a quote is examined. This phase includes:

−drawing up *an inventory of requests* and limitations;
−drawing up *a request for information*;
−the examination and *processing of the answers*;
−drawing up of a *request for proposal*;
−receiving and *processing of a suppliers' quotes*;
−*selection of suppliers* and possibly careful investigation at a suppliers' using 'due diligence.' At this stage of the procedure, a letter of intent may be given. In this letter of intent, parties record that they intend to do business with each other; that there will be no more negotiations with other parties; what the duration of the negotiations will be; that the negotiations are bound to certain vows of secrecy and which law (s) and competent court are applicable, should it not come to a contract after all. It is often

also necessary at this stage to inform the works council/union in the case of certain contracts.
–*the signing* of the contract.

In this phase, there is a period where all parties are free to break off the negotiations. This can stop for example when an investigation of due diligence takes place. In some law systems the negotiations can then often only be broken off, if one reimburses the expenses incurred by the supply organization. After handing over of the letter of intent and its acceptance, none of the parties are allowed to break off the negotiations for arriving at a contract without reimbursing the other party for its efforts and possibly part of the lost earnings.

Contents of the contract

The contents of the sourcing contract may include elements of various contracts provided for in law. It may contain elements of a sales contract, an agreement for provision of services and a processing agreement. Labour law should also be taken into account. In the part of the contract dealing with purchase and sale, it is indicated which objects are handed over. Staff may transfer to a different organization simultaneously with the taking-over of objects. The contract will in this case also touch on subjects regarding labour law. After taking-over objects, the supply organization will supply services. These services may include processing of data.

In the contract, stipulations regarding sale and purchase of objects such as tailor made goods and infrastructure and the objects to be passed on are described and the price for the objects is given. In addition, the buyer is safeguarded against claims from third parties to do with possible ownership. The purchase for his part, records the guarantees he has given with regard to the possible taking-over of employment contracts of employees in the sourcing contract.

A second part of the sourcing contract deals with the services to be delivered. This part describes these services, deals with the scope of the provision of services and the way in which one deals with more and/or less work. The actual provision of services is often further elaborated in an SLA. Next, the period of transition is determined. This is the period in which the supply organization, in the new setting starts to deliver the services. Agreements are made on the duration of the transition period and the way in which possible (personnel) risks are covered.

Furthermore this part of the contract goes into:

- the duration of the agreement;
- the price to be paid and the method of payment. A fixed price could be agreed. The price may also depend on usage and therefore be variable. One can agree on tariffs to be applied. The contract may include an annual price reduction or the sharing of realized economies;
- the way of protection and securing personal data. One may agree physical, logical and organizational measures to protect these data;
- possible secrecy of parts of the contract and possible publicity of the conclusion of the agreement;
- the use of licences. This may be a matter of transfer of ownership of a right to use, with permission of the owner. One may agree on safeguarding against claims from third parties in the field of intellectual property and on the transfer of possibly created new intellectual rights of ownership at the end of the agreement;
- possible guarantees with regard to the professional ability of the service provider, guarantees for his financial capacity and for the way of dealing with subcontractors;
- risks of damages and loss of objects;
- possible liability for damages. This involves the type of damage and the maximum ceiling of this liability. One may demand that the supply organization takes out insurance for this risk. In this insurance a so-called no claims bonus system may be included;
- dealing with circumstances beyond one's control. What are the service levels then? What is the maximum duration of possible non-availability? Can or should one in that case bring in third parties? And also, under what conditions does this result in entire or partial rescission of the contract?
- the way of dealing with disagreements. This involves escalation procedures, a possible proof of default with a maximum term for sorting out affairs, the applicable law, the competent court and a possible submission to arbitrage;
- the service level agreements ensuing from the contract. These include a description of the products and services to be delivered, the exact service levels, possible preconditions, dealing with changes of the products and services;
- the handling of innovation; the use of audits; the use of benchmarks (frequency, procedure and consequences for agreement).

Contracts in which exploitation services are supplied, also include conclusion of a processing agreement. In this agreement parties record what data is processed, for what purpose and by which means this is done.

During the contract period

Exact details of modes of operation between the demand and the supply organization are recorded in DAP dossiers. These contain working agreements and procedures. These discuss the responsibilities and competencies. These often also include details on when and where consultation should take place and which data should be present. When failing to comply with the contract, one may start by warning the non-performing party; next one may declare them liable and finally talk about penalties. These may be penalties in monetary terms, the taking-over of the management, and possible involve discounts and compensation.

Annulment of the contract

A contract is terminated at a certain moment in time. This could be a premature annulment, it may however also be a normal termination after the contract expires. In both cases, it is recommended to come to some form of agreement about the ending of the contract when concluding the contract. These agreements include:

- the settlements in case of premature termination with regard to cancellation remuneration;
- the possibilities regarding rescission, when failing to meet agreed service levels. In this a distinction can be made between imputable defects, force majeure and other cases, such as moratorium, bankruptcy and take-over of the organization by third parties;
- a possible exit strategy at insourcing or transfer of the contract to another party and the transition involved.

Extra points of particular interest

After discussing the phases of a contract, we would like to point out three special sourcing contracts. The first special contract is a contract for products and services that are delivered *offshore*. At such a contract, an organization does run risks because one has to deal with the legislation of a different country; with the agreement on a competent court; with payment in different currency; with cross-border data traffic and maybe with the commanding of compliance from a foreign contract party. A second special contract may be the conclusion of a contract for *Application Service Providing* services. In such a contract one pays according to usage. The contract includes elements of the agreement for purchasing and renting as provided for by law. Besides, this includes provisions on dealing with licences and intellectual property, dealing with availability, arranging sufficient security and the possible working out of the contract in one or more SLA's. Finally, one increasingly comes across contracts for *utility computing*. In utility computing (parts of) IT facilities such as for instance storage, processing and transport capacity are only then paid for when these are actually used. The IT facilities are permanently in the (in-house) computer centre. These are however not constantly used.

WORKING WITH SERVICE AGREEMENTS

Reasons for SLA's

Contracts are found when services are insourced from external parties. Service level agreements then provide a further elaboration of the contract. Service level agreements are however also concluded when there is no contract. In service level agreements, the performance to be delivered is clearly defined. It is clear which role each of the parties plays and who is responsible for what. It is a basis, on which communication between demand and supply organization may be designed. Internal service providers and their customers also use this tool in this particular way. The conclusion of SLA's prevents conflicts and tempers expectations, that are pitched too high. It often records long-term relationships and indicates in which way the performances are measured and may in this way contribute towards streamlining of the services. Furthermore, drawing up of SLA's provides insight into, always delivered but never paid for services (see Figure 14.3).

Supply organizations often conclude service level agreements with various demand organizations. In order to do this efficiently and to avoid repetition, one has set up a type of products and services catalogue for the supplying of

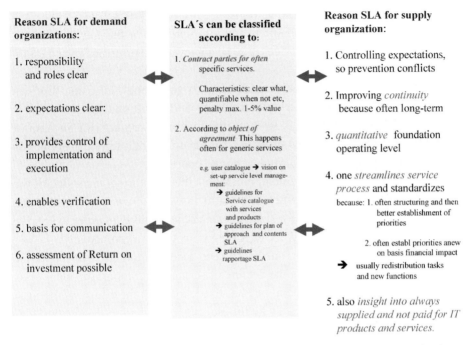

Figure 14.3. Reasons for entering into SLA's at the demand and the supply organization

generic services. This provides an overview of generic products and services. Apart from this, for specific services tailored to a contract party, a special SLA may be drawn up.

Consequences of concluding SLA's

Configuration of SLA's often leads to expenses for external advice and to costs for the set-up or reorganization of the service organization, One is after all forced to think explicitly about the mode of provision of services and the controlling of the process in order to arrive at products and services. This includes aspects of planning, organization, staffing, execution and inspection. For improving this process, the moral of the story is that real knowledge is achieved by measuring. One has to realize that nobody suffers because of good planning but many do suffer because of bad planning. For an exploitation organization the use of SLA's often results in the work becoming more quantifiable. Examples of this are that:

–the service desk is forced to register calls according to type. This often requires application of new technology, so that in the long-run agreements on the level of services may be achieved and priorities can be established;

–problem management structurally has to go through all calls; discover patterns and has to solve structural faults and report on these;

–change management has to warn the customer pro-actively in case of changes and has to take measures for ensuring continuity of services as much as possible even during a change operation;

–at configuration management, one learns that the correct recording of the configuration in many processes results in working more efficiently; that one can provide advice for standardizing objects more, in order to achieve an SLA more efficiently, for replacing objects more pro-actively;

–at capacity management, one has to keep account more pro-actively of the increase and decrease in the decline of services and report on this;

–at availability management, one has to reckon with the effects of the SLA on the architecture of the IT facilities;

–optimal cost management requires that one knows the consequences of other functional and/or performance requirements;

–at customer management, one has to have quantative rapportages about problems at one's disposal and one has to know the effect of the use of standard facilities on the service;

–at product management, one can possibly sell if necessary additional services at the demand organization. One proposes the demand organization to innovate further at success of the current provision of services.

Successful SLA's

Successful service level agreements provide 'end-to-end'-service. They include products and services that can, according to the given specifications, be realistically delivered. These involve measuring the essence of the service, in which there is a clearly visible relationship between the costs and delivery. These involve penalties when they are not met. These may be financial penalties but it is also possible that the customer is present at the regular meetings of the supplier, where his IT facilities are discussed and where he establishes the priorities. The modern SLA is easier to conclude and to manage, includes a limited number of measuring points, has transparent tariffs and leaves some room for a more flexible interpretation. Furthermore, clear-cut types of consultation have been included and there are effective processes for dealing with proposals for change. In conclusion, rapportages are recorded in these. In case of procurement of generic services, the supply organization can provide a services catalogue in which the standard services are included.

The process organization and the SLA

Implementing of such service level agreements is characterized because this implementation in larger organizations often demands the cooperation of people of many parts of the organization and sometimes also the cooperation with people from different organizations. These people share a part of the information on the IT facility and add data to this from their own perspective. When implementing a service, one has to deal with account management, architecture, development, maintenance, exploitation and with the financial department that sends the bill. Also on top of that, sometimes with various departments within a department.

Account management for instance, introduces the request for one hundred new connections, architecture designs these, maintenance implements them, the exploitation front-office performs the service desk tasks and the back-office keeps them in production. Every connection has, amongst other things, its own configuration information, customer information, its authorization information, its availability information and its cost information. It will be obvious that achieving a connection in large organizations demands elapsed time. In Figure 14.4 these implications of working with SLA's in a service process are shown.

Example

Boddeke (2003) examined the exchange of information between parts of the IT organization of the tax authorities. In the empiric part of his research, he made an inventory of the control of activities in conformity with two concluded service level agreements. For the two examined SLA's plans for improvement of quality were made and agreed with the demand organization. In the year 2003 in this organization, 60 SLA's were concluded. Boddeke (2003) ascertained that at the realization of products and services as agreed on in an SLA, the cooperation

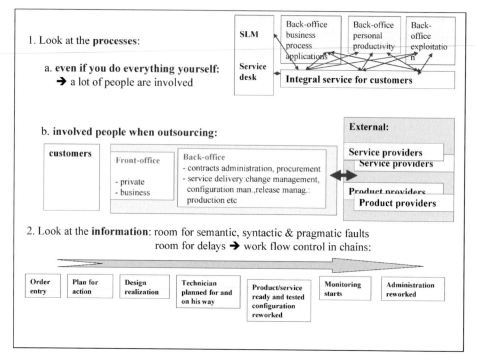

Figure 14.4. SLA's cut straight across an organization

between the various parts did not always take place in accordance with the function description of the employees in question; that the information needed for being able to work sometimes simply was not available; that control of the SLA on agreements as recorded in the concluded quality plans, did not appear on the agendas of the management teams of the organization parts involved and that at realization of the SLA, a lot of feed-forward control took place but that the feedback on the results of an action could be improved.

Example

De Jong (2003) remarks that ABN AMRO in order to improve meeting of commitments on the IT facilities between demand and supply organization to be delivered, has switched to thinking in portfolios. A portfolio is set up per business. Each portfolio requires actions in the technical domain, requires delivery of generic services and delivery of specific services. In the technical company, the striving is for standardization and consolidation. With regard to generic services, there are eleven service processes that employ eleven hundred people. Here, catalogues are used. With regard to specific services, there are tailor made contracts for supplying around thirty IT services.

SPECIFYING AND CONTROLLING SERVICE AGREEMENTS

The lessons

From the previous text, it transpires that employing SLA's can be a powerful tool but that implementation is not always that easy. The Kwintes study (www.kwintes.nl) formulates this as follows:

- 'one records agreements in SLA's and then does not use the SLA's';
- 'one draws up SLA's, sets up the organization but forgets about measuring, reporting and evaluating';
- 'one draws up SLA's, one sets up and measures but provides no or insufficient feedback to the demand organization';
- 'one does do everything but it has no consequences for the SLA.'

In addition to the previous text, it was added that making and implementing SLA's in larger organizations, demands the streamlining and gearing of the work of many organization parts. Application of IT may simplify the necessary exchange of information between these parts. In practice, this enables realizable control on the SLA's, if parties are aware that it is crucial to many processes in the service chain to have the correct basic information and that one has to keep this information optimally up-to-date.

Drawing up SLA's

The Kwintes study also phrased functional and performance requirements for the product of service provision (service pit) and for the services to be provided (the service shell). In Figure 14.5 these are shown. How does a demand organization define these functional and performance requirements for a concrete case?

IT product	Functionality	Availability	Performance	Capacity
	List of possible functions that the IT object offers to e.g. users. E.g. Salary records Email, Printing wordprocessing	Servicetime /opening hours Maintenance time,average time between incidents average availability, maximum duration incidents, minimum repair time, average repair time, maximum lost user time, maximum number incidents per period	Transit speed Reaction time Response time Accuracy Speed of an action Pages to be printed per minute On time delivery of requested functionality	Storage capacity Transport capacity Transaction capacity Maximum number of users Maximum number of times a function can be used
IT service ∗ User support	Service times /opening hours Maximum number of times the phone rings before it is answered, maximum number of missed calls	Service times /opening hours Maximum number of times the phone rings before it is answered, maximum number of missed calls	Speed with which a problem can be solved, percentage problem that are solve immediately, max. number of oustanding problems	Maximum number of users that is supported Maximum number of times user support can be called for
∗ Security	List of possible functions of security. E.g.: Physical access security Logical security, encryption, exclusivity, integrity Safeguarding data	Opening hours for certain functions	Speed with which data is recovered, maximum data loss per period Number of authorization requests per period, maximum number unauthorized access attempts per period	Maximum number of users that is supported Maximum number of times user support can be called for
•Disaster recovery	List of possible functions that have to remain functional during disaster recovery. E.g: IT object Salary records, just consulting, no alterations	Availability during disaster recovery situation What is available during disaster recovery When is disaster recovery available	Speed with which the availability is restored Audits on disaster recovery plan	Maximum duration disaster recovery situation
∗ Changes	List of possible functions of changes.e.g.: limitation change area Recognized categories of changes, development,number users,intensity usage	Manner in which changes have to be applied for	Quickness of reaction at change requests, quickness with which changes have to be implemented, maximum number disturbances as result of changes	Maximum number of changes per period Maximum size of a change

Figure 14.5. Functional and performance requirements to IT facilities in conformity with
www.Kwintes.nl

The concrete phrasing of SLA's for an organization requires making the needs for IT facilities of the demand organization explicit. This requires insight into the operating processes to be supported, definition of the requested IT facilities and defining the qualities of these IT facilities. An SLA is therefore drawn up in steps (Figure 14.6.) These steps are:

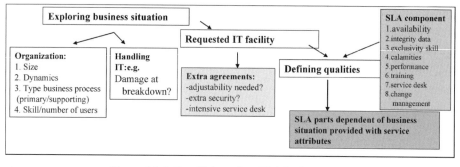

Figure 14.6. Specifying of an SLA in three steps

1. *The definition of the business situation.* Here the size of the organization to be supported is looked at, the degree in which one has to anticipate changing situations, the types of operational processes to be supported and the types of users that are going to use the facilities. In general, a limited number of situations are distinguished, such as:
   (a) a small simple organization with work that is not complex and little knowledge of IT, such as a small company or a secretarial office.
   (b) a large more stable environment, such as for example the back-office of a bank, insurance company or a benefit administration;
   (c) a professional organization. This often has an informal operating environment, executes complex tasks and has highly educated staff. Examples are management and staff departments;
   (d) a strongly innovative organization. This is characterized by its relatively short existence, because one often changes jobs and because of its mode of operating. One often works in varying teams.

   Each type of organization has its own requirements with regard to functionality and the speed with which one should have this functionality at one's disposal, the measure to which the workplace changes location, the desired availability of the workplace, the degree of security and the response (see the Kwintes requirements of Figure 14.5).

2. The *profile of the business process to be supported and the definition of the desired support.*

   A business process in general, gets three types of IT support. This includes support by the operational processes supporting applications support at personal computer use and support by means of internet facilities. The latter can be an intranet or an extranet or both. One or more types of IT can support each workplace.

   Furthermore, the work of an employee can be more or less IT dependent. In general one makes a distinction between three categories: a strong dependency, a normal dependency and a lesser one. This dependency recurs in possible extra measures in the area of front-office services, such as opening of the service desk and back-office services, where one takes care of capacity, availability and performance.

3. *The drawing up of the SLA's and the indication of the products to be delivered and their services.* Next, the products are determined and the services to be supplied with these. In general the product will be:
   –support by the ERP application;

– support by a personal productivity tool such as for instance Microsoft Office;

– use of the intranet, the extranet and access to internet;

– use of a business intelligence tool for composing control information such as for instance Business Objects;

These products are supplied with certain availability. The delivery complies with certain performance requirements and is set-up for providing a certain capacity. Apart from this, one provides user support, a certain degree of security and disaster recovery and is set-up for implementing changes in a certain way (see Figure 14.5).

Next, one describes these products and services and records agreements about the requirements. Often the supply organization has a limited number of levels of requirements products and services are delivered on. Van Boxel (2003) discussed these levels and links these with the service or product to be supplied. She states that a supply organization could set up some five levels and relates these to the levels that everyone knows, being those in an airline company. These levels are:

(a) A 'basic class' level. The supply organization want to offer a new product with a new service, that both have to be designed further. The supply organization concentrates on supplying the product and on the effectiveness of services.

(b) An 'economy class' level. The demand organization sets demands with regard to the continuity of IT products and services. These have to comply with minimum requirements. There is not just more attention to effectiveness but efficient delivery also becomes a topic.

(c) A 'business class' level. The supply organization demands mature IT products and services. The supply organization equips itself for optimally managing the products and services and delivering these anywhere. One is equipped for transparency. The customer has a controllable insight into costs, the current production, the innovation and the satisfaction of its organization with regard to the delivery of products and services.

(d) A 'business class enhanced flexibility' level. The demand organization wants to follow the market, be flexible and creative. The supply organization supplies services and products under architecture. One is able to link applications to facilities within and outside the organization. The use of web services is possible. The management organization is transparent.

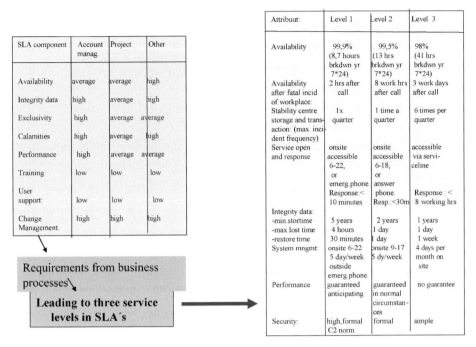

SLA component	Account manag.	Project	Other
Availability	average	average	high
Integrity data	high	average	high
Exclusivity	high	average	average
Calamities	high	average	high
Performance	high	average	average
Training	low	low	low
User support:	low	low	low
Change Management.	high	high	high

Requirements from business processes

Leading to three service levels in SLA´s

Attribuut:	Level 1	Level 2	Level 3
Availability	99,9% (8,7 hours brkdwn yr 7*24)	99,5% (13 hrs brkdwn yr 7*24)	98% (41 hrs brkdwn yr 7*24)
Availability after fatal incid of workplace:	2 hrs after call	8 work hrs after call	3 work days after call
Stability centre storage and trans- action: (max. inci- dent frequency)	1x quarter	1 time a quarter	6 times per quarter
Service open and response	onsite accessible 6-22, or emerg.phone. Response:< 10 minutes	onsite accessible 6-18, or answer phone. Resp.:<30m	accessible via servi- celine Response : < 8 working hrs
Integrity data: -min.stortime -max.lost time -restore time	5 years 4 hours 30 minutes	2 years 1 day 1 day	1 years 1 day 1 week
System mngmt:	onsite 6-22 5 day/week outside emerg.phone.	onsite 9-17 5 dy/week	4 days per month on site
Performance	guaranteed anticipating	guaranteed in normal circumstan- ces	no guarantee
Security:	high,formal C2 norm	formal	simple

Figure 14.7. Example application SLA definition

(e) A 'business class enhanced flexibility and security' level: the products and services are supplied on level 'd' but besides, even more extensive attention is paid to the aspect of security and reliability of data processing.

Example

Figure 14.7 shows the example of the Bosch machine works. The Bosch machine works in Gelsenkirchen employs 800 people and manufactures conveyor belts and other factory installations. The company is familiar with account management, project-orientated handling of orders often specifically made to customers' requests and has a number of supporting departments. The department account management, deals with all customer contacts. It also submits quotes and designs new machines. This department includes an engineering department. The projects department builds the designed machines. The Bosch company also includes a financial administration, secretarial offices, a personnel department and a legal department. Figure 14.7 shows that the Bosch company actually recognizes three types of operational processes that have to be supported. One has translated this support directly to the level on which one wants to have one's IT products and services supplied. Therefore there are three levels of delivery of IT products and services.

Monitoring an SLA

When implementing a service level agreement, this entails implementation of a number of procedures and agreements. These include, amongst other things, the tools to be used and the data to be collected, the meaning and notation of data being the most important consideration.

The data to be collected concerns data about all fields of the balanced score card. The financial data might come from a subscriptions administration but if one charges according to use, also from the operational systems. The operational data comes from, amongst others, the registrations of service level management, from the service desk, from configuration management, from change management and from problem management. The data concerning the state of affairs with regard to new products and services as ordered, originate from the progress data of innovation projects, whilst the customer perspective is usually measured indirectly by means of registering complaints, and directly by means of customer surveys.

Conditions for collecting measuring data for checking up on working in compliance with the agreements of the SLA's, are that one has a clear insight into the critical success factors in delivering the requested products and services and front- and back-office processes needed for this. One has to know who plays which part in all this and what this person's responsibilities are. That way, it is possible to arrive gradually at the right operating level. The set-up of the necessary processes for delivering the services and products, is a process that includes iterations. After a first implementation, adjustments take place on the basis of experiences that become clear by means of, amongst other things, measuring. These adjustments, aimed at arriving at a higher level of service, are manifold. An increase of the mean time between failures in the infrastructure usually leads to making adjustments to the hardware and software or to installing extra hardware. Measures for delivering new products quicker, usually regard the ensuring of up-to-date documentation of the IT facilities, taking care that software is developed methodically, that the maintenance is systematic and one uses well-trained staff.

Example

The availability of IT facilities may be defined as the time a configuration-item performs in conformity with the expectations. This availability can be expressed in

((planned service time-the downtime)/planned service time) $\times$ 100

This definition has some shortcomings. Firstly the resulting availability figure relates to a complete IT facility. This IT facility consists of parts that together form the facility. Furthermore, this number does not say anything about the exact moment the downtime occurs, nor about the number of times one is unable to work. That is to say, having just the IT facility at one's disposal does not necessarily mean that the organization is up and running again. Usually it takes a certain time to reach the standard production level after a break down.

A last matter concerns the length of time one measures for the SLA. A supply organization likes to measure for an availability figure during a certain time, for example three months or more. This enables them to correct a possible lower level of availability.

Example

The maintainability of IT facilities is defined as the effort needed for adjusting one or more configuration items. The costs for this can be charted. These expenses often depend on the product, the used change process and the knowledge and skills of the people.

CONTENTS OF SERVICE LEVEL AGREEMENTS

Contents

Service level agreements usually consist of a general part and a specific part that deals with the products and services specifically to be delivered to a certain group. In the general part the products and services to be delivered are specified, the contact persons, the general conditions and the exact escalation procedures. In the specific part the functionality of the products and services to be supplied are defined. Concerning the services to be delivered, service processes are often referred to. These may be ITIL service processes.

Dealing with SLA's for applications, demands that the demand organization knows what it wants and that the supply organization is aware of the consequences. Furthermore, the demand organization should have insight into the number of changes to the facilities per year and the frequency with which changes have to be implemented. Dealing with SLA's for the infrastructure demands of supply organizations that use the ITIL method, that they structure their services, protocol these and next control these quantitatively.

In conclusion

Davids and Faas (2003) provide a number of points of particular interest in dealing with contracts and service agreements in organizations. Their list of points is interesting because they try to anchor commitment in demand organizations (Figure 14.8). They do this for example by asking for performance declarations.

And where does this lead to (variation on Davids/Faas (2003):

1. For each contract draw up an SLA for delivery ➔ basis for communication

2. Reduce the gap between expectations and realization
   ➔ speak a language the demand organization understands,
   ➔ know who the contact persons are
   ➔ form per contract teams with those most involved

3. Document and evaluate the information of demand and supply-side.

4. Ask for performance declarations ➔ that requires everyone to consider the quality

5. Work with a contract authority on the demand-side and a service authority on the supply-side.

6. Work with SLA to be considered.

7. Take care of having the right tooling

8. Be aware of secundary services ➔ rapportages, service catalogues, consultation, improvement plans, etc

---

Figure 14.8. Points of particular attention in SLA's

QUESTIONS

1. What are service level agreements? What is the difference between a contract, a DAP dossier and a service level agreement? Illustrate your answer with two examples.
2. Who plays a role on the demand-side and who on the supply-side when working with contracts, service level agreements and DAP dossiers? Explain your answer by giving an example.
3. Which legal aspects are included in a contract and therefore also in a service level agreement as part of a contract? Explain your answer by giving an example.
4. Which phases does the conclusion of a contract include? Provide two points of particular interest for each phase when concluding a contract for IT facilities.
5. Give four reasons why the demand and four reasons why the supply organization should want to conclude service level agreements? Illustrate your answer by giving an example.
6. If we conclude that supply organizations supply generic and specific IT services, how do they ensure that they supply these generic services efficiently? What does this mean to a customer of their services? Illustrate your answer with an example.
7. What are critical success factors in working with service level agreements? Illustrate your answer with two examples. What is the effect of concluding service level agreements on the exploitation organization?
8. Why are service level agreements usually difficult to implement? Remember the processes these affect and the information that is needed for optimally interpreting a service level agreement. How did ABN AMRO enable itself to work with SLA's with regard to this issue?
9. Give the functional and the types of performance requirements for an IT product and an IT service. Give an example of each of these requirements.
10. How does one arrive at a service level agreement step by step? Give an example of each of these steps.
11. How does one track a standard service agreement? Illustrate your answer by giving two examples.
12. How are SLA's put together? What does this lead to in SLA's for applications and in SLA's for infrastructures? Illustrate your answer with two examples.

Chapter 15

Securing IT facilities (according to amongst others ISO 17799)

With the increasing impact of IT care for continuity, confidentiality and reliability of data processing also become statutory. For instance, the police have to comply with the security requirements they have set. The Superintendant performs annually an audit to see to what extent his force complies with these. The ING bank implements internally the guidelines of the ISO 17799 standard for Information security and attaches a Trusted Internal Party state to parts of the organization.

A retail chain discovered that, with regard to its IT facilities (logistics and cash registers) it demanded that after a complete breakdown of central storage and transactions, it should be entirely up and running again within 72 hours. During a test, with the help of a third party this was proven not to take 72 hours but over 96 hours. Following the test, the requirements were examined. This resulted in a new recovery strategy. In the new strategy the data in the in-house computer centre was permanently replicated on the computer centre of an external service provider. The result of this new strategy was that after a full breakdown, one was 100% up and running again within eight hours.

The considering of the continuity of IT facilities is starting to become top priority. At the start of the nineties, we thought it important to be able to repair after a disaster. That has changed vastly. The arrival of the internet, the extended enterprise, realizing what the effects of terrorism could be and even more basic, in the year 2003 the experience of a total blackout on the East Coast of the USA, has led to business continuity planning becoming a hot topic. 'Think the unthinkable' is the motto and one works out which scenarios are available to the in-house organization, in order to let IT breakdown go unnoticed. One wants to have all facilities at one's disposal, in spite of the breakdown and without delays and degradation of level. That is a must in the zero latency organization of today.

Contents of this chapter

Security is the subject of this chapter. Security of IT facilities is set up in order to guarantee the continuity of the IT facilities, in order to safeguard that data is handled confidentially and in order to contribute to working with reliable data. The chapter starts by outlining the environment in which the security of IT in organization takes place. This organization asks itself questions about the internal dealing with data. This organization has legal obligations and works with technologies that increasingly simplify access to and working with data. From the demand organization, demands are made to the security of IT facilities. This demand organization works with customers, suppliers and partners that communicate with the organization at any moment of the day and from any location in the world. The supply organization is in charge of making this happen safely. This is nowadays only possible when the security of IT is dealt with systematically.

When the demand for security is clear, it is exactly indicated what security of IT entails. To this purpose, the Bautz cube is used. Next is discussed, how organizations using the ISO 17799 guideline, can interpret their requirements with regard to security of IT facilities systematically. The lifecycle for filling in these requirements is outlined.

As soon as the framework and the interpretation are given, the requirements to continuity, confidentiality and reliability of data transaction are discussed in more detail. In this, levels of continuity are recognized and the efforts

needed for realizing these are discussed. Next the activities in the field of securing the confidentiality are defined. Here the ten principles of security are the
starting point. Next measures for increasing the reliability of data come up for
discussion.

In conclusion, the chapter discusses the certifying of the security organization and the transferring of risks to third parties by means of taking out
insurances.

SECURITY, REQUESTS OF THE DEMAND ORGANIZATION AND POSSIBLE ANSWERS FROM THE SUPPLY ORGANIZATION

The challenge

The increasing use of IT, results in general and business management of
organizations posing more and more questions, such as:

- who do I allow to perform which transactions on my IT facilities?
- how can I be sure that the person performing the transaction in reality also
  is the person that executes these transactions?
- is the data at my disposal reliable?
- do we comply with all legislation, such as for example those in the field
  of safeguarding personal privacy?
- does somebody steal goods or services from my organization? Do they for
  instance keep membership records on my website?
- does somebody destroy something on my IT facilities and how do they do
  it?

At the same time, more drastic IT solutions for security were introduced.
The use of passwords for example, was not satisfactory and chip cards with
continually changing passwords took their place. The use of biometrics started,
public key inscription (PKI) was introduced, the procedures were tightened and
one started to check compliance of these and so on and so forth.

The increase of external pressure, especially the rise of facilities to be
implemented for complying with duties as laid down in specific and generic legislation (see Figure 15.1) and the increased use of modern technology, added to the

A world of specific legislation:	Just for the continuity of IT:

Protection of Personal Data Act
Computer Crime Act
Telecommunication Act,Public Records Act
Government Information Act
Municipal Records database
Data Protection Act
Intelligence and Security Services Act
Security Screening Act
Electronic Signature Act
	- Banking and Insurance:
	  - Federal reserve, comptroller of the currency, SEC; and in
	   the Netherlands: DNB, AFM
	  - Securities Industry Association
	  - NASDAQ, NYSE, Graham-Leach-Billey Act (1999)
	  - Financial System and Major Operational Disruption
	   (Green paper, UK, February 2003)
	  - Financial service authority
	  - Australian Prudential Regulation (APRA, 2002)
	  - Basel Accord II (2001)
	- Healthcare and Drugs industries:
	  - HIPAA (USA, 1999) – CFR Part 45 (FDA)
	- Government in the USA and the Netherlands:
	  - Continuity of Operations Planning directive
	  - NIST Special publication 800-34: Contingency planning
	   guide for Information Technology Systems.
	  - Regultions Information Security Dutch Government
	- Utilities companies:
	  - NERC/FERC in the making, Telecommunication Act.
	- Industry-independent legislation:
	  - King Report in South-Africa (2002)
	  - Turnbull report (Institute of chartered accountants UK)
	  - Sarbanes Oxley Act (USA; 2002)
	  - Civil Contingencies Bill (UK)

Figure 15.1. Examples of external pressure for taking notice of security regarding IT facilities

need for switching to a more methodical approach of security. This is especially the case for so-called zero latency organizations that need IT facilities to be available 7 times 24 hours, in order to be able to operate. Yahoo, the portal, the asset formation advisor Charles Schwab and the internet auction house e-Bay, all discovered that dealing with security of IT facilities demands a methodical approach.

The policy of organizations like that in the field of security is not static; it has to be readjusted every year. The architecture resulting from this has to be certified. This architecture has a life expectancy of three to fifteen years. One has to train the organization for being able to use the measures that ensue from the architecture and have been implemented. This training has a half-life of three years. Anyway, time aspects do figure in security. A good example is the software for the permanent checking for viruses and worms within the organization. Nowadays it is better to update these continuously. Security of the IT facilities that optimise the everyday life in organizations, does therefore involve more and more dynamics. One has to 'think about the unthinkable', which is what the power failure on the East Coast of the USA taught us in 2003. For many organizations, this was the start for attaching priority to 'business continuity planning.'

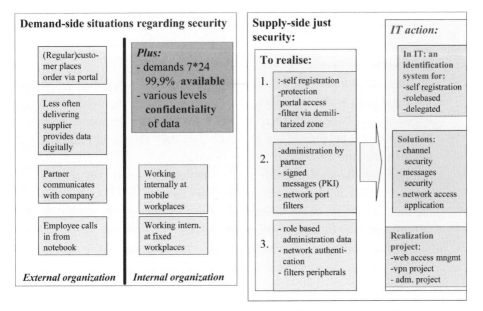

Figure 15.2. The requests of the demand organization, challenges for the supply organization

How requirements affect the supply organization

The necessity for a methodical approach can be explained with an example. In Figure 15.2 the challenges a demand organization comes across and the possible answers of the supply organization are represented in a diagram. Let us discuss this figure systematically. In this figure, we see that the demand organization has to deal with once-only customers and suppliers and with customers and suppliers with whom a more permanent relationship is maintained. Some have become partners in business. The organization and its partners are often a part of a whole that has become known as the 'extended enterprise.' An example of such an enterprise is Cisco, in which company the customers and suppliers have access to many internal databases in the Cisco organization. All parties approach the organization seven days a week 24 hours a day. All parties drop by in person, call on the phone or have contact through digital data exchange.

Types of contact

Once-only contacts enter the organization through the internet portal. In-house employees call in from outside. Partners communicate with the organization via a PKI possibility. Internally, the organization logs in using special chip cards. This mode of operating requires that one:

- has facilities for enabling once-only access;
- has facilities for dealing with employees' access. These may want to use *ID* cards both within the organization, as being able to log in from the outside through the public net. Once in it has to be decided which role they play, so that it becomes clear to which data they should have access and whether they are authorized to alter this data;
- has facilities for dealing with access involving partners. Customers can place an order with partners and partners can use the customer data of the demand organization. In that case, part of the care for reliability and the safeguarding of the confidentiality of data lies with the partners of the demand organization.

So, which facilities do demand such a mode of operating?

Consequences

In order to enable all these means of contact, one needs facilities for being able to identify parties and for determining their role. One needs technical solutions for checking incoming and outgoing messages, for protecting the access to the network and safeguarding the safe transport of data. When an organization does not have these at its disposal, projects are started for safe web access, for a safe virtual private network with partners and for configuring of the necessary procedures in the field of the administrative organization. This last project makes roles, responsibilities and modes of operating clear.

WORKING SYSTEMATICALLY AT SECURING OF IT FACILITIES

The Bautz model

A model for looking systematically at the security aspect is the Bautz cube (see Figure 15.3). This model provides three perspectives on the security

Bautz model:

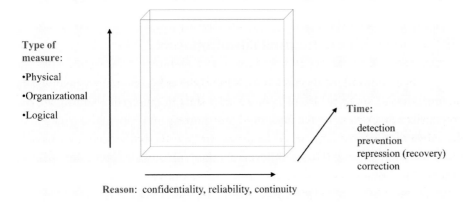

Figure 15.3. Looking at security systematically

aspect. These perspectives are: the reason for security, the type of measure to be taken and the moment in time that this measure is taken.

Let us start with the reasons for security. In principle one protects for ensuring the continuity of the use of IT, for limiting errors in storage, processing and transport of data to an absolute minimum and for safeguarding the confidentiality of the use of data.

Security measures can be physical, logical and organizational by nature. Physical measures are for instance the creation of extra water supplies in water-cooling and installation of computers in concrete rooms. Organizational measures are amongst other things, the division of the computer centre room into a section for printing, a section operations and a section where the computers are set up. For each section different requirements are applicable in order to gain access to these rooms. Another organizational measure is the introduction of segregation of function. Logical measures are the providing of passwords, the use of chip cards with changing passwords and considering single sign on.

These measures can be preventive by nature, corrective, detective and may repress violation, in which case these are repressive. Working with a double computer centre is an example of this. When one has such a centre at one's disposal, one can always immediately switch over. The incidents one protects oneself against are in 75% of all cases, actions of in-house employees and in 3% of the cases, actions of third parties. The chance of the cause being lightning, flooding, water damage, fire or any other natural cause, is around 20%. Of this 20%, half the damage is caused by flooding and the other half by fire.

Difference with the manual situation

In essence in the digital world, 80% of the work on security involves the organization of security. There is however a shift in emphasis. Nowadays, one emphasises on preventing the undesired transporting and copying of data and on the prevention of incidents in IT facilities. In these activities one does have to make use of electronic tools and has to use logging and electronic surveillance of network traffic. Before, the emphasis in the security of organizations used to be more on maintaining segregation of function and the performing of physical checks.

ISO 17799

Stiennon (2003) states that when looking at security most organizations will start from the best practices, as have been laid down in the ISO 17799 standard. In the European Union, this standard was copied into the Code for Information security of most National Standardization Institutes. This code is aimed at managers and employees responsible for setting-up, implementing and maintaining information security. The code consists of two parts. The first part is a management frame-work, which describes the measures to be taken by an organization. The second part describes the requirements, which third party organizations can use to certify that the processes in an organization or a used security product comply with a certain standard.

Management framework ISO 17799

The management framework distinguishes the ten most important areas of particular attention in the field of information security. For each of these fields it provides the objective, the basic set of standards and the activities an organization has to carry out for complying with the set standards. The ten most important areas of particular attention in the field of security in conformity with the code are:

1. The *security policy of an organization*: this indicates the target and the situation to aim for in terms of organization interests.
2. The *organization of the security*: this is where the security functions, the tasks to be performed within that function and the matching responsibilities are discussed. It also becomes clear how coherence in measures is achieved in this field and in which way and by whom agreements with third parties are concluded.
3. A *classification of and the management of capital equipment*: with regard to the objects it is defined which objects come under the security policy and who owns these objects. Apart from this, the classification of information is discussed.
4. Measures in the field of *personnel*: these measures discuss the training of the employees in this field, encouraging and checking of the desired behaviour and the security awareness, behaviour on the work floor, the policy with regard to hiring and appraising people and finally reacting to calls.
5. The measures in the field of *physical security and the environment* in IT facilities: this paragraph includes the security of and the infrastructure regarding canals, concrete built rooms etc., the controlled access at the gate, the physical security of the decentralized computers' and workplace facilities, the clean desk policy, attention for the power supply, the dealing with external data communication lines, the cooling and humidity levels of rooms, the protection of diskettes, tapes and documents.
6. *Computer and network management*: the operation procedures, the management of the technical security and the applicable responsibilities; considering and taking of anti virus measures; the handling of incidents and the rapportage on these; the protecting of e-mail, electronic data interchange, internet facilities and data.
7. *Access control*: the access control and authorization for the use of applications.
8. *Development and maintenance of applications and infrastructure*: these include the attention for security functionality and safe development and maintenance methods that result in (permanently) safe applications.
9. *Continuity planning*: this subject is about the emergency measures in case of disasters, the drawing up and managing of disaster recovery plans and taking care of adequate disaster recovery.

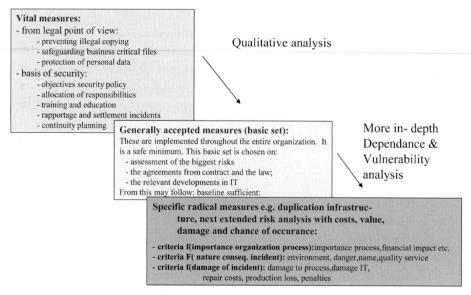

Figure 15.4. Levels of information security, implementation of ISO 17799

10. *Supervision*: taking care of observance of and checking on observance of legal and contractual rules, the security check on IT systems, performing of an IT audit and the execution of internal supervision tasks.

Levels of operating ISO 17799

In using the code, one can distinguish between the levels of measures that are found in this field. The code includes a minimum set, a basic set and possible specific measures. In Figure 15.4 these levels are shown. For getting from level 1, the statutory measures, to level 2 usually a qualitative analysis suffices. This analysis then results in a basic set of measures that are introduced in the entire organization. More radical measures require a more profound and also more quantitative analysis of possible expenses caused by failing security. One often performs a so-called dependence and vulnerability analysis. When taking the measures as advised on the basis of this analysis, one often operates systematically and from an architecture. In this the costs are weighed against the benefits. Whether measures are indeed taken, depends on the importance of the process, the nature and the consequences of the incident and the damage caused by the incident.

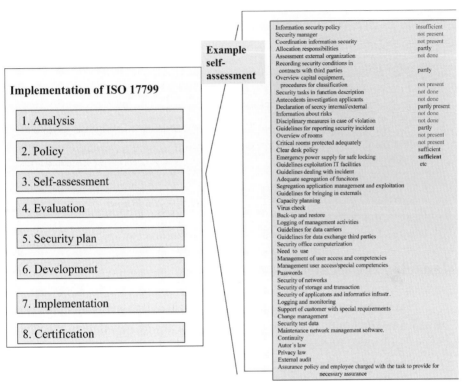

Figure 15.5. Implementation of ISO 17799, including self-assessment

Process of implementation ISO 17799

Figure 15.5 indicates in which steps an implementation of ISO 17799 in an organization can take place. First the business process and the business objects to be protected are analyzed. Next a security policy is drawn up and the organization checks how the current situation relates to the desired situation. This is called self-assessment. In Figure 15.5 it is also indicated which questions an organization asks itself at such an assessment. On the basis of the results of the self-assessment and the gap, discovered between the current and the according to the policy desired situation, a security plan is drawn up. This includes projects for changing the current situation. These projects lead to development of facilities and the implementation of these facilities. This also includes the implementation of an organization for managing security measures. After implementation of the measures an external party is asked to certify the state of the security.

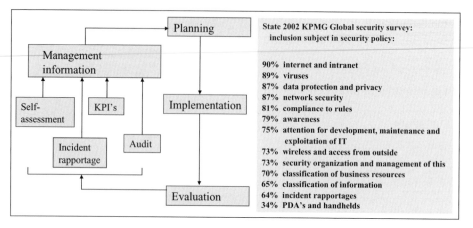

Figure 15.6. Security is a permanent process and there is still a lot to be done!

Managing the security

Dealing with security measures requires often that an organization is attentive 7 times 24 hours. An organization has to deal with new threats constantly and having to adjust the implemented measures. Figure 15.6 shows that for security, a management process of planning, implementing, checking and evaluating has to be configured. Parts of this process are the permanent monitoring of the situation on the network, having key performance indicators for services, working with incident reports and the execution of self-assessments by the management of the demand and of the supply organization.

The following proves that this is still a necessary process. In 2002, *KPMG* performed a worldwide customer survey to find out which objects in the field of security are important to organizations. From Figure 15.6 it is obvious that there are gaps with regard to classification, checking of rapportages and dealing with the latest resources.

Measures in more detail

Above we stated, that one uses security in order to ensure the continuity of the use of IT, to safeguard the confidentiality of data in using IT facilities and for limiting errors in storage, processing and transport of data to an absolute minimum. We will now discuss the measures that one can take in each of these fields in more detail.

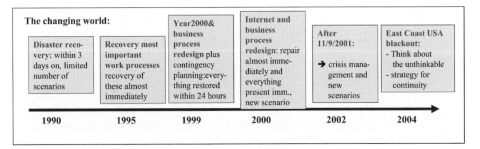

Figure 15.7. The changing requirements to business continuity management

APPROACHES OF CONTINUITY IN IT FACILITIES

Continuity

The ideas about continuity of IT facilities have changed considerably over the last ten years. This change took place step by step (see Figure 15.7). In 1990 the situation was often that an organization did have disaster recovery plans, which meant that one had all data at one's disposal again after a maximum number of days. Gradually one started to make higher demands. That started early on in the nineties, with the awareness that critical processes in banks and insurance companies were strongly IT dependent. This dependency was increased by the rise of internet and the awareness that denial of service could cost an organization millions of euros. The one-day breakdown of e-Bay and Yahoo caused by a denial of service on the 8th February 2002 cost each of these organizations several tens of millions of dollars in trade. In the year 2004, the situation has evolved in such a way that more and more organizations have decided to pay systematic attention to the effects of IT facilities on the continuity of their operational management. 'Thinking the unthinkable' has become the guiding principle. Nothing seems impossible anymore after the collapse of the *WTC* in New York on September 11th 2001 as a result of aeroplanes crashing into them and the blackout on the East Coast of the USA in 2003. In the zero latency organization of 2004, continuing to work without even noticing that somewhere IT facilities break down, has become pure preservation of life. Facilities have to be restored within two hours and all resources have to be available all at once. The Charles Schwab case proved that supply organizations could meet these requirements. Charles Schwab built—forced by bad publicity in the media as a result of a breakdown

Class:	For which products?	Service levels:
1. In the real time enter-prise	Applications, which link the organization with customers and partners. Support with direct impact on profit figures	planned 7*24 available 99.9% available (<45min/month down) recovery time < 2 hrs continue immediately on same point
2.	Applications that influence profit less directly, production chain	planned 6.75*24 hrs available 99.5% available (<3.5 hrs/month down) recovery time between 8-24 hrs maximum within 4 hrs all back on line
3.	The secundary processes, e.g. finances, personnel, archive.	planned 7 * 18 hrs available 99% available (<5.5 hrs/month) recovery time < 3 days maximum within 1 day all back on line
4.	Specific functions in departments	planned 6,5 * 24 hrs 98% available (<13,5 hrs/month) recovery time < 5 days maximum within 1 day all back on line

Figure 15.8. Levels of continuity of IT facilities (Mingay, 2003)

of a maximum of 15 minutes—an IT facility that has 99.999% availability. This building took several years and started in 2002.

Levels of continuity

Mingay (2003) has indicated that the zero latency organization, in other words the in real time operating organization of 2004, knows levels of continuity. In Figure 15.8 these are shown. Mingay (2003) distinguishes four levels, depending on the impact of the IT support. On the highest level a user does not notice the breakdown of the facility at all. One is online 7 times 24 hours, one is able to continue working as if nothing has happened and does not have to go without any of one's resources. On level 2 one has to deal with a 6.75 days per week operation. This is 99.5% available 24 hours a day. After a major incident, which amongst other thing destroys the processing facilities, within eight to twenty-four hours, one has all facilities at one's disposal again. That is how the levels 3 and 4 are defined in Figure 15.8. There is always a different percentage of availability; a different duration of the repair period and a different moment one is able to have all facilities at one's disposal again. Realizing these levels requires measures in the field of the infrastructure and the applications. In Figure 15.9 these measures can be seen. These measures amount to the following:

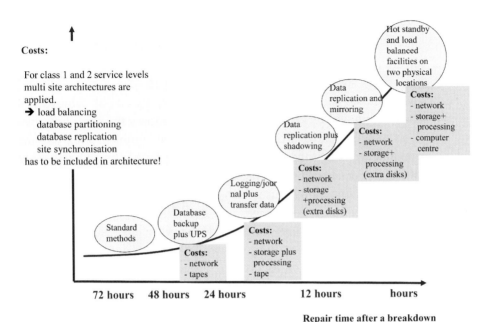

Figure 15.9. Step by step to other levels of continuity

(a) realizing a repair time after a major disaster—e.g. a fire in the computer centre—of less than 72 hours is possible using standard methods such as tape back-up and having a so-called empty shell present (that is to say, an empty room in which IT facilities can be installed). In this mode of operating, the transactions made after the last back-up do however get lost;

(b) a repair time within 24 hours after a major disaster—e.g. fire in the computer centre—can be realized with standard methods such as tape back-up and back-up of data in a disaster recovery centre. The data is transported to this centre on a daily basis. In this approach, the transactions completed after the last back-up are lost;

(c) repair time within 12 hours after a major disaster demands logging of transactions on the in-house computer centre plus providing transport of all data to a disaster recovery centre. In this case no data is lost. The last transactions that are not on the back-up are on the log;

(d) achieving repair times of less than 3 hours is possible using techniques like replication, shadowing and mirroring. Using shadowing it is possible to construct the old situation on the storage media from the stored data after a disk crash. Using mirroring all data is permanently double written.

For storage one often uses a SAN, a Storage Area Network. In a SAN all storage of data is concentrated. All transaction units have access to this SAN. If one sets up a double SAN and places these SAN's in two physically separated locations in different areas and if one replicates the data continuously, a high level of availability can be achieved. In this, one should reckon with the fact that during a fire one of the two SAN's should remain accessible. This could be a problem if one puts the computer centres in the same location. In the case of a fire, the senior fire officer decides in fact which persons are allowed to set foot in a location and he could possibly refuse access;

(e) two entirely equipped storage, processing and transport facilities, of which one acts as a hot stand-by for the other one. The storage and processing facilities are set up in two physically separated locations at sufficient distance from each other. The transport facilities have been executed in duplicate and are communicating along physically and geographically different lines with each other. One of the databases permanently updates the databases of the hot stand-by machine's.

In order to reach the levels (d) and (e) organizations therefore make use of multi site IT facilities. The data is permanently replicated and on site level synchronisation of data storage takes place. The databases have been split up in parts. In order to use the two sites efficiently, load balancing is often applied so that one site is not just hot stand-by for the other but both are hot stand-by for each other.

DEALING WITH CONFIDENTIALIT OF DATA WHEN USING IT FACILITIES

Positioning of confidentiality of data processing using IT

Safeguarding confidentiality of data when using IT facilities includes, according to Stiennon (2003) three activities, each with their own character. These activities are:

1. Activities aimed at *keeping 'the scoundrels out!'*. These activities are aimed at preventing IT facilities being broken into. These are occupied

with controlling all activities aimed at achieving a reduced vulnerability. This means possibly implementing certain procedures and modes of operating. One may also choose to use encryption.

Speaking in terms of ISO 17799, the phrase 'keep the scoundrels out' means that within this framework, a classification of capital equipment takes place and what the competencies of people should be is examined. On this basis, physical, logical and organizational measures are implemented and handed over to a managing organization. This manages the measures and amongst other things supervises compliance with the set rules.

The 'keep the scoundrels out' phrase usually includes the use of independent products. The products fit in with the security architecture as designed by the organization. The organization use encryption, firewalls, employs virus checkers etc.

2. Activities aimed at providing *'customers and suppliers with access in the correct manner.'* These activities on the one hand, aim at identity management and on the other hand, at taking care of secure communication. Identity management includes for example, maintenance of a user administration, the organizing of checks at access and the taking of measures in order to make sure a user really is who he says he is. This is known as authentication. When ensuring secured communication, remote access, communication between different sites, the exchange of data between applications and data exchange between users is enabled.

    Speaking in terms of ISO 17799, identity management requires a classification of capital equipment, the checking of roles and responsibilities of the employees, taking of physical, logical and organizational measures and the passing on of the management of these to a security organization. Ensuring secure communication implies on top of that, the taking of measures at development and maintenance of applications and taking care of access security.

    Providing 'customers and suppliers with access' in the correct manner, often boils down to taking measures on platform level. Access to facilities is often linked to a user administration. This administration registers use and also the configuration for enabling use of the facilities.

The data of the administration is often the basis for charging of the costs.

3. Activities aimed at *'keeping the enthusiasm for security alive.'* This denominator includes the execution of activities such as:

  - realization of a security policy;
  - set-up of a security organization and ensuring its continuity, as well as continuing development of the already implemented and possibly still necessary measures;
  - the allocation of roles and responsibilities to employees;
  - training of employees;
  - taking care of following up on security incidents;
  - taking care of physical security;
  - taking care of compliance with the rules and regulations, amongst other things, by performing audits;
  - advising on safety aspects in case of outsourcing.

Speaking in ISO 17799 terms, when keeping security alive, each part of the ISO 17799 standard emerges. Looking at security from this perspective is a task for the in-house management of the organization, possibly advised by a third party. The configuration and next certification of the in-house security can be an argument used when acquiring orders.

Points of departure when ensuring confidentiality

De Roos Lindgren et al. (2004) remarks that Saltzer and Schroeder in 1975 defined ten points of departure one could use when taking care of the protection of the confidentiality of data. In Figure 15.10 these points of departure are shown. These starting points are:

  - taking care of isolation of the problem. There is a channel, everyone has to pass through and this channel has the desired functionality. It carries out checks, it records etc.
  - the employment of a prudent security policy. It is better to be too careful when giving authorization than to be too generous;

Saltzer and Schroeder (1975)	**Application in network security by:**
	1. **Isolation:** exchange of data between internet and the external network only via the firewall
1. Isolation	2. **Safe defaults:** exchange of data between the internal network and internet only possible after permission.
2. Use safe defaults	
3. Completeness: no exceptions	3. **Completeness:** every visitor has to report in at the firewall
4. Open design	4. **Open design:** the architect hours of the firewall are known
5. Implement segregation of function	5. **Segregation of function:** the firewall is checked by someone other than the manager and is designed and tested by yet another person.
6. Limiting functionality	
7. Compartimentalization	6. **Limitation:** the firewall allows only strictly necessary services in.
8. Ergonomic	
9. Redundancy	7. **Compartments:** the internal network split into various domains.
10. Diversity	8. **Ergonomics:** the firewall cannot be opened by accident.
	9. **Redundancy:** the firewall consist of several components that can replace each other.
	10. **Diversity:** the firewall consists of several components that each realize the functionality of the firewall differently.

Figure 15.10. Points of departure when building an architecture for ensuring protection of the confidentiality of data (De Roos, 2004)

- preventing special situations as much as possible. Exceptions and special permissions have to be avoided as much as possible;
- the use of known, open designs. This means that experience has been gained with the design and the advantages and disadvantages of its application are known;
- the implementation of segregation of function in the organization of the security. Each of the activities designing, implementing, testing, managing and checking is in principle carried out by different people;
- there is no unnecessary functionality. A firewall or a chip card only has the necessary functions. There are no unnecessary trimmings. The design is simplicity itself;
- one makes use of compartmentalization. The IT facilities have been split up into areas. For each area different requirements are applicable.
- the facilities are easy to work with. These have been designed in such a manner; it is not too easy to create leaks. They are set up 'ergonomically secure';

–there is redundancy. In case of breakdown, another component takes over the tasks;

–there is diversity in measures. Optimal security is ensured in different ways. A mix of measures has been taken.

DEALING WITH THE RELIABILITY OF DATA IN USING IT

Reliability of data

The third reason for security is part of the care for the reliability of the data an organization works with. Ruts (2004) has listed which factors determine whether an organization runs more or less risk in this field. In Figure 15.11 these

---

Risks involving data, depend on:

A. **The industry:** banks,insurances hospitals and solicitor's offices have rules, how to deal with data

B. **The assets:** protection of built knowledge and reputation

C: **the departments:** HRM, sales, IT etc have access to informattion, one would rather keep indoors

D: **the employees:** depending on number and type that comes into contact with the information secrecy becomes more difficult

E. **The used techniques:** one can use various applications for gaining access. That increases the risk.

F. **Internet:** provides extra risk of distribution and access.

G. **Working in a so-called extended enterprise:** by sharing with partners one is also dependent on their security level

---

Figure 15.11. When does one run a greater risk in working with data? (Ruts, 2004)

factors are shown. Looking at these factors, one may conclude that organizations run increasingly more risk in having their data accessed unauthorized and maybe even modified. If an organization has not formulated and implemented an explicit policy in this field, many within an organization have access to vital data and are able to modify it. The access to this data becomes increasingly easier because organizations use IT on a large scale. Working in an 'extended enterprise,' an organization form in which one closely cooperates with partners and is often able to look at each other's files, also makes an organization dependent on the facilities that third parties have installed.

Ruts (2004) suggests finding out whether this situation is desirable and if not, an organization should be able to arrive at a more optimal handling of its data in a few steps. These steps are:

1. classifying data in classes, as free to distribute, internal only, top secret, do not print, do not forward and the defining of the following procedures per class of data;
2. the if necessary organizing of security of data per class. Each data can have three states. These states are:

   – the state 'sleep.' This is the phase in which data is stored. This storage may take place using encryption. With the use of digital rights management one can allow only certain functionaries access to this data.
   – the state 'in transit.' This is when data is transported over a network. One does have the possibility to encrypt data during transport. Next one may carry out check-ups to see how the transport of data takes place. One may look at the content and the protocols used for this transport.
   – the state 'in use.' For data with this state one can make sure that only authorized users can perform certain actions. To this purpose one may employ digital right management technology. With this technology one can recognize a user and supervise which actions he can undertake. The user can be given several different rights. The user may have copyright, they may have pasting rights, he may have storage rights, there may be validity data connected with the data; they might just have access at certain locations, they may have printing rights etc. etc.

3. the set-up of an audit policy. This includes for example the pro-active execution of log file analyses.

IN CASE ONE WANTS GUARANTEES OR WANTS TO TRANSFER RISKS TO A THIRD PARTY

The last part of the chapter discusses the certification of the security organization and the transfer of risks, against which an organization cannot always safeguard itself.

Certification of security measures

Taking security measures inspires confidence. Others are also allowed to know about this. As a consequence of this, certification of the security level was created. Certification provides an acknowledgement by third parties stating that the organization has a certain level of security. This can offer a commercial advantage. The fact is that customers sometimes do not take the risk of doing business with somebody else who has put less effort into security. Besides, it makes insurance covering the other risks in the field of security cheaper.

Certification in security takes two different shapes. On the one hand, one can certify the measures as taken within an organization. On the other hand, it is possible to certify certain products used in this field. In a certification the measures as taken are tested on the basis of a requirement. These requirements are the Code for Information security, which is derived from ISO 17799. Most governments use these Codes as a basis for testing their measures. In order to arrive at platform 3 of the code, one may use an automatic tool for performing a dependency and vulnerability analyses. Figure 15.12 shows how organizations can arrive at such a certification. On the basis of the applied security measures, the organization itself releases a declaration of conformity. This defines how security is approached and in which manner one complies with the recommendations of the code. This declaration is the basis for an audit by a third party organization, which then leads to certification.

Certification of products is often achieved by testing the product on its security aspects to the Common Criteria for IT security evaluation of the *ISO*. These common criteria include two elements. For one thing, these provide a number of functionality classes in the security field, for another these establish with which measure of certainty a product indeed has the functionality as reported. This certainty is found in a number of areas and in each of these areas it is present at a certain level (see Figure 15.12).

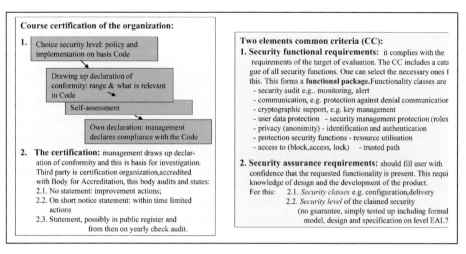

Figure 15.12. Certification of security process and of security products

Insurance

Finally, the risks one runs when using IT facilities, can be partly transferred to third parties. To this purpose, insurance is taken out. There are many possibilities in this field and insurance for larger organizations can if necessary be tailor made. In practice the choices are:

1. a general liability insurance, that covers the liability in law, the product liability and the professional liability;
2. a collective inventory insurance and a collective insurance against fraud. The first insurance covers damage caused by fire, storm, explosion, lightning and aircraft in the standard coverage and damage to the inventory and caused by burglary in the extended coverage. The second insurance covers the risk that money and/or monetary values have been embezzled or otherwise have become lost (for example as the result of computer fraud). Hacking is covered under this insurance if this involves illegality.

The above-mentioned insurances do not include damage caused by short circuits, incorrect operation, own fault, certain types of water damages, terrorism and vandalism. In case one also wishes to make the insurance compensate for the financial consequences of the occurrence of all these facts, special computer insurances have to be taken out. These insurances include all damages to do with computers that are not explicitly excluded. Besides, one can take out insurance for:

1. the extra cost involved in having work carried out elsewhere. This includes the costs for preventing, cancelling or reducing business stagnation. The remittance allows hiring extra computer time, payment of overtime, regress to manual transaction, and so on;
2. the costs for reconstruction of lost data carriers because of insured material damage. This insurance covers for example, the cost of wages and salaries of temporary workforce, the rent of a temporary computer room and the rent of computer time for reconstruction;
3. the damage suffered because of the breakdown of IT applications at a computer-controlled production process. This include the damage caused by unproductiveness or recurring expenses, loss of net profit and the costs made for restarting the organization after stoppage;
4. the claims of third parties in case one does not meet obligations as included in agreements or does not meet these satisfactorily, which cause damage for the contract partner.

QUESTIONS

1. The demand organization is forced to think about the security of its IT facilities. Within the organization it asks itself a number of questions, it becomes increasingly vulnerable because of the introduction of new IT facilities, it has to deal with special laws and has to implement general legislation. Give an example of each of these reasons for doing something about security.
2. Give an example why organizations need a methodical approach of security. Do this by looking at this from the demand-side and indicate to which facilities this should lead on the supply-side.
3. How could one look at the security aspect of IT facilities systematically? (Explain the Bautz model.) What are the shifts in emphasis in security, when comparing today's actions with those of around 1985? Illustrate your answer with an example.

4. What is ISO 17799? State the ten most important areas of particular attention of this standard and explain these.
5. How does one implement a standard like ISO 17799? Which levels of implementation can be distinguished? Why is this distinction made in levels? Which analysis is often performed before one proceeds to carry out the highest level of security? Why? Illustrate your answer by giving an example.
6. Which four levels of continuity does Mingay (2003) distinguish? How does one realize the levels 1 and 2? Illustrate your answer with an example.
7. Which three activities does Stiennon (2003) recognize for safeguarding the confidentiality of data? How do these activities reconcile with the ISO 17799 norm? What does it mean to realize these activities?
8. State at least six of the ten starting points when building an architecture for protection of data confidentiality according to Saltzer and Schroeder (1975). Give an application of each of the mentioned starting points.
9. Which three steps does Ruts (2004) propose for arriving at more attention for the reliability of data within organizations if necessary? Illustrate your answer with an example.
10. Which are the steps leading to an ISO 17799 implementation for the security of an organization? What does self-assessment entail? Illustrate your answer with an example.

Chapter 16

Standardization of content, process and product

For supporting customer relationship management we all chose the Siebel package and we still ended up with three different implementations in our organization. Set-up of a CRM competence centre would have prevented this. In that case we would have been able to support the divisions at an early stage. We would just have bought those licences for modules that are really necessary. We would not have become entangled in tailor made modules for functions, that in a release two years on are delivered as standard. Fortunately, the further evolution of technology, in this case the transition of the client-server version to the browser-based version makes this problem open to this discussion.

EDS estimates that in the year 2004, Fortune 100 companies have about 10,000 servers. The way things are going and without interference this will be 20,000 in five years. These all have Windows, Unix and/or Linux operating systems in a specific version. EDS itself annually has to deal with 200% growth of its internet

331

services. In 1997, it had to manage 21,000 servers. In 2003, this number was over 50,000. In 1997, these were used to run 10,000 applications. In 2003, this has increased to 40,000. The speed of change per application went in that same period from once a month to three times a week. If EDS ever wants to supply IT services, nowadays in the way that utility companies handle gas and electricity, EDS will have to take care of more standardization.

Upgrading of an application in the year 2004 happens as follows. First, a performance management application discovers that a critical service has a limited response. Next, a monitoring application identifies that this could be improved by adding more transaction capacity or more bandwidth or/and more storage capacity. Next, these are allocated by a third application and the new configuration is passed on to the monitoring, security and the cost charging application. At least five applications are this way involved in this upgrading. The data transfer between these applications has to be consistent. The processes have to take place within minutes instead of, as is the case, in days. This is the reason for DCML (Data Centre Mark up Language). DCML is a standard that enables sharing of information between the various management applications. DCML is applicable, regardless of the used platform.

Contents of this chapter

Coming to agreements at sufficient detail level, ensuring that one—in spite of vast growth—still can stay in control and being able to meet the requirements of tomorrow: standardization can assist in all this. The architecture of the IT facilities is often laid down in the standards to be used. This way, IT application is more controllable and new products and the accompanying services can be introduced to the market quicker.

This chapter is about standardization. It discusses the definition of standardization and the reasons for arriving at standardization of IT facilities to be applied and their matching services. It is made clear that as a result of the history, it is not always immediately possible to effectuate agreements on standardization but that it is in everybody's interest to work with standards. This is the reason for the existence of international standardization organizations and is also why governments enforce laws. The production and implementation of standards is a task for independent organizations, that do not have any personal interest in working in conformity with the set standards, which is illustrated using examples.

Next in this chapter, those areas that IT demand and IT supply organization have to deal with when considering standardization, come up for discussion. In the last part of this chapter, the possibilities for arriving at national and international standardization and the way in which this is achieved are discussed. In this framework we also go briefly into working with a specific type standard: open-source software.

WHAT ARE STANDARDS?

Definition

Jacobs (2000) defines the concept standard as: a publicly available specification of procedures, rules and requirements, issued by a legitimate and recognized authority. The standard is created by means of a voluntary, described process of consensus that results in a basis for agreement on what a specific system or a specific service should contain.

This definition of the concept implies that standards only provide the basis of a process or product. These do not include a functional elaboration of the product or process in an implementation. Furthermore, the definition means that standards are only set by recognized authorities. This makes it impossible for organizations such as the Open Group or the ASP forum to set standards. They can offer elaborations such as standards for processes and/or products to recognized organizations for standardization. This is how the M-3050 recommendation of the ITU came into being. The basis for this recommendation is the eTOM process model of the Telemanagement forum. Finally, the definition indicates that standards are set on the basis of consensus and are not enforced by law. The definition does not indicate whether a standard is of a more proactive nature, or is only then set when the market has already done its business and the standard is created more as a reaction to this.

Another definition of the concept standard is provided by Looijen (2002). He distinguishes between standards and norms. According to Looijen (2002) standards are recorded design requirements that objects of IT infrastructures and/or applications and/or organizations in the production environment have to comply with. Norms are the specifications as officially laid down by a standardization institute for products, modes of operation and the like that are eligible for application. The conclusion is that what Jacobs (2000) calls a standard, Looijen calls a norm. Next, we will use the concept standards in conformity with the definition as given by Looijen (2002). This definition also includes the norms. These standards are agreements and:

(a) agreements on products, processes and content can be entered into on various levels. One can do this on departmental, organizational, regional, national, European and international level. One can also do this at sector level, for various sectors and for all sectors in society;
(b) agreements can be complied with voluntarily, provided as guidelines and also de facto simply acted upon;
(c) entered agreements can furthermore react to a situation that has arisen. They may also pro-actively try to avoid certain situations arising.

Divisions of standards

Looking at standards this way, one may distinguish according to level of operating of a standard and to subject. With regard to level of operating one distinguishes de facto, organization wide, sector wide and de jure standards. An example of a de facto standard is MS-Office. An example of an organization wide agreement may be the agreement to use the ERP application SAP. Example of a sector wide standard may be the agreement to use the data centre mark-up language (DCML). DCML describes the relations between IT facilities and rules that are employed in their use. That makes it easier to exchange data. An example of a de jure standard is ANSI Cobol. Figure 16.1 shows international organizations that prepare or provide standards in the field of IT.

The division of standards according to subject of standardization distinguishes between standards for content, standards for products and standards for processes. In the field of content one may amongst other things, think of standards for service level agreements, plans, contracts etc. These are standards concerning text, image and speech data. With regard to products, these concern the guidelines for objects of the infrastructure, the applications and the services. With regard to processes, this usually concerns the set-up of IT organizations using methods such as BiSL, ASL, ISPL and ITIL. Regarding this type of standards,

Standardization organizations in the field of IT
e.g.:
(Jacobs, 2004)

ECTF	Enterprise Computer Telephony Forum
IETF	Internet Engineering Task Force
IAB	Internet Architecture Board
ISOC	Internet Society
IANA	Internet Assigned Numbers Authority
IRTF	Internet Research Task Force
IEEE	IEEE Communication Society
ITU	International Telecommunications Union
OMG	Object Management Group
TINA-C	Telecommunications Information Network Architecture Consortium
ACTS	Advanced Communications Technology and Services
MSAF	Multimedia Service Affiliates Forum
NMF	Network Management Forum
UMTS	UMTS Forum

Figure 16.1. Organizations, that provide and/or prepare internationals standards in the field
of IT

one must remember that in order to comply with standards in an organization does require the standard to indicate precisely how a product, context or process should be configured. This also involves questions about the method used for measuring products and their support.

VARIOUS PERSPECTIVES ON THE USE OF STANDARDS

Looking at standards from the top of an organization

Let us start with the organization itself. Why should it conform to standards? Organizations in the network economy come to agreements with each other. This is why divisions and individuals in the organization have to give up some breathing space. It costs innovative capacity. The organization as a whole should better itself from it. Dewan et al. (1995) discusses this issue. He states that organizations can take two points of view on standardization. From the first point of view, one defends the proposition that people themselves should choose the product or the service that suits their needs best. Our economic system does award ingenuity. On the other hand, from the perspective of the organization as a whole and in the year 2004 often from the perspective of a whole chain of organizations, it could be useful that those involved comply with set standardization agreements. In principle one should choose the same type of configuration items for their IT facilities; the collected data should take their departure from the same semantics, syntax and technical design and internally, organizations should use the same modes of operation for the same processes. This last mentioned point of view is used in this book, making the marginal comment that it is not always wise to stick 100% to an agreed standard. There could be valid reasons for diverging slightly from agreements.

Organizations have four reasons for choosing a large-scale standardization of processes and products. These are:

1. the *controllability*-criterion. Organizations want to be able to exchange data quickly and really want to use this without any further conversion. This is the reason for the advent of the DCML standard in computer centres. This is also the reason for an increasing use of IT in the exchange of information in chains of companies. One does not want to waste time on matching data;

2. the *effectiveness*-criterion. Organizations want to be able to compare themselves with others. Benchmarking helps improve these processes further;

3. the *efficiency*-criterion. By limiting diversity, one can conclude contracts with a larger procurement, one is able to have spare parts in stock if necessary, one has to proceed less to the conversion of symbols, can train more specifically, can introduce life-cycle management etc.;

4. the *innovation*-criterion. One is able to fit in new products and services more quickly and deliver new services around these. The whole fits in with an architecture, of which one can extend the functionality step by step and make this gradually comply with higher performance requirements.

In practice there is often a combination of reasons involved. Control of the diversity means that an organization uses less different products and/or less different modes of operation. This often results in the ability to build up and maintain knowledge on the used products and/or processes with less effort. People are employable in more departments because all departments use the same standards. Because exceptions hardly occur, less people are needed for arriving at the same level of availability, response time and 'mean time to repair.' The increase of interchange ability results in being able to repair different appliances using the same spare parts, having to deal with fewer suppliers and getting higher discounts. Finally the constructing of larger units from modules, means that one delimits divisions and agrees interfaces between various objects. By using standards for these interfaces IT objects of different suppliers can be connected.

From idea to implementation

Even though the implementation of rigid standardization might seem necessary for an organization, in practice the implementation of standards does not always go that smoothly. There are two reasons for this. The first reason lies in the current method of working of an organization. The second lies in their way of thinking. Organizations often already have products they work with and have set up their operating processes for using these products. By working with a product for a long period of time an optimal method of working has been imprinted (see Figure 16.2). Having to change this as a result of an agreement might take up some time. Apart from this, often in organizations a certain way of thinking is dominant. One has taken years to set up ITIL and arrived at an optimally set-up exploitation organization from the perspective of the supply organization. However by working within a chain and through the increasing use of standard applications, set-up of the demand does become more important.

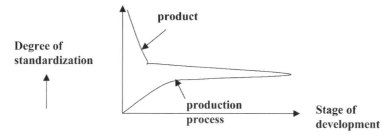

Figure 16.2. The use of a product is increasingly more rooted in the process (Utterback, 2003)

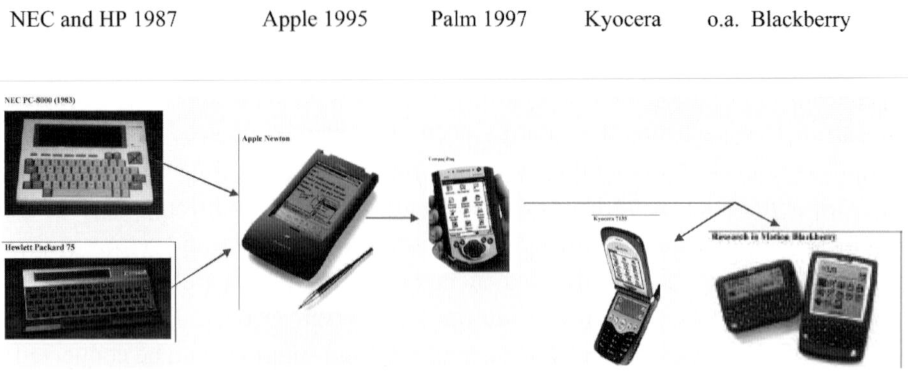
NEC and HP 1987
Apple 1995
Palm 1997
Kyocera
o.a. Blackberry
NEC PC-8000 (1983)
Apple Newton
Hewlett Packard 75

Figure 16.3. Dominant thinking and the choices made by organizations

That requires implementation of a method such as BiSL. The dominance of supply thinking has to be replaced by thinking from the demand.

Kaplan and Tripzas (2003) illustrated the influence of dominant thinking in organizations using the history of the Personal Digital Assistant (see Figure 16.3). The PDA was developed by the NEC company as a word processor. The HP company developed it from its calculator. The reason was that NEC mainly supplied to administrative organizations, whilst HP mainly had technicians for customers. Both parties targeted their product at replacing the personal computer. Both parties did not achieve their sales targets. This all changed in 1993 when it was realized that the PDA is an add-on. The rise of the Newton and the Palm made clear that PDA's are handy as diaries and for making notes in combination with a personal computer. This accelerated the development of the PDA. In the year 2004, we arrived at another crossroads.

This time, the question was whether one should produce a mobile telephone with keyboard (e.g. Nokia) or a PDA with keyboard and telephony facilities (the Blackberry). Dominant thinking and being stuck in a method of working, this way influenced the tempo of the implementation of standards.

Standards set by independent organizations

It is clear: standards are useful. But, who has to set them? In her book 'The politics of Innovation,' Deborah Spar (2003) studied the rise of various technologies and ascertained that when an invention is a great success, private companies after some time ask government bodies to break the monopoly of one or more suppliers. Having a dominant standard is valuable. One realizes vast profits and pushes others out of the market, as soon as everybody uses the product and agrees it to be a standard within their organization. This way, the supplier of the product gets the monopoly and is sooner or later confronted with measures instigated by the competition. This happened in the seventies in the mainframe market with the antitrust cases against the IBM company. It also happened in the eighties in the telecom sector with the division of ATT and in the nineties the examples are the antitrust cases against Microsoft.

Deborah Spar (2003) indicates that the demand for rules rises gradually. In Figure 16.4 this process is illustrated. Its course is as follows. First, technicians get a product on the market. Next, it is the turn of the salespeople. Through their sales they turn the product into a de facto standard. Those is the moment more and more people in government, in society, at the competition or at involved companies are saying that rules should be set. In practice it is often the competition that gives the final push in this direction and governments (antitrust) or the standardization institutes, implement the measures.

Standardization institutes often set these rules before the product is a real success. Government often do this later, when the product already has a market.

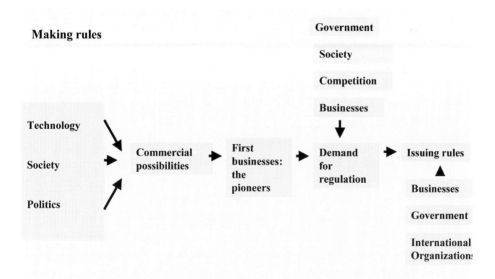

Figure 16.4. The process for arriving at making rules (D. Spar, 2003)

Effects of standards

The Center for Democracy and Technology (www.cdt.org) makes the importance of standards clear. By using examples it states that the setting of standards should not just be left to companies. It focusses its activities on the internet and the techniques needed for this. This internet was off old an environment where users had a lot of control over their communication. The users were able to surf the network freely and guarantees for privacy were in place. Seemingly small decisions of a technical nature changed this step by step. These small decisions are often made by private organizations such as the Internet Engineering Task Force (IETF). Let us present some examples of this. We distinguish here between:

(a) Recommendations made by relatively open working private organizations such as the World Wide Web consortium (W3C) and the Internet Engineering Task Force (IETF). Examples of decisions with a political dimension are:
   – The *W3C* recommendation on IP. In IP version 4 all users have a lot of anonymity and privacy because an address is not linked to a machine or user. IP version 6 deduced in the first version of the standard the address from the Ethernet card address of the user. As soon as one became aware of the consequences, a different address scheme was made for IP version 6, with better privacy protection.
   – The IETF decision on plugins. In 1999, the IETF was confronted with the possibility for including plug-ins for tapping in the internet. Ultimately it was decided by the IETF that building in plugins involved unacceptable security risks.

(b) Recommendations made by consortiums. An example of a decision as made in such a consortium that has impact on society is the standard for cable modems DOCSIS. This standard is strongly aimed at achieving fast traffic to the terminal station and slow traffic from the terminal station. By choosing this standard the use of internet for upstream traffic such as VoIP, Videoconferencing and peer-to-peer servers is limited.

(c) Products brought to the market by one single organization. Netscape developed cookie technology. It is convenient for the user but also enables others to track, which sites one visits and which adverts one sees.

The setting of standards has in the opinion of the Center for Democracy and Technology often a political dimension. That is the reason why government involvement or of a recognized independent international standardization body is desirable.

STANDARDS FOR CONTENT, PRODUCT AND PROCESS

Having established the reasons for using standards and it also has become clear that organizations should strive for compliance with international standards, set by independent standardization institutes such as ISO and ITU, we will discuss the setting of standards itself. In IT organizations standards can be set for content, for the product and for the process.

Dealing with content

IT organizations have content management on various levels. There is a level of text, speech and image. One also has a level of data. On the level of speech, text and image standard templates for contracts, service agreements, rapportages, project reports, the contents of audit trails etc are on the up. This data is stored more and more in content management applications. Figure 16.5 gives an example of the type of requirements such an application has to meet. With regard to data, the following are all up and coming: standards for indicating versions, for registration of use of facilities and for the data to be communicated etc. With regard to this, it is important to consider the semantics or the meaning of the data; notation (how many characters and which abbreviations) and its technical design (numeric, alphanumeric etc.). Usually there will also be standards in this field such as the ITU's TMN 3010 standards, the standards of the Dublin convention regarding context and the NNI standards for addresses.

Dealing with product standards

Standards for products concern the configuration items to be applied in in the building of the technical infrastructure, the informatics infrastructure and

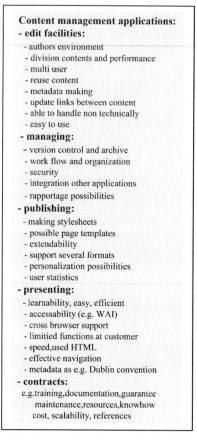

Figure 16.5. Points of particular attention when procuring a content management application

the applications. In Figure 16.6 an example applicable to such agreements within an organization is given.

Dealing with standards for processes

Standards with regard to method of working indicate how an organization deals with the procurement of goods and services, how it has set up its maintenance process and how the implementation of new versions is achieved. It is for instance possible to agree on using ISPL (information services procurement in the European Public sector) in certain fields for the procurement of goods, the

The technical infrastructure is standardized on:
- servers and storage mainframes, minis and personal computers.
  of supplier Y. On these servers the operating systems OS vs. 11.9,
  MOS version 7.3 and DOS version 9.2 run.
- for transport TCP/IP version 6.7 and network hardware of company K, version 9.3
- on the workplaces personal computers, see above
  As browser MS Explorer version 6.3 is used.

The informatics infrastructure has:
- with regard to the building environt as 3rd generation languages Cobol 1998,
  4th generation languages GG version 14.2 and regarding Object oriented
  environments the Microsoft line, version xx.3 is used.
- with regard to management tools, the tools of supplier
  YY for the service desk. Configuration management, security and
  funding, version 7.2 are applied.

With regard to applications:
- concerning the business processes YYY, version 8 is used.
- concerning individual work of MS Office 2004, version x;
- concerning communication the Siebel CRM packages version 14.2 and in-house
  Intranet and Extranet applications, version 15.6 are used.

Figure 16.6. Example of agreements on IT products

ITIL method in the exploitation process, ASL in the management of applications and PRINCE2 (projects in controlled environments) as a project management method.

Within an IT organization, standards for processes play a part in the field of exploitation management, functional management and application management. In functional management we may for example agree standards for the mode of operation, the forms to be used for change proposals and the bodies to be involved in the procedure. This approach results in fewer mistakes, clearer expectations of those involved and a transparent decision-making process. In application management standards usually concern the maintenance and development processes and/or the product/service.

Process standards for instance, discuss the procedures for dealing with change proposals and problem reports.

Apart from this, standards may be set for the documentation of products. An example of this is the WS8506 standard, which determined the set-up of system documentation for applications in various NATO armies for years. In exploitation the ITIL processes are often used as standards. These processes are elaborated in a manual, that support the operations process and a manual that describes the production planning and preparation process. The presence of these

In diagram:

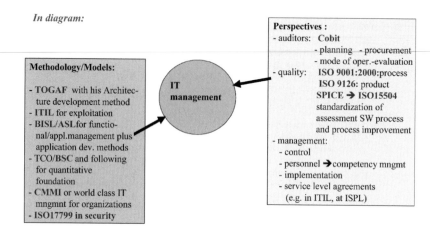

Perspectives :
- auditors: Cobit
          - planning - procurement
          - mode of oper.-evaluation
- quality: ISO 9001:2000:process
          ISO 9126: product
          SPICE → ISO15504
          standardization of
          assessment SW process
          and process improvement
- management:
  - control
  - personnel →competency mngmt
  - implementation
  - service level agreements
    (e.g. in ITIL, at ISPL)

Methodology/Models:

- TOGAF with his Architecture development method
- ITIL for exploitation
- BISL/ASL for functio-
  nal/appl.management plus
  application dev. methods
- TCO/BSC and following
  for quantitative
  foundation
- CMMI or world class IT
  mngmnt for organizations
- ISO17799 in security

IT management

Figure 16.7. Standards for set-up of processes as discussed in this book

standards leads to a shorter training period for staff, better dealing with calls, a raised availability of the use of IT and less work. Figure 16.7 provides an overview of the standards as discussed in this book used within an IT organization.

STANDARDS AND INDEPENDENT BODIES SUCH AS GOVERNMENTS AND INTERNATIONAL STANDARDIZATION ORGANIZATIONS

What can an international organization or a government do?

Agreements with regard to standardization can be drawn up about rules and measures in architecture. These may be drawn up by authorities and by international (standardization) institutes. These have impact on national and/or international level. Examples of measures that are observed internationally are the ISO and ITU standards, the rules of the world intellectual property organization (WIPO), the agreements in IETF context and granted patents. Agreements on national level are for example the standards of National standardization institutes and the legislation for protection of personal data. Agreements that result in measures with regard to architecture are available in different forms. If, for example we look at the internet, there are measures in the architecture with regard to:

(a) The *organization* of the internet. Internet works as follows. Somebody is looking for a page. This is not on the server of his internet service provider. Next, one goes to a root server. To start with there were only thirteen of these root servers early on in 2001. Ten of these were situated in the USA and three in Europe. One of these thirteen operated as a root server at a given moment. This server is managed by Network Solutions. One can ask oneself who is really in control of this server.

(b) The *infrastructure.* If we limit ourselves to the network protocol and the browser, then one finds that within the combination browser/protocol a mail application (SMTP), a hypertext application (http) and a file transport application (FTP) all operate. One may add other applications to these and take care of:

–*identification* and add possibilities for working with passwords, cookies and digital signatures. For this one may choose to use the possibilities of the server, like the program 'N2H2' does or to use the possibilities of the browser, like Microsoft does do.

–the managing of *'digital rights'*. This means that personal data is exchanged at contact and is decided whether one is authorized to take note of certain information.

(c) The *workplace.* The personal computer includes two types of architecture measures. The first type consists of filters such as Norton's internet security that obstructs access to certain things. The second type includes protection programmes that are brought in by third parties in the form of Trojan horses and automatically channel data to third parties. An example of this is the DIRT programme that is used in police circles and passes on which sites a person visits and what they do on these.

(d) The *product.* This means that measures are taken on the data carrier itself (cd rom, disk or tape) counteracting copying. These measures could for instances ensue from the Secure Digital Music initiative.

Application of international standards becomes increasingly important for organizations. These facilitate the working within chains because agreements made on the basis of these standards are accepted sooner. For this reason we briefly discuss two types of these standards, being the ISO standards and the recommendations of the IETF.

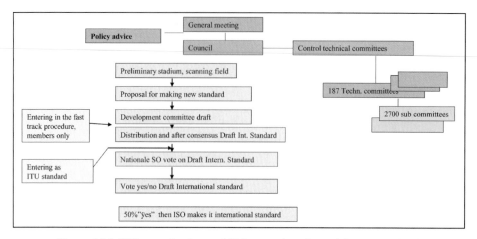

Figure 16.8. ISO organization and ISO procedure for arriving at standards

The ISO Procedure

The International Standards Organization (ISO) is a non-governmental federation of 120 national standardization institutes. The ISO includes full members, affiliate members and associated members. It came into existence in 1947 after a merger of IEC and the ISO. The IEC was founded in 1906 and set standards in the field of electro technology. The International Standards Organization was founded in 1927.

In Figure 16.8 the organization of the ISO and the procedure for arriving at an ISO standard is shown. This procedure for arriving from an idea to a standard takes a minimum of four years at the ISO. For members of the ISO the use of a fast track procedure was created. This procedure starts in the process of Figure 16.8 immediately at the Draft International Standard (DIS) phase. In this fast track, proposals are made that immediately move into the ratification phase. The ISO votes every six months. The standards that come into being usually are of a proactive nature.

The ISO is domiciled in Geneva. Eighty national standardization institutes are full members of the ISO. These include amongst others the Netherlands Standardization Institute (NNI), the Deutsche Industrie Standard (DIN), the American National Standards Institute (ANSI), the Japanese Institute for Standardization (JIS) and the Belgian Institute for Standardization (BSI). The

ISO has connections with over 400 other organizations, operating in the field of standardization. This also includes the ITU.

The ISO consists of around 200 technical commissions (TC) that each include sub commissions and working groups. One of the most important technical commissions, is the Joint TC1 of the ISO and the IEC that deals with all generic standards in the field of IT. The JTC1 carries out around 30% of all ISO activities. It has a permanent secretariat in New York. It is estimated, that worldwide around 1000 human years per year are spent on carrying out activities for the JTC1.

Recommendations of the IETF

In other organizations the procedure for arriving at a standard takes less time. Let us use the IETF as an example of this. The IETF is a division of the ISOC (the Internet Society) and an organization one can become a member of 150 organizations are members of the ISOC, as well as 16,000 individuals working and living in 180 countries.

Since 1991, the ISOC works on an international level on standards in the field of the internet. The ISOC is governed by a board of trustees and has the task to supervise development and the evolution of the internet and the social, political and technical issues this development entails. The ISOC appoints the members of the Internet Engineering Steering Group (ISEG). This group includes a research group for subjects in the field of internet in the long-term, the Internet Engineering Research Group (IERG) and an internet engineering task force (IETF) for true standardization. This task force includes working groups in various fields. These working groups work out a standard. The working groups come into being on the

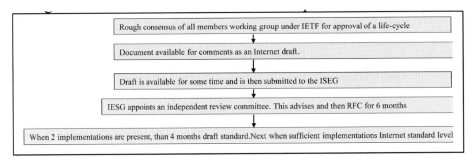

Figure 16.9. Procedure at the IETF for arriving at an IETF recommendation

initiative of the IETF area managers or on the initiative of third parties. Working groups work with e-mail. They provide a global consensus for the standard to be investigated. This next runs the course of the procedure as indicated in Figure 16.9.

Differences between the various standardization bodies

From the previous text, it emerges that various organizations are active in the field of standardization. Private organizations sometimes set a defacto standard. Examples of such de facto standards are the Adobe PDF standard and the Microsoft PowerPoint presentation standard. However, more often than not groups of organizations unite and come to collective agreements on standards. Sometimes they offer these to official standardization institutes. Examples of groups like these are the Open Group, the World Wide Web consortium (W3C), the ISOC and the Telemanagement forum. Finally, there are official standardization institutes such as ISO and ITU. These institutes often operate slower but their efforts do lead to very robust standards. All organizations have a more or less open procedure for arriving at agreements. However there are differences in the organizations and the individuals that may contribute to the concluding of these agreements.

From basic standard to implementation

Standards often provide a basic standard. For arriving at implementation of basic standards, a functional form has to be found. Basic standards describe the 'what.' They are often future-oriented, which means they sometimes have to be adjusted. Functional standards indicate a relationship within or between one or more basic standards. The functional standard selects possibilities within the basic standard. That way it forms a basis for the implementation of a function and for testing whether one complies with the basic standard.

The functional standard is often the reference when one wants to procure an object. Implementation of a basic standard and demonstration of this is needed for increasing the trust in the standard. One can show products that comply with a standard at trade fairs such as the CEBIT in Hanover (Germany). Governments can also promote the implementation of standards by asking for products and services that comply with a certain standard.

Slowly but surely the national standards disappear. European standards immediately become national standards. The European Union (EU) raises the European standard immediately to national standard if the national institutes have cooperated on development of the standard at European level. Furthermore, European standards are whenever possible the same as worldwide standards. The European industries are for this reason supported by the EU, to apply these standards immediately. Standards are, in the vision of the EU essential when one wants to build an infrastructure and organization-transgressing applications have to be implemented.

REMARKS ON OPEN SOURCE SOFTWARE

Open source software and standards

The chapter is concluded with some remarks on open source software. Open source software includes the operating system Linux, the personal productivity tool Star Office and the ERP application Compière. The sites www.freshmeat.net and www.sourceforge.net provide an overview of the main open source products and their stage of development.

Open source software is characterized by the fact that it is available for free. Because of this, open source software could very easily become a de facto standard. Use of open source software has advantages and disadvantages. In Figure 16.10 these have been listed. From the perspective of ensuring optimal quality

Advantages:

1. saving in costs: no licence costs
2. functionality easily accessible
3. choice of support
4. high quality product because way of development.
5. appeal because of openness
6. no upgrade duty
7. openness standards
8. customer participation

Disadvantages:

1. liability: no software package with licence and guarantee
2. high penetration at low visibility and limited awareness business community
3. limited trust management and no sales department: amateur image
4. often little user friendly
5. no roadmap for further development
6. risk of self support may lead to extra efforts for application management
7. specific knowledge needed for assessment product in advance

Figure 16.10. Advantages and disadvantages of the use of open source software

of services, the use of open software involves risks. These risks can be limited by providing answers to the following fourteen questions (Baten, 2004):

- how many users use this software?
- is the number of users increasing and if so by how many?
- how many people contribute to the development of the software?
- is there a release schedule for new versions and if so, what do these include?
- at what tempo do these new versions become available?
- how does the distribution process of versions of the software run and how is version verification organized?
- what is the architecture in which the software is developed and maintained?
- which other licences do I need for running the programs?
- what knowledge do I need of informatics infrastructure e-products as used by the program?
- who supports the software? Where are they located?
- are there any user forums for the software? And if so, where?
- do we have any basic knowledge of the product in the in-house organization?
- is the product supplied with documentation, what is its quality and is this documentation updated?
- is there any coordination of functionality of the software when working on a new version?

Answering these questions can lead to the conclusion, that dependency on the open source software in question is less desirable from the point of view of the performance requirements as stated, with regard to reliability, flexibility, quality and speed of delivery. The cost element of using open source software is often not the deciding performance requirement.

QUESTIONS

1. Which definition of the concept standard is used? Why? In which does this definition diverge from the Jacobs definition?

2. Standards can be categorized according to level of operating and design. Elaborate this categorization and give an example of each category.
3. Which four reasons are there for an organization to use standards? Illustrate each reason with an example.
4. Why is the implementation of an agreement on standardization not always that easy to implement for an organization? Discuss the use of the current processes and products as well as the effect of a dominant way of thinking.
5. Why should standards have to be set by independent organizations? Provide the views as given by Deborah Spar and the views of the Centre for Democracy and Technology (www.cdt.org). Illustrate your answer by giving three examples, including one of an antitrust case, one of a private standardization organization and one of a standard made by a private company.
6. On which levels do organizations have to pay attention to content? What does this mean for standardization? Illustrate your answer with an example of standardization of content on each of two different levels. What can content management applications contribute to this?
7. What can governments and international (standardization) institutes do in the field of standardization? Illustrate your answer by giving three examples. Each example should cover a separate category of measures.
8. What are the differences with regard to contents of standards, with regard to process and with regard to those involved, when looking at various standardization bodies such as for example ITU, ISO, IETF? Illustrate your answer with an example.
9. State at least five questions an organization should ask itself when it wants to make use of open source software. Which performance requirements for products does one weigh against each other when using open source software? What is often the outcome? Illustrate your answer with two examples.

Part 5

IT management tomorrow

Chapter 17

IT management en route to 2027 (a.o. ITIM)

In the age of the steam engine (1840), the activities that made use of the energy of this engine were placed close to this engine for reasons of efficiency. The layout of a plant was determined by the source of power. That all changed with the rise of electricity (1880). This meant that activities could be grouped together in such a manner one achieved an optimal flow of goods through the production process. It took a few decades before this new source of power was optimally used. In the year 2004 the networks enable us to think about an optimal positioning of IT tasks. What will this lead to?

Internet reduces transaction costs in markets. However, internet also reduces coordination costs within organizations, which makes control more efficient. According to Coase—a Nobel Prize winner in the field of economy—most inventions change the costs both in the organization, as well as the costs on the

355

market and—again according to Coase—in general those costs that result in better control, will also increase the size of the organization because one will insource more tasks.

Two views are dominant in the world of IT. Should IT facilities be seen as a utility or as an option for investment that should be controlled through portfolio management? The utility function becomes possible because of, amongst other things, the rise of grid computing, web services and self-healing technical infrastructures. It states that for every organization, computer facilities have to be available that comply with the set functional and performance requirements. The view that IT is an option for investment results in IT being controlled as such and applies portfolio management on IT tasks and projects.

Jeffery et al. (2004) investigated to what extent organizations on the highest level organized the control of the demand for IT. This is also called IT portfolio management. In a survey concerning portfolio management, to which he had answers from 130 respondents of American organizations with an average turnover of 8 billion dollar and an average annual IT expenditure of 2.9% of that sum, he discovered the following. 41% of the large organizations have no central overview of running IT projects. 46% has gaps in the description of their IT objects. 47% is unable to track their IT projects centrally. 57% does not have any criteria for determining whether a project is a success and 68% does not work out, whether the ex ante predicted advantages have been achieved ex post.

Contents of this chapter

New technology enables different organization forms. Coase stated this in his transaction theory. For IT (service) management this means that locations of tasks become discussable, that looking at IT supply is proposed as procurement of utilities and in general the demand for control of IT as an investment opportunity becomes topical.

This chapter discusses IT management in the years to come. Parallels are drawn with the experiences in physical transport, in information transport and in the energy sector. It is ascertained that IT does have elements of a utility. More than 60% of all IT costs are costs made for all employees of the organization. In that case, use of IT does work de facto as a utility. Furthermore, many organizations have become that IT dependent, that supplying of IT facilities should be just as reliable as supplying a utility.

From the experiences in the transport and the energy sector, one can learn that in each of these sectors one tries to control the supply with the demand. For this reason, one makes a distinction in each sector between the present infrastructure and the products and services to be delivered on this infrastructure. One sets up demand organizations. One sets up supply organizations. At the same time, the infrastructure facility is often placed under public control that is, if it was not already or becomes a public company.

Next, the view that states that IT facilities should be offered as a utility is discussed. This way of thinking makes requirements on the technology. It does, amongst other things, require more mature web services, large-scale application of self-healing IT facilities and being able to make easy use of grid computing.

Next to this view there is another view, which sees IT management as the controlling of options. An organization or chain of organizations controls a portfolio of line and project tasks. Various levels of IT portfolio management are explained. With regard to this it is stated, that in this way of thinking requirements are made to the dealing with sourcing and the caring for knowing and forgetting knowledge. At the same time, the attention for projects that ensure reliable infrastructure facilities should not be forgotten.

The chapter ends by outlining the route that IT management will possibly take over the next years. The field IT management will encounter administrative developments. It will have to choose its way within the technical possibilities as provided. However, an organization will have to be constantly aware that IT application is needed and therefore warrants the price that has to be paid.

IT DIFFERENT FROM OTHER INFRASTRUCTURE SERVICES, SUCH AS TRANSPORT, TELECOMMUNICATION AND ENERGY?

Parallels

Infrastructure facilities have been around since time immemorial. We have learned to organize these. Transport of goods has been done for centuries. Automatic transport of information has been known since the invention of telegraph in the nineteenth century. At the same time, during the industrial revolution one learned to work with new power sources. In the year 2004, one can therefore look back on developments in sectors that have yielded reliable infrastructures, as well as options for the organization of those infrastructures for society. If one sees parallel developments here, it is likely that these developments will also take place within the infrastructure facilities in the field of IT. To discover these parallels we shall examine the developments in the railways sector, the telecommunications sector and the energy sector in a specific country. This country is the Netherlands.

Physical transport

In the Netherlands of old, a lot is invested in physical transport. The Netherlands is a trading nation. In the centuries preceding the nineteenth century, one used the waterways that were everywhere for physical transport. Private companies used these and utilized towing barges for providing transport services. In the nineteenth century the railways undercut these towing barge companies. To this purpose, a railway service was set up next to the towing barge service. Private companies did this. The railways then undercut the towing barges using their speed and higher degree of comfort.

Next, cities wanted to be connected to the growing railway network. However, nationwide coverage by the railways was only possible with the help of the State. The investments were huge and the business case was not a positive one for all lines. Around 1860 the State got on board and the State railways were created. These operated state railways. Apart from those, there were also private railways. In order to prevent total chaos, the State soon enforced a certain degree of standardization. This standardization resulted in market organization and that is how, just the State railways survived.

The State railways had to deal with new technology such as diesel engines and signalling equipment. This enabled faster and safer use of the railways. At the same time they had to defy the competition of bus and car. Towards the end of the twentieth century, this resulted in a utility that operates fast and relatively reliable. For achieving more efficiency and faster introduction of innovations, it was then at managerial level decided to divide the State railway company. Two organizations were created, one that manages the 'rails' and another one that uses the 'rails.'

Information transport

This same division between the infrastructure itself and the use of the infrastructure came into being in the field of the transport of information at the end of the twentieth century. The history of this transport in the Netherlands has many parallels with the history of the railways. The transport of information using telegraph as a professional activity, originated in the first half of the nineteenth century. Private companies that often also operated a railway line did this. The telegraph poles were set up along the rail track. Telegraph was partly used for indicating the approach of a train. The situation changed in 1852. In order to connect the telegraph networks of the Netherlands to those of Prussia, the kingdom of Prussia demanded that the organization that managed the telegraph facility became a state company. That is how the state company for telegraphy came into being. This state company at a later stage took over the delivery of the post and the care for telephony, which is how the state company for Post, Telegraph and Telephone was created. This gradually ensured a nationwide telecommunications infrastructure.

This state company was privatised at the end of the twentieth century. In this, a distinction was made between the infrastructure and the services. The infrastructure is still managed by the old company. New telecommunication companies are allowed to use this for supplying their services at cost price. A new public body ensures that competition in telecommunications can run according to market principles.

Division of infrastructure and services, which creates new supply organizations, has caused the telecommunication sector to explode, especially in the mobile telephone communications. In the last decade of the twentieth century there was great expansion in the demand for services.

The energy sector

The procedure in the energy sector is not the same as that in the transport and the telecommunication sector. This sector of old, has a large degree of multiformity in sources of energy. One has a choice between energy from gas, oil, timber, coal and hydropower; as well as nuclear energy and solar energy. This multiformity in sources has its repercussions on the market of energy providers. In this market, public utility enterprises and private companies operate side by side. Besides there is public influence. The importance of energy for our society does demand some degree of regulation. This regulation results in amongst other things, the granting of concessions for extraction of energy, public influence on the price-fixing with the suppliers and in some areas in public influence on the distribution network. In the Netherlands for instance, the government organization Tennet controls the network that takes care of delivering electricity from suppliers to clients. In the year 2004, the energy sector has been organized in such a way that a demand organization can shop nationwide in order to fulfil its energy demand. This means that one becomes a customer with a distribution company. This company procures its electricity from a production company. Delivery takes place through, amongst others things, the network managed by Tennet.

THE PARALLELS AND THE LESSONS

IT as well?

In physical transport, in information transport and in energy there is a division of organizations into organizations that take care of infrastructure facilities and organizations that use the infrastructures for delivering their services and/or products. Firstly, one wants to enable control for the supply from the demand. One expects this to result in an optimal development of this demand. The model is the same in every sector. The infrastructure is put under public influence or public supervision. Various types of supply organizations are set up and all start to operate nationally and/or internationally.

The impact on IT

It is not so far fetched that these developments will also occur in the IT sector. Figure 17.1 shows that:

(a) one arrives at *division of facilities* in the IT sector. This book makes a distinction between infrastructure and application objects. Apart from this, it recognizes tasks at the supply and tasks at the demand-side. At the demand-side functional management is placed and at the supply-side

1. **Divide:** IT facilities include products and services:
  1.1. products ➔ infra and applications on the infrastructure
  1.2. services ➔ organization demand-side = functional management
  ➔ organization supply-side = application management and
  exploitation
  Often utility, sometimes sector-specific, chain or organization.

2. Many types of organizations in all sizes ➔ points of attention:
  1. establishing priorities 2. knowledge 3. innovations
  4. organization 5. methods 6.organizational support

  ➔ **looking from demand** at projects and line organization
  ➔ **portfolio** of projects te be managed.

3. Increasing use of networks will put **infrastructure largely under government control**: licences, vulnerability analyses, legislation etc

➔ *rise of strongly professional IT control. And what is professional? =*
  f(organization or chains of organizations or sector)

Figure 17.1. Parallels in IT

exploitation and application management. With regard to the objects, a distinction is made between objects where a large degree of standardization is possible—such as the objects of the technical infrastructure—and objects where this is possible to a lesser degree. These last-mentioned objects include applications that provide organizations with a strategic advantage. Using this division, one may also distinguish between services that are strongly capital intensive and services that are more labour intensive; in services where the location of delivery is of importance and in services where this is less important. Working with all these divisions, it becomes clear that within the IT utilities can be recognized apart from specific facilities. The specific facilities can be made for one single organization, for one single chain of organizations or for one or more sectors.

(b) organizations increasingly look at the necessary IT facilities **from the demand**. In order to provide for these, organizations carry out tasks by making projects and by working within the organization. These tasks can be looked upon as a portfolio of activities. For *controlling this portfolio* one has to establish priorities and decide on:
  – innovations in the IT field;
  – the organization of the IT facilities;

–the necessary skill for carrying out the work;

–the methods to be used;

in addition to which, there must be both internal and external organizational support for these decisions.

(c) with the rise of inter-organizational networks, the society as a whole becomes increasingly dependent on reliable IT facilities. This results without a doubt in **more regulation, more control and more monitoring by government authorities**. This is evident in licences for networks, in the publishing of vulnerability studies, in new legislation etc.

An utility function will also be recognized within IT and increasingly a more professional allocation of tasks will take place. This demands the set-up of a demand organization. In clustering the demand and making demand link to supply, professional criteria will be used. In the long-term, the application of IT should contribute to the objectives of an organization. IT contributes to these as IT application enables more efficient or effective working. With IT one is also able to support the production of new products and/or services. And finally by application of IT an organization can improve control of its organization or the chain of organizations, in which it is part of.

Not every contribution IT application makes to organizations can be assessed that well in advance on its financial proceeds. Ex post, it is also not always possible to translate the proceeds in financial terms. This is the reason why one often speaks of the value of IT, instead of proceeds expressed in monetary values.

Shifts in emphasis in IT

Moschella (1997, see Willcox et al.) has listed these changes in the thinking about IT. In doing this, he distinguished four periods. These periods are (see Figure 17.2):

1. the period of the system-focussed thinking (1964–1981). In this period the supply organization took the lead. It prescribed what the possibilities were. Support using IT meant in fact support using mainframes. The law of Grosch, that states that one gets four times as much capacity by spending twice as much money, supported this mode of working;

Subject:	System-oriented 1964-1981	Personal computer 1981-1994	Network-oriented 1994-2005	Content-oriented 2005-?
Who?	Organization	Professional	Consumer	Individual
Technology	Transistor	Microprocessor	Bandwidth	Application
Principle:	**Grosch:** 4x more power at 2x the price	**Moore:** price/performance doubles every two years	**Metcalfe:** costs per extra node linear, value exponential	The more **information intensive** the more exponential the change
Supply:	proprietary	standard products	value added services	customer specific services
Focus:	computer centre	pc-network	public networks	virtual working
Leaders:	computer suppliers	suppliers of components	telecommunication companies	content suppliers
Focus of the demand:	efficiency	productivity	providing service	working within a network: virtual

Figure 17.2. Shifts in emphasis over the years

2. the period in which the professional is provided with IT facilities (1981–1994). The personal computer comes into fashion. The law of Grosch is replaced by that of Moore. This law states that the price/performance of microprocessors doubles every two years;

3. the network-focussed period (1994–2005). In this period the consumers occupy centre stage. They get increasingly more new services at their disposal. The law of Moore is replaced by the law of Metcalfe. This states that the costs for an extra node in a network increases linear to the number of nodes. Parallel to this, the value of the network as a whole goes up exponential because of the addition of a node.

4. the period in which not the technique itself but what one uses it for is at centre stage: content is the magic word (from 2005). In this period the possibilities for executing tasks differently by using IT are the central point. The more information-intensive the processes in an organization are, the larger the potential changes in modes of operation are.

Figure 17.2 shows these shifts. The movement over the years from technique to content becomes clear. Closely related to this is a trend for looking at IT facilities as being utilities, apart from the trend for thinking more and more from the demand for IT and the value the application of IT has to an organization. It also becomes clear that this value often ex ante or ex post cannot be appreciated in money. Top down control of the portfolio will be done less on money than on the added value of the application of IT for the organization, the chain of organizations or for a community.

TWO VIEWS ON DEMAND AND SUPPLY OF IT: THE UTILITY VIEW AND THE PORTFOLIO VIEW

The trends cause the further investigation of both views on the demand for and the supply of IT facilities.

Utility computing departs from the demand organization, getting IT application that complies with the functional and performance requirements it has set. The demand organization charges this IT application according to the use one makes of it. The supply organization(s) on-charge the costs for developing and managing services in the use of the provided services.

IT portfolio management implies that the demand organization regards the application of IT as a portfolio of projects and line tasks. Periodically a budget has to be reserved for each task. At every reservation, a task or a project can be reconsidered. Portfolio management can be introduced at every level in an organization. For a project or task, each way of financing the costs may be applicable.

Next, both views on application and control of IT will be examined further, starting with the view that IT can be controlled as a utility.

LOOKING AT IT FACILITIES AS UTILITIES

Utility computing

Many companies have their own definition of utility computing. Figure 17.3 compares these definitions. The figure shows that utility computing depending on which organization one works with, may amount to:

1. the supply and on-charge of the demanded IT facilities (infrastructures, applications and organization) according to use;

Utility computing: each one has its own term!	
- CA	Managing On-demand Computing
- IBM	On demand computing
- HP	Adaptive enterprise
- SUN	N1 Architecture
- Microsoft	Dynamic Systems Initiative
- Dell	Scale out
- Veritas	Utility Conputing
- EDS	MyCOE (Consistent Office)
- EMC	Business service management
- Gartner	Real Time Infrastructure
- Forrester	Organic IT Computing
- Giga	On demand
- Metagroup	Adaptive Organization
- Managed Objects	Business Service Management
- Mercury Interactive	Business Process Optimization
Also: Agile infrastructure	

Figure 17.3. What's in a name? Many expressions refer to utility computing

2. the supply of IT management services (also known as managed operations);
3. the supply and on-charge of transport facilities according to use;
4. the supply and on-charge of storage services according to use;
5. the supply and on-charge of processing services according to use.

The central issue is that the demand determines the use and one pays for a service. The demand organization is allowed a large degree of flexibility. When examining these definitions it becomes clear that utility computing in practice, often concerns the supply of infrastructure services.

Ross et al. (2003) states that utility computing defined as supplying and on-charge of the demanded IT facilities accordingly, becomes more and more a reality. They also find that the technology needed for utility computing is becoming more mature. Grid computing enables the shared use of technical infrastructures. The progress in autonomous computer technology produces self-healing IT facilities, which makes it possible to realize an increased reliability of IT facilities. Finally, standardization of web services and web technology makes it easier to link applications.

Result of the rise of utility computing

Ross et al. (2003) also remarks that utility computing may lead to a different focus of the demand organization. Utility computing can provide the demand organization with more flexibility of operating. However, this flexibility comes at a cost. The risk profile of the IT application changes. Utility computing entails handling the IT organization differently. Application of utility computing demands that the demand organization has a certain degree of standardization with regard to operating process and used IT products. Application of utility computing requires measuring of the use of IT facilities and coming to agreements with the supply organization(s) with regard to this. Application of utility computing may lead to an organization:

(a) running a *strategic risk*. It is more difficult to compete on a business process if the competition can hire the very same IT support. Yet, maintaining an operating process that is not a core activity may lead to waste and lack of focus.
(b) that runs a *transition risk*. One has to adjust one's operating processes to the products and services that are delivered;
(c) runs *technical risk*. One introduces standard interfaces between facilities. These standards have to be implementable.

Ross et al. therefore arrives at the conclusion that especially those organizations that have a need for flexibility, benefit from utility computing. In order to make use of utility computing successfully, these organizations clearly have to manage the risks they might run. Utility computing requires a clear organization of the demand, a transparent mode of operating and reliable measurement of IT service provision. Organizations that wish to apply utility computing have to be able to handle a certain granularity of their IT services. This granularity is only then possible, when one has a clear architecture for the in-house IT facilities at one's disposal.

Utility computing and the theme of this book

The demands that are made on the use of utility computing are the backbone of the theory as discussed in this book. In Figure 17.4 this theory is

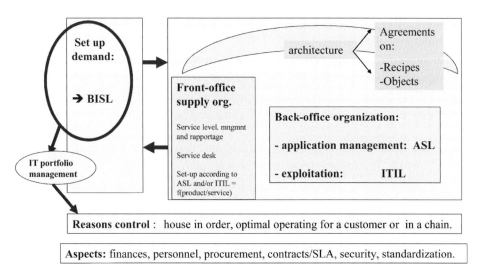

Figure 17.4. The demands on utility computing and the theory of IT management

shown in a diagram. The diagram indicates that optimum use of IT requires the demand for and the supply of IT to be clearly organized. This way one can control the application of IT and clearly motivate. The use of IT becomes transparent. It is clear whether the application of IT helps to carry out internal tasks (house on order) optimally, whether it facilitates activities in a chain of organizations or whether the reason for using IT is that it becomes easier for customers to use the services and products of the organization. In order to arrive at the use of IT one establishes priorities. When weighing these up, one will often have to deal with financial, personnel, procurement and other aspects of the tasks and/or projects in question. Establishing priorities of IT application is done similar to the choosing within a portfolio. Flexible application of IT finally does demand that, in controlling IT one departs from an architecture for the IT facilities.

CONTROLLING IT AS A PORTFOLIO OF LINE TASKS AND PROJECTS

IT portfolio management

The second view on functioning of the demand, states that the demand organization controls the use of IT as a portfolio of line tasks and projects.

Jeffery et al. (2004) investigated whether and how this mode of controlling is implemented in organizations. Jeffery et al. arrives at the conclusion that organizations can control their IT portfolio on a number of levels. On the basis of *empirical* research into 130 organizations with an annual turnover of over eight billion dollars and an average expenditure on IT of 220 million dollars per year, they distinguish four levels of IT control. These levels are:

1. ad hoc or *reactive* control. This means that there is now central control of IT. The organization decides at its own discretion;
2. one *is aware,* how and where IT is applied. On central level all information on IT line tasks, IT projects and their progress is known;
3. one *controls* the application of IT. In this case there are well-defined procedures for screening and ranking IT tasks and projects. Financial and non-financial methods are applied. The demand and supply organization periodically looks at alignment of the application of IT with the targets of the organization;
4. *the business determines* the application of IT and ensures that this is in line with the targets of the organization. There are frequent reviews for discussing the costs of the application of IT and its proceeds. The portfolio is also weighed up like this. The IT application is tracked along its entire cycle.

Figure 17.5 shows this empiric classification by Jefferey (2004). Furthermore Jeffery et al. (2004) remark that IT portfolio management requires that one organizes a decision process. By this, they mean the providing of rules for informing on IT tasks and projects; having the opportunity for achieving adjustment of a portfolio; clarifying the way decisions are made about the portfolio; the actual deciding on the portfolio and the announcing of and checking on the compliance with these decisions.

The ITIM model of the general accounting office

A more limited view on IT portfolio management emerges from the ITIM, the IT Investment Model of the General Accounting Office of the government of the USA. The General Accounting Office set up a theoretic model that indicates on which level organizations decide on their investments in IT. The purpose of this model is to contribute to organizations looking at IT as an investment option and decide on the application of IT as a portfolio of invest-

Stage:	One knows what one is doing	Controlled	Synchronization with business
Standardization	The objects are welldefined and documented	IT portfolio divided in types projects, e.g. house in order, facilitate customer etc.	
Centralization	All projects centrally storedand updated.		Use of supporting applicationsin portfolio management Real time updates on portfolio.
Organization of the demand		Well defined procedure for screening and ranking:	
Financial criteria		Use of financial methods like Net Present Value, ROI and Internal Rate of return (IRR)	
Alignment with strategy:		Annual reviews between demand and supply for discussing IT alignment	Frequent reviews between demand and supply for link with strategy (monthly)
Active control of portfolio			Discussing costs and proceeds The portfolio is also weighed up like this.
Measuring advantages			Tracking of proceeds after the processis in production. Tracking over entire cycle.
Feedback, how it is going More advanced estimation			Feedback on alignment with strategy using score cards. Including options in choice, measuring value over all production years.

Figure 17.5. Levels of implementation of IT portfolio management

ment opportunities with varying proceeds. In that case, they do not constantly decide ad hoc whether or not individual projects will take place or on individual programmes of projects. They decide on the portfolio of all programmes and projects as a whole.

The ITIM model includes five levels of operating. In Figure 17.6 these levels and the critical processes on each level are shown. Furthermore, the ITIM model goes further than the Jeffery model (2004) as emanated from empiricism. It gives attention to more subjects, such as for instance life-cycle management of investments and it has an extra phase. In this extra phase the own investment processes are benchmarked with those of other organizations. The ITIM model is a direct result of the Clinger–Cohen law of 1996, which asked authorities to indicate their performances in the field of IT.

IT portfolio management looks top down at the portfolio of IT tasks and projects. The demand organization decides. It investigates sourcing of IT and reckons in its decision-making process with the progress in the field of utility computing. Its decisions result in the building of certain knowledge in-house

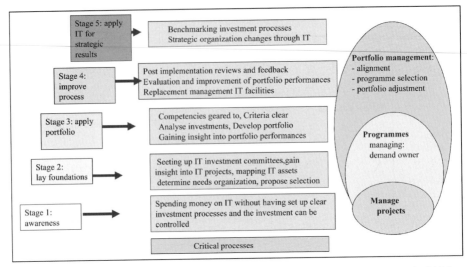

Figure 17.6. The ITIM model of the General Accounting Office (see Bloem et al., 2004)

and other knowledge disappearing. Knowing is just as important as being able to forget.

Conclusions IT portfolio management

In Figure 17.7 the model for IT portfolio management, as applied in this book is shown. An organization chooses at a certain level for organizing the demand. From the demand priorities are established. These priorities lead to

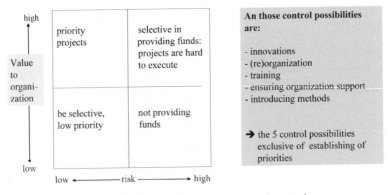

Figure 17.7. IT portfolio management in practice

innovations, to an organization of IT, to attention for knowledge advancement and knowledge run-down, to operating in conformity with methods and to activities for creating organizational support for projects and tasks and to maintain this. Tasks and projects with a low execution risk and a high value to the organization will be performed with a high priority. Tasks with a low value and high risk will not get any funds.

TRENDS AND EFFECTS ONE WILL ENCOUNTER IN CONTROLLING IT

Considering sourcing

In this control it must be realized that organizations operating within the network economy have more and more opportunities for obtaining part of their product from elsewhere, for having part of their processes executed by others and for arriving at a product in cooperation with other organizations. We call this respectively product, process and network modularisation. Figure 17.8 provides examples of this.

This figure shows an organization, where the product 'IT management', that an IT supply organization supplies, is divided into part products. This is a

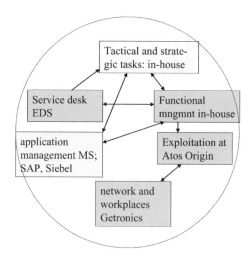

Figure 17.8. Examples of chains in supplying IT services and products

form of product modularisation. In order to be able to deliver the products and the services to go with these, processes are defined. These processes are carried out by specific organizations. This is known as process modularisation. Seen from the viewpoint of the suppliers of the processes, one works within a chain for achieving delivery of the complete 'IT management' supply.

Figure 17.8 explains clearly that even in simple chains, a web of relationships will be created. The outsourcing organization maintains contacts with each organization that contributes to the IT application, with the exception of the organization that takes care of the management of networks and workplaces. The supplier of the exploitation facilities looks after this contact.

Figure 17.8 also explains that this working within a chain requires consideration on the relationships to be entered into. Parties often conclude contracts of their own free will or enter into partnerships. The relationship as formed does however have a more hierarchic nature. There is one party that, often indeed after consideration, determines in which manner the product is realized and what its quality should be.

Gearing work within the chain requires the sharing of information between all cooperating parties, the measuring and discussing of performances. The outsourcer might, like in Figure 17.8, have to manage a whole range of supplier's relations. One or more relationships could after some time develop. These then become more or less strategic alliances, in which a supplier on his own or as one of the few supply organizations of IT facilities will function. This will result in a different contact pattern of the supplier with the customer. Relationships will then have to be shaped at different levels in both the customer as well as the supplier organization.

And next

Furthermore, the situation in which many employees of organizations can log in from anywhere in the world and than gain direct access to their own facilities does no seem that far away. In Figure 17.9 this situation is shown. Customers enter via a portal and are next lead to the applications they are authorized for. There is a central identity management and one uses an access authorization application. This application arranges permission and on-charge of costs, whilst at the same time keeping an eye on performance aspects such as

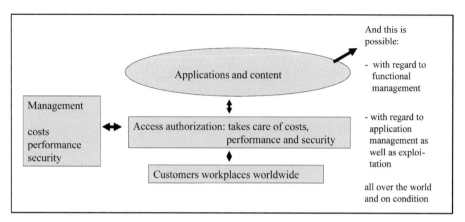

Figure 17.9. Tailor-made facilities in every workplace wherever in the world (variation on Turlings, 2002)

response time and availability and the access security. The demand organization of tomorrow will decide on these facilities. The supply organization will have to realize these. The applications function on central servers that are situated in various locations for reasons of security and continuity. Choices have been made concerning the in-house execution of application management tasks and exploitation or outsourcing of these or parts of these by the supply organization.

Offshore sourcing

There are many ways of sourcing. In the network economy professional reasons more and more decide where outsourced tasks are to be carried out. New forms of outsourcing come into being, such as for example offshore sourcing and business process outsourcing. Offshore sourcing is the contracting out of the development of software to companies in countries with cheaper labour or special skills. This is often outsourcing to countries in Eastern Europe or in Asia. This subject is placed on the agenda more and more, when parties talk about the outsourcing of tasks in the field of application management.

From experience with offshore sourcing, we learn that for projects with a clear structure and when little contact with users is necessary, this practice can work very well. In off shore sourcing there have to be clear contact points, both on the side of the customer and the supplier. During the project, the customer should have his own representatives on location. Finally, the in-house organization has to be informed on the culture of the country where the supplier is domiciled and of the prevailing work ethics (Creyghton et al., 2003).

Business process outsourcing

Apart from offshore sourcing, the contracting out of an entire process of an organization also occurs more often. This involves getting both the actual business process as well as the necessary IT application from outside. In Europe this is mainly a growth market in the United Kingdom. Companies that take the lead in business process outsourcing in the United Kingdom are mainly to be found in the sectors banks, oil and gas and telecommunication. On average, the concluded contracts run five years or more. This trend implies for the outsourcing parties that they do not always talk directly to the supplier of IT services. A consortium of organizations, of which one party is entirely responsible and controls the other parties, often implements such a contract.

These new possibilities for outsourcing require attention to the control aspects of outsourcing in general. The demand organization has to set up an outsourcing organization, that answers questions of the supply organization; one has to control the execution of contracts on the basis of qualitative and quantitative data and sometimes one has to set up a transitional organization, when one changes suppliers.

Large contracts versus selective sourcing

It will be obvious that there are many possibilities in the field of sourcing and that every form of sourcing does effect the demand organization. Ross et al. (2003) has listed the differences between the concluding and controlling of a large sourcing contract and the concluding and controlling of a relatively small contract for the demand organization concerned. They ascertain differences with regard to the shaping of the relationship between demand and supply organizations, with regard to the standardization of the services and products, with regard to the choice of and dealing with the providers and the type of activities that are outsourced (Figure 17.10).

	Real partners, large contract:	Selective sourcing:

Relation:	Formal: a. defining measuring method
	         b. link agreements to measuring
	         c. include supply in control
	Informal: a. configuring contacts
	         b. possibly take share in
	            supply organization
	         c. permanent interaction and
	            cooperation
		Limit outsourcing to tasks that can be
		      clearly defined and measured.
		Exploitation: SLA`s and permanent measuring
		      application management: limited duration
		      projects and clear specification output.
		Regular benchmark on costs/quality
		Evolve by concluding new contracts not
		      by adjustment existing ones.

Transaction:	Standaardization of product and service. Disciplined execution processes	Strongly standardized IT environment Clearly defined interfaces between divisions. Supply organization accepts rules regarding processes and standards.

Strategy:	Distinction core/non core activities
	Increasingly better support of business
	      processes by IT.
		Understanding in advance core/non core activities
		Outsourcing technique, not business knowledge
		Increasing insight into strategic operating
		      with IT and recognition of possibilities
		Including of protection in contract of use of
		      acquired knowledge in supply organization

Technique/ supply organization	Due diligence execution.
	Choosing large suppliers for ensuring
	      one stays in business. Include
	      a possibility to change supplier.
		Limiting dependency on one single supplier
		Have an exit strategy in case supply organi-
		      zation ceases to exist.
		Specification of standard interfaces for enabling
		      switching

Figure 17.10. Differences between outsourcing contracts

ORGANIZING OF KNOWING AND FORGETTING

Knowing and forgetting

A second point of interest in control of IT application is the dealing with knowledge. IT organizations are organizations and organizations consist of people, of whom the majority choose to strive together for an ideal or objective that is verifiable. In these organizations, individual learning and learning as a group takes place. This way, knowledge is improved so that the aim of an organization becomes easier to achieve. These knowledge processing and rejection processes can be controlled. This is called knowledge management (Weggeman, 1997). Knowledge management is important. The requirements that the more introvert IT demand and supply organizations, working in the industrial economy had to meet, were different from the requirements an IT organization in the more open network economy has to meet. In these organizations the demand is often designed separate from the supply and the demand works with internal and external IT supply organizations.

Management of knowledge is necessary for various reasons. Firstly, one wishes to extend vital know-how of the organization further. Another goal is to guarantee that knowledge present in one person is also present in the group of persons around this person. This way, it is ensured that when someone leaves the company, the knowledge does not leave with this person but remains within the group. Finally, the active management of knowledge enables this knowledge the organization builds up, to be more controlled, kept up-to-date and consciously lost.

Types of knowledge

IT management roughly recognizes four types of knowledge. These types of knowledge are given in Figure 17.11. The distinction between the different types of knowledge is determined on the one hand by the ease of replacing the knowledge and on the other hand by the value of the knowledge to the organization. Controlling knowledge one can, using the matrix the matrix of Figure 17.11, take measures per category of knowledge. These are:

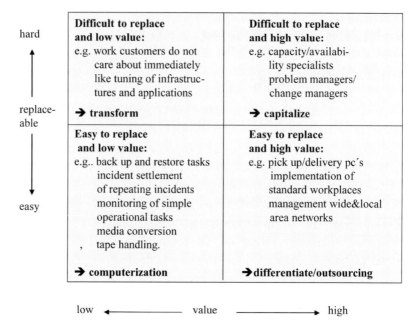

Figure 17.11. Degree of value and degree of replaceability of knowledge

(a) knowledge of *high value that is hard to* replace, is knowledge one wants to continue with. This has to be recognized and divided into knowledge clusters. This knowledge should be passed on, made explicit, enriched with knowledge from outside and next applied again internally. To this purpose, one often sets up teams;

(b) knowledge *of low value that is hard* to replace one should remodel. When this is knowledge that in the long-term could easily be replaced by use of IT, this should be done. When this is knowledge that could be developed into knowledge of high value, one should enable this development;

(c) knowledge of *low value that is easily replaced*, lends itself to be computerized. In this field, nowadays often temporary employees and part-timers are employed. In this quadrant, one finds the known-error databases, the tape robots and the top ten questions asked at the service desk;

(d) knowledge of *high value that is easily replaced and does not represent added value* for an organization, includes activities that either have to be disposed of or have to be further developed. In the first case one proceeds to outsourcing. In the second case, one tries to deliver extra knowledge. One could, for instance, extend the service deskwork by providing advice and training.

Giving attention to developing and disposing of knowledge in the field of IT management seems necessary, in view of the speed in which changes take place in this field. There could be gradual changes in the necessary knowledge. New knowledge clusters have to be set up, the knowledge in some clusters does not need any further development and sometimes acquired knowledge can be disposed of.

INCREASINGLY HIGHER DEMANDS ON RELIABILITY OF IT FACILITIES

More robust IT

The increased attention for availability of individual objects and of groups of objects is the third trend IT organizations come across. More and more robust infrastructures and applications will be introduced to the market over the coming years. In this, autonomous techniques such as self-healing of IT facilities play a part.

Basis of considering robust applications and infrastructures is the model in Figure 9.10 (see Chapter 9). This model originates from system analysis. It indicates quantitatively that double execution of systems strongly enhances the reliability of their functioning. Robust IT facilities can therefore be effectuated by reducing the chance that one object fails. One can also achieve this by placing various objects for the same task parallel. The latter enables self-healing of IT facilities. One does have redundant facilities and in case one of these breaks down, another one is always available. Other developments for increasing the availability of IT supply concern the reduction of the repair time.

Developments

The developments en route to more robust IT facilities are:

(a) For *individual objects*. In this field one tries to produce hardware that is provided with possibilities for self-repair and possibilities for 7 times 24 hours monitoring. When faults occur, an error message is immediately issued. Next, the status and use are periodically reported. This way, also small, non-fatal faults may emerge and possible overload is quickly discovered. Testing on software is done automatically on line end-to-end. When faults occur or in case of new versions, one uses possibilities for on line and remote updating of software.

(b) For *groups of objects* that together form an IT facility, architectures of IT facilities have a duplicate in vital locations. The IT facilities are lined-up spread across two or more locations. Using replication techniques, the various data collections remain geared to each other. Version control with regard to software is invested in and executed more centrally and concentrated. Besides, one sees other forms of reconfiguration of infrastructure arise. Grid computing can be regarded as the most advanced form of redundancy of server capacity. In grid computing, organizations make use of various servers for supplying transaction facilities. If one of the servers breaks down, the others ($n - 1$) take over. The same happens in networks where, with many paths available, when one path breaks down, the network searches for another available path and usually finds one.

(c) With regard to *the IT organization*. The IT demand and the supply organizations are worldwide accessible from central call centres 7 times 24 hours a day. At repairing faults one gets if necessary, immediate assistance of a second and a third line service desk. IT facilities are racked 24 hours a day. Training in the use of IT facilities is offered on every workplace through the internet. The history of an object is recorded, which means that occurring disasters can be re-enacted. Customers are informed in advance and during an incident, about the duration and state of affairs. Furthermore, the customer of an object is always informed in advance by the IT demand organization about innovations in the hardware and software. This information concentrates on the task of the employee and indicates whether further training is necessary and how this can be achieved. For this purpose, web services are often used.

THE ROAD TO 2027

Technical and administrative developments

This chapter indicated that one could look at IT application in two different ways. Organizations can regard IT as a utility. They can also see it as a portfolio of possibilities. In the next years, these IT facilities will become increasingly more reliable and organizations will become more dependent on their functioning. In Figure 17.12 it is indicated how, on the basis of the current state of affairs, one may see the development of this subject.

Examined from an IT governance point of view

As seen from an IT governance point of view, over the next years *IT organizations* will come across the following developments:

 – Having to organize the demand for IT. This may lead to declustering of demand and supply. In this, the supply can be subdivided into supply in the field of application management and supply in the field of exploitation.
 – The impact of increasingly strict legislation such as the Clinger–Cohen law and Sarbanes–Oxley legislation. This means that organizations have

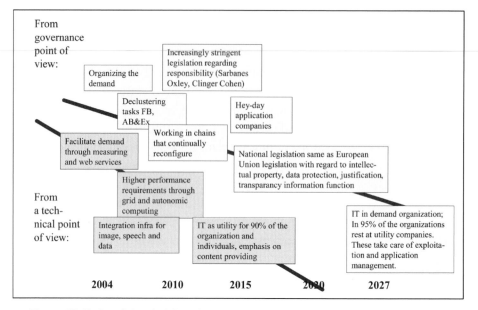

Figure 17.12. Possible administrative and technical developments until the year 2027

to take extra measures in order to be able to optimally justify themselves to stakeholders.

– The results of working in chains of organizations. This leads to higher demands to the reliability of IT facilities, the continuity of those facilities and ensuring the confidentiality of information.

– Having to comply with increasingly more international legislation. The legislation with regard to intellectual property protection of privacy, financial rapportage, tax legislation etc will be more and more on an international level.

– The application of IT will be experienced by at least 95% of all organizations in 2025, as the application of a utility.

Seen technically

The road to 2027, technically seen, leads to integration of techniques in the field of speech, image and data processing. Higher reliability and improved continuity of the provision of services will be realized by means of improved (end to end) monitoring, the developments in autonomous computing (e.g. self-healing) techniques and grid computing.

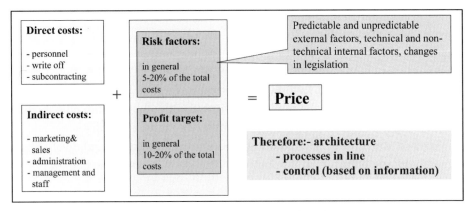

Figure 17.13. Each demand has its price

However, be aware

On the road to 2027, it will be the demand organizations that make decisions about the use of IT that supply organizations provide the facilities for. Demand organizations will not always be able to indicate in advance, what the advantages of a specific expenditure on IT could be. The costs for this will however be often easier to explain. Figure 17.13 shows how the price of IT services is determined by supply organizations (De Bruijn, 2004).

QUESTIONS

1. Which developments are to be expected in the IT sector, when looking at the historical development in the sector of physical transport, in the sector of information transport and the energy sector? How is the IT sector already prepared for these?
2. Which two views are there on the demand and the supply of IT facilities? What is the difference between both facilities? How does this work out in expenditure for IT in the demand organization? Illustrate your answer with an example.
3. Which organizations need to use IT application as a utility and why? What are the risks for an organization, if one wants to use IT as a utility? Illustrate your answer by giving an example.

4. What is IT portfolio management? On which levels do organizations in the year 2005 execute this portfolio management? Is this portfolio management important to every organization? Explain your answer.

5. What is the ITIM model for portfolio management? Why is this model more limited than the model Jefferey et al. provide? Explain your answer.

6. What is the impact of the possibilities of the network economy on sourcing of IT facilities? Illustrate your answer by giving three examples.

7. What are the differences for an organization if it concludes a relatively large outsourcing contract or if it selectively outsources tasks in the field of:
   - organization of the relationship;
   - designing the transaction;
   - the impact on the strategy of the organization;
   - the choice of a supplier.

8. Why is knowing and forgetting of knowledge important to IT management? How does one handle knowledge of high value that is easily replaced? Illustrate your answer with an example.

9. What are the developments on the road to more robust IT facilities when looking at:
   - the individual hardware or software object;
   - a group of objects;
   - the IT organization.

APPENDIX A

Short case studies about the contents of a chapter

INTRODUCTION

Below, 17 case studies are given. These case studies provide a practical application of the material in a certain chapter. The case studies have been put together because in the practice of teaching, after an hour of theory, there is a need for group-discussion on the impact the theory has on everyday practice. After an hour of discussion, with the questions at the end as a focal point, the group is requested to report.

When discussing the case study the following procedure can be followed:

(a) the class is asked to read the case-study before the chapter is discussed;

(b) after discussing the chapter in question the students are split into groups. Each group is given the task of answering the questions at the end of the case-study;

(c) after an hour to an hour and a half of group work the class is called together and two of the groups report on their answers to the questions. It will then often be clear, that groups don't agree;

(d) the lecturer will discuss these differences of opinion and can do this using the elaboration of the case-study, to be found on the lecturer's pages of the website http://www.ict-management.com.

Part A. 1. IT management: the basis

CASE-STUDY CHAPTER 1

A.1. The basis: ERP at the Royal Ahrend (tasks and objects)

A.1.1. View on the support by IT

Ahrend has the following view on its applications:

> *Applications, that are using or are going to use the set-up infrastructures, will increasingly start from a structure of components. The application architecture of an organization is constructed from building blocks that are often procured from somewhere else. The more this component approach becomes a trend, the more software factories will develop, where components or entire applications using these components or applications are procured to fill in their own application architecture.*

This was the reason Ahrend at the start of the nineties decided to introduce Baan's ERP-package for the support of its operational processes. This ERP-package can when applying all its modules, support virtually all processes in a production company. Through the application program interfaces, this package can also be linked to other program components.

Introduction of an ERP-package often requires streamlining of the organization. After introduction of the ERP-package this provides applications, in which data about the entire organization are saved in correlation. Order planning can be done quickly; elapsed times of productions become shorter because of the larger overview and the control of the organization as a whole become more quantative. In principle, Baan's ERP-package will support Ahrend later on in all primary and secondary processes. In Figure A.1.1 this situation is reflected. Horizontally are the secondary processes, vertically the primary processes, like sales, procurements, services, and so on.

A.1.2. The Royal Ahrend

Ahrend produces furniture for furnishing offices. In addition it sells office supplies. Ahrend employs about 1800 staff; working in about 40 branches spread

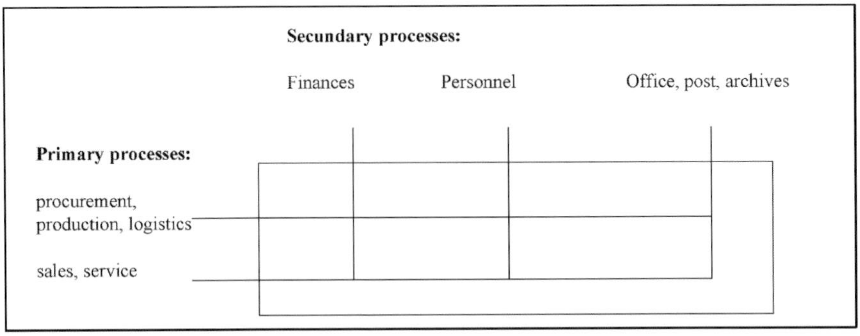

Figure A.1.1. Support and use of the same data

over 10 countries. In the sector 'furnishing' Ahrend has two furniture factories in the Netherlands (Sint-Oedenrode and Zwanenburg) and twelve sales centres. In total there are 30 Ahrend sales centres in this sector in Europe. These are found in Belgium, Germany, the Netherlands and the United Kingdom. Ahrend has in this sector implemented the Baan package. The choice for implementing the Baan package was made at the start of the nineties. At that time the information function was no longer considered efficient because:

- through acquisition of companies in a number of branches one knew of deviating IT infrastructures;
- there was a multitude of sometimes incompatible applications operational;
- at the different locations IT management was either not organized or not organized the same;
- at progressing growth the input of IT had to be flexible, scaleable and future proof;
- the importance of IT was strategic when looking at the possibilities for making planning and elapsed times transparent;
- there was a large need for achieving more integration of the primary processes production, sales and services and the secondary process finances;
- one simply wanted to have better management information.

The choice for the Baan package was prepared by an team consisting of managing directors and managers of all disciplines within Ahrend. This group of people from the operational processes logistics, sales, marketing and finances was completed with application experts (the later managers of the demand organization) and IT management. In this team one came to thinking in integrated processes. This resulted in considering a more integrated information function.

Simultaneously with thinking about different support in the field of IT, organizational measures were taken, such as the closing down of the furniture factories, whereby at the introduction of the ERP-package only two factories were left.

A.1.3. The start at the implementation in 1996

In 1996 in the factories in Sint-Oedenrode and Zwanenburg the business administration was done in various variations using the IBM Mapics package and with own software. The factories had their own functional managers and application managements for these. Mapics runs on a AS/400 infrastructure with operating system OS/400. In the sales departments in Belgium and the Netherlands one uses the software that the company developed itself and the Consist FIS financial application. These applications also run on a AS/400. In England an IBM RS/6000 Unix-machine was installed, own staff supported the management of this computer. In Germany no more than an advanced drawing package was used. In the other countries various local facilities were available.

A.1.4. The infrastructure and the applications

In the first place the financial and logistics administration of the factory in Zwanenburg was transferred to the ERP-package. Next, the administrative departments of the sales offices in the Netherlands followed. Last the factory in Sint-Oedenrode and the other sales offices were dealt with. This careful approach was chosen because within Ahrend a very high availability of the ERP-application is required and simultaneously with the introduction of the ERP-package the infrastructure and organization of IT were changed.

After implementation of the ERP-package Ahrend has a multisite Baan-environment that works on an infrastructure consisting of:

(a) Four clusters, that is to say a cluster for the factory in Sint-Oedenrode, one for the one in Zwanenburg, one for the sales offices and a cluster for testing of new versions and training staff. The test environment for Baan consists of three parts: a functional test environment, a users test

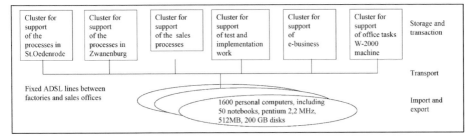

Figure A.1.2. The technical infrastructure of Royal Ahrend

environment and an exploitation test environment. Apart from this there is a cluster operative for the office environment and a separate cluster for e-business activities. Since 2003, Office XP is installed in the workplace.

(b) The underlying network has been executed in duplicate. The network between the different branches was in 2002 entirely filled with ADSL-network connections. By way of this network 32 local networks are linked to the infrastructure. The technical infrastructure consists of RS/6000 machines with the operating system AIX (= IBM's Unix). Excluded from this are the office facilities that run under Windows 2000. All servers are lined up in the Ahrend-computing centre in Nieuwegein. Server and network facilities are because of availability considerations executed in duplicate (see Figure A.1.2). In the workplace people work under Windows XP.

A.1.5. The organization of the IT management

From 2003 people work with the applications within Ahrend. For Baan, the Baan 6 release is used and one has concluded a maintenance contract for this with the Profuse Company. Since October 2002 an Enterprise-agreement was concluded with Microsoft. The e-business environment was created under Microsoft's dot.net. Since 1998 Ahrend is active on the Internet. Initially with a website that provided customers with information and enabled them through email to contact Ahrend. In 2001 this site was further developed into a proper e-business environment for the Ahrend Office products division. Secretaries usually order the products of this division. In 2003 the possibility to configure office furnishings online was added. Ahrend finds the site for Office products a success, whilst the last mentioned opportunity is moderately used. On the one hand this may be caused by the way in which the site has been put together, on the other hand it could be the way in which the site support the sales process. This recent site was made by the IT department at head office without involvement of any people in the field. Since 2003, 40% of Ahrend's returns and 80% of the Office products division are achieved through orders on the website.

The management of Ahrend's IT facilities is organized as follows:

(a) the exploitation is carried out under control of Ahrend. Ahrend's own people take care of the incident management, problem management, change management and the release management, as well as the ITIL service delivery tasks. For these tasks 13 people are employed on a 7 × 24-hour basis (5 shifts of two people plus reserves). With IBM a maintenance contract was concluded for both the storage and processing facilities as well as the internal network. The external network is managed by KPN (Dutch telecom), whilst for the workplaces at 1850 euro per year a service is rented from PinkRoccade. PinkRoccade supplies for this money a 99.5% available Office workplace, connected to the Ahrend-network.

(b) The IT department coordinates the functional management of the applications. This also has a second-line service desk for the Baan application. The rest of the substantive management lies with the Ahrend staff at the head office. In order to be able to execute the second-line service desk, the problem management and rest of the functional management, ten Ahrend employees have gone through the entire Baan training programme. Three of these employees have mainly concentrated on the financial part, four on logistics and sales and three on production. These functional managers have in turn trained so-called core-users. These are users in the Ahrend branches that need more than average knowledge of the ERP-package. In every branch three of these users have been trained. These are the primary service desk for the location in question. (c) The application management of the MS Office environment lies at Microsoft; the application management for the e-business application lies with an Ordina subsidiary. The application management for the ERP-application lies for 95% at Baan. The Ahrend IT department in this field takes care of:
   – the connection between the Baan application and the e.business environment; the daily preparation of management information tasks from the data collections of the Baan-application. At every workstation within Ahrend this information may be accessed and processed using the Business Objects package.

- the configuration of new versions of Office, Business Objects and Baan
  by setting the right parameters and supervision of the implementation
  (including any conversions if needed);
- looking after the contact between Ahrend and Baan.

A.1.6. What does the baan ERP-package mean to Ahrend?

On the side of organization one may state that the implementation of strongly parametrisable packages like the Baan ERP-package, may demand significant adjustments in the set-up of the IT-infrastructure and the IT-organization. At Ahrend, between 1995–2000 step by step, all application development and management tasks in the factories and the sales offices were outsourced. These days, development is tackled in a small way centrally and application management is performed when necessary. In the business organization the following effects of the decision to arrive at the ERP-package and implement e-business facilities can be seen:

- Changes in the organization are supported faster and better by IT facilities;
- the productivity of employees has increased because of better information being available, that is also available quicker. The item information in particular has become more reliable, whilst also the data on the history of customers is significantly more detailed. Apart from this the management is able to obtain cross sections of the results quite easily including the yield and costs per product per company division;
- a decrease of fax and telephone communications between sales offices and factories and a decrease in the use of photocopiers;
- the e-business sales channel now gets around 70% of the orders (in numbers) and around 40% of the turnover. The site is visited 2000 times a day by organizations for ordering goods. These include many authorities, who order on the basis of framework contract, as concluded by the Government Procurement Offices of Different European Countries.

Questions

1. What are the objects of management in Ahrend?
2. How does one see Ahrend slowly entering the network economy?
3. What is the impact of general and business management on the IT-supply organization of Ahrend? What shows that this doesn't always happen optimally?

4. How is the triple concept of management model configurated at Ahrend? What does this mean?

5. Elaborate how the various points of view on IT management emerge at Ahrend.
   −how does the angle of authority affect?
   −how does the angle of the methods affect?
   −how does is the angle of change affect?
   −how does the angle of system's theory affect?

6. Indicate in which way Ahrend may enter the era of 'any one, anywhere and anyplace' (ubiquituous) computing with regard to IT management?

CASE-STUDY CHAPTER 2

A.2. Architecture: the local community of Emmen and its IT architecture

A.2.1. The municipality Emmen

Emmen is, with 108,000 inhabitants the largest municipality in the Dutch province Drenthe and after Groningen the second largest of the North-Netherlands. The town has an extensive concentration of industries (the largest in the north) and a lot of glasshouse vegetable and flower culture: no less than about 280 hectares of market gardening. With all its facilities Emmen is the centre of the region Southeast Drenthe and southern Groningen, an area with over a quarter million people. Typical for Emmen is the combination of urban elements in natural surroundings. Space is still a very common thing. Thirteen smaller and larger villages surround the heart Emmen, with about 55,000 inhabitants. The total surface area of Emmen is the same size as the triangle Rotterdam-Den Haag-Leiden. However, you still find unspoiled areas of natural beauty around Emmen.

Emmen has a modern centre, with stylish shopping malls: De Weiert and De Vlinder. The much talked-about pedestrian bridge Traverse connects the existing zoo Noorder Dierenpark in the centre of Emmen and the extension of the zoo on the Noordbarger Es (opposite the centre).

Because of this special structure and the geographical decentralization of the villages and neighbourhoods that together form the town Emmen, the inhabitants of the separate villages and neighbourhoods have their own recognizable identity and they want to keep this. IT and Internet could play a part in this and in the form of the portals make a contribution to virtual community formation. The result is that, apart from the fact the municipality Emmen wants to serve people increasingly better via electronic means; initiatives are born for making citizens more familiar with the diverse possibilities of IT and Internet. This is offered in an accessible way. The social proceeds of this application of the Internet is the fact one promotes contact between citizens and this leads to the formation of virtual communities.

A.2.2. Organization of the municipality Emmen

In Figure A.2.1 the organization of the municipality Emmen is shown. In the Emmen organization about 1000 people are employed, not including those that teach at the schools. Of these 1000, about 500 are working in offices, such as the local government, civil affairs, social affairs and economical affairs. For them the use of a workplace with sufficient IT support is a must. Without this support their work would be almost impossible.

For controlling the organization and for being able to supply services to natural and legal persons (such as societies, foundations and companies) the municipality Emmen needs information. In Figure A.2.2 the information model of the municipality is shown.

Because of its size and need for information the municipality Emmen cannot do without using IT. Emmen fully realized that in 1990 and has since then standardized its infrastructure and applications to a high degree. Furthermore the municipality concentrated and centralized the exploitation of IT facilities in an IT department. This department comes under the directorate public contacts and general and technical support. The IT department is the mediator between the internal departments of Emmen and the suppliers of IT facilities. Functional management for the various applications is housed within the policy departments or support department of the various directorates, assuming these are not

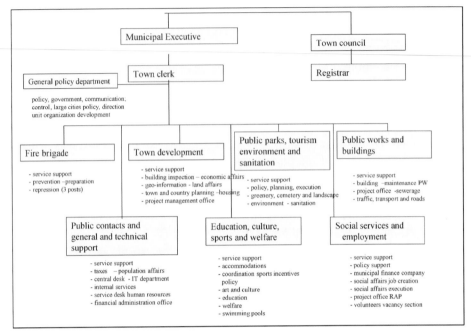

Figure A.2.1. Organization municipality Emmen

Emmen-wide used applications. In that case, this functional management rests with the General policy department. In the field of building Internet applications, producing management information, development of conversion software and maintenance of interfaces between a number of applications, the IT department of Emmen carries out application management tasks. They sometimes perform these tasks themselves; sometimes these are outsourced.

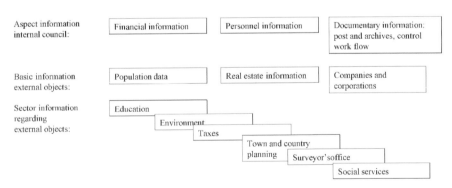

Figure A.2.2. Information needed within Emmen

A.2.3. The objects to be managed

Emmen's vision on IT applications is the following:

> *With applications, that either make use or will make use of the installed infrastructures, increasingly more, a construction of components will be the starting point. The application architecture of an organization is constructed from building blocks that are often bought elsewhere. The more this component approach becomes fashionable, the more software factories come into being, where customers buy components or entire applications and with these components or applications fill in their own application architecture.*

This was the reason Emmen decided after an extensive exploration of the market in 1990 to standardize the support of its operational processes on PinkRoccade packages. Emmen uses these packages of the support of its internal processes for finance and personnel and is considering entering into a trial for an application that supports digital archiving. The municipality also applies the PinkRoccade-solutions for its basis registration in the area of population, cadastral information and legal persons. Finally, Emmen has applied sector applications by PinkRoccade for supporting assessment of rates, the tasks of the social services and that of the building inspection authorities.

Apart from the PinkRoccade applications across the whole council, there are about twenty more dedicated applications. These have also been installed on the central server. As personal productivity tool Emmen uses Microsoft Office XP. The intranet and extranet are configured with Microsoft building tools like MS Frontoffice.

The technical infrastructure of Emmen consists of a twin-centre configuration of storage and processing facilities. These are organized as indicated in Figure A.2.3. By making storage and processing units available in several places, Emmen diminishes the risk of losing these facilities through fire or flooding. With regard to the network, a physically separated access to the KPN traffic control centre is used. The workstations are kitted out with Dell pc's with 256 Mb internal memory and 2.3 MHz processors. Emmen has 800 fixed workstations and 150 notebooks.

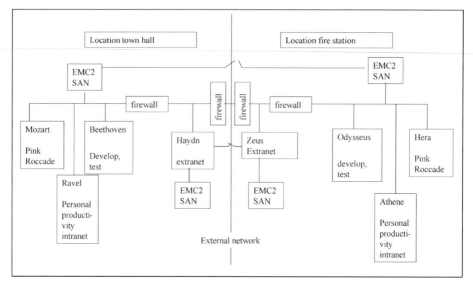

Figure A.2.3. Emmen's storage, processing and transport configuration

The Emmen IT facilities include:

(a) Four mid-range servers IBM xSeries 450 with 16 GB internal memory running with the operating system IBM Linux. These servers are lined up in a manned data centre in the Emmen town hall. The same configuration is lined up in an unmanned computer room built in the fire station. All internal servers are connected with two SAN's (storage area networks). Furthermore, the extranet server has its own SAN. These SAN's are to be found in each of the data centres. The SAN's each have 1 terabyte direct accessible disk memory and 2 terabyte off line tape memory. This tape memory is situated on an EMC2 tape robot. Using this the data of all transactions and many policy documents made under MS Office over the last 5 years can be retrieved.

The use of the servers is as follows:

−on server 1, the Mozart, the PinkRoccade-applications run;

−on server 2, the Ravel, the personnel productivity tools and intranet applications run;

−on server 3, the Haydn, the extranet applications run;

−server 4, the Beethoven, is used as machine for developing and testing new applications or changes to applications. This server has a development test, a functionality test, a users test, an exploitation and a last but one production environment.

Furthermore every server has its back-up in the twincentre. These back-up servers have been named after Greek gods or demigods. These are called respectively the Hera, the Athene, the Zeus and the Odysseus. The configuration and its line-up are drawn in Figure A.2.3.

(b) An Avaya-telephone exchange with voice response and call-centre possibilities. The Avaya-switchboard is directly connected with the network. The voice response and call-centre possibilities are used for the internal service desk for IT, the fire alarms, the service desk of the social services and that of civil affairs. It can also be employed in emergencies, like disasters and other incidents for supporting the information centre tasks.

A.2.4. The organization for IT support

Since 1995 one works in Emmen with the above facilities. For the applications the policy is used of always being one release behind the most recent version of the supplier. With every supplier of an application a service level agreement was concluded. The management of Emmen's IT facilities is organized as follows:

(a) the exploitation is carried out by Emmen itself. The own staff mans the service desk, looks after the incident management, problem management, change management and release management, as well as the ITIL service delivery tasks. For these tasks during office hours (Monday until Friday from 08.00 until 16.00 hrs.) 10 people are employed: 5 on the service desk and incident management and the rest on back-office-tasks and tasks in the field of service management and service reports. Emmen has concluded a maintenance contract with IBM for both the storage and processing facilities as well as the internal network. The external network is managed by KPN, for 1850 euro a year per workstation a PinkRoccade service is provided. PinkRoccade supplies for this amount a 99.5% available Office workstation connected to the Emmen network.

(b) the functional management of the applications is coordinated by the IT department. In order to be able to carry out the second-line service desk, the problem management and the rest of the functional management twenty Emmen employees have passed through the entire PinkRoccade training programme. Three of these employees have mainly dedicated themselves to the financial application, two on the personnel application and the rest on the remaining applications.

(c) the application management of the MS Office environment lies at Microsoft; for the application management for the e-business application there is cooperation with an Ordina subsidiary. The application management for the other applications rests for 98% with PinkRoccade. Emmen takes care of the connection between the PinkRoccade applications and the e-business environment if necessary.

A.2.5. Evolution in the process of service providing

Emmen (www.emmen.nl) tries to make its services run increasingly via the Internet. In Figure A.2.4 the functionality of the Internet service counter is illustrated. To this purpose, it has formulated three goals. These goals are a better information function towards the citizen, arriving at digital service providing and using the website as a means to involve citizens more actively in council policies and council politics. At the last goal one could think of interactive policy-making. The website is seen as a means of communicating with and towards citizens. The three goals are based on communication surveys and an internal organization innovation project at the council.

A lot of care is devoted by Emmen to dealing with the flow of e-mails, which is encouraged and tracked with a workflow management system. The products and services offered are between 90 and 100 of the in total 300 products of the product list of the Association of Dutch local Councils. These are in general the slightly simpler products. Transactions as electronic part of the products are not (yet) possible. It is however possible to apply for products, like a birth certificate from the register. Non-council services are not offered, apart from the digital marketplace. The fact that there are no other electronic services available in Emmen and no further steps are taken for developing the digital city, is caused by the absence of a large-scale broadband (glass fibre) network infrastructure.

The communications department carries out the functional management of the site http://www.Emmen.nl. The functional management controls the application management and the exploitation. At a future connection of front-office and back-office other departments will also get involved in functional management tasks. The functional management is not controlled deliberately.

Products and services . Internet Service Counter

Internet Service Counter

Welcome to the Internet Service Counter of the municipality Gemeente Emmen. This is were you can find information on the services provided by your council. I you want an explanation of the functioning of the Internet Service Counter? Click here.Do you wish to be assisted personally at one of our physical counters, please do have a look under 'personal assistance' for more information on for instance the various counters, opening hours and servcies provided.

Find a product:

Subject:

Reports, Complaints & Objections
Environment & Waste Enterprise
Education & Training Sport,
Recreation, Culture & Art
Traffic & Transport
Entertainment
Work & Income
Living and housing
Care & Welfare

Show all products

Occasion:

(Back) to school
Losing income
Starting a business
Birth
Buying a house
Immigration
Retirement
Travel
Death
Moving house
Work
Illness

Top 10:
Road closures
Pasports
Moving
Population data
General information
Sunday opening hours shops
Birth certificates
Archives
Taxes
Opening hours shops

Figure A.2.4. The increasing use of Internet at services provided by Emmen

The measuring of data only happens at the front with the use of a statistics package. Early on in 2004 it was measured there are 500 single visitors per day. For a properly functioning extranet including operational costs, the future costs are assessed at 1 million euro annually for a municipality of the size of Emmen. The operational costs of this are about 700,000.

A.2.6. The set-up of the central IT organization

The IT department of the Emmen council knows front-office and back-office-tasks. In the years between 1997–2000 the exploitation task of this department has been designed in conformity with the ITIL method. This happened

Goal: - *using indicators **getting** quality level **clear.***
- *make work supply for management **manageable***
- *start up **exchange of knowledge** about calls dealt with.*

Actions:
1. Process plan made for implementing ITIL processes long-term:
2. Processes for service desk, incident management, problem management, change management and configuration management set-up and supported by package for service support.
3. All calls reported to central service desk and classified according to:

- incidents	= workplace at standstill
- complaint	= workplace not fucntioning optimally
- administrative change	= registering and authorize users
- object change	= new on replacing hardware and software

All calls coming in through post or email were scanned
4. Acquired knowledge entered into knowledge database

Problem: without service level agreements the order of settlement if often fairly random and more difficult calls are left until later

Figure A.2.5. 1st phase introduction ITIL

in two phases. These phases and the actions undertaken within these are shown in Figures A.2.5 and A.2.6. In the first phase, that lasted six months, the various processes were designed and insight into the level of operating of the IT department was achieved. In the next phase one strived to arrive at the level as desired by the customers of the IT department and also to maintain this level.

Goal: achieving the quality levels as required by the business, therefore:
a constant reduction of the average time for dealing with a call.

Actions:
1. Setting up **service level management** and concluding SLA and establish per type call max. time for resolution (incident 4 hours, complaint 20 working days, admin. change 10 working days and change object max. 20 working days)
2. Allocating priority to each call and indicate ultimate date automatically! Service desk ensures calls do not copy.

Result:
Phase 1: structure, insight into work supply and excahnge knowledge: but: strongly varying average time for dealing with calls because of priority to incidents and random order of settlement plus adjustment.

Phase 2: after adjustment quicker access to data ensures increased efficiency and more focussed influence on quality of management.

→ reduction of and more stable resolution time (incident 19x shorter, complaint 3.5x, adm. change 9x and change object 2.5 x)
→ same approach fte's at growing number of locations but same number of calls. Increase number of work stations from 280 to 320.

Figure A.2.6. 2nd phase introduction ITIL

After 2000 this level was gradually improved, so that these days the availability of the IT facilities in the planned time is over 99.9% (i.e. on average less than 1,41 minute per day down) and the average response on a workstation 99% of the case-study-studies is less than 0.9 seconds.

Questions

1. What are the management objects in Emmen?
2. Indicate how within Emmen the tasks of Functional management, Application management and exploitation will be set up.
3. What is the service pit? And what is the service shell in the PinkRoccade-applications? What is this in the Internet service counter?
4. Which functional requirements does whom demand of the PinkRoccade-applications? Answer the same question for the Internet service counter. What are the differences?
5. Which performance requirements do who demand of the PinkRoccade-applications? Answer the same question for the Internet service counter. What are the differences?
6. Describe the IT-architecture of Emmen.
7. How would Gartner typify this IT organization? Why?

Part A.2. Traditional IT service management: organizing demand and supply

CASE-STUDY CHAPTER 3

A.3. The process approach: Houston energy and Atos Origin (processes)

A.3.1. Houston energy's market of energy products (*variation on the Enron case-study in O'Brien, 2002*)

Imagine Reinout Thiadens' daily job! Reinout is sat behind five 21" computer screens in an air-conditioned villa at the Rockefeller street 1 in Houston. On his screens he gets day-in, day-out an enormous amount of news, weather data and prices for future contracts of gas, coal and oil pouring in. Futures are contracts enabling procuring in the future at a certain price a certain volume in gas, coal or oil of a certain specified quality. All the information comes pouring in via his headset, via a normal telephone; he is connected to his customers and via a sort of upright standing phone with his suppliers and his colleagues. Colleagues within earshot also shout things to him from time to time.

Before the Houston Energy Online system (HEO-system) was installed, Reinout was only able to conclude a contract for supply of energy 30 to 50 times a day. These days he can quote a price for energy 30 times a minute. Through using Internet, Reinout concludes about three times as many contracts a day. The HEO-system has vastly increased the possibility to process data, whilst the possibilities for reusing data have been enormously extended.

A year after the HEO-system was installed on 12 March 2000 Houston Energy sells 100% more gas futures, 75% more oil futures and 10% more coal futures. The profits made by Houston Energy went up by 50% to a net profit of

20 million guilders per annum, whilst the number of staff remained the same (40 people in the entire company).

A.3.2. Houston energy and its market approach

Houston Energy profits from various trends. One of those is the fact that companies outsource the care for non-core processes. Another is the fact that there is pressure to keep the costs of transactions as low as possible.

Houston Energy came into being in the eighties. The government started a deregulation of the energy market and the prices started to fluctuate at a large scale. Houston Energy then saw possibilities for creating a market for trading in futures for coal, oil and gas. Houston Energy was able to match demand and supply of coal, oil and gas by making large suppliers make undertakings to sell their commodities through this market, by concluding contracts with transporters for coal and oil transports and by having its own grid of long distance pipelines. Energy can promise to supply gas of a specified quality during two months to a buyer at an agreed price. It can do the same for coal and oil.

By splitting up every transaction into parts and buying every part as cheaply as possible, Houston Energy limited the transaction costs between producers, transporters and customers. The point of view of Houston Energy is that working on the market is one large information processing process. Input of this process are millions of demand and supply signals. Output is a contract with a price. Using IT, Groningen Energy can process these signals many times faster than before. Before the web happened, Houston Energy survived on its market knowledge and the market's relative impenetrability. These days it arrives at a profit by the much larger turnover and a very clear price transparency.

A.3.3. How does Houston energy operate?

Houston Energy has a number of standard forward contracts for specified oil, coals and gas products. These contracts have:

 −a variable commencing date;
 −a duration of respectively two months, six months and a year;
 −the specified qualities per commodity;

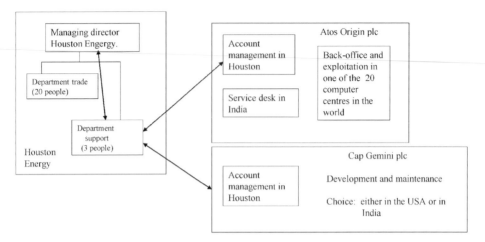

Figure A.3.1. Sourcing of IT by Houston Energy

After concluding the contract, agreements are made about the location of delivery. These costs are added to the future costs. All products are that way packaged in a number of standard contracts.

Houston Energy is for its IT exploitation entirely dependent on Atos Origin. This company takes care of the exploitation of infrastructures and applications for Houston Energy. With regard to the development and the management of its application HEO, it has concluded a contract with Cap Gemini, Groningen branch. In principle the contracts between Houston Energy, Atos and Cap are as shown in Figure A.3.1. At Houston Energy the head of administration controls the IT companies. The functional management of all applications (as far as Houston Energy is able to carry out functional management) rests with the general manager of Houston Energy. Houston Energy uses its own HEO, configured under MS dot.net, and Microsoft personal productivity tools. At the workstations IBM pc's are installed and communication with Atos and Cap Gemini takes place via a network consisting of ADSL-high-width-broadband lines. Application management for the HEO-application is done by CAP Gemini. Atos' service desk is open 24 hours a day. From all over the world, 10.000 calls daily come into Bangalore, where the desk is situated. 300 of these come in from the Texas, USA, during Texas office hours. Every call costs about 6 minutes to deal with. During 9 hours per workday (Monday to Friday) there is a special team of eight people that deals with customers from Texas (USA). These nine hours coincide with 08.00–17.00 Texas time. Outside these hours the calls are also answered in English, but not by members of this service team. Every Indian works 9 hours a day, 4 days a week and is at all times available for answering questions in English. There are 225 Indians employed at the service desk.

Questions

1. Indicate, what the average waiting time is for calls from Houston during office hours. What is in general the average waiting time before a call is answered?
2. Why do you think Atos and Cap are organized this way? What tasks will Cap Gemini and Atos have located close to Houston Energy?
3. Why have Atos and Cap organized themselves process-focused? What is the advantage and what is the disadvantage of this type of organization?
4. IT-tasks differ in volume and diversity. How are these two entities taken into account at the design and the control of the front-office-tasks of Atos (account management and service desk)?
5. Why does Houston Energy have to organize its IT, the way it did? Are there any other options?

CASE CHAPTER 4

A.4. The demand-side: chain synchronisation in retail, the Stop & Shop case (BiSL) (*using facts from an article by P. de Bie in J. van Runen et al., 2002*)

A.4.1. Introduction

Stop & Shop is an organization with 399 superstores. Stop & Shop has his head-quarters in Quincy, Massachusetts (USA). It was founded in 1914 and was in 1982 the first that introduced the superstore concept in New England.

Stop & Shop specifies centrally the superstore assortment and the corresponding pricing. The approximately 12,000 articles in this assortment are procured from 800 suppliers. There are roughly two types of supplier. The first category delivers the goods directly to the supermarket. This goes for 20% of the volume and mainly concerns meat, milk and bread. The other 80% is delivered to the shops via a Stop & Shop distribution centre.

The category direct deliveries does still include articles that could possible be supplied cheaper via the Stop & Shop distribution centre. The amount of goods that can be delivered to a shop in one delivery and the location where the goods are produced largely determines which articles. It is after all still expensive to have to drive to one single store with a half empty lorry in order to deliver the goods.

When talking about Stop & Shop, we talk about 800 (suppliers) × 7 (distribution centres) × 399 (superstores) around 2 million chains, whereby for instance:

- many suppliers have their own individual product, their own individual production line, their own specific returnable pallets, their own rules with regard to the return of goods or packaging and their own preferences for times of delivery;
- Stop & Shop's distribution centres demand spacing of deliveries over the day and over the week. Besides they want as much as possible delivered using standard pallets with a standard height.
- the superstores sometimes have to be supplied before the customers arrive because the lorries otherwise can no longer unload at the backdoor. Furthermore these sometimes struggle with a lack of warehouse space, which results in having to supply more often.

Every store order currently arrives electronically at a distribution centre and has to be supplied within 10 hours.

A.4.2. What does Stop & Shop want with its logistics?

In principle there are the following rules to be considered:

- getting the goods in should be as easy as possible for the storekeeper and should cause as little disruption of the sales process as possible. This means fewer suppliers at the backdoor and therefore limitation of the number of suppliers that take the goods directly to the stores;
- the storekeeper should have no worries about the freshness of the produce. This requires a high turnover rate in the Stop & Shop distribution centres and a minimum number of distribution centres. Furthermore not too much fresh produce should be delivered at the same time, so this can be processed adequately at delivery. The total delivery should therefore be spread over a number of individual deliveries;

– ordering the goods should not cost the storekeeper too much time. Apart from this, the customers should never have to go without the products they expect. For this reason, a forecast is made, which is compared to the supply that is present in a shop. The difference is rounded up in order units and by the storekeeper transmitted to Stop & Shop's distribution centres or the supplier.

A.4.3. Measures

The introduction of efficient consumer response (ECR) has smoothed the road for chain partners to compare their work processes and next attuning these processes. At this attunement it may become clear that some actions are unnecessary. An example is abolishing of money back deposits on many products.

Furthermore chain partners together look at the frequency and quantity per delivery. Year after year the view is confirmed that a chain should use full pallets and as many pallets as possible. This means that the manufacturer produces full pallets of products and these pallets should in fact as a whole arrive at the store via the distribution centres. For this reason the distribution centres have been constructed higher from 1990 onwards, which created more possibilities for working with pallets.

Apart from all this, the moments of delivery of articles become increasingly important. Tailbacks and delays at distribution centres cost a lot of money. By making good use of the right time-windows these can be minimized.

A.4.4. Information function within the chain

With the ECR-approach the differences in work processes and approach at the various partners in the chain become clear. It also becomes clear that the savings as realized with ECR, often one-sided land with one party.

It is desirable that the transport of goods throughout the chain is transparent and checkable and is uniform to some extent. If every supplier comes up with a different system, the storekeeper will have to create an administrative department just for performing invoice checkups. In the long run one should therefore create an optimal situation within the chain.

In order to realize this optimal situation concerning process and information function, Stop & Shop has started consultations about this with the suppliers of fresh goods and the other suppliers. In the sector fresh products there are about 10 major suppliers per distribution centre, delivering 95% of the goods. In the remaining sector there are about 20 suppliers per distribution centre, supplying 95% of the goods.

A plan for achieving an optimal information function within the chain within three years has been drawn up for all suppliers. In conformity with this plan 60% of the suppliers as well as Stop & Shop itself have to make adjustments to their applications. These adjustments will cost Stop & Shop 1 million dollars. Each and every supplier also has to invest. These investments range from 100,000 dollars to 800,000 dollars.

A.4.5. The information function within Stop & Shop

Fred Jensen is information manager at Stop & Shop. Fred has been in this position for two years and was present at the last budget round. His department consists of ten people, who are involved in functional management for the whole of Stop & Shop. In practice they perform all the tasks in user management and functionality management, as given in the BISL-model.

Fred is also present at every supplier's consultation and is a member of the internal steering committee for use of IT, of which the entire Stop & Shop management team is a member. Fred reports to the general manager. The steering committee for use of IT consists of Stop & Shop's general manager, the financial manager, the logistics manager, the personnel manager and the retail businesses manager. This steering committee meets every fortnight for half an hour, immediately after the management consultation on Monday morning.

The use of IT at Stop & Shop's information function includes their own application for distribution and logistics. The aspect systems for finances and personnel originate from SAP. Application management and exploitation are done by the Albert Heijn department of IT services or are outsourced. Where SAP is use, SAP takes care of part of the functional management and almost all application management.

The computerization plans for this year include introduction of a new version of the operating systems at the places of work at a cost of 0.5 million euro; a new release of Microsoft Office at 0.75 million euro, a new version of SAP at 0.60 million and an upgrade of the internal logistics and distribution applications at 1.5 million euro. In total the plan has earmarked 3.35 million euro for innovation. The day-to-day management of the applications inclusive of exploitation and replacement of the hardware of the infrastructure costs around 10 million euro. The total budget is therefore 13,35 million euro.

The developments within the chain force Fred to find means in the short term for funding the changes in the distribution and logistics applications. The general manager is the owner of all applications.

The users at Stop & Shop are in general happy with their IT facilities. Newer versions and releases are therefore usually implemented by Fred in order to prevent legacy and for making 'everyday life easier.' Really big efficiency benefits by means of a better use of IT cannot be realized, unless looked upon at supply chain level instead of at the level of Stop & Shop as a whole. The current releases and versions solve some minor problems and in general result in an efficiency gain of about 0.5%. A lot more could be gained if one succeeded in reducing the mistakes as made by users when entering data. About 76% of the errors in data are caused because procedures are not followed or applications are used inadequately.

Questions

1. One of the results of research into, amongst others, Stop & Shop was that one should ensure that producers get their products on the suppliers' shelves as quickly as possible. Looking at supply chain level that would be the cheapest solution for the chain as a whole because one is able to restock using full lorries at all times and has to make the trip less frequently. What does this demand of the information systems? What does this mean to the cooperation between parties? How would you solve this? Please, examine:
   – necessary synchronisation of the data;
   – changes to the IT facilities for getting the right data in time;
   – the decision process in the chain;
   – the technology to be chosen.
2. How is functional management organized at Stop & Shop? What does Fred Jensen do? Do you consider this situation optimal? Why do you? Why don't you?
3. Which BISL tasks will become important to Stop& Shop? Why? Illustrate your answer by giving an example. Is Stop & Shop equipped for this? Why is it? Why not?

4. What is legacy to Stop & Shop? Why? How does Stop & Shop try to get rid of this? What do you see concerning result focused implementing?

5. How would you adjust your computerization plan for adjusting the application for chain integration? Why don't you just do this project as well?

CASE CHAPTER 5

A.5. The supply-side: the ABN AMRO dealing room (ASL)

A.5.1. Introduction

ABN AMRO is the thirteenth bank in the world by total assets. It employs over 110,000 people. In the year 2000 it made a profit of over 2 billion euro. The bank is divided into three large business units. One unit for large customers, one for consumers and smaller business relations and one for assets management and private banking. Large customers are multinationals, governments and large care organizations. They are supplied with banking, treasury and financing services. Part of the business unit large customers, is the Amsterdam Trading Floor. This Trading Floor supports treasury services and trades in stocks and bonds. 150 million euros is invested in the Amsterdam Trading Floor. The Trading Floor has 500 computerized workstations and uses over 300 applications. Every day, over 25 billion euro worth of transactions are concluded at the Trading Floor.

A.5.2. The applications at the amsterdam trading floor

At the Trading Floor three different types of applications are known. There are applications that support the primary and secondary operational processes. There are personal productivity tools and one has access to the ABN AMRO intranet and the ABN AMRO extranet. The applications supporting operational processes enable immediate conclusion of trade transactions that arrive at the Trading Floor from the ABN AMRO officenet. These also provide access to up-to-the minute market data, one can use to develop market-making activities.

Input of data happens both manually as well as by means of spoken word. Personal productivity tools support individual tasks and enable working with complex spreadsheets, word processing software and mail programmes.

Between 1998 and 2000 the euro was introduced in these applications; these were made suitable for use on the new Trading Floor and achieved year 2000 compliancy. Requirement during all these actions was that the Trading Floor would be able to continue functioning uninterrupted.

The Trading Floor applications have to be easily acquired and operate fast and efficient at the lowest possible cost. With regard to IT, ABN AMRO aims to reduce the costs by providing insight into these. The business units that use the IT services therefore have to pay for these.

A.5.3. Management at the amsterdam trading floor in the year 2001

With regard to technology, the situation at the Amsterdam Trading Floor is as follows. Personal computers using the Windows 2000 operating system are installed at every workstation. Part of the central servers use the Unix operating system. The rest runs on VMS. KPN and BT network facilities and Nortel telephony equipment is used.

As far as IT management is concerned, the services of the IT department of the business unit large customers is used. This department comprises of a 150 people in size and has a budget of 63 million euro a year. This department focuses on achieving a high degree of service at as minimal a risk as possible at the exploitation of the applications that support the processes on the trading floor.

The IT department is organized in processes aimed at supplying services. These services are for instance:

- planning, specification and implementation of products and services by means of functional management;
- building of the products and services or assembling these through application management from services supplied by various suppliers;
- delivering exploitation products and services and controlling the services.

Within the IT department the tasks functional management, application management and exploitation are executed for all organization units of the division large customers. Front-office processes are set up in this IT department. Within these front-office processes three account groups take care of supplying IT products and services.

One of these account groups is involved in functional management tasks for the three ABN AMRO Trading Floors. These trading floors are set up in New

York, Hong Kong and Amsterdam, which enables round the clock trading. The account group carries out all functional management tasks for all applications of the trading floor. This also includes the functional implementation of applications. The technical implementation is performed by the department application management trading floor applications or by the company that has been hired for managing workstations with MS Office. In the first case, this department application management cooperates with the exploitation department Amsterdam Trading Floor of the IT department. In the second case, the IT department controls the external company.

The application management trading floor applications department is a separate department within the IT department's application management group. It takes care of the specific trading floor applications. The IT department has moreover a separate department for exploitation of all IT for the Amsterdam Trading Floor. In this exploitation department a service desk is included. This desk can be called with all queries regarding the use of IT. All trading floor applications are included in this IT, as well as the used personal productivity tool MS Office 2000 and the ABN AMRO intranet and extranet.

At the Amsterdam Trading Floor the service performances at management of IT facilities are measured permanently and adjustments are made accordingly. The measuring is also necessary because the bill for the services is directly related to the service level. An availability of the service of 99.999% with a response time in 99.99% of the time of less than 0.3 seconds 5 days a week, 24 hours a day operation is a requirement.

Questions

1. Describe how the ABN AMRO Amsterdam Trading Floor has set up its application management.
2. If you could indicate ambition levels for setting up application management and these would be as follows:
   - level 1: all tasks are performed. From a business point of view it is not necessary to actually set up the processes or use an agreed working method;
   - level 2: the processes are important. This is why significant initiatives have been taken to make these less dependent of humans. For the major part this was realized. There are templates for working methods, guidelines and the processes are safeguarded explicitly at the major points.

–level 3: the processes are that important; these are set up properly or have to be set up properly. The working methods are described, clear and relevant measuring standards are agreed and the process is continuously managed with regard to contents and standards.

–level 4: not just the processes are set up but there is also a continuous focus on improvement and optimisation. Not just a clear process set-up is provided but also an active system that constantly evaluates the processes on possibilities for improvement and introduces these in short cycles into the organization.

3. At which level does the application management for the applications of the ABN AMRO Amsterdam Trading Floor function?
4. Compare the set-up of application management with the set-up of application management as it emerges at ASL. Which are your findings? What would your action be?
5. What is legacy at ABN AMRO? How is this legacy phased out?
6. How does one or how should one deal with the management of versions and documents at the Amsterdam Trading Floor?

CASE CHAPTER 6

A.6. The supply-side: the World Port Centre and its applications (ITIL)

A.6.1. Introduction

The containership Theo 1946 sails through the Channel near Dover carrying a load of 5000 containers. The captain is aware that loading and unloading at Maersk in Rotterdam is going to take seven hours. Two hours later all 5000 containers will be on the train travelling along the Betuwe high speed railway line on their way to the Ruhr, the final destination for his cargo from Morocco. The first containers will reach the Wuppertal harbour within fourteen hours after arrival in Rotterdam. The communication with Intis, an IT facility of the Rotterdam World Port centre, in combination with the Maersk loading and unloading facilities, something he can thank his agent for, the Wijnne and Barents freighting department and the facilities of the Dutch Railways enable this super fast loading and delivery. All parties involved in the transport, that is Wijnne Barendts, the ship owner, the Rotterdam WPC, customs, the Maersk trans shipment company and the Dutch railways all work together to make the time it takes to get a transport from door to door using a ship competitive with transport by plane.

Two hours ago he sent all loading manifests off to his agent in Rotterdam. Using Intis this agent probably already has the import and export documents at the ready, obtained clearance of the freight to be unloaded and obtained permission for the required export and paid import and export duties.

Rotterdam has rebuilt its facilities entirely from scratch in the years after the Second World War. Supply chain management left its marks. Links in this chain were the creation of the container port (1965), the fundamental computerization of the administrative transaction (in phases from 1980 to 2008) and the building of the Betuwe line (2007).

A.6.2. Trade documents

Transport is information intensive, especially with the current security requirements. It is impossible for a ship without papers or a train with no documents to enter Europe. Information on cargo actually consists of information about:

- the cargo itself: type, value, port of origin, destination;
- the trading parties: owners cargo, recipients of the cargo, customs, agent, shippers, ship owners, banks, underwriters, port authorities;
- the concluded transactions: the transfer of data and goods at various moments, including transfer of storage, payment of services and rights and also sale of cargos;
- the means of transport and the people involved: date of construction ship and tests, vehicles and trains, captain, engine driver, driver.

Trade documents provide connections by means of manifests, loading bills, letters of credit, bills of entry and all other possible receipts and certificates of indemnification and reports. For the port of Rotterdam this concerns clearance papers for about 1200 vessels a day, which may each contain over 100 different types of cargo. The transport by train or inland shipping to Belgium or Germany is not included in this.

A.6.3. Intis: An infrastructure facility topped with an application

Intis connects all parties in the Rotterdam port, involved in transport of incoming and outgoing cargo. Because of Intis the elapsed time of documents in the port has been reduced from a maximum of four days to a maximum of ten minutes. This made the planning of the transport much more reliable and effective. Ships, trains and vehicles can be sure there is no delay when loading and unloading at a time set in advance because of absence of the required document. Delays caused by paperwork rarely occur anymore. Intis therefore reduced the transaction costs for dealing with the paperwork by 75%. However it did take ten years before Intis was used optimally.

WPC Informatica b.v., a 100% subsidiary of the WPC, takes care of the application management and the exploitation of the IT facility Intis. WPC Informatica b.v. is controlled by the directorate WPC Harbour transport. WPC Informatica employs 100 people, 60 in application management and 40 in a 7 × 24 hours service in exploitation.

The organization of WPC Informatica is divided into three parts:

1. the service level management and reports on service contracts;
2. the front-office, including a service desk and that delivers implementation support to organizations for products and services;
3. the back-office or the factory, where in one department the back-office tasks for the exploitation of infrastructures and applications are carried out and in another the application management. The latter includes innovation and extension of existing infrastructures and applications.

At WPC Informatica ITIL is used as the method for designing the processes in the exploitation and ASL for the processes in the field of application management. There is a common service desk and common incident management.

A.6.4. Operation of the front-office and the back-office of the exploitation department

The service desk itself can resolve relatively short calls. For calls that require over 20 minutes, the norm is to pass these on to the back-office. The calls are entered into a service desk application, called 'HP-ops support,' that supports the ITIL processes service desk, problem management, configuration management, change management and service level management at WPC Informatica.

The WPC service desk, that provides a 7×24 hour service, daily registers about 700 calls. 650 of these involve non-functioning infrastructures; about 50 of these are reports on applications. 80% of these calls are resolved by the customers themselves using the internet facility 'top ten' and the possibility to restart all by themselves using password facilities. Type, location and time of these incidents are largely registered automatically. The user supplements this registration with extra information if necessary.

The average elapsed time for dealing with a call is in 95% of the cases less than five minutes when using the on line facilities. If an operator is required, the elapsed time from the call to providing a solution is two hours in 95% of the cases for a report on infrastructures and 8 hours for a call to do with applications.

The service desk in this case registers for every call:

- the time the 'HP-ops support' system was brought into action;
- the time the calls were accepted into the second line;
- the time, a solution was found for the problem and communicated to the customer;
- the time the customer was called to ask whether they were happy with the solution.

The service desk uses only one person for answering calls. Three people work on solving incidents, calling customers when incidents are resolved and carrying out problem management.

The configuration as managed by WPC Informatica for its network has at least 300 devices supplied by Cisco. For WPC and WPC Informatica at least 1500 pc's, a server farm for Citrix metaframe, four large mini configurations and 2000 lines, leased off KPN, are managed. The network hardware is lined up at various locations along the Nieuwe Waterweg. Using intranet the network traffic on the fixed net is monitored. 95% of the incidents can be resolved remotely. For dealing with the rest of the incidents on the network a 7×24-hour-service contract was concluded with Alcatel. The call-out time for this contract is maximally 2 hours. No MTTR was agreed. Yearly about a third of the configuration is changed. That involves installing different hardware and (re)configuration of the software. Furthermore, Cisco annually releases new versions of the network software for the network. In this field WPC Informatica b.v. has a policy of being a maximum of two years behind with new versions.

A.6.5. Functioning of application management

At WPC Informatica b.v. the service performances at management of IT facilities are permanently measured. Based on the measuring, adjustments are made in Intis. This measuring is also necessary because the bill for these services is directly linked with the service level. An availability of the service of 99.999% with a response time in 99.99% of the time of less than 0.3 seconds during five days a week 24 hours a day operation is a requirement.

Currently Intis consist of an infrastructure on which front-office and back-office applications are running. The back-office applications date from the eighties and nineties. The front-office applications were built from 2001 onwards using IBM's Websphere technology. These are connected to the back-office through the message broker IBM MS-Queue.

Change in Intis is achieved using application management. The back-office has a department day-in/day-out management, a department maintenance/renewal and a staff department services and applications of tomorrow. Intis is confronted with a large increase in the use of mobile workstations, with security as a high priority. Intis is a 100% WPC-subsidiary. WPC is a public limited company of which 100% of the shares are owned by the city of Rotterdam. Intis has no competition in its field. It does however have to deliver services in conformity with the market and the times. The port of Rotterdam has to be first in chain computerization.

Questions

1. What is your opinion on this organization on dealing with calls? Which information with regard to control do you think is generated? What do you think will happen, when the information about calls is made available externally as well as internally at WPC Informatica?
2. Formulate some proposals for improvement, using the process approach. WPC Informatica b.v. has technical facilities such as a call centre with Avaya CMS, an intranet and an extranet, possibilities for speech recognition etc at its disposal. What could enhance services at WTC?

3. Indicate how configuration management and change management are implemented at WPC Informatica. Indicate how the communication between service desk and configuration/change management passes off.
4. How would you set up a change in Intis and why? How does such a change in Intis proceed? What is the task of application management in this? What is the task of exploitation?
5. Why is considering ITIL important to WPC Informatica b.v.?

CASE CHAPTER 7

A.7. Organizing IT tasks and IT sourcing at Union Insurance in montreal (*adaptation of Drouven, 2001*)

A.7.1. Introduction

Union Insurance is a Canadian mutual insurance company. It has its headquarters in Montreal. The company deals in life, health and indemnity insurances and has 90 offices all over Quebec. It sells insurance by telephone, post and on the internet. Union Insurance has an annual turnover more than 1 billion euros. Union Insurance currently manages 17 million policies and employs 3500 staff. The IT environment includes large Siemens servers for property and casualty insurance, large Unisys servers for health insurance, Compaq minis for the life insurances and Unisys minis with EMC2 storage media for all new products and services. In the workplaces, personal computers running Windows 2000 and Windows XP as operating systems are used. The network operates using TCP/IP.

In 1997, Union Insurance started to outsource the management of its workplaces and servers and also the management of its network. This outsourcing was contracted out to two suppliers. One supplier converted the workplaces from operating under DOS/Novell to operating under the operating system Windows '95 or Windows 2000 using the network protocol TCP/IP. Next, this supplier took over the management of these workplaces. The other supplier changed the network from a network using the SDLC protocol into a network using TCP/IP. All point-to-point connections were also linked to the network. This supplier also took over the management of the installed products, in this case the network.

A.7.2. Outsourcing of workplaces and networks

For the management of workplaces and servers a framework contract with underlying service agreements was concluded. In these service agreements precise agreements were made about the service to be provided. The various types of consultation on various levels within the organization were also established. The services were set up in conformity with the ITIL methodology. The manager of the workplaces and servers also controlled the network manager. To this purpose, he/she came to agreements with these managers, which were recorded in service level agreements.

This experience with outsourcing taught Union Insurance, that the implementing in phases of technological change and the execution of the corresponding training programme, as a consequence of the approach chosen by Union Insurance and the supplier might run successfully. The supplier's expertise and the way the relationship supplier/Union Insurance was set up both played a part in this.

The transfer from the conversion project to the organization set-up for daily management was not flawless. On top of this, the on-charge of IT costs was a constant source of resentment in this daily management and the control of the supply organization did not run smoothly because of the shared responsibilities at Union Insurance. This control was also influenced by the take-over of the supply organization by a foreign organization and the resulting change of management. All this led to the operational ITIL tasks not living entirely up to their promise. Finally, Union Insurance discovered that the supply organization often made an appeal to the supplemental work clause and that in the control of the contract; this was not dealt with adequately.

Going through the positive and negative experiences with outsourcing once again, Union Insurance concluded in 1999 that the relationship with the supply organization was mediocre, that the costs more and more got out of hand, that the agreed service levels consequently were not achieved and that there was an increase in interventions at managerial level. Things became that bad, that Union Insurance considered going to court. In 1999 this resulted in the management contract being dissolved.

Union Insurance learnt from this life cycle of outsourcing that just having a good contract is insufficient. Control of a supply organization involves contract management and contract management is a trade. In this case of a good contract and good management, the space as built in by both parties is filled

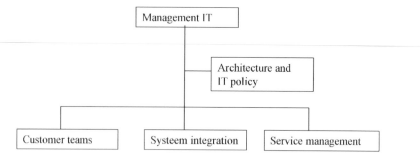

Figure A.7.1. The Union Insurance IT organization

in to everybody's satisfaction. An outsourcing contract should include a certain amount of dynamics.

A.7.3. Set-up of the Union Insurance IT organization

As a result of the experiences with outsourcing, Union Insurance adjusted its IT organization. The focus of the IT organization was aimed at the day in, day out management, in which the new services and products were always procured on the market or the development of these was put out to tender. Union Insurance set up an in-house IT organization with a core consisting of policy advisors, account managers, project managers, information architects, system integrators, service managers and IT infrastructure specialists (see Figure A.7.1).

The service management department is set up for controlling the day to day management by third parties. It manages the budget, has extensive powers and closely cooperates with the customer teams. The department consists of service managers for process control and IT infrastructure specialists for quality control. Their work is supported by an application for the ITIL processes service desk, configuration management and problem management.

Union Insurance also has accommodated the knowledge necessary for arriving at outsourcing contracts in a permanent team, that includes employees from various divisions of the organization. This team consists of a lawyer, a service manager and a system integration specialist. This is ad hoc, supplemented with financial and human resource knowledge.

Each life cycle of outsourcing starts by setting-up the demand organization. Next, this organization draws up a request for proposal. On the basis of this proposal, suppliers are invited to submit a quote. This quote results in a declaration of intent from Union Insurance. On the basis of this, the process continues and framework agreements and service agreements are drawn up. These contracts if necessary, include the transfer of configuration items and people to the manager, a transition period is agreed and agreements are recorded about the dates on which the agreed service levels have to be achieved.

Questions

1. Give an outline of the demand and supply organization for IT at Union Insurance.
2. Has Union Insurance set up its IT organization in conformity with the model for smaller organizations or in conformity with the model for larger organizations? Explain your answer.
3. In which areas could the Union Insurance IT organization be improved? What does attract the attention, when for example looking at the functional management organization? Compare this with a management organization set-up in conformity with the BISL method?
4. In your opinion, which reasons did Union Insurance have for arriving at outsourcing? How do you think, Union Insurance set up the organization of the outsourcing? Which processes are crucial in this process and how is this shown?
5. How does the Galbraith model fit in with the situation at Union Insurance? Explain your answer.

Part A.3. Controlling IT Facilities

CASE CHAPTER 8

A.8. Controlling IT facilities: the shared service centres at Philips semiconductors *(adaptation of van Dalen, 2004)*

A.8.1. Introduction

Philips Semiconductors employs 60,000 people worldwide. The company has 80 fully staffed computer centres all for development and maintenance of applications used in the building of microchips. The total expenditure of these centres is over 100 million euro per annum. Philips Semiconductors aims to reduce these costs by 30%. It wants to achieve this by introducing shared service centres. In principle, the Compass program that these centres will realize from 2004 onwards, involves the following:

(a) realizing corresponding services and products. The services are designed with the use of the ITIL process model;

(b) ensuring identical control. For this purpose ratios as shown in Figure A.8.1 were developed.

(c) the set-up of one competence centre for development of procedures, set-up of task forces for special projects and auditing of compliance of the centres;

(d) the set-up of five control centres for the 80 physical computer centres. These physical centres are not staffed. Using this set-up, it is possible to work 24 hours a day in the control centres.

```
Service desk clients per Full time equivalent employee (FTE)
Windows Servers per FTE
UNIX servers per FTE
Productive hours per FTE
Overall management span of control
FTE contribution to Competence Center related management processes
Number of sizes of Shared Service Centra's (SSC) (1000-6000 clients)
Availability management (hours per 1000 clients)
Build and test
Business assessment process (hours per 1000 clients)
Capacity management process (hours per 1000 clients)
Change management process (hours per 1000 clients)
Configuration management process (hours per 1000 clients)
Cost management process (hours per 1000 clients)
Customer management process (hours per 1000 clients)
IT strategy development process (hours per 1000 clients)
Operations management process (hours per 1000 clients)
Release to production process (hours per 1000 clients)
Service level management process (hours per 1000 clients)
Service planning process (hours per 1000 clients)
Incident management process (hours per 1000 clients)
Problem management process (hours per 1000 clients)
```

Figure A.8.1. Key performance indicators for a shared service

A.8.2. Control of an SSC

Each SSC has the same tasks and processes. Furthermore, each SSC in controlled in the same manner. Control is carried out on the basis of key performance indicators. In order to realize these, timekeeping has been introduced for all 6000 people in the entire IT organization. The processes of the service centre are developed in one central competence centre. Each of the 80 locations may expect extra services from an SSC. These extra services are supplied over and above the normal SSC services. The SSC manager is controlled by general management and is not controlled by business management.

The key performance indicators relate to all areas of the SSC. These indicators exclude development of applications, administrative support, telephone expenses, consultancy fees and special services such as video conferencing.

The competence centre also provides control for the SSC's. The competence centre control aims at five or more technical fields and three specific application areas. The technical fields are the front-end servers and storage, the back-end servers and storage, the networks, security and continuity and generally used applications such as for example MS Office. The three application areas are production, engineering and business applications. The competence centre actually takes care of all BISL areas. It operates as a functional management organization for the SSC's.

A.8.3. The SSC's

Each SSC controls 14 physical computer centres. Each SSC realizes the products in the worldwide-standardized service catalogue. It has also concluded service level agreements with each of its customers.

Experience teaches that these SSC's in various fields, need to develop towards a different level of service provision. These levels of development concern the exploitation of IT facilities, the rapportage on these, the control, the services and dealing with the concept of 'demand and supply organization.' The various distinctive levels are like those recognized in the EFQM model: activity-oriented, process-oriented, system-oriented, chain-oriented and transform and excel.

Questions

1. In general outline, how will the IT control of SSC's be put together? Who takes care of functional management, who looks after application management, who is responsible for exploitation? How is the relationship with stakeholders outside Philips? Who are they?
2. There are six possible areas for control:
   –establishing priority;
   –innovation choices;
   –organization including sourcing;
   –skills;
   –organizational support;
   –methods.
   (a) using the diagram of 'high priority current applications/low priority innovation,' indicate where the Philips' SSC project is situated;
   (b) how has Philips positioned the choice between radical and incremental innovation?
   (c) which organizational choice was made? Which knowledge therefore needs to be present?

    (d) what does the case say on guidelines and methods? On organizational support?

3.   When looking at the level of operating of this shared service, what possibilities do you expect for filling out a Balanced Score Card?

CASE CHAPTER 9

A.9. House in order: evaluate and improve, Canteen Vending Machines (CVM) Kyoto (Japan)

A.9.1. Introduction

Kyoji Komachi, director of CVM, is considering Autall, a computer application, developed for improving the service to the customers. CVM is in Japan, second with regard to market share in the market of canteen machines. CVM wants to progress towards a more customer-oriented approach, so much so that of all funds quoted on the Nikkei stock exchange, over 80% of the drinks and snack machines will be purchased from CVM. CVM is organized in two divisions, being:

    −a design, manufacturing and installation division;
    −a maintenance division.

CVM includes two product ranges. CVM 'snacks' for soft drinks and snacks and CVM 'warm' for coffee, tea, soups, hot chocolate etc. Since early 1983 all machines are fitted with microprocessor-based control units. These enable proactive maintenance on the machines, the storing of maintenance and repair data that is then transported to the central CVM database.

A.9.2. The Vending machine business

The market for new CVM machines is strongly dependent on the number of new buildings that customers put into use. The service market on the other hand is very stable. However, there are a number of companies active in this market. The choice of a service company is often made on the basis of price-performance ratios. This means that large numbers of machines could switch service organization all at once.

A.9.3. IT and operating customer-oriented

CVM installed around 75,000 machines in Japan. For servicing these machines, 100 people day in day out are on the move. This service division installed its first computer in 1975 in its in-house IT supply organization, in order to enable sending invoices for maintenance. From 1980, possibilities were added to this application for enabling viewing stock of parts on line, checking debtors' balances and requesting service contracts.

In 1985, CVM started to investigate to what extent IT would be able to support a department that could deal with customers' requests day and night for solving breakdowns in machines. At the time, outside office hours CVM utilized an external company for taking these calls. This company had insight into the schedule of the service division and therefore was able to send a mechanic. During office hours CVM took care of this. Customers usually relate the quality of the CVM service to the time it takes a mechanic to arrive. CVM had the experience that the external company was less focussed on keeping this time as short as possible.

After an investigation in 1988 in Kyoto, a call centre application was installed for supporting the central call centre. In 1988 this application was extended with an e-mail facility. The customer can ring a free phone number or send an e-mail. These arrive at CVM, the call is registered and if necessary a mechanic is sent. Mechanics are often responsible for breakdowns and precautionary maintenance at certain customers. CVM knows that using a dedicated mechanic saves around 2% on the annual average service costs of a machine because of the reduction in extra visits.

A.9.4. The autall application

Autall is an application that supports maintenance work. In the first version dating back to 1984, Autall only contained a customer database. In the current version, Autall keeps a record of all service data, amongst other thing by reading out all the microprocessors. Autall makes the work of the service division visible and ensures a better service to the customer. The Autall reports, provide insight into the performance of the mechanics and into the problems with certain types and series of machines. Furthermore, Autall is connected with an early-warning system that gives special attention to machines that breakdown more than twice a month. Autall enables cost price calculations for services per customer and per machine. All departments of the CVM service division use Autall. This division is staffed by 130 people.

A.9.5. Impact of autall on the processes in the CVM organization

The use of Autall is of influence on the CVM organization. Let us examine this influence.

At the IT department, the pressure for supplying consistent service has increased. It turned out that if Autall was not available for an hour, the work of the staff slowly ground to a halt and around 25% of the effectiveness of the mechanics' work was lost. Therefore, for achieving the functional and performance requirements for the support by IT, the budget for IT was increased by 170% over the 1990–2003 period. The central, 7 times 24 hours call centre, is staffed with highly educated employees. At commencement of employment, Autall trains everyone for six weeks in the use of computer and telephony equipment, in dealing with telephone calls, the CVM organization receives and provides some information on the vending machine business. This knowledge is periodically updated. Operators are taught to update the Autall data during contacts with customers and to enter additional customer data. The management controls actively on the level of the conversations with customers by means of evaluation and advice to the operators. The call centre gets around 300 calls a day about breakdowns. During office hours, four operators are on call and outside office hours there are two. The service mechanics report via the microprocessors when they arrived at the breakdown and when this was solved. They also report in writing which actions they took. That way it is centrally known in writing, which mechanic serviced which machine and what action he took. The sales department has customer data and service data at its disposal. It supplements this with information from customer contacts, which means that a picture emerges of all machines that are in use at a certain customer.

Questions

1. The CVM service organization is dependent to a high degree of the support by IT facilities. Which functional and performance requirements are demanded from the products that deliver these facilities and the process of delivery?
2. In which ways can one look at this process of delivery? Which level of service provision does the IT supply organization have with regards to process?
3. What are the requirements the IT organization has to meet in conformity with ISO 9000-2000?
4. Is it necessary to minimize the operation risk of non-availability of IT facilities? How is this achieved?
5. How would an accountant check the processes at the IT facilities of CVM?

CASE CHAPTER 10

A.10. Innovation from customer and chain perspective: the french land registry on line

A.10.1. Introduction

By collecting data on registrable property in France, keeping this up to date in public registers and on cadastral maps and next placing this data at the disposal of society, the Land Registry provides clarity regarding to whom a specific property subject to registration belongs to and what its characteristics are. By property subject to registration, is meant immovable property or real estate (such as houses, apartments and other buildings and works that are permanently fixed to the ground) and moveable property (such as ships and aircraft). The Land Registry wants to develop further as a professional, market-oriented organization into a central organization for real estate and geo information and do pioneering work in this market. It also wants to increase the accessibility and availability of its information and guarantee the quality of this for its professional and private customers. In all this, cooperation with other organizations in the property market is of importance.

The Land Registry bases its strategy for the coming years on a number of targets. One of these targets is more and better attention for its customers'

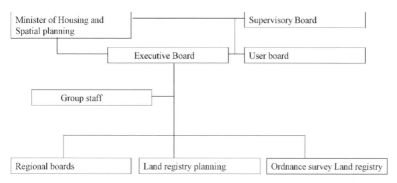

Figure A.10.1. Organization Land Registry

requests. Information and communication technology ensure that it becomes increasingly easier to link property databases. For the customers of the Land Registry, this means that it is easier to realize their specific wishes. Besides, one wants to offer one's customers a choice of distribution channels. For instance, by making Land Registry information and products available on line on the internet to both private persons as well as companies. Another target of the Land Registry is to extend its existing activities wherever possible. The merger with the French Ordnance Survey as per 1 January 2004 is an example of this, which means an important extension of the activities of the Land Registry and of the services and products for the private and corporate market.

A.10.2. Organization and turnover of the land registry

Since 1994 the Land Registry is an autonomous administration authority within the French government organization. The Land Registry carries out its tasks with approval from the Ministry of Housing and Spatial Planning. The Supervisory Board oversees the day-to-day running of the concern that is in the hands of the Executive Board. With regard to affairs of general interest, the Executive Board is advised by the User Boards. The Land Registry operates on the long-term policy plan and the Charter Public Responsibility. The Land Registry cooperates with a number of organizations in the domain of real estate, for increasing the informative value of the data as registered by the Land Registry. Quality and privacy are important values with regard to this (Figure A.10.1).

The head office of the Land Registry has its seat in Paris and consists of eight staff units, being:

1. Office Executive Board. This office advises on and facilitates policy and company judicial, internal, and external communication for the entire Land Registry organization.
2. General and technical services: this facilitates and advises all staff units on financial management, human resources execution tasks, information function, multimedia, graphic services, central procurement, general and technical support services and accommodation.
3. Finances & Control: this management supports and advises the Executive Board in the financial operational management of the Land Registry.
4. Information policy and Projects: this management is responsible for the IT policymaking and planning and the realization of new systems. Besides, IPP advises on IT developments.
5. IT services. This management offers IT services that guarantee continuity, quality and professionalism of the systems and translates customer requests into IT services and IT solutions.
6. Land Registry International. This is an advisory body that places knowledge and experience at the disposition of countries where land registry systems are less well developed (especially the former French colonies in Asia and Africa).
7. Personnel & Organization. This is responsible for the development of an integral personnel and organization policy. This policy influences the primary and supporting operational processes and contributes to a good work atmosphere.
8. Real estate information & Geodesy. This management sets the course as regards to professional contents for the policy concerning products and services of the Land Registry and determines the preconditions for the execution.

The Information policy and Projects management outlines the IT policy and develops new applications. In the IT services management, IT infrastructures and applications are managed. This is where the tasks application management and exploitation take place. The management dealing with matters such as for example finances and control, real estate information, land development etc. each execute their own functional management (Figure A.10.2).

In 2002, the Land Registry realized a turnover of around 780 million euro. On 31st December 2002, the number of structural jobs was around 8000

Sale of around 60.000.000 information products in 2002 distributed over the following customers (approximate numbers)::	
Building industry	1.500.000
Housing corporations	180.000
Utility companies	500.000
Financial houses	2.800.000
District water boards	360.000
Municipalities	1.100.000
estate agents	9.000.000
Accountants and administration offices	560.000
Bailiffs and collecting agencies	625.000
Central government	1.200.000
Private individuals	400.000
Other	2.500.000
Office of notary	38.000.000

Figure A.10.2. Turnover at various groups of customers

people and the number of temporary ones 800. The number of (part-time) employees with permanent employment was 8400 and the Land Registry employed around 900 persons temporarily. Of all employees, 77% were male and 23% female. The average age of a Land Registry employee in 2002 was 47.16 years; in 2001, the average age was 46.51 years.

A.10.3. Deliveries by the land registry and the customers' wishes

In 2002, the Land Registry supplied around 60,000,000 information products to various groups of customers. The most important customers of the Land Registry are the office of notary (63% of the volume) and estate agencies (17%). Since 1/1/2004, the Land Registry can supply maps on every scale between 1:500 up to and including of 1:250.000. Utility companies and councils use the first type of map in metropolitan areas. The last-mentioned map is for example that one uses as a basis for their roadmaps. In a customer satisfaction survey in 2001, the customers hinted that they did require a number of improvements in certain areas. In the years after 2001, this resulted in the following actions:

1. Improvement of the accessibility and user friendliness of the on line approach to Land Registry information. To this purpose, Land Registry-on-line was introduced towards the end of 2001. This is a service based on internet technology, that initially enabled professional customers to gain

access easily and efficiently to Land Registry information from every workplace. From the summer of 2001, customers have in phases been enabled to switch to Land Registry-on-line. By now, almost all customers have done this. Furthermore, the opening hours have been extended. On work days one can get access to cadastral information until 21.00 hrs and on Saturday from 09.00–16.00 hrs. In conclusion, the quality of their support during the extended opening hours has improved.

2. Introducing innovations in products and services. The following innovations came onto the market:
   - More search possibilities have been added to Land Registry-on-line, such as direct access through the appropriate map. Because of this, the cadastral information about rural, agricultural plots, without need for an address or postcode has become more accessible.
   - The registration of information on ships is renewed and is opened through Land Registry-on-line.
   - Private persons are also allowed to consult information using the website of the Land registry after making an electronic payment.

3. Ensuring clarity of services and invoices based on this. Regarding this, a start was made with:
   - publishing of delivery times. Delivery times have been set per product or service and are for example to be found on the internet site of the Land registry. There is also a product catalogue. In this catalogue, all products are described, including tariffs, delivery times and method of application.
   - sending one single invoice for Land Registry services per period. Previously, customers received an invoice from every Land Registry region they were doing business with.
   - ensuring the on time dealing with complaints and objections. For all objections and complaints, within three days after receipt, a written confirmation of receipt sent. Next, the elapsed time of resolution is tracked centrally.

A.10.4. Medium-term perspective 2004–2008

The long-term policy plan 2004–2008 is set up annually by the Executive Board of the Land Registry based on article 22 of the Organization Act Land

Registry. This plan is, before approval by the French minister of Housing and Spatial planning, presented to the User Board for advice and decreed by the supervisory board. In the plan as approved by the minister and drawn up in 2003 amongst other things, the following targets are mentioned:

1. optimising the execution. To this purpose, the office of notary will be enabled to deliver deeds electronically. This method of delivery results in a saving of 12 million euro on a yearly basis. Furthermore, the quality of operational processes will be strongly controlled. Links with other public information such as the municipal personal records database and Chamber of Commerce registers will be realized.

2. the development of the existing public task. For this purpose, there will be a merger with the French Ordnance Survey. In France, this will result in large-scale maps of the Land Registry and the small-scale maps of the Ordnance Survey ending up under the same roof. Furthermore, the registration of statutory limitations and sale agreements is prepared.

3. emphasizing more on the use of the information. For one thing, action will be undertaken for expanding the number of connections of Land Registry-on-line, for another the information will be made more accessible by introducing national personalized access, a more flexible delivery of geographical information and the development of supplementary services concerning land development. Finally, there will be more attention to the private market. This will, amongst other things, be realized by installing an 'internet counter' for the benefit of integrating Land Registry-on-line in governmental internet counters.

This long-range plan results in renewal of the primary operational systems for the cadastral registration. In 2002, a choice was made for gradual construction and implementation of parts of the new system next to the existing system. Point of departure is the continuity of the service to customers. When adjustment of information products is necessary, a reasonable transitional period will be used in consultation with coordinating customer groups.

Currently the national registration of personal data and addresses is developed. Based on this, national personalized access at the on line information function will become possible (the project Cadastral registration of personal data) and the further extension of Land Registry-on-line. Besides, a first step has been taken towards the set-up of a separate national database or information distribution, which over the next period should result in a Cadastral Information service with integrated cartographic and administrative information. Next, existing output products, including the 'Massive Output', will be renewed. Apart from this, the further realization of the computerized public register takes place. The renewal of the registration functions of the present primary operational systems will be further prepared. The actual realization of this will be outside the plan period, as well as the realization of one single national computerized public register (the current computerized public register is set up per branch).

The aim is to keep the IT expenditure at the same level. For this purpose, simplification of the technical infrastructure and reduction of the diversity in applications are necessary. The increased use of IT (internet) in opening up cadastral information requires more attention for security. Because the operational processes both internally as well as externally connect with each other more closely, larger mutual dependencies are introduced and new security risk come into being. For this reason the Land Registry updates the internal security guidelines three times a year, which is in keeping with the code for information security (ISO-norm). In order to be able to guarantee the security of information systems in case of a disaster, from 1 February 2004 the exploitation of the applications is divided over two locations.

A.10.5. IT organization and objects

The Information Policy and Projects management consists of 400 people. It outlines the IT policy and develops new applications. The IT services management of 600 people takes care of the exploitation of IT infrastructures and applications: the Land Registry uses technology for this that is accepted in the market. The operational processes for finances, personnel and procurement are supported by the SAP ERP application. For the support of its primary processes, the Land Registry has developed its own mortgage system, a property registration system and a system for supporting mapping processes. Their own staff maintains these last processes. Recent developments in the Land Registry are (apart from the above-mentioned in observing the customers' wishes):

– the rollout from February 2002 of the system for scanning analogue deeds and processing and storing these digitally (Scan-Elan): This means that the operating processes are from 1 January 2004 largely prepared for the

arrival of electronically delivered deeds. The introduction of electronic
delivery of deeds is only waiting for amendment of the Land Registry act.

– the set-up of a nationwide cartographical information database and the
set-up of one single national personal and address registration.

– increasingly reducing IT costs, in which for the fourth year running relatively more money was spent on innovation than on management and
exploitation. In 2002, the expenditure was 58.9 million euro, a reduction
of 1.5 million euro compared to 2001.

– the complexity reduction in the technical infrastructure. The decentralized
computer centres in the branches are therefore dismantled and concentrated at the head office in Paris and standardization of hardware at the
workplace has been worked on.

Questions

1. Work out the four different areas of a service for the Land Registry-on line
   service. This includes e.g. interaction and work, necessary basic facilities,
   relationship achieved and the result.
2. Which trends in provision of services do we see return at the Land Registry?
   What does this mean to the front- and back-office of their IT facilities?
3. Which phases can one distinguish when realizing a service such as Land
   Registry-on-line? Explain these phases by means of a case study.
4. How does one see elements like location, chain and attention to functions and
   roles return in Land Registry-on-line?

Part A.4. Aspects of IT management

CASE CHAPTER 11

A.11. The financial aspects: use of benchmarks at housing corporation IN in Duisburg (*variation on a lecture by P. van Dijk and A. de Vries, 2004*)

A.11.1. The IN housing corporation

The IN housing corporation was created in 2000 after the Public Housing corporation Duisburg and the Student housing foundation merged. It is a non-profit organization. Its customers are people on a low income, students and people that need extra care. Its main activities are amongst other things, letting of houses and rooms, district management, maintenance of housing and project development.

IN has 11,500 letting units. IN employs 160 staff. IN has an annual turnover of 46 million euro. The organization wants to professionalize and for that reasons invests strongly in IT facilities. Recent IT projects are for instance, the introduction of e-mail and internet, the renewal of the networks, storage and processing facilities, the introduction of a documentary information system, the implementation of a data warehouse, the set-up of a service desk and making the website interactive.

IN has 140 workplaces all supported by IT. IN employs four IT employees, utilizing a computer centre with twelve servers. These servers operate under the operating system MS Windows 2000. These servers run about 30 different applications. Applications and system software are automatically distributed to the workplaces.

The management of the telephony and the data networks are extraneous to the work of the IT department. In 2003, the exploitation budget for IT was 800,000 euro. The investments come on top of this. In 2001, these amounted to 250,000 euro, 1,000,000 euro in 2002 and 400,000 euro in 2003. Because of the proposed replacement of applications by an ERP application, the budget for 2004 is 1,500,000 euro.

A.11.2. The benchmark

The IN housing corporation annually takes part in the benchmark for IT expenditure of the housing corporations. In total 23 housing corporations in Germany, take part in this benchmark. Taking part in the benchmark costs each corporation 2000 euro. The benchmark is based on a TCO model. The process of the benchmark runs as follows:

(a) the participants each receive a cost model. It is expected that they indicate on this:
   – the expenditure for the IT organization;
   – the expenditure for the workplaces inclusive of workplace applications;
   – the expenditure for the local area network (LAN);
   – the expenditure for the wide area network (WAN);
   – the expenditure for storage and processings inclusive of applications;
   – the expenditure for speech facilities;
These expenses are split into non-recurring investments and annual expenses.
(b) Next, the participants have 10 weeks for filling out the forms. During these ten weeks, there is a meeting in week six, where questions can be asked about the data to be filled out and exchange experiences.
(c) In week 10, researchers collect the questionnaires at each corporation. On this same occasion, a personal validation talk takes place.
(d) Finally, all the data is processed and the results are presented in week 12.

An external company, in cooperation with the Network IT of the housing corporations, set up the benchmark. In this respect, these information managers of the housing corporations regularly meet. For being able to execute the benchmark, it's scope and target were defined in advance. Next, every organization in the target group registered its IT expenditure in conformity with the standard definitions to be used in the benchmark.

The benchmark lists for all organizations together and for each separately:

- the IT expenditure per rented unit per housing corporation (average of 91 euro);
- the number of rented units per workplace (average 97 rented units/ workplace);
- the IT expenditure (including speech) per workplace (8475 euro on average);
- the ratio between workplaces number of employees; (1.07 on average);
- the percentage of IT costs of the annual turnover (1.96% on average);
- the number of employees per IT employee (40 on average);
- division of expenditure per object category (infrastructure, applications, organization, other);
- division of the expenditure per type of object (organization, I/O, LAN, WAN etc.).

A.11.3. Participating in the benchmark

IN participates in the benchmark for IT costs. It wants to know whether its high IT costs are justifiable; it want to view its position with regard to its colleagues; it wants to exchange experiences; it regularly wants to have a finger (held) on the pulse and see whether perhaps there are economies possible it has not noticed.

In order to be able to partake in the benchmark, IN had to adjust the way it records it's data. The definitions have been straightened and in accounting, the registration of expenditure is standardized on the benchmark. Extra data has also been added, such as the tax write-offs that previously were not registered per object. After these preparatory actions, it takes IN about two days to fill out the questionnaire.

IN uses the results of the benchmark, in which it participates for the third time in 2004, for looking critically at its expenditure. Furthermore, it wants to be able to explain peaks in expenditure. For example, the IT expenditure per rented unit is 118 euro, the costs per workplace 10,000 euro and the costs for IT as percentage of the annual turnover 2.9%. That means that IN has higher costs than the other corporations. It explains it by its sizeable IT renewal programme. IN expects that consolidation of the twelve servers and the coming introduction of an ERP package—which means that for the exploitation of certain applications it no longer needs to use an external company—will reduce the costs rapidly from 2005 onwards.

Questions

1. Which data does this benchmark supply? Which not? What is the disadvantage of using this TCO model?
2. What does this mean for those concerned at cost data? How does this fit in with the trends?
3. What is your view on using benchmarking in IN? Where is this application successful? Where are the possible gaps?
4. Does the IN supply organization on-charge its costs to the demand organization? Why does it? Why not?
5. Which cost model is used? What does this mean? Does IN behave accordingly? What does this show or does this not show?
6. What does IN do at introduction of on-charge of costs?

CASE CHAPTER 12

A.12. The personnel aspects: experiences with competency management at Italian Insurance
(adaptation of gompers, 2000)

A.12.1. Introduction

Italian Insurance is an insurance bank with offices in the twenty largest cities of Italy. In order to become an international player, the strategy of Italian Insurance is aimed at offering its insurances to its customers entirely via the internet within two years. Italian Insurance bank wants to be the on line supplier of mortgages, insurances and, in the long-term, other financial services. This strategy is a challenge for its IT demand and supply organization. Because of the large-scale use of internet technology, this organization is more closely involved in the primary process and its customers.

In order to be able to provide the services, the management of the IT organization has started a massive renewal programme. This programme consist of five parts, being:

1. renewal of the architecture of the IT facilities;
2. implementation of professional application development methods and redesign of the management organization, in which for application management the ASL method and or functional management BISML are implemented. This implementation will take the context of Italian Insurance into account;
3. improvement of the exploitation of IT facilities and set-up of these using the ITIL method for a basis.
4. at reorganization of the IT organization, a demand and a supply organization are set up. In the front-office of the demand organization, a service desk is set up, which can be approached by the entire organization. The supply organization will have a front-office with a service desk exclusively for the demand organization. Operations between demand and supply organization take place based on service level agreements. The demand organization and the supply organization will be separated. Each reports to a different member of the Executive Board. The demand organization reports to the member of the Executive Board responsible for Operations. The supply organization comes under the executive that is responsible for the general and technical support services.
5. grading up the employees by means of the introduction of competency management. In this, the necessary functions and corresponding knowledge and skills are defined. Employees are allocated to new functions, often with the requirement to develop the necessary behavioural skills within a certain period. In this lifecycle, their own manager and an external organization coach them.

There are various reasons for the management of the IT demand and the IT supply organization to enter into competency management. Firstly, one wants to use mainly in-house people for designing the necessary changes. Especially the IT supply organization includes at the start of the lifecycle of renewal, many external employees that cannot be replaced by internal employees just like that.

The in-house employees do indicate they want to take over tasks of these outsiders but also know they will first have to acquire the necessary skills. The management of the IT demand and the IT supply organization therefore went looking for a system that provides more insight into the knowledge and skill present in their own employees and assists in setting up development and career paths. The systematic approach to competency management and especially the method as was carried out at Dutch Telecom company KPN and reported in the literature were very appealing. In this, one wishes to emphasize the cultivation of the ability to change in the individual employee and all this because the management does expect the current change to be quickly followed by more change.

A.12.2. Approach to the introduction of competency management

To start with, Italian Insurance applies competency management to groups of employees. These are the management team of the demand and the supply organization and the service managers of various service processes in the supply organization. The service managers are chosen because they play a central part in the realization of service management and implementation processes; the management team because the managers play a crucial role in the creation of the ability to change in the IT demand and the IT supply organization. The IT demand and the IT supply organization have function profiles for the service desk manager, the problem manager and the configuration manager. However, experience teaches that these function profiles do not present any handles for controlling these managers. The function descriptions do define the tasks that these managers have to execute but do not go into the result that is expected of them. It is also difficult to ascertain what training these managers should have. This requires knowledge of the process in question and some consensus on the skills that are important for the execution of the function.

Italian Insurance uses competency management for making a concrete translation from the design of the front-office and back-office processes for functional management, application management and exploitation into process and function competencies. This is the basis for the competency profiles for the service managers responsible for the various processes. Based on the process for change management, it has been determined which competencies the manager responsible for change management has to comply with.

Italian Insurance will achieve competency management for both the new demand as well as the new supply organization in conformity with the following step-by-step plan:

1. A meeting is held, where the core competency of the new IT organization is determined and an answer is formulated to the question which knowledge, which behaviour and which skills one has to have at one's disposal for substantiating the started changes.
2. By means of interviews, workshops and the process design, the process competencies are determined. This answers the question which knowledge, which behaviour and which skills are required for a service desk process, a configuration management process, a change management process etc.
3. Next, the function profiles are set. One defines which technical and which personal behavioural competencies are required for an individual function such as the one of service desk manager etc.
4. Next, the competency profiles of the current organization and its employees are determined. To this purpose, the competencies and talents at group and individual level are assessed.
5. This analysis generates input for a process that determines which of the set requirements, the current functionaries comply with and what their discrepancy is with the requested competencies. On this basis, it becomes clear which development these functionaries have to go through and which knowledge and skills they have to acquire.
6. Next, action is taken for bridging the differences as noticed. This entails making plans for education, defining career paths, providing training, recruiting, coaching and job rotation.
7. At the same time, the human resource tools are adjusted, so these optimally play along with the new method of personnel management and the management is trained to use these tools.

Questions

1. The IT demand and the IT supply organization of Italian Insurance has chosen for competency management. Looking at the approach of competency management, do you consider this approach suitable to every IT organization? Explain your answer.

2. What are in your opinion, the preconditions for making such an approach successful? To what extent do elements like context and role of a functionary play a part? Explain your answer.
3. Which competencies are in your opinion of importance in more tactical front-office tasks, in respectively the demand and the supply organization and do these play a part in the more technical back-office tasks?

CASE CHAPTER 13

A.13. Procurement of IT facilities: procurement at Diesel Engines International. (DEI GmbH) in Berlin.
(variation on a case in Applegate et al., 2003)

A.13.1. Introduction

DEI GmbH realizes a turnover of 3 billion euro and has its head office in Berlin (Germany). The company is market leader in the field of diesel engines, both standard models as well as engines made to customers' specifications. DEI GmbH has sales departments all over the world and 75% of its turnover comes from export. DEI GmbH is a profitable company. For twenty years, DEI GmbH distributed a dividend of 6% per annum to its shareholders.

Towards the end of 1999, a team of junior managers realizes that the streamlining of procurement and sales processes through internet technology support could provide great advantages to DEI GmbH. It recommends to do this gradually by first taking care of a web infrastructure which allows customers to access the website, communicate with the DEI GmbH and place orders. Next, the back-office applications have to be web enabled. To this purpose, the legacy applications should be replaced by an ERP application. At the same time, the technical infrastructure with regard to storage and processing should be located at a modern IT service provider. The reasons for these recommendations are:

1. the current computer centres of DEI GmbH are not accommodated to ensure 99.9% availability of facilities 7 times 24 hours. The thought of housing a small number of high availability servers for the sales department is enough to make the current staff nervous.

2. the complexity and limitations of the current legacy applications seems to result in these being replaced in their entirety. In that case, it might be recommendable to start all over again at an entirely new location.
3. IT service providers are because of their specialization on hosting, capable of achieving service levels that are far better that what the in-house IT department of DEI GmbH could achieve. In the long-term, this could also result in cost savings.
4. the external hosting facilities are already in place, so one can start immediately and does not have to wait for renovation or extension of DEI GmbH computer.

The first application to be implemented is an application that enables DEI GmbH-dealers to supply orders and see their status. Next, a similar facility will be provided for procurement. This will be continued with extensions and facilities for the after sales and maintenance department, after which the entire information function, both intern and extern of DEI GmbH, will become web enabled.

A.13.2. The selection of an IT service supplier

DEI GmbH sets up a selection team for advising on the choice of the hosting provider. The requirements the hosting supplier has to meet are laid down in a request for proposal (RFP). On the basis of this, offers have been invited and three suppliers were asked to explain their quote in a presentation of two hours. This explanation took place during a visit to the sites of each of the three finally selected suppliers. These three suppliers were selected because they have space available for hosting of the necessary facilities within the time DEI GmbH would like and are within 30 kilometres of the head office in Berlin. The storage and processing hardware and software were procured by DEI GmbH, installed at the suppliers and exploited by them.

The main requirements in the request for proposal are:

(a) the following storage and processing facilities are placed at the hosting supplier:
  −a double HP server with 1 terabyte of working memory;
  −a double Cisco firewall;
  −four Cisco routers;

The complete set-up is fitted in three cupboards, each measuring 0.80×0.80 m and is connected to power and network services.

(b) demands to the supplier for hosting services are:
   - the entire installation has to be set up in one place;
   - the supplier should have demonstrable skill and experience in implementation and operation with regard to the hardware and software facilities, DEI GmbH places at the service suppliers';
   - extension of the installation with the same dimensions should be possible within two days;
   - 7×24 hours a day security with security guards, access control, closed circuit TV, back-up power using diesel aggregates when the mains power fails and highest standard of fire safety;
   - electricity connections through two independent circuits, UPS present for first power failure and after 5 minutes, the diesel aggregate taking over with sufficient capacity for 72 hours back-up;
   - network facilities upgradeable to 100 mega bits a second with TCP/IP address for at least $2\times$ current number of connections. From the computer centre two separate cables run via separate routes to the first Deutsche Telecom (DT) local exchange.
   - protection against Denial of Service attacks from the internet.

(c) During the selection process the selection group collected data on the suppliers. This data can be found in the appendix. This appendix includes:
   - general data on the suppliers;
   - summary of the quote they submitted;
   - impressions gained during the on site visit to the suppliers;
   - offered service level agreements;
   - price details.

A.13.3. Management considerations when choosing

The management of DEI GmbH realizes that the chosen supplier as a standard should have facilities at their disposal that ensure 100% availability of 24×7 hours facilities for power, gas and water; that they should offer security facilities including 7×24 surveillance in and around the building; that they should offer acclimatized rooms and fire protection, that they should be able to cooperate with every external network supplier and that they should keep a service desk operational every moment of the day.

Furthermore, the management realizes that companies are often reluctant when it comes to outsourcing because they have objections with regard to the security of the data, the flexibility of the provider, the performance of the service provider, the organization of its services, transparency and costs.

Questions

1. Compare the reasons DEI GmbH have for procuring IT with the reasons as provided in this chapter. What do you notice? What is the reason for this?
2. If you compare the procurement of IT services as done by DEI GmbH with the procurement processes, documents and the dealing with risk, as would occur at application of ISPL, which differences do you notice?
3. Looking at the model Griffioen (2002) uses for defining the level of operating of the procurement and sales organizations, at which level is DEI GmbH and at which level is each of its possible suppliers?

APPENDIX TO DEI G mbH CASE

Data on the suppliers of hosting services

A.B.13.1. General data and impression of the suppliers

Supplier 1 is a national player, established in 1998, financed by Gilde. The company owns computer centres in Berlin, in Hamburg and in Bremen. These computer centres all include about 2500 square metres of computer floor. The computer centres in Hamburg and Bremen are full up. However, there are rumours that a number of customers because of financial difficulties have to break their contracts. The computer centre in Berlin is 60% full. In 2002, supplier 1 has sacked 20% of his staff. In the quote to DEI GmbH, supplier 1 refuses to discuss their financial situation. However, it is known that this company does have some financially healthy organizations for customers.

During a visit to the Berlin computer centre the following emerges:

– the computer centre is situated on the second floor of a large office building. The building is in a suburb of Berlin, far from motorways or industry with harmful substances. It was possible to just enter the building using the goods entrance. There is no closed circuit TV installed. The air-conditioning is invisible (maybe on the roof) and the diesel aggregates have been set up safely.

– in the building itself badges are needed. The porter gives these out. There is generous use of closed circuit TV but nobody is actually present in the monitor room. It is ascertained that maintenance staff opens the door to an external supplier so they can enter the building without seeing the porter.

– the hardware and software are placed in cages. Electricity is supplied from underneath the raised flooring. Via a patch panel in the cage telecommunication connections are available.

– redundancy and security. Electricity and communication are at 99.999% availability level. At least three employees, very expert in the field of security and networking were spoken to.

– the ITIL processes service desk and service level management are implemented on a defined level.

– objections: from time to time it is ascertained that people do not stick to the rules. Food is found in computer rooms. At least twenty employees of contractors are walking on the computer floor.

Supplier 2 is a local supplier, established in 1996. The company has good relationships with all network suppliers. In the ten years of its existence the company has made losses during three years. This was in 1996, 2001 and 2002. The company blames the last two years of losses on the fast expansion of its computer centre with 2000 m^2 extra (now 4000 m^2 computer floor), just when the internet hype was ending. In 2003, it expects to be 80% occupied again and making profit. With the expansion of 2000 the limits of the capacity in the high security bunker have been reached. Next, increases in capacity will lead to the set up of computer centres at different locations near and around Berlin, which will enable offering physical disaster recovery facilities.

Visiting the supplier in a neighbourhood of Berlin the following becomes clear:

– the computer centre run by supplier 2 is situated in a building that is entirely used by supplier 2. The building is in the industrial estate of the neighbourhood close to the Berlin University. The computer floor is in a concrete bunker in the cellar, protected against water damage and secured against external disasters. The site was tested by two certification institutes on effects such as a possible fireworks disaster and bombardment. The first building is at 40 metres from the perimetre. The supplier owns the entire terrain. There are two porters: one at the entrance to the terrain and one at the entrance to the building. There is no visible closed circuit TV. The air-conditioning cannot be seen (maybe on the roof) and the diesel aggregates are set up safely.

– in the building: the walls are covered with fire retardant Kevlar. Security is behind bullet-proof glass. Two colleagues watch the closed circuit TV-monitors. Biometry is used for security of people that enter between 18.00 pm and 6.00 am. There is a lot of security and strict procedures. Bags are checked. Sweets and coffee cups are not allowed in the computer room. Identity cards have a photo and a guard has to open the cage before we can have a look at this.
– the hardware and software is placed in cages: same as supplier 1.
– redundancy and security. Electricity and communication at 99.999% availability level. All electricity, communication and airconditioning equipment is placed in a closed room with access control and registration. At least three employees, very expert in the field of security and networking were spoken to.
– the ITIL processes with regard to service delivery and service support are largely recognizable in the organization of supplier 2.
– objections: none.

Supplier 3 is an independent division of the Deutsche Telecom (*DT*) Company. This supplier has in the Berlin area, computer centres in three locations. This means that disaster recovery facilities can be offered if there would be a large fire in one of the computer centres. Each computer centre has about 3000 m² of computer floors. Being a DT division, the suppliers' returns are consolidated in the annual DT account. The chairman of the DT Executive Board has guaranteed DEI GmbH in writing that supplier 3 will be a division of DT at least until 2010.

During the visit to the Berlin 1 branch the following is noticed:

– the computer centre of supplier 3 is located in a building, of which floor 2 and 3 of the three-floor building are in use with supplier 3. The building is on the outskirts of Berlin, 50 metres from the motorway Berlin-Hamburg, 75 metres from a very busy restaurant. Lorry traffic patronizes this restaurant. It is possible to enter the building via the goods entrance without any problems. (Later on, it transpires that suppliers doing some work cause this. The security that has to watch this part of the building was temporarily absent.) There is no evidence of closed circuit TV. The air-conditioning is invisible (maybe on the roof) and it was possible to walk into the building, where the UPS and the diesel aggregates are lined up. Before entering, we waited—this should have been seen on the closed circuit TV—but nobody approached us. A builder was noisily sinking piles into the ground for the building of neighbouring buildings.

−Inside the building: the first security circuit is the security of the building itself. Security is not aware of the presence of a computer centre on floor 3. Next, we approach the desk on floor 2. This desk is not staffed and not equipped with bullet-proof glass. One could easily climb over the desk and gain access to the facility. Closed circuit TV and biometrics are visible. One is already inside, when the visitor's ID cards are made up. The road to the computer floor is open and the door to the computer room is also not locked.

−hardware and software are placed in cages. The necessary electricity and communication are provided from above. The top of the cage is not closed, which makes it possible to get to other installations. There is a 50-centimetre gap between the barrier and the ceiling.

−redundancy and security. Electricity and communication on 99.999% availability level. All electricity, communication and air-conditioning equipment is situated in a locked room with access control and registration. At least three employees, very expert in the field of security and networking were spoken to.

−The day in, day out operation of the facilities in the computer centre is controlled from a central monitoring room from Berlin branch 2.

−the ITIL processes at operational level are easily recognized in the organization of supplier 3. The processes at tactical level are present at a defined level.

−objections: the facility is really still too much in construction to enable a well-rounded opinion. It is expected that one is at least at the same level as supplier 1, when DEI GmbH need the services (within 3–4 months). The general impression is that this company does not yet entirely master the hosting business.

Demand:	Supplier 1	Supplier 2:	Supplier 3:
Financial data company: - annual report - partners in service:	not available suppliers utilities	strong financial position none	KPN moving forwards again security company
Space offered:	3 cages, of which the dividing partitions have been removed for turning into one space	3 10% smaller cages of which partitions removed (168 foot 2)	50% less connected space (280 square feet)
Right to purchase extension:	no	no, unless immediately purch.	available
Facilities: - electricity - security - communication:	OK OK OK	OK OK OK	see site visit possibly within 2 months possibly within 6 weeks
Price: - rent room - set-up costs - set-up communication - communication	19500 euro/month 6500 euro once-only 1200 euro once-only 1200 euro a month plus 525 euro/month per mbps over 10 MB/second	20400 euro a month 7800 euro once-only 1500 euro once-only 1500 euro a month plus 589 euro a month per mbps over 10	9800 euro a month 10800 euro once-only 1600 euro once-only 900 euro a month plus 412 euro a month for each mbps over 10.
- right to expand:	not available	see above	1500 euro a month
Charged extra:	extra network monitoring advice and professional services on project basis	extra network monitoring, discovery of creeping in, security audit and handling diagnosis performance load testing, advice and professional services on project basis.	advice, monitoring and prof. services on project basis

Figure A.13.1. Main points in the suppliers' quotes

A.B.13.2. Tender and price details

In Figure A.13.1 the relevant tender and price details are given. With regard to the service level agreements to be concluded the situation is like this:

Supplier 1

– downtime is defined as the situation where over 50% of the customers' messages unplanned are not processed during 15 continuous minutes.
– Lack of response is defined as the situation in which there is over 0.5 seconds delay between the entering of the signal on the network of the provider and the signal leaving that network.
– incidents are reacted to within two hours in the form of response and availability and the problem is solved within 4 hours after the diagnosis of the problem if the reason lies with the service provider.

−Each period of downtime results in crediting one day of service costs. Each time, the diagnosis or repair does not take place within the agreed time, an additional day is credited for every four hours delay. Per month, no more than ten days can be credited. The supplier determines whether there is a right to credit.

Supplier 2

−downtime: same definition as supplier 1.
−Lack of response is defined as the situation, where there is more than 0.7 seconds delay between the signal entering the network of the provider and the same signal leaving said network.
−there is a reaction to incidents within two hours in response and availability and the problem is solved within 2 hours if the reason lies with the service provider.
−each period of downtime results in crediting of one day of service costs. Each time, that diagnosis or repair does not take place within the said time; an additional day is credited for every two hours delay. Per month no more than seven days can be credited. The supplier determines whether there is a right to credit.

Supplier 3

−downtime: is defined as the situation when more than 30% of the customer's messages unplanned are not processed during 15 continuous minutes.
−Lack of response is defined as the situation when there is more than 0.5 seconds of delay between the signal entering the service provider's network and that signal leaving said network.
−there is an answer to incidents within two hours in response as well as availability and the problem is solved within 2 hours if the reason lies with the service provider.
−Each period of downtime results in crediting three day of service costs. Each time diagnosis or repair does not take place within the agreed time an additional day is credited for every two hours delay. Per month no more can be credited than the amount one would normally have to pay if no crediting took place.

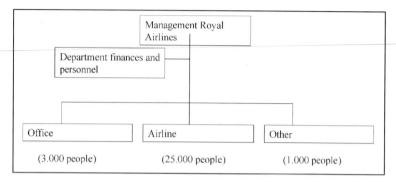

Figure A.14.1. The organization of Royal Airlines

CASE CHAPTER 14

A.14. Service level agreements at Royal Airlines

A.14.1. Introduction

Royal Airlines is a company within Air France. It provides scheduled and charter flights. The primary process of Royal Airlines is running regular services within Europe and on the transatlantic route. The organization of Royal Airlines is shown in Figure A.14.1. Royal Airlines has about 30,000 employees and a turnover of about 12 billion euro per annum. Royal Airlines outsources its workplace services to Workplace International, a division of Getronics. In close cooperation between Royal Airlines and Workplace International an SLA has been drawn up for enabling exploitation of the more than 4000 workplaces of Royal Airlines.

A.14.2. The services to be supplied

The IT facilities of Royal Airlines consist of a technical infrastructure and applications. The technical infrastructure includes a TCP/IP network with Cisco network hardware, central storage and processing facilities on HP computers and on the workplace 5000 HP pc's. Royal Airlines has an application that support financial, personnel, archive and primary processes. Apart from the primary processes supporting application, these applications are all part of an SAP implementation. SAP is a Standard Enterprise resource Planning package. The primary processes application is a standard application for passenger reservation, check-in of passengers and for transporting cargo. Furthermore, Royal Airlines has installed MS Office in every workplace for supporting the individual work and an extranet application for communication with its customers. With the extranet application customers can book on line, review their bookings and get information on Royal Airlines' services and products.

The IT services to be provided are the complete exploitation of IT facilities including service desk as well as the supplying of products and services for the implementation of new versions of the applications and new infrastructure items. The Royal Airlines' users of services can be divided into office staff, the airline and the other users.

A.14.3. Users of IT facilities

The users group office staff, which includes the ticket sales department and the staffs in head office, attach a lot of importance to the secondary applications, the extranet and the personal productivity tools. Breakdown of the IT immediately grinds the work to a halt and results in considerable delays in, amongst other things, the sales process. There are a lot of changes in that sales process. One has to deal with worldwide markets, with customers increasingly using extranet and many new services and products. The user group consists of young highly trained employees. It is localized centrally and concentrated. The profile of the user group is: an innovative organization. The confidentiality of the data is of average level. This is mainly the data of people that order tickets and reservations for airfreight.

The user group airline makes limited use of the IT facilities. It is strongly dependent on a functioning e-mail system but that is often as far as it goes. There are strong dynamics in the department because of the vast number of charter flights. The complexity of the work is average because people constantly have to react to new situations. The users in this group are between 25 and 50 years of age. This club flies all over the world and includes worldwide-stationed local station managers. It has a fairly simple stable structure. The measure of confidentiality of the data is average.

The user group 'other' consists of the employees of the Schiphol station, the employees of the maintenance services, catering staff and the employees in

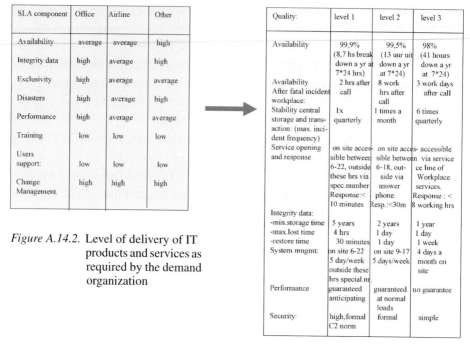

SLA component	Office	Airline	Other
Availability	average	average	high
Integrity data	high	average	high
Exclusivity	high	average	average
Disasters	high	average	high
Performance	high	average	average
Training	low	low	low
Users support:	low	low	low
Change Management.	high	high	high

Figure A.14.2. Level of delivery of IT
products and services as
required by the demand
organization

Quality:	level 1	level 2	level 3
Availability	99,9% (8,7 hs break down a yr at 7*24 hrs)	99,5% (13 uur uit down a yr at 7*24)	98% (41 hours down a yr at 7*24)
Availability After fatal incident workplace:	2 hrs after call	8 work hrs after call	3 work days after call
Stability central storage and trans- action: (max. inci- dent frequency)	1x quarterly	1 times a month	6 times quarterly
Service opening and response	on site acces- sible between 6-22, outside these hrs via spec.number Response:< 10 minutes	on site acces- sible between 6-18, out- side via answer phone. Resp.:<30m	accessible via service ce line of Workplace services. Response : < 8 working hrs
Integrity data: -min.storage time -max.lost time -restore time	5 years 4 hrs 30 minutes	2 years 1 day 1 day	1 year 1 day 1 week
System mngmt:	on site 6-22 5 day/week outside these hrs special.nr.	on site 9-17 5 days/week	4 days a month on site
Performance	guaranteed anticipating	guaranteed at normal loads	no guarantee
Security:	high,formal C2 norm	formal	simple

Figure A.14.3. Service levels as
defined by the supply
organization

the secretariats; their dependency on IT is usually average. Breakdown of IT almost never means breakdown of the primary process. This work is largely growing in size. The work itself is not very complex. The users are usually young and do have experience with the applications. One can typify the user group as a simple structure. Confidentiality of the data is average.

A.14.3. The service level agreements

In Figure A.14.2 the requirements to IT facilities are shown for the various groups. Opposite is the level of services and products as supplied by the Royal Airlines supply organizations to the demand organization. These are shown in Figure A.14.3.

Questions

1. Execute the step-by-step plan for arriving at a specification of an SLA for the various services to be delivered to Royal Airlines by Workplace International.
2. Indicate whether adjustment of service levels to be delivered by the supply organization of Workplace International is needed for Royal Airlines. Do remember that buying of tickets on the internet has really been fashionable since 2000 and the service levels have been determined around 2001 and have not been changed since.
3. Do you advise Royal Airlines to produce a user catalogue of services to be procured? Why? Why not? Consider the views of the ABN AMRO bank in this field. How would you apply this view to Royal Airlines?
   How would you like to realize the security of the SLA at Royal Airlines? What are the problems with such an SLA at Royal Airlines?

CASE CHAPTER 15

A.15. Securing IT: the ING bank and its TIP status (trusted internal party). (*variation on goudriaan, 2001*)

A.15.1. Background

ING is a worldwide operating banking and insurance company. ING is characterized by the fact that, until recently each business unit within the ING Group was able to retain its own character. ING has organized its security of IT facilities as follows:

- on the level of the executive Board of the ING Group the security policy is established;
- realization of the IT security policy takes place per management centre. A management centre can include a number of companies (next called business).

–each business unit can choose the status of Trusted Internal Party (TIP) on the network of the ING Group or for a non- TIP status. In the last case, a business unit is connected to the ING network via a firewall.

Business units are allocated the TIP status if they comply with an adequate implementation of the ISO 17799 standard and if an audit has been done by a central body or an acknowledged external EDP auditor on possibly present external connections. This audit should result in a certification, which proves that there is a sufficient level of security of IT facilities.

A.15.2. Minimum level of security

Within ING the security is minimally on the level of platform 2 of the Code for Information security. If one reaches this level, one does comply with the basic requirements that are the same for the entire ING Group. At implementation of the code, each business unit and each management centre decides through self-assessment its position with regard to the code. This self-assessment is called 'gap' analysis within the ING Group. Next, if necessary projects are started for closing the gap between the desired level and the current level of security of IT facilities. As soon as, in the opinion of the management the desired level is reached, certification is applied for.

In this certification, the quality of the implementation of the code is audited by the Corporate Audit Services of the ING Group or by an acknowledged external agency. This audit can for the business unit result in a certification of conformity with ISO 17799 and therefore to a TIP status.

The management of the level of security of IT facilities and further improvements in this field as a result of developments in the general ING policy, is done by the management centres. These each have an in-house organization unit, that takes care of the local implementation of the ING policy and the management of the present facilities, a steering committee for information security, including security of the IT facilities used in the information function and an allocation of responsibilities.

Besides every business unit within a management centre has also, its own steering committee information security. On this level one decides whether one wants a TIP or a non- TIP status, about the in-house operational security policy and about its implementation. The security policy of a business unit is reviewed by the Corporate Audit Services of the ING Group.

Questions

1. Explain how the organization of the information security at ING is put together.
2. Explain why business units would choose for a non- TIP status.
3. When is a TIP status valuable to a business unit within ING? Explain your answer comprehensively.
4. What effort is involved in complying with ISO 17799, for a business unit that primarily sells insurance via all thinkable sales channels? Explain your answer. Use for an example the business unit life and household insurance for private persons. This uses the following sales channels: sale through agents and sales as direct writer by means of the internet and using a call centre, that also uses e-mail amongst other things.

CASE CHAPTER 16

A.16. Standardization: experiences with the introduction of E-Mail and dcml at Brasiliana chemistry
(adaptation of Jacobs (2000) and Howes (2003))

A.16.1. Situation

Brasiliana Chemistry is a large chemical concern with production facilities in twenty countries, three research laboratories, head offices in Rio de Janeiro and sixty sales offices in almost all capitals of western countries. The introduction of e-mail in this organization with 30,000 workplaces with computer facilities was done in phases. The first decisions for starting to use e-mail were made in the laboratories. After that, two production plants introduced e-mail and next a number of smaller sales offices and head office. This method of implementation of e-mail resulted in a very heterogeneous e-mail environment in the year 1995.

A.16.2. The road to standardization

Let us list the experiences Brasiliana Chemistry had with e-mail. The first Brasiliana Chemistry e-mail users got to use e-mail as a by-product with other products of a project. E-mail was introduced as a tool for simplifying cooperation between members of project teams in three laboratories (one in Edinburgh, one in Rio de Janeiro and one in Minnesota). Bit by bit, the use of e-mail became more popular and the advantages within the laboratories became clearer. Elsewhere in Brasiliana Chemistry parallel to this development, comparable developments took place. Because of the lack of central control this would be the situation until 1995.

In 1995, e-mail users realized that more central control of e-mail facilities was necessary. They experienced compatibility problems as soon as they wanted to send messages from one part of the organization to another part. Because of its bottom-up strategy, in 1995 Brasiliana Chemistry installed more than 10 e-mail solutions. In some cases, these were mutually connected with gateways. Because these gateways were not able to transfer the entire functionality of one e-mail application to the next e-mail application, this often resulted in loss of functionality. The ensuing meagre communication quality between the various departments was an ever-increasing problem.

In order to arrive at central control, a managerial decision is required at Brasiliana Chemistry. The management had to be convinced that a mailing facility of the size such as Brasiliana Chemistry needed, requires an annual budget of 30 million guilders for training and upgrades and that investing in this will bring benefits in the long-run. In 1995, the management was convinced of this and a two-year budget was allocated to the central IT department of Brasiliana Chemistry. This central department in head office was given the task to integrate the various e-mail solutions. The central IT department decided to tackle this as follows:

– a central backbone network facility is implemented;
– a programme is run through aimed at reducing the number of types of decentralized e-mail solutions in the period 1995–1999 to just the use of Lotus solutions, including Lotus Notes.
– during the conversion it is ensured that all users in the organization can mail each other 7 times 24 hours and that the same gateway is implemented everywhere. This is the gateway that, when transferring a message to a different network, causes the least compatibility losses.

The users decide the tempo of the change. The sales offices are converted first, next the plants and finally the laboratories.

A.16.3. The period following 1999

As soon as the integration was completed in 1999, the e-mail services were connected with other possibilities. The users gained access to an intranet, the extranet and the internet. In 2003, instant messaging and video conferencing over the backbone were introduced as new services. Furthermore, it becomes possible in every workplace to use those operational processes supporting applications that one needs for one's particular task. In 2004, the ambition is focussed on Lotus Notes services, internet services and the operational processes supporting applications appearing as one single entity of facilities to the users.

In the year 2004, larger and smaller computer centres, that all cooperate are set up at 25 locations worldwide. The initial e-mail service has been renamed and is now called collaborative services. The requirements to the services that come under collaborative services have been considerably raised between 1995–2004. In the year 2004, it is required that of all sent messages 99.999% worldwide has to arrive within 2 hours and there has to be an absolute guarantee that none of the messages go missing in the network. To this purpose, Brasiliana Chemistry implemented extensive back-up and recovery facilities.

The Brasiliana Chemistry IT facilities in the year 2004 include about 2000 servers, 5 terabyte of SAN capacity and 30,000 workplaces. One intends to control the 25 locations from three computer centres that pass the baton around the clock. One centre is located in Amsterdam, one in Minneapolis and one in Kuala Lumpur. At the same time, one wants to optimise the exchange of data between the various management applications. In this context, introduction of DCML is considered. At the moment, the exploitation is managed as follows:

1. The permanent running application for measuring response times end-to-end discovers a performance problem. It points this out.
2. Next, an employee starts the monitoring application. This analyzes whether the bottleneck is in the application or in the infrastructure. If the problem is in the application the supplier is called in. If the problem is located in the infrastructure then an advice for adjustment of either

the processing capacity or the storage capacity or network capacity or a combination of these three follows.

3. The advice is next implemented manually, after which the new resources are registered in the on-charge application, the configuration management application, the security application and monitoring application.

This mode of operating is currently necessary because the various applications do not all use the same user data and the same method for registration of objects. Different suppliers supplied the applications.

Questions

1. What are the advantages of standardization for Brasiliana Chemistry? Why does it take some time for Brasiliana Chemistry to implement the proposed standards?
2. Which type of standards should a company like Brasiliana Chemistry use? Illustrate your answer with an example. What does this generate?
3. What is the importance of DCML to Brasiliana Chemistry? Why? Why does this importance increase because of the growing requirements to IT and the introduction of utility computing?
4. Work out what the results of a standard e-mail service are for Brasiliana Chemistry, assuming 1 mail per person per day and the fact that in the year 1997 around 1% of the e-mails did not arrive, whilst in the new application each mail is logged and is checked twice a day whether the sent e-mail did arrive or not.

Part A.5. IT management tomorrow

A.17. En route to 2027: the t(echnology)-based organization of Hong Kong Pacific Consultantcy (HPC) (*variation on and addition to Lucas, 1996*)

A.17.1. Situation

Yelei Zhang, one of the salesmen of courses in management development of the organization, advice and training institute Hong Kong Pacific Consultantcy, is on a Boeing 787 en route to a new prospect. Immediately after lift off in Shanghai, Yelei plugs in her notebook whilst flying to Beijing. Next, by clicking an icon he selects the inflight service menu. In this menu, he reserves a port in fifteen minutes and fills out his customs forms. The details known to the airline company have already been filled out on this form. He notices that it is indicated with 95% certainty that the flight will arrive at Beijing on time. He closes the programme.

Next, he clicks a different icon, makes a hotel booking for the duration of his stay, and books a taxi from Beijing airport to Beijing centre. Lastly, he calls his husband and on the screen watches his children play in the living room in Tokyo.

A.17.2. Selling in the year 2010, passing on orders

Next, he gets to work, activates electronic mail and listens to a message from Bert Bos, a partner of HPC. He states that professor Locke of Hong Kong University, mailed him. Locke states that the CEO of China software told him during his stay in Beijing, that he thinks his management is insufficiently armed against the competition. He is interested in a tailor-made programme for his company for training the company's 100 most important employees. If HPC gets

461

to work quickly, it might be able to get this order without competition calling. If this programme is executed successfully there might also be future orders.

Bos also states that he checked the HPC customer database and ascertained that there were not that many orders from China software over the last few years. He remarks that Yelei worked with this CEO five years ago, when he was still in charge of Macao software. Bos furthermore changed Yelei's diary and made an appointment with the CEO, pointed out Shan Chen as a contact in the Hong Kong Pacific Consultantcy Beijing office and Mary Zhung as assistant.

Next, Yelei listens to the e-mails that Locke and Chen sent. Chen indicates in his mail various contacts of HPC within China Software. One of the projects HPC was involved in, concerned productivity in software development. From this project, a recommendation arrived for training the management and building a software development laboratory in Asia. Yelei then checks Chen's profile. Chen appears to be a specialist in raising various areas of expertise within HPC but as a person he is a bit unpredictable.

A.17.3. Actions

Yelei next sends an e-mail to Hong Kong Pacific Consultantcy's Japanese partner, who worked on this order for Empire. He is in the middle of a cruise in the Carribean but can be reached through e-mail. Yelei passes him the information Bos sent him and asks him for a summary of the advice from the project in question. Next, he downloads the presentation of the project and highlights the important sections. He mails his findings to Chen.

In the meantime, Mary Zhung sent Yelei a file on China Software with a summary of their organization, their suppliers, their customers, their competitors, their products and services, their weaknesses and strong points etc. After reading this file, Yelei enters into a conference call with Mary Zhung and a specialist in management training from Stanford University California. Yelei wants to arrive at a list of names and companies, universities and independent consultants that are qualified to teach in this type of programme. He wants data on fees, availability, area of expertise of the lecturer and evaluations of students of the lecturer in question. Furthermore, she retrieves video clips of each candidate lecturing an audience of managers.

Before ending the conference call, Mary Zhung loads a multimedia presentation on to Yelei's computer. HPC recently used this presentation for selling a similar training programme for managers. Finally, Yelei asks Mary Zhung to draw up a list of people that could participate in the programme. After this, he concludes the conference call. Yelei then calls a tutor in Singapore and asks whether he can use his video clip tomorrow in her presentation at China Software's CEO.

Finally, Yelei contacts Kolormagic, a Kuala Lumpur-based company that can produce high quality multimedia presentations for its customers. Kolormagic takes the commission for making a presentation on board. Yelei spends the next few hours discussing the topics with the multimedia specialist in question. The specialist promises her a roughly outlined presentation by the time he gets to Beijing. Locke, Chen and the Japanese partner will all be able to see the concept presentation, before Yelei and Chen talk to the China software CEO.

A.17.4. The set-up of demand and supply in Hong Kong Pacific Consultantcy

HPC is an international organization, advice and training institute. HPC consists of 30 people, providing these services often in cooperation with third parties. The head of finances and personnel looks after the application of IT in HPC. He and his deputy are responsible for the demand organization. They outsource all their IT activities. The Geronics company was given a contract for application management. This company supplies an application suite for medium-sized organization departments. This suite includes:

- a financial application with ledger, accounts receivable, accounts payable, statement of profits and losses, invoicing and budget possibilities;
- a personnel application with a human resource application and a salary portal facility. The salary application redirects to the Pigeon salary service on the in-house IT facilities of the Getronics company;
- a planning and project control application with planning facilities and booking of time on projects using timekeeping;
- a personal productivity tool with MS Future Office facilities;
- an intranet and extranet functionality.

The suite runs on the EDS transport, server and storage facilities. EDS was chosen because of its worldwide presence. Within HPC one has access to the facilities of the application suite through a browser. Head of finances and his deputy organize from the HPC office the authorizations for the HPC employees and customers and look at the use of the facilities of the application suite by them and their reliability. Taking care of the import and export facilities such as notebooks, fixed workplaces and printers is done in-house by HPC.

Although an extended form of ASP, such as sharing the application suite with many more Getronics customers is a possibility, HPC has chosen to work in its own application environment. The reason for this is that this mode of operating provides an optimal integrity with regard to data processing and storage. HPC transports all data encrypted over the network. The used end servers are set up for this.

Contracts have been concluded with the supply organizations, in which costs are charged for the application based on the number of users of a module with regard to the exploitation based on user transactions.

A.17.5. Epilogue

Yelei draws up a summary of the things she has done with regard to the China software project and sends this, together with the name of the wine that China software's CEO favours to Chen and to the HPC database. He gets his port and sets the alarm for 10 minutes before landing. After this, he goes to sleep.

Questions

1. Which elements are included in the use of IT facilities of utility computing?
2. Is IT portfolio management a tool that can be used in HPC? Why is it? Why not?
3. How does HPC deal with outsourcing of IT facilities? Is this a question of selective sourcing or not? What does this mean?
4. Does HPC deal optimally with 'knowing and forgetting' of IT knowledge? Explain your answer.
5. Which demands that the IT mode of operating that HPC uses, make on its IT facilities?

APPENDIX B

Extended case studies for group assignments

INTRODUCTION

Group assignments, where students study cases as a group are an integral part of an IT management course. It is important that students in groups apply the subject material on extended practical case studies outside the lectures. These case studies demonstrate the practical significance of IT management to organizations. They show the IT management issues from various angles and as such are good preparation for future practice.

Advising on the desired solution of a practical problem can, when not tackled effectively, be very time consuming. This is certainly the case if the group, which has to arrive at a solution jointly, is of a certain size and does not operate not (yet) very focussed. This is the reason for the following guidelines, when dealing with a case:

1. Make sure you are well prepared when you go to a group meeting. Prepare yourself as follows:
   - read the lecture material concerning the case thoroughly and make, if necessary, a summary;
   - glance over the case twice and then write down the main problems of the case;
   - in the meantime answer the questions roughly in brief;
   - recognize you might have too little information for some and too much for other problems. This is always the case in practice but doesn't stop any organization from entering into the decision-making process.

2. Go to the group meeting. Organize this meeting by appointing someone to lead the discussion and by assigning another to take notes of the meeting. The meeting then goes as follows:
    - the discussion leader opens the meeting and asks those taking part to each give their opinion concerning the first question of the case;
    - the discussion leader sums up everybody's opinion and states possible differences of opinion. These differences are brought up for discussion;
    - every difference of opinion is fully discussed and final conclusions are formulated;
    - after determining a position on all questions, the group's position on the case is finally determined;
    - by mutual agreement a division of tasks is agreed for transferring this position onto paper;
    - a date for the next group meeting is set.
3. At the next group meeting(s) about the case, the solution of the case is discussed and agreements made about possible corrections.

The solution for the practical problem is judged on style and content. Concerning style the advice has to be very readable and has to include all the points mentioned in the paragraph 'questions' of the case. The advice is on average less then seventeen pages and may be about 3000 words long. For a more extensive answer generally penalty points are given. After all, in every day practice organizations are also punished for taking too long when formulating their problems and solutions. If their own colleagues within the organization don't do this, the competition will definitely shoot down these dawdlers in flames.

With regard to the content, the solution for a practical case can be tested, for instance by asking the following questions:

- Does your answer indicate you master the subject matter?
- Is the solution new or does it contain good original elements?
- Does the group take the right risk by presenting this solution?

Introducing the elements originality, innovation and risk at assessing case-solutions meshes with the existing reality. Innovations and risk can be rewarded but are sometimes punished.

Part B.1. IT management: the basis

B.1.1. "IT worry free": an IT supplier to small and medium-sized enterprises (IWF) (*Variation on the Everdream case, Eiserman, 2003*)

B.1.1.1. Introduction

Pietro Agnelli is CEO of the company 'IT worry free (IWF).' IWF is a company that supplies subscriptions for computer services to small and medium-sized organizations. For the fixed monthly sum of 75 euro these organizations can have at their disposal a standard personal computer workplace on the internet. This workplace has been fitted with a certain amount of software. Figure B.1.1.1 describes what the company has to offer.

The basis of IWF is the idea that by putting a completely standardized personal computing workplace at someone's disposal, taking care of a daily back-up of files through the internet on a central server, and automatically downloading new software versions, the IT problems experienced by customers of the service will be limited to an absolute minimum. IWF promises to take care of supporting the customer and will not outsource this task. Apart from the standard services, IWF provides access to other services through its business centre (this centre is called 'the Business shop,' abbreviated tBS). The business centre is part of the Marketing and Sales department.

```
Hardware:      HP personal computer with pentium 4 2.4 Mhz processor, 512B RAM
               30 GB disk, DVD drive and CD read/write, 19 inch colour monitor
               ADSL internet connection (if not available ISDN)
    Optional:  Brother laser printer 10 pages per minute
               HP impact printer with 3 pages per minute
               HP colour printer with 3 pages per minute
System software: Windows professional XP operating system incl.
               MS Explorer 6.1 and Windows media player
Applications:  Personal productivity tool MS Office XP
               Davilex accounting and personnel administration application
               Norton Security, Adobe acrobat, Winzip, Real player

    Optional: website possibilities via own ISP (internet service supplier) facility

Training on line in the supplied software, resp. Windows, Internet Security, Office
           and Davilex (web based training via ADSL).

Business center: provides advice, extra handholding, set- and possible installation and imple-
               mentation of extra applications and local networks. Furthermore, it supports
               possible e-commerce and e-business extensions of customers.
Support:       7*24 hour a day support through a service desk. Daily backup of crucial data
               on request. The desk top could be taken over by the service desk.

Contract duration: 36 months.
Price per workplace including ADSL subscription: 75 euro a month.
```

Figure B.1.1.1. What IWF has to offer, as far as accessible to customers. Besides, this as part of the informatics infrastructure e-business support software there is the application 'Solve it together'

B.1.1.2. Background of IWF

Two brothers, Gerald and Carl Talamini, started IWF in 2001. They started a computer shop for small and medium-sized businesses in Rome (Italy) and soon found that:

- these businesses often had difficulty to maintain IT installations because the existing ones were usually outmoded and moreover provided with really old applications;
- in 99.9% of all case studies, all these companies' wishes in the field of IT could be fulfilled by new high end personal computers on which standard applications are installed;
- what these companies really wanted was a type of 24 hours a day no-hassle-guarantee for their IT support at a reasonable price.

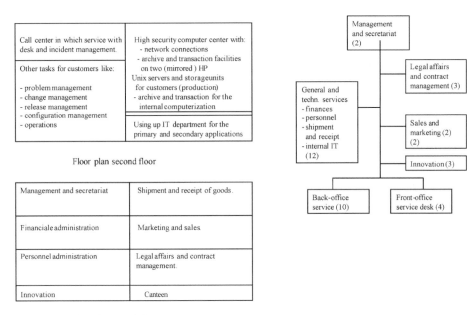

Call center in which service with desk and incident management.	High security computer center with: - network connections - archive and transaction facilities on two (mirrored) HP Unix servers and storageunits for customers (production) - archive and transaction for the internal computerization
Other tasks for customers like: - problem management - change management - release management - configuration management - operations	
	Using up IT department for the primary and secondary applications

Floor plan second floor

Management and secretariat	Shipment and receipt of goods.
Financiale administration	Marketing and sales.
Personnel administration	Legal affairs and contract management.
Innovation	Canteen

Floor plan ground floor

Figures B.1.1.2 and B.1.1.3. Left: organization IWF (39 people); right: floor plan of the building and location of the departments

Knowing this, they started IWF. The business model of IWF is taking care of a superior IT-experience by reducing customer's problems to practically nothing and solving problems quicker and more attentively than the competition.

B.1.1.3. Organization of IWF

In Figure B.1.1.2 the organization of IWF is shown. In Figure B.1.1.3 one can see the location of the departments in the IWF-building on the Via Napoli in Rome. At the IWF-service desk the Siebel CRM-application is in use. With regard to the processes finances and personnel Peoplesoft is used; as personal productivity tool Microsoft Office is employed and on the internal intranet a tailor made application runs. The functional management of this tailor made application lies with the marketing and sales department. The application management and the exploitation lie with the internal IT-department.

The technical infrastructure of IWF consists of processing and storage facilities on Superdome HP Linux servers each with 1 GB internal memory and

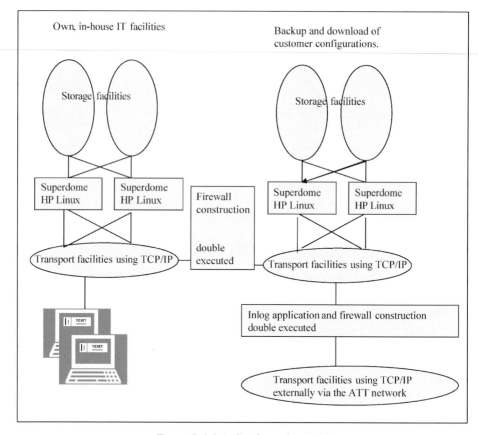

Figure B.1.1.4. Configuration IWF

1 terabyte external memory on disc. The internal workstations all have access to the CRM and the Peoplesoft-application, as far as is needed for performing their tasks, and to the personal productivity and internet applications.

The architecture of the computer facilities of IWF is shown in Figure B.1.1.4. In this architecture a clear distinction is made between the facilities for customers and the facilities for supplying the IT services and the functioning of the internal organization of IWF.

B.1.1.4. The IWF strategy

IWF wishes to simplify the IT experiences of small organizations. It wants to supply superior service by decreasing the number of problems customers come across by solving occurring problems as quickly and thoroughly as possible. In order to achieve this goal IWF is doing two things. Firstly customers are only offered a limited choice of options. Secondly a disk with certain safety facilities is made. This disk is partitionned into three parts. One part contains the system and application software, a second part contains a mirror image of that software and a third part contains room for customers to save their own specific data and possibly their own applications. Furthermore the monthly price of 75 euro, as charged by IWF, seems attractive. IWF however, does have competitors that charge prices from 50 euro a month. These offers lead to problems because of their lack of support and the strict demands the suppliers pose, with regard to the applications and data the customer is allowed to add to the hardware.

IWF aims its marketing efforts at organizations of less than 20 workstations and at distant departments of larger organizations. For these last mentioned customers, IWF can take care of the availability of special applications, possibly special monitors for users and extra training. The activities are carried out via "the Business shop."

In the long run it is expected that the profits of IWF will consist of 70% of the profit made on subscriptions and of 30% from the sales of extra products and services. IWF supplies computer services, which are in principle scaleable. The prices of the subscriptions may come down but as soon as one is accepted as the trusted supplier of services, an infrastructure is in place, which means that other services may be supplied to the same customers as well.

Through direct selling and value added resellers one tries to reach the customers. These value added resellers get 6% of the value of the contract that they sell.

B.1.1.5. Example of processes of the front-office service desk and of incident management

In Figure B.1.1.5 an example is given of the way of thinking and working within IWF. Every personal computer (pc) is delivered by the company with a specific service desk icon. The user can either call the company or fax a message or send a letter or, in case the pc still works, contact the IWF service desk via the icon and the ADSL-network. After clicking the service desk icon the user has the option to chat or send an e-mail. The customer's message then goes through the process as seen in Figure B.1.1.5.

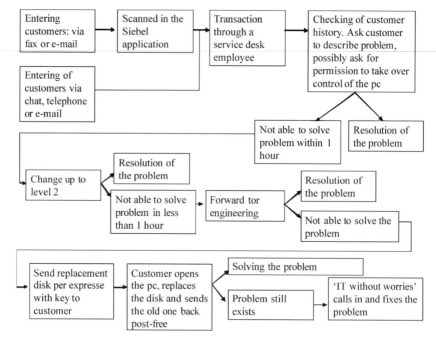

Figure B.1.1.5. Work process at the IWF service desk

Every IWF-pc contains e-support software, that has been made by IWF. The software is loaded on the costumer's computers as well as on those of the IWF service desk staff. This software, called 'Solve it together (SIT)' has three functions. These functions are:

1. self-healing functionality for simple repairs and data and programme recovery;
   – enabling overtaking the operating of personal computers, being able to perform remote diagnosing of problems and together with customers going through system and application possibilities;
2. saving faults and usage. This enables the perform planned service actions, not just when faults occur, collect customer information and providing advice focused on better use, and to include the experiences with the use of personal computers in the development of services and products.

3. It is checked daily whether the customers save their data on an external medium. If this is not the case, the IWF software makes a backup of the data for the customers on its own infrastructure.

Questions

1. Describe the objects of management at IWF.
2. Where does the responsibility in fact lie for the functionality and the performance of the IT facilities? Where lies the responsibility for the quality of the data, customer organizations save on the IT facilities?
3. Why is the type of facility that IWF offers a typical facility one might come across in the network economy? How would one implement such a facility on an organization that operates along the lines of industrial economy?
4. Name two strategic and two tactical reasons, why a demand organization should take a decision for using the services and products IWF offers.
5. Apply the service pit and service shell idea to IWF. Indicate what functional requirements and what performance requirements the product and the services of IWF comply with. Look at these functional requirements from four different perspectives.
6. How do the products and services IWF provides, fit in with the future ideas about:
   –the working methods in a demand organization?
   –the working methods in a supply organization?
   –why didn't these fit in very well with the views on IT management of the eighties and nineties? Illustrate your answers with examples.
7. Give the four angles on management from the IWF perspective. Distinguish between the IT support of the internal processes and the products and services, IWF supplies to its customers. What differences can be noticed?
8. Which external influences have impact on the IWF services and products? What does this mean for the sales of their products? What is the impact on IWF of the view that IT to its users should appear like a utility (utility computing)? What is the impact on IWF of the fact that labour-intensive tasks often disappear to low wages countries?
9. How do the services and products, supplied by IWF, fit in with the performance requirements as defined by ISO 9126 in combination with the Quint-report? How do these fit in with the performance requirements

that come across from the logistics and operations management fields? For this, go through all performance requirements and the way in which IWF outlines these.

10. Which GAP's might appear when supplying products and services by IWF? Give an example of all five GAP's. Next, indicate how one finds out about the appearance of such a GAP and how one can counteract such a GAP or not.

11. What is the architecture for IT facilities when looking at the internal IT facilities of IWF? What is the IT architecture at IWF, when looking at products and services supplied to third organizations? What are the differences between these architectures?

12. How did IWF realize its internal architecture of IT facilities?

13. How does the realization of the architecture for supplying products and services to third parties by IWF fit in with Gartner's views on this, respectively the Nolan Norton group's views on this? Explain your answer.

14. Test the internal architecture of IT facilities and the architecture for supplying products and services to third parties against the TOGAF-model. What catches the eye? What is missing? What are the differences between the results of both tests?

B.1.2. The 'health for all' group: IT in the hospitals of San Francisco *(variation on: 1. Harvard case 9-303-097 F.W. McFarlan en R.D. Austin, revised 26/2/2003; 2. Davenport, t.h., et al.: just in time delivery comes to knowledge management, Harvard Business Review, july 2002; 3. lecture about the it organization at the Orbis hospital, Alberts, 2004.)*

B.1.2.1. Well! Well!

'The good news is, that the primary care did not suffer.' That is how Tom Brilliant, Chief Information Officer of the 'Health for all' group, started his management briefing about the fact that the IT of the 'Health for all' group had been down three-and-a-half days and all employees of the 'Health for all' group had to revert back to work processes supported by paper. Many of those processes hadn't been used for over a decade. The care for patients maybe hadn't been as quick over the past three-and-a-half days but no problem had been reported linked to the IT not working. Many lessons were learnt though and the experience showed that some subjects do need more attention.

B.1.2.2. The 'Health for all' group

The 'Health for all' group is a team of professionals in the health care, striving to provide personalized care. Members of the 'Health for all' group are 10,000 workers and 1500 physicians in various health care centres and hospitals in the San Francisco area in California, USA. The 'Health for all' group came into being in 1997 as a result of mergers, through which a hospital organization was created with an annual turnover of 1.8 billion dollars. The organization is the number one size-wise in California. Reason for the merger was the ability to procure more cheaply and achievement of cheaper work processes, so the continuity of the organizations involved is guaranteed.

In the years after the merger, the work processes in the various hospitals were improved, a very successful joint procurement was achieved and one arrived at the development of an extremely advanced use of IT, which was considered one of the best in the industry.

In 2003 the senior management of the 'Health for all' group consists of a CEO/Chief Legal Officer, a Chief Financial Officer and a Chief Information Officer. The 'Health for all' group provides in the year 2003 IT support for itself and for various other hospital organizations. Since 1998 Tom Brilliant has been CIO of the 'Health for all' group. The moment he arrived in 1998, 160 people worked with a budget of 70 million dollar for IT. They spent a lot of their time on the millennium problem. In the year 2004 there are 140 different people left.

Tom Brilliant graduated from the University of California, San José, in the subjects computers and economics. Afterwards, at the University of Seattle he simultaneously studied mechanical engineering, electrical engineering and medicine. In 1996 he moved to Minnessota to start a practice and take his PhD in medical informatics at the local university. He also became the head of 45 internet specialists at the 'Health for all' group. Tom Brilliant is both engineer and physician.

B.1.2.3. The IT organization of the 'Health for all' group

The IT organization in the year 1998 had a strongly decentralized decision process and a large multiformity with regard to infrastructure and application objects. Each of the participating organizations had its own tailor made products, dating back to the period before the merger. The applications were of extremely different quality. There were also extreme differences in working methods. In situations where one hospital was using an ultramodern application, another hospital was still using paper for the same process or segment. In 2003 all this had changed and all organizations in the 'Health for all' group are using the same IT support, whilst the costs for IT have remained the same. In the year 2003 the 'Health for all' group has, according to what they say:

- the most advanced network in the health care sector;
- the most advanced e-mail system in the health care sector;
- the most advanced speech and mobile communications system in the sector;
- the most advanced computing centre in the sector;
- and the most advanced web infrastructure in the health care sector.

The IT facilities support, amongst other things, the work of 1500 physicians, process 10 terabyte of data per day and know the medical history of 900,000 patients since 1977. There are 140 people working in the IT organization. All applications are web enabled and it is possible to see each patient's files, X-rays, echogram etc online via the web. The IT organization has a 7 × 24 hours running, entirely automated exploitation at its disposal. Power back up consists of three diesel generators, which were for that matter hardly used over the last three years. In the last quarter of 2003 clustered HP Superdome servers running under Linux version 8.2 replaced the last remaining IBM mainframe. The storage of data is done on central EMC Storage area networks. There are separate configurations for exploitation and for developing, maintaining and testing of applications. Physicians get free e-mail accounts and they also have cordless message services (with Black Berries) at their disposal.

The IT products and services at the 'Health for all' group are seen are extremely critical for the support of the work processes and the loyalty of the employees. In May 2002 the IT organization of the group was number 1 in Information Week.

B.1.2.4. The IT objects and the organization in detail

The functions in the hospitals of the 'Health for all' group can be divided in a number of clusters:

(a) clusters of medical functions, such as:
   – the clinical functions. These functions include: the admission planning, the admission preparation, the clinical reception, the nursing, the medical reporting, the medical quality control and the medical appointment coordination;
   – the examine and the treatment functions. This includes, amongst other things, the actual execution, arranging and planning, preparing of, reception, reporting, preparation of medicine and quality control;
   – the outpatient functions. This includes amongst other things assisting, arranging appointments, preparation of surgery hours, reception and referral;
(b) the administrative supporting, including:
   – the administrative and commercial functions. This includes amongst other things registration and statistics, bookkeeping, procurement, operation administration and invoicing, salary records, files management, library management, administrative quality control, application assessment and ordering, procuring registration and progress check.
   – personnel functions like staffing, applying condition of employments, education and training, personnel care, assessment employees etc.
(c) the functions for the 'hotel business' and the 'accommodation':
   – civil functions like food supply, goods management, civil maintenance, transport and distribution, welfare facilities, civil security, communication etc.
   – technical maintenance functions like the maintenance itself, the applications for and the planning of, quality control, the operating and control and the project management.

In order to be able to carry out all these functions, information about, amongst other things, patients, appointments, possessions, employees, medicine, treatments, invoices and payments, orders, suppliers and schedules is needed.

The applications as used by the 'Health for all' group supported the above-mentioned functions. In all hospitals of the 'Health for all' group the

ERP-system SAP version 4.7 is used standard for support of the financial, personnel and procuring functions (the functions under b). This standard version of SAP is integrated with a hospital version of SAP supplied by the Berlin Company Medizin plus (also uses SAP version 4.7.). This version supports the medical functions (the functions under a) and the functions for the hotel business and the accommodation (the functions under c). The applications with regard to personal productivity tools are directly connected with MS Office XP. The hospitals have intranet and extranet. This intranet and extranet was developed by the 'Health for all' group itself. The 'Health for all' group itself carries out functional management, application management and exploitation.

Since 2001, the IT organization of the 'Health for all' group is concentrated and centralized in San Francisco. It is subdivided in two parts, a demand organization and a supply organization.

B.1.2.4.1. The IT demand organization

In order to live up to the high expectations regarding IT application, the 'Health for all' group has set up a demand organization. This organization deals with the functionality of the IT facilities. It examines at strategic level, which applications have to be set up in future, what their functionality should be, justifies these and plans them. It examines the suppliers one would like to work with, the requirements of the partners in the chain and the chosen organization of IT. At tactical level it controls the implementation of the new applications and the management of daily use.

The demand organization consists of 60 people that are divided into four groups. Three of these groups are engaged in tactical and operational tasks in the medical, administrative and civil domestic domain. The fourth group takes care of the strategic tasks. Each group dealing with operational tasks has a service desk. The service desks are:

- for the medical functions 20 people, available 7 days a week 24 hours a day;
- for administrative functions 5 people, available 5 days a week 8 hours a day;
- for civil functions 3 people and available 5 days a week 8 hours per day.

The same ratio, with regard to dedicated workforce, goes for the change functions at operational level. In this field twenty people are employed. Apart from management, there are seven people available for functions at strategic level. Finally, five people are employed in the demand organization for carrying out management tasks.

B.1.2.4.2. The IT supply organization

B.1.2.4.2.1. The organization

The IT supply organization of the 'Health for all' group consists of 80 employees. These are divided into an exploitation group and an application management group. The application management group carries out the parametrizing for the SAP-package, develops the internet applications and does the application management for the Business Objects applications, that look after the management information of the 'Health for all' group. The total group consist of 55 people. The exploitation department of the 'Health for all' group consist of four parts: the operations group of 20 people, the change management group of 8 people (amongst whom also the network group), the monitoring group of 5 people and the strategic group of 2 people.

The operations group take care of the exploitation of the desktops and notebooks, networks and processing and storage facilities. For installation jobs and solving hardware problems at the place of work a contract was concluded with the Micromagic Company. The exploitation department itself takes care of the daily operations of the network, storage and processing facilities. This is done in a 7 days 24 hours roster. The change management group looks after the implementation of new versions of applications and infrastructures.

B.1.2.4.2.2. The managed objects

The technical infrastructure of the 'Health for all' group is sketched in Figure B.1.2.1. The 'Health for all' group has three identical computer centres. When a computer centre goes down, one of the others has sufficient capacity to take over the tasks of this computer centre. Normally every computer centre has a third of the load of the group. All day long the data collection of the group is replicated on the Storage Area Networks (SAN's). This way, each of the three SAN's has a complete, almost up-to-date copy of all data of the 'Health for all'

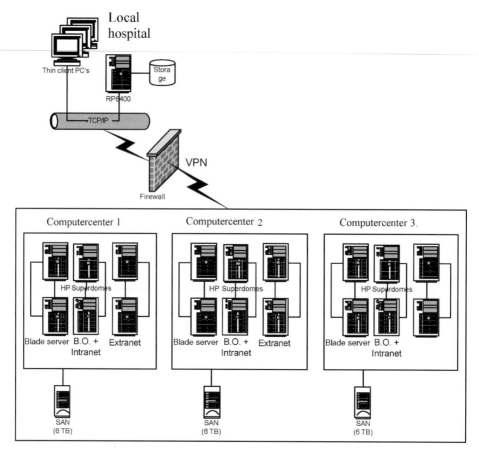

Figure B.1.2.1. The technical infrastructure of the 'Health for all' group

group. There are contracts with Cisco, EMC2 and HP for maintenance of objects they supplied.

At all fixed and mobile workstations of the 'Health for all' group thin clients are used. This means that the processing of local tasks takes place on blade servers. The network of the 'Health for all' group consists entirely of Cisco hardware.

The HP superdomes in each computer centre are set up:

1. for application management and functional testing;
2. for exploitation of SAP;
3. for the documentary information function;

4. for intranet and extranet applications;
5. for business object applications.

Apart from this, HP blade servers have been set up for support of the personal productivity tool MS Office, that runs under Citrix metaframe (thin client working method).

B.1.2.5. The fatal date: 13 November 2002

In the days leading up to 13 November 2002 a researcher of the 'Health for all' group starts to experiment with a knowledge management application, based upon the sharing of files, like a type of Napster for medical science. The application is designed for localizing data and copies these automatically over the network. No sooner had he installed the application at his workstation or he was called away because his wife was having a baby. He took three weeks paternity leave. He left the application in non-tested and non-tuned condition. The application started to explore its environment and started copying data at an increasingly larger scale. On the afternoon of 13 November 2002, the application transported terabytes of data across the net.

These massive data transports monopolized the services of the central network control. No other data came past the switch and the network no longer replied to requests from other parts of the network. These concluded from this they had to find alternative routes over the network. And so they did! The problem was however that the network had been extended step by step and as a whole ran out of the architecture. Parts started to duplicate each other's tasks and the result was the creation of an endless loop. This caused the whole network to grind to a halt. Nothing worked any more. Physicians had to resolve to judge combinations of medication on their effectiveness. Radiology technicians were given a crash course in operating the basic version of the machine. Case histories had to be told by the patients themselves. The telephone replaced emails. Work processes using paper became operational once more and senior staff member taught younger ones how to use these. In one foul swoop the hospital organization turned into an organization of the seventies.

For the IT group this meant all hands on deck. Tom Brilliant personally led the operation. By pulling all the stops, the network was back on line by 14 November 2003 at 4.00 a.m. but as soon as it worked it started to hang again.

After a further attempt on Thursday 14 November 2003 it was clear the IT organization of the 'Health for all' group could not solve the problem without outside help.

By 4.00 p.m. on 14 November 2002 the help of network hardware supplier Cisco was called in. Cisco looked after the maintenance of all hardware and considering the importance of the leading medical centre it was not hard to get the full attention of the advanced support-engineering group. This group brought the incident to the attention of Cisco's CEO who promoted the incident to CAP status. This meant putting Cisco's SWAT-team into action. When a SWAT-team is sent this means a Boeing with network hardware and engineers takes off from Santa Clara. At the same, time experts left from North Carolina for San Francisco. These people and hardware together were able to, if necessary; install an entire new network for the 'Health for all' group. Thursday 14 November 2002 late in the evening Tom Brilliant met the Cisco-people at the airport. By then, the IT group and Brilliant had been non-stop in action for 24 hours without achieving anything.

On arrival the Cisco-team immediately took over control, this in conformity with the CAP-status. Cisco froze all changes. Cisco became the owner of the problem and the 'Health for all' group delegates all authority with regard to the network to Cisco. The team brought in specialists from all time zones and according to the 'follow the sun' principle they worked 24 hours a day on solving the problem. From Friday 15 November 2003 it was decided to work in hand mode, for the time being, as long as it was uncertain whether the network functioned. This was because, switching constantly seemed to put the patients more at risk.

On 18 November 2002 the network operated as per usual. Step by step the usual applications were started up. The work processes with paper were only then replaced, the moment the IT system had functioned perfectly for 24 hours.

B.1.2.6. Lessons to be learnt from the incident

It was clear that the 'Health for all' group in the last ten years had become heavily dependent on the use of IT. Tom Brilliant however also learnt the following:

1. make sure you have experts regularly check whether your network is configured correctly;
2. make sure you don't have to depend on one single official in your IT group;

3. keep your network knowledge up-to-date. The 'Health for all' group network was state of the art in 1993. At the end of the nineties it had grown out of its shell and the network group, that hadn't kept its network knowledge up-to-date, did not see the problems coming;

4. beware of users with just sufficient expertise; they may become dangerous;

5. organize a rigorous control of changes in the network. After the incident a network change and management committee was installed with participants from a number of disciplines, which has to approve every change in the network infrastructure. Fundamental changes are put to Cisco first. Changes are these days implemented between 2 a.m. and 5 a.m. on Sunday morning and test and recovery plans have to be demonstrably present, before changes can be made;

6. adapt to changes in the environment. As IT staff, one should constantly ascertain what the effects on the IT infrastructure are of changes in the environment;

7. there are limits to maximally meeting demands of the user organization. An example of this is that the user organization is not able to hire its own IT people for just putting a video quickly on the net through IP. The IT group will do this after consulting Cisco;

8. have back-up procedures in place you can trust;

9. having back-ups of components is not enough, one should also have alternatives for approaching these. Using modems with dial up via telephone part of the IT, be it slower, could have functioned. However these were not in place;

10. perform life-cycle management for your network components. Routers, switches and other network components will only last up to four years;

This incident taught the 'Health for all' group that the IT support consists of thousands of parts and that each part has to function in harmony with the other parts.

B.1.2.7. Perspectives on using IT at the 'Health for all' group

Hospitals function in a dynamic environment, where IT can be of significant importance. Let's give an example. The knowledge in the field of medicine changes day in, day out. A specialist in the hospitals of the 'Health for all' group has to have some knowledge of about 10,000 illnesses and syndromes, 3000 possible medications, 1100 lab tests and of many of the roughly 400,000 annually published articles in his field. Even if an internist would want to read just the articles published by the University of San Francisco Medical School, 202 of those would be on hypertension, 139 on asthma and 313 on diabetes. A physician should really know something about around a million little facts and these facts change all the time. Not knowing might result in making mistakes.

Studies in the San Francisco hospitals early 2000 proved that:

– five percent of all patients reacts wrong to prescribed medication. Of these 43 percent is of a serious nature. The cause of these reactions can be partly prevented because over 50% of these are caused by prescribing the wrong medication;
– of the six most requested lab tests in intensive care 50% is clinically unnecessary.
– over 50% of the prescriptions for a certain drug used for heart conditions are wrong.

In order to really do something about these facts the 'Health for all' group want to include the knowledge of science in the daily work process of its doctors. This can be done, by integrating this knowledge into the IT applications the doctor uses. This approach to the problem is expensive, takes a lot of time and is not without risks.

For doing this, one often starts by applying more IT support in prescription of treatments and lab tests at a patient's first visit with a complaint. Applying more IT, especially when recording the treatment and the tests to be taken is important because this is the translation of the doctor's diagnosis into actions to be taken. At this moment, supplementing knowledge from other sources is at its most valuable. Use of IT when recording treatment and prescription of tests enhanced the efficiency of working and reduces the chance of mistakes. The power of the desired IT input lies in the fact that it works real time. Knowledge is immediately combined, the moment the doctor needs this knowledge the most.

We could continue like this for a long time. Input of IT at the 'Health for all' group can also improve the logistics process. A recent advice to the Ministry of Public Health in the Netherlands provides examples of this. Combination of data and speech with input of Voice-over IP networks can furthermore lead to reducing phone costs etc. etc.

Questions

1. Describe the management objects of the 'Health for all' group.
2. Where does the responsibility in fact lie for the functionality and the performance of the IT facilities at the 'Health for all' group? Where does the responsibility lie for the quality of data that various hospitals store on the IT facilities?
3. Why is the IT support as offered by the 'Health for all' group typically a facility one could come across in the network economy? How would one implement such a facility in an organization that operates along the lines of industrial economy? What did the 'Health for all' group forget to think about with regard to this? Do you consider the way the 'Health for all' group has set up its IT infrastructure a wise one? Why? Why not?
4. Name two strategic and two tactical reasons why a decision for using the services and products of the IT supply organization has to be made by the IT demand organization of the 'Health for all' group.
5. Apply the idea of the service pit and service shell to the IT supply of the 'Health for all' group. Indicate which functional demands and which performance demands the product and the services of the 'Health for all' group meet. Look at these functional demands from different perspectives.
6. In which way does the way in which the IT products and services of the 'Health for all' group are supplied fit in the future ideas on:
   – the way in which demand organizations operate?
   – the way in which supply organizations operate?
   – why don't they fit in as well with the views on IT management of the eighties and nineties? Which view on IT management does the 'Health for all' group apparently have? Illustrate your answers with examples.
7. Give for the 'Health for all' group the four angles on IT management. Give an example of every angle.
8. Which external influences have impact on the services and products of the 'Health for all' group? What is the impact of the idea that IT for its users must seem like a utility on the IT of the 'Health for all' group? What does

this mean for the IT organization of the 'Health for all' group? (utility computing). What is the impact on IT supply organization of the 'Health for all' group of the fact that labour intensive tasks mostly disappear to low wages countries?

9. How do the services and products of the IT supply organization of the 'Health for all' group fit in with the performance requirements, as defined by ISO 9126 in combination with the Quint-report? How do they fit in with the performance requirements that come across from the logistics field and operations management? Check all performance requirements and their implementation with regard to this.

10. Which GAP's could appear when delivering products and services by the IT-departments of the 'Health for all' group? Give an example of all five GAP's. Also indicate, how one discovers the appearance of such a GAP and how this GAP then can be counteracted.

11. What is the architecture for IT facilities looking at the IT facilities of the 'Health for all' group? What grabs the attention when looking at these IT facilities and what should therefore be worked at? What are the consequences for the managed objects?

12. How did the 'Health for all' group realize its internal architecture of IT facilities?

13. How does the realization of the architecture for supplying products and services by the IT organization of the 'Health for all' group fit in with the views Gartner, respectively the Nolan Norton group has on the subject? Explain your answer.

14. Test the architecture of IT facilities of the 'Health for all' group to the TO-GAF model. What do you notice? What is missing? What are the differences between the results of both tests?

Part B.2. Traditional IT management: organizing demand and supply

B.2.1. Turbo trade: Advice in the field of asset management (*variation on Applegate et al. (2003), Charles Schwab*)

B.2.1.1. The Turbo Trade Company

The Turbo Trade company started in 1973, immediately after the oil crises. John Thorpe decided to establish the assets advice organization Turbo Trade, when in Australia the regulations on advise on stock and other asset forming products were changed.

Turbo Trade offers a wide range of investment possibilities, which are realized by others. Turbo Trade provides advice, as to which of these should be acquired. In order to make sure there is no clash of interest, staff do not get paid a commission per transaction but a fixed salary with a bonus based on the performance of the team as a whole.

Turbo Trade is a pioneer in its sector. In the seventies it was the first company purely operating as an asset formation advice organization with a chain of local offices. It was the first to offer a 7 times 24 hours transaction possibility and a detailed online asset survey service. Turbo Trade leapt on the fact that, as the customer is more self-servicing, it becomes more important to have online facilities at one's disposal. This is also obvious when looking at the past with regards to technological innovation (Figure B.2.1.1).

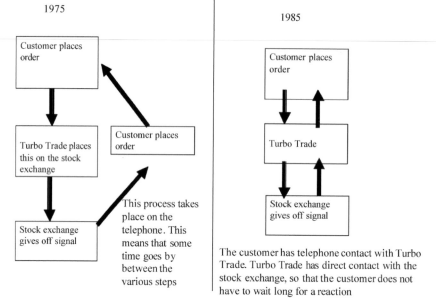

Figure B.2.1.1. Changes in Turbo Trade's way of operating between 1975 and 1985

B.2.1.2. Application of IT at Turbo Trade

At the beginning a customer placed an order at Turbo Trade, next Turbo Trade placed this on the stock exchange, waited for the signal whether the transaction was realized and rang the customer back. In the eighties every office obtained direct contact with the stock exchange.

That is the moment Turbo Trade set up its IT department. Building, maintenance and exploitation of IT facilities were from then onwards executed under the direction of an in-house IT organization and with regard to the primary applications entirely by the in-house IT organization. Up until then, the maintenance of the applications and the exploitation of IT infrastructures and applications at large was outsourced. For its core of competition advantage, being their innovative application of IT facilities, Turbo Trade did not want to be dependent any longer on third parties.

In order to become and stay leader in the innovation field of the sector, Turbo Trade next launched a number of applications. That way Turbo Trade in 1988 provided its customers with the same financial information it had at its

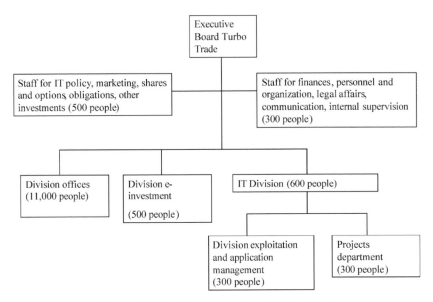

Figure B.2.1.2. The organization of Turbo Trade

disposal. In 1995, Turbo Trade delivered an online trading programme, Fasttrade, suitable for use on the Windows 95 platform. This enabled customers to trade online themselves. Finally in 1998, Turbo Trade Direct went online. This is an internet sales channel that is unrelated to the existing sales channels.

B.2.1.3. Organization

As mentioned, in 1980 Turbo Trade set up its IT supply organization, the IT division. In the year 2003 this organization has grown into an organization of about 600 people. As is shown in Figure B.2.1.2, the IT division is subdivided into two large divisions, being exploitation and application management and development projects.

The IT division concentrates on application management and exploitation tasks. Functional management of the applications is carried out by the staff of the Turbo Trade head office, with the exception of the service desk task for the applications used by customers. This task is initially taken care of by the front-office of the division e-investments or by the employees of the division

offices. If they receive queries in the field of IT facilities, they are unable to
answer; they contact the service desk of the IT division. This then provides the
office in question or the front-office of the division e-investments with a possible
answer to the query.

The exploitation department is subdivided into a front- and a back-office.
The front-office deals with all questions in the IT field, originating from the Turbo
Trade organization. The back-office ensures that the Turbo Trade applications
and infrastructures have an availability of 99.9999% and a fast response time.
Over the past years this has been given a lot of attention. As the following
testifies:

> *Turbo Trade's decision in 1999 to offer full internet trading to
> all customers at a fixed low price led to a serious strain on Turbo
> Trade's IT facilities. It is ascertained that the computers have
> to process about 4000 transactions per second. The large IBM
> mainframes really appear to be utilized to the limit and Turbo
> Trade is forced to invest 20 percent of its annual turnover in IT
> projects, application management and exploitation.*
>
> *Trade on the internet appears to have more peaks than
> normal online trade and is therefore more sensitive to inci-
> dents and possible lack of capacity. One has to both integrate
> more security measures as well as apply more transport, stor-
> age and processing capacity than was calculated using the old
> models. Instead of having a capacity of the size that is three
> times than the average daily trading volume, one has to tar-
> get a capacity of three times the size of the average trading
> volume per hour. The Executive Board decided because of this
> to install a capacity of 10 times the size of the average daily
> volume.*
>
> *Furthermore, the 99.2 percent availability is too low. The
> consequences of down time are more serious in the internet
> era and the bad publicity in the various Autsralian television
> programmes. Radio news and newspapers take care of the rest.
> Turbo Trade is forced to lower its performance requirements to
> non-planned and planned non-availability of its services from
> 0.8 percent (being ten minutes per day) to less than ten seconds*

per day. This process took two years and was completed in January 2003.

In practice this means that Turbo Trade has for each critical component in its exploitation environment, the same critical component permanently on hot stand-by. This way, availability of 99.9999% is achieved. This means that in a certain period of for example 30 days, only 0.0001% non-planned non-availability of the exploitation environment for applications and infrastructures that are in production occurs. In 30 days, one has $24 \times 60 \times 30 = 43,200$ minutes. At 99.9999% availability one is therefore during this period not available a maximum of 4.3 minutes.

B.2.1.4. Architecture for IT facilities

The Turbo Trade IT architecture consists of infrastructure objects, the application that uses this infrastructure and the organization for utilizing the objects and develop these (Figure 2.1.3). The technical infrastructure consist of:

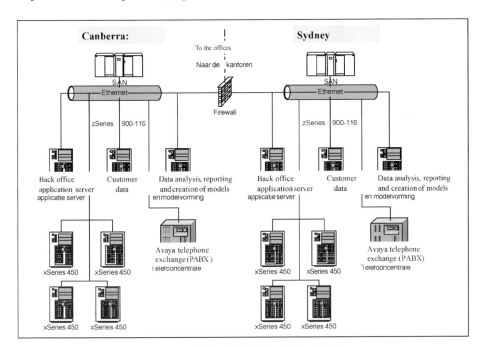

Figure B.2.1.3. The ICT at Turbo Trade

(a) Two computer centres: one in Sydney and one in Canberra. Both are connected by means of a fast data network of 1 gigabyte/sec. In each computer centre there are:
- three mainframe servers, IBM zSeries 900-116 with 40 GB internal memory running on the zOS operating system. One single server is used for all applications in the back-office of the offices, a mainframe server for all customers the e-investments division and a mainframe server for data analysis, reporting and model creation. All three mainframes are coupled with a storage area network (SAN), in which all data for processing is stored. This SAN consists of 2 terabyte online accessible disk memory and 6 terabyte staged memory. This memory is situated on an EMC2 memory robot. Using this all data of all customer transactions of the last 10 years can be recovered.
- four mid-range servers, IBM xSeries 450 with 16 gigabyte background memory running under Microsoft Windows Server 2003 per Turbo Trade sales region and for the e-investments department. These servers support authorization and authentication of employees and customers. Besides, on these servers the actual processing of office applications such as MS-Office takes place;
- an Avaya-telephone exchange as well as voice response and computer telephony integration facilities necessary for supporting the call centre applications in the various sales offices, the regional call centres and at the e-investments division. The Avaya-exchange is directly connected to the network. Within Turbo Trade since 2003 calls are made using Voice over IP.

(b) each of the workstations in the offices has a Windows-based terminal. This terminal is connected through a TCP/IP-data network with the two mainframe computer centres and from every terminal printouts can be made on a network printer. Furthermore each of the workstations is kitted out with call centre functionality. Apart from this, employees on external duties advising customers can call in using their mobile phone and use their laptop for accessing the network of that Turbo Trade office and its mainframes.

The architecture of the Turbo Trade applications consists of two parts. These are the front-office applications and the back-office applications. When developing new products and services one often encounters the question how to connect the new front-office application with the existing architecture of back-office systems.

The availability of the Turbo Trade IT infrastructure is measured on an end-to-end basis. It amounts to 99.9999% at an average response time for the internal Turbo Trade end user of less than 1.25 second in 95% of all cases. For the internet customers this is 1.75 seconds per screen that has to be sent.

B.2.1.5. Applications

Turbo Trade uses the Turbo Trade trade system (TThands) for supporting all it's primary processes. This application is a tailor made application. TThands consists, like many other applications at Turbo Trade, in principle of three parts. That is the data input using input media in the offices with corrections etc, the data processing and the data output on paper or otherwise. The processing part and the output system are batch applications. The input system is an online application. This application has been developed on in the internet age to a front-office application, using internet technology. Through a portal, customers and employees enter the Turbo Trade applications and is determined which facilities one can use in TThands (Figure B.2.1.4).

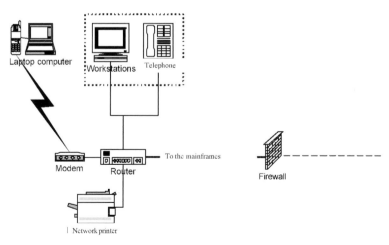

Figure B.2.1.4. The IT facilities in a sales office

Turbo Trade's in-house management executes the functional and the application management of these applications. Microsoft Office XP is applied as personal productivity tool and on all personal computers Windows XP operates. For support of the financial and personnel function within Turbo Trade, the standard application People Soft was procured. Large parts of the functional management and almost the entire application management of these are taken care of by the People Soft company. For extra management rapportages, tailor made applications are in place.

Regarding management tools, the HP ITSM tool set for service desk, configuration management and problem management is utilized. The tailor made applications have all been built using Oracle building tools and use Oracle databases. For making management reports, Cognos and SAS building tools are applied.

B.2.1.6. From decentralized control of the IT division to the BISG department

The Turbo Trade management observes that the Turbo Trade environment becomes increasingly dynamic and that spread across the entire organization, functional management tasks are performed. This does not always result in transparency in decision-making with regards to IT. There is really no IT portfolio management at Executive Board level, whilst IT application is vital to a company like Turbo Trade in order to survive. Therefore it has been considered to convert the staff department IT policy as part of the staff of the Executive Board, into a staff department Business Information Systems Governance (BISG). This department will execute the Turbo Trade BiSL tasks.

The BISG department will have to interpret the demand-side for the IT division for the various departments and divisions. They will act as contact for the IT division. One expects to need approximately 150 staff functional management. BISG should bundle the demand of the various departments, carry out clear IT portfolio management and operate as the strict client for the IT division.

The heads of the staff departments and the directors of the various divisions have strongly supported this development. It did mean diminution of their autonomy but the achievement of cost advantages and the resolution of countless problems were deciding factors for going through with this. At the lower control levels, one has not always yet reached this conclusion.

The BISG department is still a small organization in the process of development. An enormous amount of questions are an issue within the BISG department. One has more or less carte blanche for setting up the organization. One has to deal with issues like:

- what activities will BISG have to carry out?
- does it have to limit itself to just directing or will it also have to execute tasks?
- what organization structure should be used?

The situation of the BISG department is complicated by the fact that the divisions are ultimately responsible for the use of the information function in their organization. The funding counts as a large part of the divisions' budget. BISG has to get the costs of the information function paid from the various divisions. That is how the BISG group and the IT division are financed.

Questions

1. State the objects of management at Turbo Trade. Describe their IT organization, discussing the responsibilities and the execution of the functional, application management and exploitation tasks.
2. What do you observe at Turbo Trade with regards to the current set-up of functional management? What is your opinion on this organization? Do you agree with the Executive Board for wanting to arrive at a different set-up of functional management? What are the reasons for your answer?
3. What does the introduction of BiSL mean to Turbo Trade? Where are or will be the various processes as dictated by BiSL situated? What does this functional management organization look like after introduction of BiSL? What are the differences with the current organization? Will this change pay for itself?
4. What do you observe at Turbo Trade with regards to the set-up of application management? Why should Turbo Trade give this more attention? What processes do you recognize at Turbo Trade with regard to application management?

5. What would a set-up of application management at Turbo Trade look like? What would this look like process-focussed? Which objects have to be present with regard to application management?

6. Why is organizing application management important in the long-term? Which processes have to be set-up by then and what is Turbo Trade doing about this? Run through the processes and indicate why Turbo Trade should set up a certain process at strategic level.

7. What does day-in, day-out management entail in ASL? What data do these processes share?

8. What do the maintenance and renewal tasks of ASL entail for Turbo Trade? How do new IT facilities get into production?

9. Indicate which demands could be the most important to the customers of the IT division at the exploitation of IT facilities? How are these demands worked out by the exploitation department? Which processes did it set-up to this end? What is the relationship between the ITIL and the ASL processes?

10. How would you control the exploitation of IT facilities at Turbo Trade? What serves as handles?

11. What is your opinion on the design of the version policy at Turbo Trade for applications and infrastructure software? Why?

12. Which manuals will be present in the exploitation department?

13. What is the progress of a showstopper for applications through the Turbo Trade organization? In which way is a change proposal for the informatics and one for the technical infrastructure processed? How does a change proposal for applications affect this organization?

14. The internal Turbo Trade service desk registers daily around 150 help desk calls. 130 of these are calls about non-functioning infrastructures; about 20 are calls to do with applications. The average time for dealing with a call is in 95% of all cases 10 minutes for a call to do with infrastructures and 2 hours for a call concerning applications. The service desk notes for every call:

    −the time it entered the front-office system;

    −the time, the call was accepted in the second line;

    −the time, the solution was found for the problem and this was passed on to the customer;

    −the time, the customer was called, to ask whether he was satisfied with the solution.

The service desk uses one person for answering calls. Two people work at resolving incidents, calling customers afterwards when incidents are solved and on problem management.

What is your opinion on this organization regarding dealing with calls? What control information do you think is generated? This information can be seen by the whole of Turbo Trade via the intranet. Formulate a few improvement proposals using the process-approach, where Turbo Trade has all possible technical facilities such as a call centre with Avaya CMS, an intranet and extranet, possibilities for speech recognition etc. What could enhance the service at Turbo trade?

15. With intranet possibilities the network traffic using the fixed net is watched. 95% of all incidents can be solved remote. For resolving the other incidents to the fixed data net, a 7 × 24 hours service contract with Unisys was concluded. The call-out time for this contract is maximum 2 hours. No MTTR (mean time to repair) was agreed.

    Every year about a third of the configuration is changed. This means installing different hardware and configuring the software. Furthermore, Cisco annually releases new versions of the network software to the network. The Turbo Trade policy is to be maximally two years behind with new versions in this area. Indicate how configuration management and change management are implemented at Turbo Trade. Indicate how the communication between the service desk and configuration/change management runs.

16. At a new release Turbo Trade uses the principles of Result-directed Implementing (RDI). Explain what this means for an application like Microsoft Office.

17. What is the disadvantage when an organization always works with up-to-date versions? What is the advantage? Also remember the consequences for informatics and technical infrastructures. What is legacy at Turbo Trade? How is this legacy phased out? How can legacy be prevented at Turbo Trade?

18. How does one, or should one deal at Turbo Trade with management of documents and versions?

19. How does the organization of Turbo Trade fit in with the model for organizing of IT management in larger organizations?

20. How does Turbo Trade handle outsourcing? What type of outsourcing does Turbo Trade know? What does that mean to the key processes in this domain?

B.2.2. TT FRONT PANELS: A SUPPLIER IN THE AUTOMOTIVE INDUSTRY (*A VARIATION ON SALONER et al., 2002*)

B.2.2.1. Simple and fast information and the car industry

'Soon, the last customer will walk through a dealer's off line showroom.' Although internet car trading is still in its infancy in the Netherlands, in the year 2002 it was possible to speak of a certain growth in this type of trade, also because of the advent of online purchase possibilities such as AutoOnline BV. These days, these online points of sale rapidly change character. Where these previously just referred to traditional garages that then completed the sale, these days this slowly changes and they are turning into companies that control the whole purchase, including financing, extra guarantee, delivery and insurance. The traditional dealer can often only deliver the car at these companies. This action only provides limited contact with the customer.

Apart from this, garages have to deal with the manufacturer's websites. These websites are capable of fully supporting sales to customers in the short term. Manufacturers set up these sites for various reasons. Firstly, the online companies are a way of getting in direct contact with the end users of the products. Secondly, they fear that the customer contact otherwise entirely shifts to cyber companies that have no ties with any particular manufacturer.

In 1999 in the USA, about 2.7% of car sales were realized on the internet, compared to 1.1% the previous year. In 2000, about 5% of all car sales were expected to be completed on the net. Up to now the sales via the web mainly entail referral to a dealer. Besides, 40% of the buyers consult the internet for more information, before buying a car. It is expected this figure will be 66% in 2001 (www.JDPower.com). Anyway, nobody expects the online sales channel will entirely replace the off line dealers' showrooms. The concluded franchise agreements and the legislation these are based upon, form a hindrance in this respect. These protect the traditional dealers and besides, these dealers also have their own websites.

Apart from application of internet techniques at the interface with the customers of a company we also know these in other parts of the business. This also includes the procurement of goods and services.

	example make	2003		2002		2001		2000	
segment	and model	abs.	%	abs.	%	abs.	%	abs.	%
A-segment	Fiat Seicento	41.570	8,50%	51.992	10,18%	51.839	9,78%	66.421	11,1%
B-segment	Opel Corsa	110.566	22,61%	114.309	22,38%	103.283	19,48%	118.371	19,8%
C-segment	VW Golf	107.856	22,06%	118.043	23,11%	129.684	24,46%	157.353	26,3%
D-segment	Ford Mondeo	90.7871	8,57%	103.568	20,28%	116.114	21,90%	126.526	21,2%
E-segment	BMW 5-serie	19.583	4,00%	25.298	4,95%	28.392	5,35%	29.150	4,9%
F-segment	Mercedes S-klasse	4.407	0,90%	5.398	1,06%	4.949	0,93%	7.174	1,2%
G-segment	Audi TT	3.013	0,62%	3.488	0,68%	4.521	0,85%	7.628	1,3%
H-segment	Ferrari	774	0,16%	906	0,18%	1.004	0,19%	1.074	0,2%
I-segment	Rolls Royce	162	0,03%	135	0,03%	287	0,05%	349	0,1%
M-segment	Renault Scénic	66.303	13,56%	50.689	9,92%	54.547	10,29%	48.976	8,2%
N-segment	Chrysler Voyager	15.041	3,08%	13.908	2,72%	13.644	2,57%	14.467	2,4%
T-segment	Jeep	17.507	3,58%	13.608	2,66%	13.312	2,51%	11.639	2,0%
V-segment	Ford Transit	9.953	2,04%	8.640	1,69%	8.091	1,53%	7.886	1,3%
Unknown		1.448	0,30%	762	0,15%	620	0,12%	609	0,1%
Total		488,970	100.00%	510,744	100.00%	530,287	100.00%	579,623	100.00%

Sales new per segment

Figure B.2.2.1. Car sales in the Netherlands Nederland (www.bovag.nl, source RDC)

B.2.2.2. The car industry

In 2002, 510,000 new cars were sold in the Netherlands (www.bovag.nl) (Figure B.2.2.1). This is 4% less than the previous year. Apart from this, an extensive trade in second hand cars exists. In 2000 the number of traded second hand cars was over 960.000 (see www.bovag.nl). The car trade furthermore generates turnover in other industries. We mention the trade in financing, insurances, extra guarantees, adverts, parts and accessories.

A number of manufacturers worldwide dominate the automobile market. These include GM, Opel, Daimler Chrysler, Volkswagen, Renault, Honda, Nissan and Toyota. GM for example, produced 7.56 million cars in 1998. These car manufacturers have production facilities all over the world. Besides they own production facilities of other manufacturers. Ford is for example owner of the British Aston Martin and Jaguar, owns the Swedish Volvo and the Japanese Mazda. GM is owner of the British Vauxhall, the German Opel and the Swedish Saab. Furthermore, GM has shares in the Japanese Isuzu and Subaru.

Car production is both capital as well as labour intensive. The material costs for manufacturing a car are 45% of the price, the labour costs 25% and the rest is sales, research and development and administration. In general, the profit margin is 6.5% before taxes (1994–1998). Car manufacturers direct their resources mainly at design, engineering and production of cars. Design targets a beautiful appearance and functionality, engineering targets performance and handling.

B.2.2.3. Designing, manufacturing, marketing and distributing

Design and manufacturing of a car are time-consuming processes. It takes between 18 and 36 months for a car to be taken into production after the first drawing is made. Car manufacturers have a complex chain of processes, starting from the purchasing until the delivery of the car to the customer. They have thousands of suppliers (supplying for instance steel, plastic, glass, electronics, oil and chemical products). The BMW Z3 Roadster for instance, has over 3000 parts.

Although manufacturers subcontract the manufacturing of increasingly more parts, they still continue to manufacture many themselves. Engines and transmission are often regarded the heart of a car and manufacture of these is rarely left to another.

Production facilities are usually designed for producing batches of a certain type car. Every plant has several production lines and every line produces a particular model in many varieties. Even though 80% of each type is standard, every car has options concerning specification, such as colour, interior, engine, wheels, stereo systems and so on. The Daimler Chrysler Neon model comes in 2800 variations. In order to limit this number, manufacturers usually ask their customers to choose from particular packages.

The manufacture of cars demands a 30–60 day planning horizon. Production parts for 60 days are in stock. The production is determined on the basis of orders of dealers and customers. Orders of dealers make up 80–85% of production. In all other cases the car is produced after a customer's order. Customers prefer to have the car immediately and are not prepared to wait 30–60 days for delivery.

Optimal utilization of the production capacity dictates a minimum production at a plant. This production is based on cars sold and the forecast. This forecast is mostly based on research that is minimally one year old, when the cars reach the dealers' showroom. The forecast is therefore usually 30–60% wrong, which leads to surplus and shortages.

Cars are distributed through a network of dealers, working on the basis of a franchise contract. This contract allows selling cars of a certain make and to service these in a certain area. The dealer is under obligation to sell particular numbers of cars and provide a minimum level of service. Dealers keep a 60 day stock. They are dealing with delivery times of between 1 and 2 months.

Manufacturers and importers support their dealers with promotional campaigns. In general, the car industry purchases the major part of the advertising market. Manufacturers spend on average 2000 euro per car on discounts and other incentives both for customers as well as dealers. Furthermore, manufacturers have permanent market research done on trends and consumer wishes. Each model is as much as possible targeted at a specific target group and, although preferences are often linked to age, sex and income, there are also differences based on region, marital status, profession and other factors. In 2001 for instance, the sale of business cars in the Netherlands was greater than the sale of private cars (see www.cbs.nl).

In general, the distribution costs amount to about 30% of the retail price of the car. 50% of these costs are directly related to importer or manufacturer (advertising, promotional discounts, low interest loans etc.), the other half is dealer related (financing and insurance of stocks, labour costs, sales bonuses, overheads and profit).

B.2.2.4. The car retail trade

In Dutch retail trade there are two types of retailers: the specific dealers with an 80% market share and the remaining ones with a 20% market share. In total, there are about 6000 car companies and these provide work for about 57000 employees. In all companies mentioned in Figure B.2.2.2 there are 87000 in total.

Looking at the retail trade one may conclude this is consolidating. The cause for this lies in the fact that less franchise contracts are concluded; in companies closing down; the increasing capital intensity (more variety in cars in stock, more complicated electronics and therefore more expensive testing equipments etc.) of a dealership and garages being bought up by large dealer companies. The manufacturers and importers have the problem that large dealers rarely limit themselves to one single make and do not care much whether the customer buys a Volkswagen or an Opel.

BOVAG

Division	Number of members per 31-12-2003
ABA (Auto Bedrijven Associatie)	3.224
NDA (Nederlandse Dealer Associatie)	3.029
TWB (Tweewielerbedrijven)	1.755
BBT (Branche Behartiging Tankstations)	1.050
VAN (Verkeersopleidingen Associatie Nederland)	690
AVL (Autoverhuur Ledenassociatie)	663
TDA (Truck Dealer Associatie)	357
AMR (Afdeling Mobiele Recreatie)	235
WAS (Autowasbedrijven)	144
AWB (Aanhangwagenbedrijven)	108
VNM (Verenigde Nederlandse Motorenrevisiebedrijven	80
TOTAL	**11.335**

Source: BOVAG members administration

Figure B.2.2.2. An overview of all types of Bovag members (www.Bovag.nl)

B.2.2.5. Manufacturers, the internet and their customers

Manufacturers try to use the internet in four different ways. These ways are:

1. They concentrate their purchase operation as much as possible through Covisint, an electronic marketplace that connects the direct and indirect suppliers of the large manufacturers with each other and with their customers. GM and Ford spend over 80 trillion dollar a year on procurement of goods. By going through Covisint they hope to speed up elapsed times at procurement and reduce costs.
2. Fitting internet and e-mail into cars. By subscribing to a service, the smart phone can be used, e-mail sent and internet used. Besides, in the long run it will become possible to send performance information of the car, so preventative and more systematic maintenance can be done.
3. The mutually connecting of data collections of sales, marketing and distribution means that sales will be more targeted and relationships are maintained.

4. Creating websites, in order to bring in more online customers. On the GM website www.BuyPower.com customers can compare GM models to those of the competition. Ford presents possibilities for 'e-prices' etc. Apart from that, alliances with Yahoo and other portals are started. Ford for example, bought a 25% share in the Microsoft www.Carpoint.com website.

Sites that sell cars have the problem that a customer, after having bought a car wants to see this delivered immediately or at least within the week. Even if that particular car would be for sale somewhere, the manufacturers would not have the applications to find this car and to deliver this. When a manufacturer has to manufacture the car first, the customer has to deal with a long elapsed time. This elapsed time between order and delivery varies in the USA between 20 days (Toyota) and 52 days (GM).

GM aims to reduce this time to 10 days. In this period of ten days, the assembly of the car will take up to about 30 hours. The set-up of the assembly, fitting of specials and transport take up the rest of the ten days. Reducing this elapsed time would increase customer satisfaction and reducing the stocks. With a 50% reduction in stocks, the price could come down by 10–15%.

B.2.2.6. The next years

It is clear that in the information era manufacturers, suppliers and dealers exchange a lot more information with each other on products and customers. A dealers' business model probably becomes increasingly dependent on income from a subscription to services that is concluded at purchase of the car. Just like the suppliers, these dealers increasingly become a link in the production chain from steel plate to a car for the customer.

TT front panels is a link right at the start of this chain. TT front panels has its headquarters in a factory in Wolfsburg. It also has a factory in Detroit. It produces front panels for the car industry. 90% of its trade (1,500,000 panels a year) is bought by GM, Opel and Volkswagen, each for an equal share (30% each). The remaining 10% turnover is divided over 20 car manufacturers. GM and Opel buy through Covisint. Volkswagen is part of a competing buyer's cooperative. The remaining manufacturers are spread across both buyers' cooperatives. Buyer's cooperatives of car manufacturers like Covisint enforce procedures on their suppliers for the administrative settlement of purchase transactions. TT front panels was that way forced to introduce the SAP ERP system. Unfortunately the implementation of SAP within the two buyer's cooperatives is not the same. Because of this, TT Front panels has to keep two order and delivery flows going next to each other.

B.2.2.7. TT front panels (TTFP) in the chain

TTFP manufactures its products in two factories that are in principle identical. Each factory could take over the production of the other factory. Selling to the car manufacturers is mainly about concluding framework contracts with the buyers' cooperatives. Sales offices in Detroit, Wolfsburg, Kyoto, Seoul, Paris and Manchester are responsible for this.

TTFP has insight into the procurement applications of its customers and ensures that the stock levels of the various car-manufacturing plants for certain assortments of TTFP products continuously stay at a certain level. In doing this TTFP takes over the stock keeping task and the supply of the manufacturers. TTFP plans its production such that there are always full truckloads on their way to customers whilst at the same the minimum stock level of articles is not exceeded. The car manufacturer pays for the supplied articles at assembly. This is detected because each dashboard is fitted with RFID (radio frequency identification), which detects the movement of stock.

B.2.2.7. The technical and informatics infrastructure at TTFP

The technical infrastructure at TTFP is shown in Figure B.2.2.3. In the head office in Wolfsburg a twin computer centre is lined up. This is a computer centre consisting of two equal parts at different locations, in this case at about 300 metres distant from other on the same terrain as the head office. Each part of the twin includes two Hewlet Packard (HP) Superdomes with 2×64 Intel Itanium 2 processors operating under HP Unix release 11i version 2. Each transaction centre has a central EMC2 storage area network, on which 2 terabytes in data is stored. These Compaq servers are connected through the TTFP-network with HP Superdomes with 16 Intel Itanium 2 processors in all sales offices (each

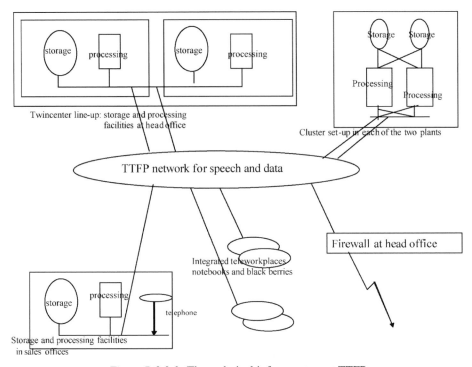

Figure B.2.2.3. The technical infrastructure at TTFP

once) and in the two factories (each twice with cluster technology for storage). Furthermore, there is a connection with the central Avaya Definity telephone system (executed in duplicate), where to every Definity two voice-reponse systems are each connected with 50 voice-response lines. 300 workplaces are connected to the HP Superdomes at head office, all equipped with HP personal computers (Proliant type). In the factories there are per factory 30 workplaces and per office about 50 workplaces connected to the network. TTFP has circa 1000 employees, of whom 90% have a personal computer in their office. The operating system Windows server 2003 is installed at the workplaces as well as the central servers outside headquarters.

The informatics infrastructure at TTFP is composed of an Oracle basis as regards the operational processes applications and for the intranet and extranet and the connection between these applications and the operational processes applications, if tailor made software is needed, the software from the IBM-line such as Visual Age is used.

The applications at TTFP consist of three parts. The operational processes supporting applications, the personal productivity tools and the communication supporting applications. The operational processes applications can be divided into primary and secondary applications. Secondary applications are the applications for supporting financial, personnel and office processes. Primary applications serve the sales, distribution and production. For sales, personnel, financial and distribution processes the mySAP.com software is implemented. The salary records are kept at the PinkRoccade group. For personal productivity tools and communication supporting applications the Microsoft products are available. MS Office is used and own applications were made for the intranet and extranet applications. For generating control information at the workplaces the InfoRay product is used. InfoRay was chosen because of its user friendliness and the many interfaces with all possible data collections it offers in the standard model.

B.2.2.8. The organization of IT at TTFP

In principle TTFP procures all its software externally. This may happen in the shape of a package but it may also be tailor made commissioned by TTFP. The TTFP IT department consists of 60 people, subdivided into 10 in the departments for application management, 40 in functional management, 8 of those at the service desk and 5 in content management for the intranet and extranet and 10 in exploitation. The application managers at head office make the connections between the packages, the functional managers carry out tasks of functional management and the people in exploitation take care of, amongst other things, the taking in and keeping in production of the IT facilities.

In the exploitation of TTFP, the ITIL processes of the service delivery and the service support set are implemented. Every connected employee can download data about the average availability and the response of locations during the last hours up to and including five months ago. Problem calls are reported daily. The costs for the services are available per network facility, per workplace, per office, per factory department, per factory, per head office department and for head office on a weekly basis according to used facility. The given authorizations are on the internet, as well as the configuration data — at least of the supported configuration. It is also indicated at least two months in advance, which changes in the applications are taken in production and what this means for the users within and outside the TTFP organization. All this data can be found on TTFP's intranet. The implementation of ITIL with regard to the availability of control information for customers at TTFP, from the users point of view comes across as the best of traffic information: up-to-date, correct and you can put your trust in it.

The ITIL process approach is implemented for changing infrastructure facilities and applications. In principle these changes run evolutionary and from location to location, so the investments are overseeable. The TTFP service desk is accessible via the intranet and the telephone from 7 am until 11 pm, five days a week (two-shifts-operation). Outside office hours the systems in the factories and at head office are permanently scanned for occurring faults, which would stop the system working. At the occurrence of such a fault (on average ten times a week) in 98% of all cases this is resolved remotely. In 2% of the cases, one is only able to do this by going to the computer centre in question.

B.2.2.9. The evolution with regard to IT application over the next years

In the technical field, TTFP strives for an entirely quantative control of the management of its infrastructure, so preventive measures can be taken for increasing the performance of this infrastructure. Furthermore, TTFP want to achieve an entire integration of data and speech transfer on its internal network. One expects this to be realized before 2007. The aim of this exercise is to avoid the high telephone rates and to realize data transfer of whatever type using international networks. Besides, TTFP also want to make the facilities of operational and executive applications (made using InfoRay) available to customers.

Organizationally TTFP concludes that the environment of TTFP becomes increasingly dynamic and is more and more confronted with the need to come to agreements on the information function in chains of organizations. The current IT organization—that could actually be split up into a department for functional management in which the demand is bundled and a department that by means of the execution of application management and exploitation takes care of supply—acts too much internally oriented. Furthermore, it is far too operationally active. Finally, demand and supply sit on each other's lap, so as to speak. This way, there is really no decent IT portfolio management within TTFP at such a level that the application of IT can be assessed the same as any other investment by the organization. All this, whilst application of IT becomes increasingly vital to TTFP for survival. TTFP therefore wants to divide its IT organization into a demand and a supply division. Both divisions come directly under the Executive Board of TTFP.

The new IT demand department has to look after the entire IT demand-side for the entire organization. It will act as a contact point for the IT supply department. IT demand will have to bundle the demand of the different departments, perform clear IT portfolio management and operate as strict client for the IT supply department.

The heads of the staff departments and the managers of the various divisions have strongly supported this development. This way, they hope to get a department that is a better partner in their discussion with customers about connection or integration of applications between TTFP and the customer; achieve cost benefits and solve countless daily problems with the current IT through a larger degree of transparency in the decisions in this field. At the control levels beneath, one is not always that far advanced yet.

There are an enormous amount of questions within the new IT demand department that need answers. One more or less has carte blanche for setting up the organization. Issues one has to deal with are for instance:

- which activities should be carried out by the IT demand department?
- should it be limited to directing or should it also perform executive tasks?
- which organization structure should one use?

The situation of the IT demand department is hindered by the fact that the divisions are ultimately responsible for the use of the information function in their organization. The funding is largely part of the divisions' budget. The IT demand department has to get the costs of the information function paid for by the various divisions. That is how the new IT demand and supply departments are financed.

Questions

1. State the management objects at TTFP. Describe their IT organization and discuss the responsibilities and the execution of the functional, application management and exploitation tasks.

2. What do you observe at TTFP with regard to the set-up of functional management? What is your opinion of this organization? Do you agree with the TTFP management, for changing the IT organization? What are the reasons for your answer?

3. What does introduction of BiSL mean to TTFP? Where will be/are the various processes as prescribed by BiSL situated? What does the functional management organization look like after introduction of BiSL? What are the differences with the current organization? Does this change pay for itself?

4. What do you notice at TTFP with regard to the set-up of application management? Why should TTFP pay attention to this? Which processes do you recognize in TTFP with regard to application management?

5. What would a set-up of application management at TTFP look like? What would this look like process-oriented? Which objects should there be regarding application management?

6. Why is organization of application management important in the long run? Which processes should be set-up by then and what is TTFP doing about this? Go through the processes and indicate why TTFP should set up a certain process at strategic level.

7. What does day in, day out management at ASL stand for? What data do these processes share?

8. What are the ASL maintenance and renewal tasks as far as TTFP is concerned? How do new IT facilities come into production?

9. Explain what requirements will be the most important for the customers of the IT division at the exploitation of IT facilities; and how the exploitation department has worked out these requirements. Which processes has it set up for this purpose? What is the relation between the ITIL and the ASL processes?

10. How would you control the exploitation of IT facilities of the TTFP? What are the handles in this case?

11. How do you think the version policy at TTFP for applications and infrastructure software is designed? Why?

12. Which manuals will be available in the exploitation department?

13. How does a showstopper for applications run its course through the TTFP organization? How is a proposal for change for the informatics infrastructure and how is one for the technical infrastructure processed? How does a change proposal for applications run through this organization?

14. The internal TTFP service desk registers daily around 150 help desk calls. 130 of these are calls to do with infrastructures that do not work; about 20 of these are calls to do with applications. The average time for dealing with a call is in 95% of all cases 10 minutes for a call to do with infrastructures and 2 hours for a call about applications. The service desk keeps a record of every call stating:
    – the time the call was entered into the front-office system;
    – the time, calls were accepted in the second line;
    – the time, one found a solution for the problem and passed this on to the customer;
    – the time the customer was called in order to find out whether they were happy with the solution.

    The service desk operates with one person for taking calls. Two people work on the resolving of incidents, call customers when incidents are solved and on problem management.

    What do you think of this organization of dealing with calls? What control information you think is generated? This information can be seen by the whole of TTFP on the intranet. Using the process-approach, formulate some proposals for improvement, where TTFP has all possible technical facilities such as an Avaya call centre with CMS, an intranet and an extranet, possibilities for speech recognition etc. What could enhance service at TTFP?

15. Intranet possibilities are used to watch the network traffic on the fixed net. 95% of the incidents can be resolved remotely. For fixing any other incidents on the fixed data net a 7 × 24 hour service contract with Unisys was concluded. The call-out time for this contract is maximally 2 hours. No MTTR was agreed. On a yearly basis, about a third of the configuration is changed. This means installing different hardware and configuring the software. Furthermore, Cisco releases new versions of the network software every year onto the network. The TTFP policy is to be a maximum of two years behind with versions in this field. Indicate how configuration management and change management are implemented at TTFP. Explain how the communication between the service desk and configuration/change management runs.

16. At a new release TTFP uses the principles of Result-directed Implementation (RDI). Indicate what this means for an application such as Microsoft Office.

17. What is the disadvantage when an organization always works with up-to-date versions? What is the advantage? Also consider the consequences for informatics and technical infrastructures. What is legacy at TTFP? How is this legacy phased out? How can TTFP prevent legacy?
18. How does one deal with, or should one deal with management of versions and documents at TTFP?
19. How does the organization of TTFP fit in with the model for organizing IT management in larger organizations?
20. How does TTFP deal with outsourcing? Which type of outsourcing does TTFP use? What does this mean for the key processes in this field?

Part B.3. Controlling IT facilities

B.3.1. Easy service: Catering and other necessities home delivered

B.3.1.1. Introduction

'Our company is built up brick by brick using the most modern technology in a process of trial and error. Every mistake teaches us what is possible and what is impossible and that way we discover the online business of the future.'

That is how Terry Clockwork's company operates, the Easy shopping experience, in short called Easy Service. Terry Clockwork originally was a re-tailer. From the eighties onwards, he built a chain of 200 fashion shops, the Clockwork's exclusive fashion shops. Towards the end of the eighties he had enough of the rag trade and bought a media company. As owner of this company Sunnytale, he produced a daily newspaper and a weekly. From 1997, this media company also supplied on-line services under the brand name 'Kingdom Services.' At the end of 2002, the media company employed 1000 people, including 300 journalists.

Terry had always dreamt of starting a home delivery service, alongside his fashion and media enterprises. That is why in mid 2001, Terry started the 'Easy Service' company. This was, to start with, a grocer that used the internet to get to his customers. He targeted clientele consisting of people in the middle to higher income bracket. The Greater Borough of London seems perfectly suited to a company like this. There are around 10 million people living in this part of the England and the telecommunication infrastructure is very good, certainly after the arrival of ADSL and GPRS, the new standards for landlines and mobile communication.

The existing Tesco, Woolworth, Marks and Spencer and Albert Heijn supermarkets do not always have an extensive assortment, nor are they always to be found where there is easy parking. 'Easy Service' promises delivery of goods at any requested time of the day on the same day as ordered, in cities where traffic delays are common and where parking is a constant problem.

Easy Service as a business proposition has a number of qualities. It is an entirely virtual company in a region where shop floor space does not come cheap. Besides, Easy Service can sell apart from groceries other high profit margin items such as computers, clothing, consumer electronics and financial services.

B.3.1.2. The set-up of easy service

Because he had never sold groceries before, in 2000 Terry decided to hire Carl Sundgren as chairman of the Executive Board of Easy Service. Carl Sundgen worked for Ahold (the company behind the Albert Heijn supermarkets) for fourteen years, of which nine years at their interests abroad. For instance, Carl worked for Ahold in the logistics of their American acquisitions and he was managing director of their companies in South-East Asia, including those in Hong Kong and Singapore. Starting with only six staff, in six months Carl developed Easy Service into an organization of 400 people. There was a lot of criticism, such as: 'London is no Hong Kong or Singapore, where people live all squeezed together and high-rises are the order of the day. We make sure our borough of London holds enough green. Tesco tried this business model before and they had only 3000 orders a day in the London area in the middle of 2000. Why would Easy Service make a success of it now?'

On the 21st June 2001, Easy Service opens its electronic grocery shop on a business to consumer basis. The public interest is overwhelming, not in the least because of the advertising campaigns that are run at the same time in Terry's media company. A permanent challenge for the management is the costs of logistics. In spite of the limited assortment of 200 items, there is a high investment in distribution centres. Carl Sundgren started with one single central distribution centre with 10 satellites all over London. Furthermore, 200 delivery vans of the type Opel Corsa have been acquired. These are sprayed a bright yellow.

B.3.1.3. The logistics of easy service

Apart from the delivery aspect there are other logistics aspects with regard to the Easy Service business. Most of its supply companies survive on long-term contracts with suppliers as Tesco, Woolworth, Marks and Spencer etc., that have 70% of the market in the England. These supply companies are reluctant to supply to Easy Service. Furthermore, Easy Service cannot afford to invest in large stocks of many different products. They simply cannot have 4000 different items in stock, like a normal shop does.

B.3.1.4. Reaction of other grocers

Giving discounts and advertising constantly in the Sunnytale newspaper provoked the competition. The import of soft drinks resulted in large stocks at local distributors, whilst the large supermarkets started campaigns such as 'three for the price of two,' 'money back, if you find this cheaper elsewhere' and '1000 cheap daily necessary products.' Next, they discontinued their ads in the Sunnytale, same as some of the supply companies did. This way, the Sunnytale lost 25% of its income. However, Terry Clockwork was of the opinion that:

> *The shops advertise in the daily newspapers. The supermarket will also come back in the long run because the daily is the number one newspaper for advertising in. We get, from the same number of daily printer newspapers around 28% more income from adverts.*
>
> *The online shop does not just have a high growth capacity as a shop. It is also a new way of doing business. It is a disruptive innovation: it is completely new and does not fit in with anything. A web-based shop soon has room for new alliances and partnerships in the short and the long run. A shop in a location is either there or not: that is it. They can match our prices; they cannot charge delivery costs, however they cannot form or change new alliances, affiliates and partnerships as quickly as we can.*

B.3.1.5. Handling costs

In September 2001, Easy Service lost 25,000 euro a day. It needed 10,000 orders a day to break even and only managed to get 4000. In December, this amount had dropped to 25,000 euro a month. In the intervening months, the problem with the website was remedied. This had been down regularly and also the entering of orders did not link optimally with the back-office delivery system. There were gaps in the system with regard to the transferring of customer orders to the administration, whilst the entering up of stock also showed some faults. This meant that the business had to be closed every Monday in order to sort out the chaos in the information function of the week before.

In November, the technical infrastructure of Easy Service was doubled and the software errors from the front- and back-office applications were remedied. The call centre was extended in order to deal with the 30,000 telephone calls. Only approximately 7% of all orders were placed via the internet and one had not anticipated the importance of hiring and training the call centre staff. Furthermore, this call centre was only manned from 7 in the morning until 10 in the evening. The use of the telephone appeared to be easier for the customers than using the internet and Freriks also started to realize that not enough people in London had a pc. In London there are in general about 30 computers per 100 inhabitants, 70 people in a 100 that own a mobile phone and about 20 internet users per 100 inhabitants.

This results in Easy Service having many unexpected expenses then and now. What Easy Service saves on shop buildings, it spent on vehicles. Instead of 200, it had to have at least 250 vans because of the increasing traffic jams, whilst the costs involved in the three shifts in the call centre (transaction rate of 150 calls per person a day) soon mounted up. Easy Service had reckoned with 15,000 calls and in reality it had 30,000!

To simplify things, the number of distribution centres was reduced to 3. This reduced the personnel costs, although still half of the (400) people were working in logistics.

B.3.1.6. New opportunities

In March 2002, Easy Service sold 2000 different items. What had changed in the meantime? Let us ask Sundgren:

Easy Service started out as a 'business to consumer' home delivery service for 200 items. But we had more and more questions from customers that besides cola and loo paper also wanted to order their office supplies from us. They explained that they wanted one stop shopping and did not want to have to order from four different suppliers with equally as many invoices. That is how Business to Business started and how we found out that this segment is much more profitable than going into battle with the supermarkets in the business to consumer (B2C) market.

In London our customers are small companies. The market in the field of office supplies is rather complex in this area and our business to business (B2B) customer group in a short space of time grew to about 7500 companies.

In order to attend to these customers really well, we went further and formatted a team of account managers that address the secretaries of the customers directly. This team consist of 20 people at the moment. Besides, we allow our customers a 30-day credit period. This allowed B2B to become 40 percent of our turnover and B2C became 60 percent.

In 2002, Terry has planned an expansion of his retail concept to other densely populated area in Europe, such as the Ruhr, Berlin, Paris and the suburbs around Paris. Criteria for choosing these areas were:

- a certain density of population;
- a middle class of sufficient size;
- a large city because, according to Terry, only in a large city 'time' becomes an aspect that threatens the quality of life accordingly.

A concept such as the Easy Service concept does rely on the predictability of delivery and that is only possible using excellent logistics. Easy Service does not target the gift market, such as flowers, chocolates etc., the market of popcorn and video or dry cleaning. Easy Service just aims for the mainstream of the home delivery market. They want to develop this market using local parties and if necessary set up franchises. Terry expects by transfer of skill and ideas to be able to get hold of about 20 to 30% of the ownership of such an alliance.

B.3.1.7. The part played by sunnytale

Six months before the launch of Easy Service, the Sunnytale started to develop publications and services on its website targeting their reader's life style. At the start, this website did not have any links to the websites of Perry Sport, Mediamarket, Barnes Corner, Auto by tel, cinemas and theatres, Free Record Shop, McDonalds, Ford garages, the London bookshop, British Airways and Kingdom Travel. However, the chairman of the Sunnytale Executive Board did see possibilities for cross selling. Halfway through 2001, the Sunnytale site had become a portal with shops of 12 companies in its electronic market. Furthermore, clicks on the site gave discounts on purchases from Easy Service. Finally, the site provided room for advertising, chat and the daily news of the Sunnytale. The site was frequented by English people outside England that have the goods they order online sent.

B.3.1.8. Brick shops and the virtual world

In the short space of time, Easy Service and Sunnytale used the internet, they learnt a number of things. Terry can sum these up briefly:

When we started Easy Service and the Sunnytale site, all we knew is that we wanted to make life easy for people. We had no experience whatsoever in doing business online. We did know that we did not want to copy things such as planning and projects of the offline business online. In the online world we wanted to work more trial and error focussed. We discovered that in the online world it does not matter what you sell, as long as it is really present. In other words, if you sell convenience it really does have to be a convenience. We discovered also that people use the online world because it is convenient, whilst the offline world is the place where they come into their own emotionally and socially.

Conducting business using e-commerce and doing business from a fixed location are two entirely different things. That has everything to do with the customer experience. Online customers do not look at choice, price or priorities. They order products from Easy Service that are heavy, voluminous and big. They do not buy biscuits and crisps. Those are impulse buys; people do not use the web or the telephone for.

With these experiences under his belt, Terry and his staff try to set-up their online presence in such a way, it opens new avenues for his offline business. He words this as follows:

One should look at one's offline business from an online perspective. In doing that, the online force is a catalyst for the offline world. The convenience, the availability to everybody and the culture based on innovation enable services that complement the offline environment.

England today is like the online business in the USA three years ago. Things are going well enough and are just waiting for restructuring. The offline companies have a price/profit ratio on their items of 3 to 4; for luxury items, books and cars they have to deal with long delivery times, they have to deal with stock and goods on credit. In the online business the turn around speed is a lot faster, we have to deal with payment by credit card in advance, the home delivery time for cars, books, CD's etc. is often a factor 4 or less and the price/profit ratio 30 to 35. Online shops force these companies to consider their added value.

B.3.1.9. The organization of Terry Clockwork's company and its IT application

The Terry Clockwork company (TCW) consists of the media company the Sunnytale, the fashion company the Clockwork's exclusive fashion shops and Easy Services (Figure B.3.1.1). All are part of the TCW plc company. At company level, amongst other things, the IT strategy is determined. The Chief Financial Officer (CFO) is responsible for this. In this strategy:

(a) a clear-cut suppliers policy developed with regard to the partners with whom business is conducted in the field of IT objects. TCW plc only deals with Logica CMG, as far as the hiring of people is concerned,

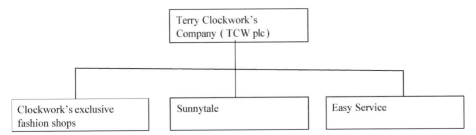

Figure B.3.1.1. The organization of TCW plc

with regard to network capacity only uses BT, regarding infrastructure objects for data only uses IBM, for speech infrastructure Avaya, with regard to the standard applications for logistics, personnel and finances SAP and for personal productivity tools MS Office. For business specific applications such as editing applications for the Sunnytale and the applications for the call centres the applications as used most commonly in that sector are used. For the call centres that is the Avaya CMS application in combination with the Siebel customer relationship management application;

(b) a clear distinction is made between the support of the internal operational processes at TCW plc and its companies and the support of the processes that are directly connected to the customers. At the internal processes standard my.SAP.com and standard MS Office are utilized. Based on Microsoft technology an intranet was developed that is maintained by the company's communication department and by the three divisions each for their own separate division. In the fashion shops and the holding, only SAP and Microsoft software and this intranet are operational. Sunnytale and Easy Service use their own applications round their call centre operation, as well as the Siebel and Avaya standard software. Furthermore, the Sunnytale uses a standard application for supporting the editing, layout and typesetting process of the media products.

(c) The TCW plc management committee establishes priorities with regard to IT facilities. This committee includes the chairman of the Executive Board of the holding, the senior officials for finances (CFO) and personnel (CPO), the three managing directors of respectively the Sunnytale, the Clockwork's exclusive fashion shops and Easy Service.

B.3.1.10. IT Objects

The TCW plc IT facilities are designed as follows:

(a) the exploitation of the internal systems of TCW plc is carried out at the Atos Origin computer centres. To this purpose, a service level agreement was concluded stating an availability of 99.99% during 5 times 12 hours a week, a response time in 99% of all cases in all workplaces of less than 1 second and an average security level;

(b) every fashion shop has two or three cash point terminals connected with a central personal computer. This can be called up at any time, which enables the drawing up a profit and loss statement at any given moment and a balance sheet for Wolbers fashion shops. Every branch manager and the head office of the shops have access to all data regarding the Clockwork's exclusive fashion shops.

(c) the Sunnytale building houses two IBM RS6000 systems in cluster for supporting editorial work, layout and typesetting. At each workplace one has access to these systems as well as to the internal systems of the Sunnytale. At head office one has access to all internal applications of the company and the divisions. At every workplace thin client terminals are set up and at logging in the necessary applications are downloaded.

(d) by means of an identification application each system is connected with the TCW plc backbone. When an employee of one of the divisions or the holding logs in, it is first checked in a central identification application whether they have access to the infrastructure of the company (see Figure B.3.1.2).

B.3.1.11. The organization of the IT facilities

TCW plc has a central organization for functional management, application management and the exploitation of IT facilities. This organization reports directly to the CFO. The divisions are obliged to obtain all their IT facilities through this central organization. On-charge of the costs for IT facilities takes place by this central organization on the basis of direct costing.

Figure B.3.1.3 shows the central organization. In this organization all service management functions for exploitation tasks have been placed in two

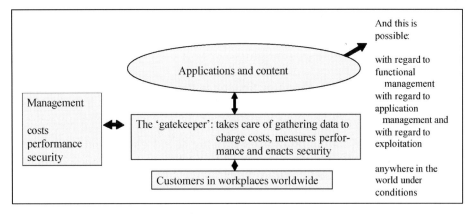

Figure B.3.1.2. The 'gatekeeper' application

separate departments. Outside these departments the tasks service level management, finances and IT security are located.

Questions

1. What are the possibilities that the Executive Board of TCW plc has for controlling the IT facilities of the company. How are these applied? Work out at least four of the six possibilities.
2. How are the demand for and the supply of IT structured at TCW plc? What does the force field look like, in which one operates? What does this signify?

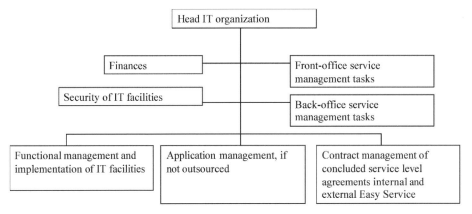

Figure B.3.1.3. The IT organization of TCW plc

3. Is the use of IT important to TCW plc? In which manner does this become visible in the organization of the IT facilities? What does this importance mean for the TCW plc management? How does this transpire from its mode of operation?

4. What does the information function, on which the IT organization controls its operational processes probably, look like? How is that proved?

5. Provide a plan for IT facilities for TCW plc. Indicate what the contents of this plan are, what the process for arriving at this plan is and who should be involved in the drawing up of this plan and in which way they should be involved.

6. Give four different perspectives from the various stakeholders in the field of IT management and position CMMI, ISO 9001:2000 and the CobiT approach.

7. Explain the quality management system ISO 9001:2000 and apply this to TCW plc. What is TCW's position if we hold this company against the ISO 9001:2000 yardstick? Explain your answer.

8. What are the minimum requirements for certifying an organization according the ISO 9001:2000 standard? Does TCW plc comply with the requirements as set by ISO 9001-2000? Where does it, where not? What would you advise TCW plc if they want to have the activities in their IT organization certified? Explain your answer.

9. Which levels of operating are known to CMMI? What does this mean for the operating processes in the field of service management? Choose two service processes and indicate at which level TCW plc operates in each of these processes.

10. How does TCW plc deal with project and with operational risk? Illustrate your answer with two examples.

11. What does the approach of the CobiT method mean with regard to auditing of IT organizations? Which four areas does the CobiT method recognize? Indicate how TCW plc performs if we measure this company using the CobiT benchmark? What would you advise TCW plc with regard to this?

12. How does TCW plc deal with the performance requirements to IT products and services, as used by Easy Services? Illustrate your answer by giving an example.

13. Which four principles are behind the development of IT services, such as Easy Services needs? What choices does one therefore have for setting up such an IT product and such an IT service?

14. TCW plc wants to introduce a new IT supported service: the company-wide recognizing of and supplying to a virtual customer. Which process for implementing this service would you recommend to TCW plc? Explain your answer.
15. How would you set up service management for this new service? Would you advise TCW plc to accommodate the new service with Easy Services or would you set up a new subsidiary company? Explain your answer.
16. Apply the step-by-step management plan of Looijen on the development and the implementation of this new service.
17. What does the rollout plan for this new service look like?
18. What would you advise TCW plc, if they want to make use of new applications for this new service and the accompanying business intelligence application as smoothly as possible? The new business intelligence application delivers online, on request management information about the service. Which process of introduction does one choose and how is the introduction process controlled? Why?
19. Who are involved in the development, implementation and management of this new product and this new service? Why?

B.3.2. THE IB GROUP: IMPLEMENTATION OF EDUCATION REGULATIONS OVER THE YEARS

B.3.2.1. The IB group in the year 2004

The execution of the Student Grant Act (WSF) in The Netherlands rests with the IB Group. The organization of the IB Group is shown in Figure B.3.2.1. A Supervisory Board supervises the activities of the management and advises where necessary. The Minister of Education appoints the five members of the Board. The Supervisory Board appoints the general manager. This general manager has the final responsibility for the IB group. Together with the four managers he forms the management team of the IB Group. These managers manage the following departments:

– *Customer service.* The management Customer service takes care of the services for the individual customers of the IB Group: pupils, parents, students and people that pay back their student loans. This service is organized

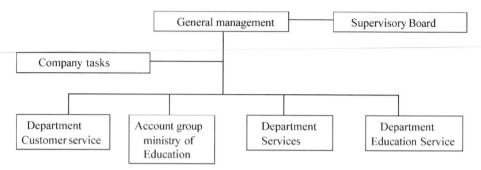

Figure 3.2.1. Organization IB Group in the year 2004

according to the principle of integral customer transaction: regional teams take care of an entire group of customers within their own region.
–*Education service.* The management Education service is responsible for the provision of services to institutions of primary, secondary, vocational and higher education, to umbrella organizations in teaching and to exchange partners, such as the general management Central Financial Institutions and the National Insurance Institute. One of its tasks is the introduction and management of the 'education number,' a personal individual number for everyone in The Netherlands receiving education.
–*Services.* The units of the directorate Services support the entire IB Group with services, products and policies in various fields. Services consist of five divisions: Communication, Personnel & Organization, Administration & Process management, Business and Safety, Health and Welfare.
–*Information and Communication technology.* The department Information technology of the Services directorate was set up in 2004 as a separate directorate.

Apart from this, there are the staff unit Company tasks and the account group for the ministry of Education. The staff unit Company tasks advise the general manager and the management team on finances, planning and control, legal affairs, policy and audit. The account group is responsible for the relation management with the Ministry of Education and for the implementation policy for the legal tasks of the IB Group. To this purpose, the account group consults the ministry about (changes to) the implementation of tasks and the programme funds needed for this implementation.

In 2004, the IB Group employs 1560 people. Annually, 2.6 billion euro is remitted in Student Grants and 0.8 billion euros collected. Besides, an amount of 0.12 billion euro in services is supplied to the Ministry of Education.

One of the services of the IB Group is taking care of the payments and collections within the framework of the Student Grant Act. To this purpose, the IB Group has a front-office, consisting of regional offices and a call centre in Groningen. The transaction of incoming forms takes place in the back-office. The telephonic contactability is in 2004 80% of about 7500 incoming calls a day. Besides, the front-office deals with 2200 e-mails a day. It is expected that the number of personal contacts will decrease. The customer will increasingly use the internet via their own internet portal: My IB Group.

The Student Grant Act was introduced in 1986. Next, the history of this act will be discussed and the way in which this act changes. Amendments to this act are coordinated and controlled by the directorate Student Grants of the Ministry of Education, Culture and Sciences (OCW). This directorate was established in 1988, at the same time the IB Group came into being.

B.3.2.2. The WSF over the years

The WSF (Stb. 1988, 252, WSF) has a longwinded history. After the amendments Student Grants (January 1974), the outlines for a new system of Student Grants (February 1981) and the starting points for a new system of Student Grants (May 1982), in June 1984 the amendment Outline for a new system of Student Grants was presented to the Lower Chamber (Dutch Lower Chamber, sessions 1983–1984, nos. 1–2). This amendment was the basis for the bill regarding the WSF that was presented to the Lower Chamber in August 1985. Chapter II of the WSF that concerns all full time students between the ages of 18 and 30 years of age at a recognized educational institute largely came into effect on 1st October 1986. This chapter replaced in outline a system of scholarship, interest-free loans, child benefits and subsidies for the students in question. The new act did increase the group of people qualifying for a grant because the new act affected more types of education (further education and secondary vocational training). On the basis of the WSF, every student between 18 and 30 years studying at a recognized institute, was eligible for a basic grant.

The WSF was adjusted over the years. Most well known are the adjustments that were necessary for the introduction of the public transport annual ticket in 1990 and that for the introduction of the performance grant in the period 1993–1995.

B.3.2.3. Changes in organization and tasks in the field of the WSF

The policy responsibility for the Student Grants rested in the seventies with the Directorate-General Higher Education of the Ministry of OCW. In 1984, this responsibility moved to the Central Directorate Student Grants in Groningen (Centrale Directie Studiefinancieringen or CDSF). The directorate CDSF is from then on responsible for both the policy as well as the implementation of the regulations with regard to the Student Grants. In the first half of 1988 this situation changed because the implementation of the WSF met with problems and a crisis team was appointed for solving these problems. This crisis team was under the guidance of a delegate administrator appointed by the Minister. This administrator was until 1 July 1988 responsible for policy and implementation.

By taking three measures in particular, the delegate administrator and his crisis team mainly solved the crisis. The first measure consisted of giving students loans. The second was setting-up a new organization and the third was improving communication with customers. To this purpose about 30 regional offices Student Grants were set up. The new organization was the IB group. It had departments for:

- implementation tasks with regard to the WSF;
- implementation tasks with regard to the subsidy costs of study for pupils of the ages between 12 and 18 years;
- for paying benefits to education personnel;
- for implementing student stop regulations;
- for collecting school fees and
- for organizing exams.

This larger organization had also room for a number of real staff departments amongst others departments for customer communication, for IT, for Personnel and Organization and for Finances. All these departments reported directly to the general manager.

Mid 1988, the policy task for Student Grants was located at the directorate Student Grants at the Ministry of Education. In the combined action between policy and implementation, the tools of the implementation test was created. Each change in legislation that is devised by the ministry is put to the IB group. It tests this change on the following aspects:

- how do I communicate this to my customers (communication)
- what does it mean to my organization (implementation)
- what are the implications with regard to the information function and the consequences for the adjustment of the computerized systems (informatics)
- what does the change cost once-only and permanently; (finances)
- what does the change mean as regards the rules? (legal)

In 1994, the IB group becomes an independent government body. With the privatization of the IB Group, a Supervisory Board was also set up.

After the privatization of the IB Group, the former general manager left. He was succeeded by one of the deputy general managers. The new general manager was given two tasks. The first was to ensure a more integral customer approach; the second concerned the finding of a wider clientele for the IB Group.

As part of the first task, the organization of the IB Group was changed from product-oriented to process-oriented. The customer became the focal point. To this purpose, integral customer transaction teams were set up. Also it was tried to support the new organization optimally with new IT applications.

Within the framework of the second task almost nothing was achieved. Therefore, this setting of the task was changed around 2001. The motto became 'the result counts' and the focus became providing an optimal performance with regard to the implementation of education legislation by order of the Ministry of OCW.

In 1997, parallel to the changing of the IB group organization to its current form, the department in charge of paying benefits to education personnel was branched off the IB group organization. This department became a division of a newly set-up government social security organization.

B.3.2.4. The IT support of the operating processes

The IT support of the Student Grant Act has up until now seen four different periods. The first period is the one before 1988, the second is the period 1988–1995, the third is the period 1995–2000 and the fourth period started in 2000. Each period has its own characteristics with regard to control, IT facilities and organization.

In the period before 1988, the directorate Organization of the ministry in Zoetermeer decided about the application of IT. They decided to outsource the development of the WSF application to CAP Gemini and to use Getronics for the necessary exploitation. In 1986, Cap Gemini supplied a mainframe application, made in 'proven' architecture. The application was made in the third generation language Cobol and used a hierarchic IMS database. The WSF application operated on the mainframes of Getronics. The exploitation was controlled from the IBgroup. At the end of 1988, only the part 'grant' of the application was in production. The part 'collect' was partly present in the form of a design.

In the next period 1988–1995, the IB Group has its in-house IT department. The IT manager is a member of the management team. In 1988, this manager chose three things. Firstly, he wanted a reorganization of the recently set-up IT department. 120 external consultants were sent home within two months after he took up his duties. The IT department became that way transparent and had sufficient finances for funding the innovation of infrastructure and applications. Secondly, he wanted to develop applications in-house and utilize these. He chose to do this in the fourth generation language Synon on the IBM-AS/400-platform with employees the IB Group trained in-house. These were mostly recruited from the Groningen University. Finally, he wanted to build all future and present applications of the IB Group using its own people. His approach resulted in Minister Ritzen of Education writing to the Lower Chamber on the 28th April 1994:

Results

> With the technical infrastructure and the approach to the computerization of the IB Group, it was possible in spite of a strong increase in the number of systems, in connected workplaces and in quality of the information function and the data processing, to bring down the costs of the application of information

> *technology. From the figures at my disposal about the costs of the computerization of the ministry of Education, it proves that especially the costs in the IB group have been reduced considerably: from 55 million euros in 1988 to 19 million euros in 1993.*

In this period, apart from the choice for the IBM platform, the choice was also made with regard to telephony. In 1993, the IB Group became the first European customer of Avaya for call centre and telephony applications. In February 1995, all regional offices ran on their own telephone network using ISDN lines. The period is characterized finally with regard to management by a methodological approach, quantifiable control of project, twice weekly consultation between IT management en project management about progress of projects and short communication lines.

The next period 1995–2000, characterized itself by the focussing on the demand-side for IT. The IT department became therefore a sub department of the newly established services department, the manager left and a new departmental head of IT was appointed. The IT department was reorganized and an extra management layer was added. The development of applications and the maintenance of applications were separated and each situated in their own subdivision.

In 1997, this department started, by order of a project organization that was set up for arriving at an integral customer approach, with an integral innovation of IT applications. The head of the department became project leader of the IT project. For the duration of the project, an interim manager became head of the IT department. The latest technology was brought into action for the project, the so-called object-oriented technology. This ambitious lifecycle of system innovation did not become a success. In February 1999, a substantial exceeding of the budget was ascertained. It was then decided to limit the technological innovation to the development of a new system for the benefit of the WSF and to forget about innovation of the systems for collecting of student debts and tuition fees, the advance on study costs, selection and placement of first year students, Central Register Enrolment Higher Education and Central Register Educations Higher Education. In spite of intensive talks between Minister of Education and the Supervisory Board, *second opinion* research into the adjusted project plan and the introduction of more decision moments and means for tracking the project efficiently, in January 2000 it turned out that the adjusted plan would also not deliver the desired results within the planned time and the available budget. Initially, on the basis of two counterchecks one insisted on concluding the development phase but by mid 2000, it was definitely decided to desert the idea of replacing the existing systems in one go by an integral new system. Instead, a scenario was chosen in which the desired innovation takes place step-by-step. Furthermore, it was decided to no longer realize this gradual innovation by means of a separate project but to place this within the line organization. The failing of this IT project costed 27 million euro.

The period 2000–today is characterized by the getting in line of the organization around IT. The annual report 2002 of the IB Group states, there have been two external investigations into the IT function. One investigation targeted the control and organization of the IT function. The second is a benchmark inquiry that compares the IT function with that of comparable organizations. These investigations result in various organizational adjustments, including the appointment of an IT director directly reporting to the general manager and head of the newly formed department Information and Communications technology, per 1 January 2004. In order to link the back-office applications with the front-office in this period, the IT product IBM MS queue was chosen. This product is capable of connecting new front-office and old back-office applications with each other. The front-office applications were next extensively extended. This evolutionary approach of organization change using IT resulted in 2003, in the portal My IB Group, in which students can sort out more and more IB Group services without the intervention of employees. On 26 February 2004, it also resulted in the European Commission choosing the IB Group as one of the better European examples in the field of electronics service provision by governments.

B.3.2.5. Check- and countercheck

Over the years many authorities have carried out counterchecks at the IB Group and with regard to the WSF. We mention:

- the investigation of the Dutch National Audit Office into the exceeding of expenditure as a result of the introduction of the WSF in 1989;
- the Arthur Anderson investigation in 1990 into the implementation of the support of the WSF by IT and the correctness of an implementation test by the IB Group;
- the Compass investigation in 1992 into the quality of the IT organization by order of the general manager of the IB Group;

−the Berenschot investigation in 1989 into the exorbitant increase in costs for IT at the Ministry of Education in 1989;

−the investigation carried out by Professor Keuning of the Free University in 1994, if so and how the IT directorate could become part of a newly formed directorate Services. Client was the general manager of the IB Group;

−the KPMG investigation into the quality and the future of the IT organization by order of the general manager in 1995. KPMG remarked that the IT applications were very advanced however the user organization was not;

−the Getronics investigation in 1997 into the quality of the WSF application. The result was: the WSF application is in perfect order and does not have to be replaced;

−the investigation of the Expertise centre in 2001 into the integral innovation of applications;

−the investigation of the Dutch National Audit Office in 2001 into the quality of the information function at Cadans and the IB Group. The Audit Office concludes gaps in the internal supervision, the quality of the basic data, the general IT checks and in the reports to the Minister. There are for instance no quality criteria for the computerized systems and the surrounding organization;

−the privatization evaluation in 2003, carried out by Cap Gemini and downloadable from www.ibgroep.nl.

B.3.2.6. The IT facilities of the IB group in the year 2004

In 2004, the departments Customer service, Education service and Services have set up their own demand organization. The department Information and Communication technology acts as IT supply organization. For the company staff and the account group Education it also acts as a utility company. It supplies them with the basic IT facility consisting of intranet/extranet facilities and personal productivity tools.

The processing and storage facilities of the IB Group consist of the IBM-I-series, running under the operating system OS/400 release 5, version 2 for all business process supporting applications and internet applications. The personal productivity tools operate under Citrix metaframe on IBM-e-servers (blade solution). The network operates using the TCP/IP protocol at a speed of 100 mb/second. The data and image processing and storage facilities are through the TCP/IP-network connected to the telephone facilities. These facilities utilize Avaya hardware, including a Definity telephone exchange.

The entire storage and processing infrastructure for processing of data and images has been executed in double. There are two computer centres at 200 metres distance. Both keep a complete copy of each other's data storage using replication technology.

All applications are exploited by the IB Group itself with the exception of the application, which supports the awarding of Student Grants. This runs in service at IBM. The IB Group is connected with the IBM computer centre online.

The primary applications of the IB Group are made by the in-house supply organization. The secondary applications are procured from third parties. FMS is used for finances and for support of personnel and salary tasks; Pigeon of the Getronics group is used. Personal productivity tool is MS Office.

Questions

1. Give the theoretical possibilities the IB Group has for controlling the companies' IT facilities. How do they apply these? Look at the situation in 1985, in 1994 and 2004. Work out at least four of the six possibilities.
2. How are the demand for and the supply of IT structured at the IB Group in 1985, in 1992 and in 2004? What does the force field look like in which one operates? What does this mean?
3. Is the use of IT important to the IB Group? In which way does this show in 1985, in 1993, in 1997 and in 2004 from the organization of the IT facilities? What does this importance mean to the directorate of the IB Group? How does this emerge from their mode of operating?
4. What does the information function, on which the IT organization controls its operational processes probably, look like? How does that show?
5. Provide a plan for IT facilities for the IB Group. State what the contents of this plan are, what the process for arriving at this plan is and who should be involved in the drawing up of this plan and in which way they should be involved.
6. Give four perspectives from the various stakeholders in the field of IT management and position CMMI, ISO 9001:2000 and the CobiT approach.

7. Explain the quality management system ISO 9001:2000 and apply this to the IB Group. What is the IB Group's position in 1985 and 2001 respectively if we hold this company against the ISO 9001:2000 yardstick? Explain your answer.

8. What are the minimum requirements for certifying an organization according the ISO 9001:2000 standard? Does The IB Group comply with the requirements as set by ISO 9001-2000? Where does it, where not? What would you advise The IB Group if they want to have the activities in their IT organization certified? Explain your answer.

9. Which levels of operating are known to CMMI? What does this mean for the operating processes in the field of service management? Choose two service processes and indicate at which level the IB Group operates in each of these processes.

10. How does the IB Group deal with project and with operational risk? Illustrate your answer with two examples.

11. What does the approach of the CobiT method mean with regard to auditing of IT organizations? Which four areas does the CobiT method recognize? Indicate how the IB Group performs if we measure this company using the CobiT benchmark? What would you advise the IB Group with regard to this?

12. How does The IB Group deal with the performance requirements to IT products and services, as used by the directorate Customer Services? Illustrate your answer by giving an example.

13. Which four principles are behind the development of IT services, such as the directorate Customer Services needs? What choices does one therefore have for setting up such an IT product and such an IT service?

14. The IB Group wants to introduce a new IT supported service: the service My IB Group for education institutions. Which process for implementing this service would you recommend to the IB Group? Explain your answer.

15. How would you set up service management for this new service? Would you advise the IB Group to accommodate the new service with directorate e-Portals to be set-up a new for students and education institutes or would you house this with the directorate Education Service? Explain your answer.

16. Apply the step-by-step management plan of Looijen on the development and the implementation of this new service. What does the rollout plan for this new service look like?

17. What would you advise The IB Group, if they want to make use of new applications for this new service and the accompanying business intelligence application as smoothly as possible? The new business intelligence application delivers online, on request management information about the service. Which process of introduction does one choose and how is the introduction process controlled? Why?

18. Who are involved in the development, implementation and management of this new product and this new service? Why?

Part B.4/B.5. Aspects of IT management/IT management tomorrow

B.4.1. INTERNATIONAL ELECTRONICS: INTRODUCTION OF ERP AND ASPECTS OF IT

B.4.1.1. Introduction

Dr. Manmohan Singh starts in 1995 as Chief Executive Officer at the International Electronics (IE) company in New Delhi. One of his sources of concern are the IE management information systems that do not necessarily work together and suffer from years of evolution of IT application that was never optimised. Dr. Singh thinks that the future of the company depends on his skill for simplifying the IE organization and making it transparent. The key to all this is the implementation of better IT support. Dr. Singh hires Dr. P. Banerjee as Chief Information Officer, an IT professional he has worked with before.

International Electronics is a company with history. Established in 1888, it has developed into a multinational with interests in over 60 countries. The company has four divisions: light, medical instruments, components and consumer electronics. In each division around 30,000 people work. At the head office in New Delhi about 1000 employees are at work. IE is in the top three with regard to turnover and quality of its products in all the fields it is active in. In spite of this strong position in the market in which IE operates, the company has a legacy regarding IT application that limits its operating flexibility and its possibilities for growth.

IE supports in various parts of the organization comparable processes with other applications and infrastructures or like Dr. M. Mukherjee, Chief Financial Officer, says:

IE has over 700 applications in its offices in India alone. Offices have set up different operational processes to achieve almost the same goals. IE has no sight of the stock that is present at any one location. One looses sight of the products as soon as these are shipped from a factory to a local national organization. Should we ever want to dispose of part of the company, the problems are that IT connects it with invisible tentacles to other parts and it is hard to even get the data for being able to make a rational disinvestment. This use of IT renders us extremely inflexible.

Indications of the inflexibility are:

- indication of deliveries of goods by suppliers or to customers at an exact time on a specific day is impossible with the current applications;
- orders have to be entered simultaneously and in duplicate in different applications. This provides double the work but also results in unnecessary mistakes (e.g. in the order entry application for delivery, in the service application for maintenance contracts and in the sales information application for compiling the sales targets);
- the faulty interfaces between the applications made it almost impossible to have at disposal on a central level elapsed times of orders, exhaustion of stock, purchase of similar products and services etc. This way, there are hardly any performance indicators on a worldwide basis;
- effectively controlling of international accounts such as ABN AMRO, Woolworth, Hospital Engineering, Wall Markt, etc. is virtually impossible because no overview can be made of their market and it is impossible to conclude worldwide contracts for things like light (services), sales of hospital equipment and consumer goods.
- balancing of the books takes weeks and it is difficult to indicate which parts of the organization makes a profit and which parts not.

Dr Singh wants to control a transparent organization. IE in Berlin should be the same as IE in Johannesburg or IE in Hong Kong. Just the language and the legislation may be different.

B.4.1.2. The road to enterprise resource planning (ERP)

The manager of the division Light, Dr., A.Gandhi, supports Dr. Singh's views. His division is fast growing and the old applications of the division Light are in the long run not capable of supporting this growth. Dr. Gandhi is a strong supporter of getting into projects with governments at world scale, in which IE takes full responsibility for turnkey provision of road systems, bridges, squares and stadiums with lights. IE supplies the products, takes care of the design, implements, trains the local maintenance people and provides support. The new division operates worldwide and supplies both products and services. This change from a company that supplies products to a company that supplies products including implementation and service cannot be slowed down because of gaps in the supporting IT.

The other division managers support dr. Gandhi's views, so the project for implementation of an ERP system gets the go-ahead without the necessity for extensive justification studies. The implementation takes place with the following starting points:

- even after the implementation the various divisions light, components, medical equipment and consumer electronics should be distinguishable;
- the company divisions make as much as possible use of shared services such as those for ERP implementations (ERP competence centre) and computer centres and of standard thin client workplace facilities;
- the configuration of the ERP application is as original as possible. There are no significant changes made to the package that the supplier delivers. Experience teaches that adjustments always take up a lot of time, are expensive and make development into next versions of the package more difficult and also that the supplier usually provides most of the desired functionality in the long term in next releases and versions.

This resulted in each division getting its own implementation of the application for sales and delivery of goods. Within the division this implementation concerns the entire division. At the same time, the implementations of the applications for outstanding invoices, ledger, balance and profit and loss account, assets and some parts of purchasing become standard for the entire organization. This enables having an up to the last minute up-to-date overview of stock, balance, profit and loss. By changing the standard package as little as possible it does result in internal processes across the whole of IE having to be adjusted.

B.4.1.3. The preparations for the implementation of the ERP package

IE chooses the package that Dr. M. Singh and Dr. P. Banerjee have experience with: Oracle Financials. In doing this, IE does not choose a 'best of breed' strategy, which would lead to a suite of applications that are all connected through interfaces. The reason for this choice is that IE does not want to have to deal with different service contracts, with different version policies per package and the various connection and integration problems that come with the choice for a combination of packages of different suppliers. IE states that Oracle Financials complies with the requirements and chooses Oracle Financials.

Before the implementation of the Oracle Financials package is started, a steering committee under chairmanship of Dr. Singh is set up for the project. This steering committee determines the business model that Oracle Financials will have to support. This business model, that indicates how the internal processes are set up, works according to the rules of Figure B.4.1.1.

These rules result in amongst other things, the same bookkeeping systems worldwide, in a central customer registration and a single registration of

1. the orders are entered and executed by the divisions;
2. the divisions are owner of the relations with the customers;
3. the division decides where the order is entered;
4. the division decides the sales channels and the fact whether and how stock is kept;
5. the same aggregated information is avaialable at both the level of the divisions as the level of the holding on worldwide scale;
6 the same application for outstanding invoices, ledger, balance and profit and loss is used by each division of the organization;
7 property of the customer data lies at the level of the holding;
8 credit exposure is controlled on a worldwide scale;
9 the accounting with regard to import tariffs and excise duties is safeguarded at holding level and
10. regional distribution and administration service centers are used

Figure B.4.1.1. Starting point at implementation of Oracle Financials worldwide IE

product and service codes. These worldwide agreements enable in the long run, the realization of a data warehouse, which makes it possible for IE to control its worldwide operations in almost real time.

The IE project organization was constructed around a few key figures. In each division and per continent, part project leaders were appointed from the user organization. These had to have in depth knowledge, both in the field of the operational processes as well as in the field of the functionality of Oracle Financials. The general project leader is Dr. Singh. As CEO he carries weight within IE. The program manager used to be the head of the IE strategy office. In the steering committee of the project that meets once a week live or via video conferencing, the CIO, the CEO, the program manager and the managers of the four IE divisions have a seat the committee. Within each division there is an introduction project, that is controlled by a steering committee under the leadership of the division manager and in which the departmental head in question and the part project leader of the division have a seat on the committee. Each project group has an external Oracle Financials consultant and an employee of the IE IT management. This management is led by P. Banerjee (see Figure B.4.1.2).

Dr. P. Banerjee spends 60% of his time on the Oracle Financials implementation and has devoted his best people to the various project groups. He takes tough decisions, from the outsourcing of the exploitation for Oracle Financials, to the obligatory utilization of the competence centre for Oracle Financials, to standardization of workplaces, retraining or removing of employees. The division managers play a deciding part in the driving and pushing through of the project; they make their key figures available and solve political problems. They fulfill a crucial role in selling the project within the in-house organization.

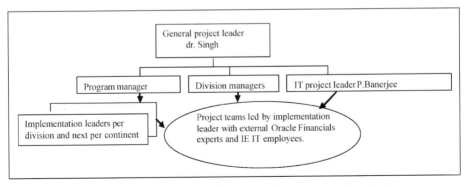

Figure B.4.1.2. Project organization for the implementation of Oracle Financials

Implementation is carried out strongly result-driven. The target is constantly to realize a clear functionality including the appropriate adjustment in the organization within a certain time. Program management has been given the task to ensure that in spite of the small steps, all this stays on course. Because of this set-up of the project, one regularly gets feedback from the users, is able to fit in possible new versions of Oracle Financials and regularly gets results, which reinforces the idea they are headed in the right direction. Therefore, it is more important to IE to stick to the planning than it is to stick to the budget. Dr. Singh means that this basically brings the company more money in the medium term.

B.4.1.4. The actual implementation

The implementation of Oracle Financials is carried out using five part projects. The first project is the rollout of a new financial system, the next four projects are the rollout of the order management and the outstanding invoices application in each IE division. Each project first tries to get the basis functionality working in India, next in each of the other countries and finally to connect all countries worldwide.

The financial system

The aim of the implementation of the financial system is the realization of the same image worldwide for all financial data within IE. In order to realize this, changes have to be made to various operational processes. These changes are carried through under the name standardization and simplification. These changes include for example:

- a standardization of the financial reports;
- the elimination of obscure processes for transfer pricing (a term used for describing all aspects regarding price-fixing within the company between related company entities; usually applicable on transfer of tangible and intangible property within an organization);
- the abolishing of independent local national organizations and replacing these with offices that are not controlled as a profit centre but on

commission and that are managed by a local office manager who operates more like a branch manager;
- the acceptance of English as the language within IE. With the customers one can speak their own language but within IE everyone speaks English.
- concentrating of the financial back-office tasks in specific locations in the world.

The order management/outstanding invoices application

The implementation of these applications progresses in the same way as the implementation of the financial system but this needs more adjustment to the specific situation of a division. The reason for this, is that dealing with orders in this day and age for example for the division Medical equipment and the division. Light is also a type of weapon in the competition with others. Furthermore, the order management system of Oracle Financials does not right now include all the functionality IE needs and although this is planned for future releases of Oracle Financials, IE cannot wait for this. That is why a multi lingual application was built next to Oracle Financials, which enables the support of the local languages and ensures compliance with local legislation. Because of this solution the Oracle Financials package was not adjusted but every time during printing the data tasks from the database, are provided with the appropriate layout and printed in the language of the country in question and in conformity with the legislation of that country. This way, a uniform implementation of Oracle Financials can take place worldwide.

The implementation of Oracle Financials starts with the division Consumer Electronics. This division has the items with the fastest rate of circulation and items of a commodity-like nature. The division manager Dr. B. Tilak has asked to be the first division where these applications are implemented. Dr. Tilak views this implementation as a motor for renewing his out-of-date operational processes. From IT point of view this division is also a wise choice. The division targets the production and sales of a relatively small number of standard products that are produced in stock. Compared to the divisions Medical Equipment and Light it has simple operational processes. These divisions operate with a lot more items and there could be a small number of very complex orders that have to be validated and attuned. Furthermore, those divisions just like Components manufacture to order. By starting at consumer electronics, the basic functionality can be tried and tested. Because this is a first implementation and the technology is new to IE, the implementation will be hard enough as it is. The first implementation helps to build up knowledge and experience, which is important for the next implementations.

Subsequently, it was the turn of successively the divisions Light, Medical Equipment and Components. In these divisions the new business model is aimed at shipping the items directly to the customer.

This is the same for the division Light. This new business model results in significant changes in the local IE organization, which was used to order, assemble in-house and next ship the goods. The changeover to new applications did no go without any problems. It was decided to carry out an extensive test programme ahead of the implementation. Under this programme on Saturdays in five locations at once, live tests are carried out on all applications in order to simulate the practice as closely as possible. Besides, after conversion of all data to the new applications, Light stopped the order management system for one week in order to get rid of all impurities and to make sure that it was 100% safe to go live. Because of all this, the implementation took about twice as much time as planned, time that was mainly spent on learning to handle the application and testing. However, when they finally did go live, there were hardly any problems.

Light was followed by Medical Equipment. The implementation went speedily and was less prepared than the one at Consumer electronics and Light. Consequently, the complexity of the order entry means that more people are needed than was originally planned and that more knowledge was needed for configuration of the installations and the introduction to the system. Last but not least, the division Components followed.

B.4.1.5. Functional management, application management and exploitation at the shared service environment of the new ERP package

Simultaneously with the introduction of Oracle Financials, IE reorganizes its in-house IT departments. The functional management for Oracle

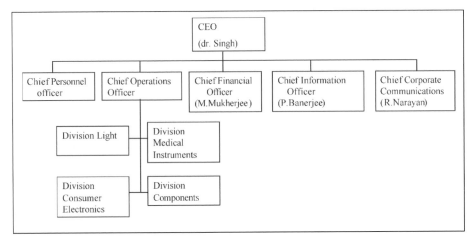

Figure B.4.1.3. Internal organization IE

Financials is localized at a central staff department of CFO Dr. M. Mukherjee in New Delhi, including the functional management of the functionality that is made specifically for the various divisions. Dr. P. Banerjee is the CIO and responsible for the contracts with different externals, the implementations and possible innovations using IT and the responsibility for the application management. In Figure B.4.1.3 the new organization structure in IE is shown The application management for Oracle Financials is 99% the responsibility of Oracle, excluding tailor made software. The contract for the application management is awarded to Atos Origin.

Apart from a standard package for the ERP, IE also has a standard functionality for personal productivity tools in the workplaces. For this, they use Lotus Notes with the Amigo Plus word processor. Started as a package that had to facilitate e-mail worldwide, these days Lotus Notes provides the support for knowledge management, instant messaging and group decision support. New functionality in this field is implemented by IBM Global Services. The functional management of the personal productivity tools rests with the same department as the one that takes care of functional management for Oracle Financials.

With regard to management information, Business Objects is used. Application management for this package is carried out by Business Objects. Functional management comes under the same central department as the one taking care of the functional management of Oracle Financials.

IE has also finally a worldwide operating intranet and extranet. The functional management for the intranet functionality also rest with the above-mentioned department functional management that comes under the CFO. With regard to the extranet functionality, this rests with the extranet department that comes under the responsibility of the Communications management of the Corporate Communications Officer (CCO) Dr. R. Narayan. Application management for intranet and extranet is executed by IBM global services.

Atos Origin also runs, on the basis of a 'managed operations' the three worldwide operating IE computer centres. The computer centres are the property of IE. The network capacity for wide area networking is leased from India Telecom and ATT. These contractors are controlled via Atos Origin.

In Figure B.4.1.4 the structure of the department functional management has been drawn. In the building in New Delhi, where this department is domiciled, there are also rooms set up for IBM global services that carry out their tasks from these rooms. In Figure B.4.1.4 the set-up of this application management and exploitation task is shown. The objects to be managed by Atos Origin for the technical infrastructure and the ownership of the user rights for the applications are procured directly by IE.

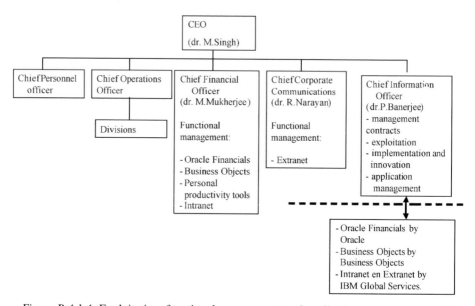

Figure B.4.1.4. Exploitation, functional management and application management at IE

B.4.1.6. The three worldwide shared service centres and the network and workplace objects

On the workplaces within IE, thin client personal computers are installed. Each time someone logs on, the necessary applications are downloaded from the shared service centres. The log-on operates with a personal chip card that is inserted in a chip cardholder in the keyboard, combined with a personal password. Next, a VPN connection is set up that goes through the firewall and provides access to the computer centre in question. IE operates in the workplaces with Oracle Financials, business objects, tailor made software, Office XP under Windows XP. The entire IE network uses the TCP/IP protocol. The network capacity is hired from Indian Telecom and ATT. These contractors are controlled via Atos Origin.

In the three IE computer centres, 6 HP Superdome 32 servers with each with 16 partitions and 64 GB in internal memory are lined up. These Superdomes are lined up per two in a cluster configuration, in which each of the three clusters has a specific primary task. The first cluster is dedicated to the exploitation of Oracle Financials, the second supports the use of business objects and the intranet and the third supports the extranet facilities. The Superdome clusters are mutually interchangeable.

Furthermore, each of the three computer centres can take over the tasks of one of the other computer centres, in case one should break down. Each Superdome is connected through a Fiber channel with a Storage Area Network (SAN). This Storage area network has a capacity of 6 terabyte. The data are via the worldwide network replicated to every SAN in every IE computer centre. For personal productivity tools, every local national organization has set up a local HP cluster RP8400 with per country varying internal external direct attached memory. These clusters are controlled remotely from one of the three IE computer centres. Every computer centre focusses on a region. These regions are Asia/Australia, Europe/Africa and the Americas. The objects of management are shown in a diagram in Figure B.4.1.5.

In each computer centre a small production department is set up. This performs the possible local operations tasks. The front-office and back-office with regard to exploitation are set up in New Delhi. This is where in the back-office the operational problem management, configuration management, change management and release management tasks take place. Furthermore, it carries

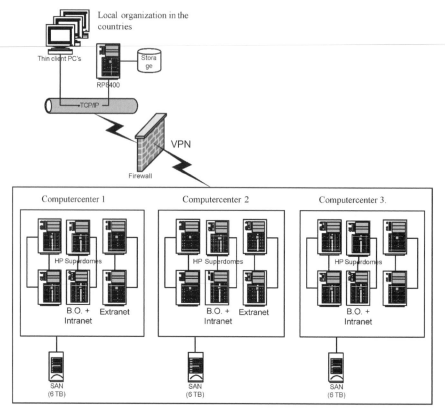

Figure B.4.1.5. Objects of management at IE

out tasks at tactical level in the field of capacity, continuity and availability management. Therefore, Atos advises IE with regard to the technical infrastructure to be set up. Atos from New Delhi also performs the front-office tasks to do with service level management, financial management and rapportage and service desk.

B.4.1.7. The result

Looking back, the implementation of Oracle Financials is a success. IE is capable of doing business at a level that was impossible with the old applications. The business can indicate that there are improvements because of the implementation of Oracle Financials. New indicators are available, such as the number of days in which the order is certain to be delivered, delayed deliveries, worldwide stock levels etc. In more than one division the number of orders that can be delivered on the same day has increased from 20 to almost 85%. The elapsed time for obtaining approval for supplying an organization without payment in advance has been reduced from over 24 hours to less than a minute. The improved data integration also enables analysts to delve in data various levels deep, which provides better insight into sales trends and internal performance. The balancing of the books towards the end of a fiscal period is quicker and because of the availability of information, managers take faster and better decisions. Even the lowest levels in the IE organization can see the advantages. Previously, they spent 90% of their time collecting data. This has now been reduced to 10%, which means the rest of the time can be spent on analysis and presentation.

Looking back, Dr. Singh and Dr. Banerjee remark that the implementation of Oracle Financials provided IE with access to a new level of operating: operating on a worldwide scale. By implementing Oracle Financials worldwide as a standard one is able to grow.

Questions

1. IE owns or is owner of a user right for all infrastructure and application objects. It is also responsible for all application management. In fact it hires manpower from third parties for executing tasks in the supply organization. IE has hired these people on the basis of five-year contracts at a fixed price. In this contract it is agreed that the costs for managed operations at the same amount of work should come down by 9% per annum.

   Explain in which way IE could internally on-charge the costs for IT. Which organization does IE have to set up for achieving internal on-charge? How could IE benchmark its costs with other multinationals? What are with regard to this the problems with the figures? What is useful with regard to using key performance indicators? In which fields would this be possible within IE right away? In which not? Where in IE could you apply activity based costing?

2. To what extent should there be a relation between IE's strategy and the way in which one achieves on-charge of IT costs? Which types of strategy are there at IE? What does that mean to the method to be used for on-charge of IT costs?

3. How would you optimise the organization of IT management from cost perspective if you were IE? If you were Atos Origin? If you were IBM Global services?

4. From the case, it does not emerge that IE has set up competency management within its IT organization. Do you share the idea that competency management is nice but actually is not important to IE? If so, why? If not, why not and which competencies should IE certainly set up?

5. Under which conditions could competency management in IT tasks be successful at IE? Which competency should IE set up? What does the career path for people that work on these tasks look like?

6. Atos Origin may also consider competency management. In your view, which competencies are important when executing tactical tasks for the front- and back-office organization? Illustrate your answer with three examples.

7. Why is procurement of IT facilities important to IE? Of which definition of procurement do we speak in that case? What are routine products to IE? What are strategic products? What is the importance of this difference?

8. What is the role of the internet at procurement of IT products within IE?

9. How would you apply ISPL within IE? How does risk management in procurement within IE come up for discussion?

10. Which roles do you see in IE at the management of service agreements? How do you view these roles in concluding contracts? What is the legal framework for IE's managed operations contract?

11. What are the reasons that IE records agreements in contracts and subsequent service level agreements? What reasons do IE's partners have? What are for IE critical success factors for concluding SLA's? Why?

12. What is the problem of an SLA between the IE demand and the supply organization for example for the exploitation of IT facilities? Illustrate your answer by giving an example.

13. Specify a plan for arriving at a service level agreement step-by-step for the application management and for the managed operations of the Oracle Financials application for IE with respectively Oracle and Atos Origin. Do the same for the Lotus Notes application with IBM global services.

14. Indicate which service levels you consider to be important for the management application that uses Business Objects? Do you recommend IE to

produce a user catalogue for its IT service products and services? Why? Why not? Who is going to produce this?

15. How would you monitor and safeguard the concluded SLA's with the various outsourcing partners, if you were IE?

16. At securing IT facilities, reliability of the facilities is of major importance. Provide a calculation of the advantage that 99.5% availability, a response in 99.999% of less than 5 minutes for asynchronous e-mail and almost 100% certainty with regard to the secure sending of e-mail has for IE. With regard to this we assume the following data:

    – one e-mail per employee (IE has 127,278 employees: this is a random indication of 1 January 2003 at 16:00 o'clock) is sent per day;

    – in the old organization where in every country it had its own control of the exploitation of IT facilities and its own computer centres, there were different e-mail applications as seen from IE central, a 99.9% chance of deformation of the message and a 98% chance the e-mail would reach the recipient within one day. In 1% of all cases the recipient never got the message.

    – the value of an e-mail varies. In general, by sending e-mails, a manner of communication that is asynchronous by nature, messages are sent that reach the recipient and cause the speeding up the elapsed time of actions. On average, per sent e-mail 25 euro on expenditure caused by delayed decision-making not being informed of prices etc is saved.

    – in the new situation each e-mail is logged and analysis of the send and receive pattern is possible.

17. Which challenges does IE encounter at the IT demand-side with regard to information security? What does this mean to the IT supply-side?

18. Explain how the information and IT security is probably organized within IE. Which efforts does IE have to make if one wants to comply with the ISO 17799 standard? Explain your answer.

19. Which level of continuity of IT facilities would you set up with regard to Oracle Financials? What does this entail for IE?

20. How does IE score with regard to architecture of their security concerning the ten points of Saltzer and Schroeder?

21. Which actions did IE undertake for arriving at standardization? Discuss in this respect the standardization of information (content) and the standardization of IT products and processes. Explain your answer.

22. Which advantages and which disadvantages are a result of this way of standardizing? Explain your answer. What is the importance of compliance with
international standards for IE?

23. In your opinion, what comes under utility computing at IE? How is IT portfolio management designed at IE? At which Jeffery level does this portfolio
management operate?

B.4.2. Ministry of defence in Denmark: Business intelligence and organization of IT (*Variation on Kamps, J. (2004)*)

B.4.2.1. Introduction

The Ministry of Defence considers the optimal protecting of the employees against contagious and life threatening diseases as a requirement for
being able to guarantee the deployment of its people. Within Denmark there
is no great danger of such diseases and the government has been able to expel
many illnesses by means of the child vaccination programme. Nowadays, the
danger of contagious diseases is on the increase again. There are a number of
reasons for this. In the first place, the influx of foreigners from high risk countries
to Denmark, secondly the fact that citizens form Denmark visit risk countries
during their holidays and finally the military spending time in deployment areas
all over the world.

The World Health Organization (WHO) and the Denmark government
have drawn up a list of occurring diseases in risk countries. This list has been
copied by the Ministry of Defence and is further accentuated. The supplying and
administering of the vaccinations against these diseases to servicemen is regarded
a task of the employer. Every soldier is therefore vaccinated for various occurring
diseases before he is deployed. In principle the responsibility for supplying the
vaccinations rests with the medical service of the Royal Denmark Army. All
vaccinations are administrated by the Military Health Care Service. Only they
are authorized within Defence to administer vaccinations.

B.4.2.2. Supporting IT application

The doctors are supported by the Immunization module (I-module). The I module is a tailor made application and especially developed for being able to record the immunization of the Royal Denmark Army and the Royal Denmark Air Force and to safeguard the validity of the immunization, resulting from the vaccination. Therefore, this is a registration system. This application can be accessed from all (about 40) health care centres. Details are entered directly online into this system.

From the registration in the I-module, reports are generated on the degree of immunization of the individual soldier and for entire units. Some of these reports are meant for the doctor in the health care centre and some for the officers of the (administrative) units.

Making extra queries or having these made is time-consuming. These queries have to be made by the Defence IT Organization. Furthermore, the internal procedures for passing the various layers within the organization for acquiring authorization also cost a lot of time. The implementation of changes to the application is also problematic. The functional management of the package rests with the Denmark Medical General and technical services company. The technical and application management is carried out by the Defence IT organization. This means various organization divisions are involved.

B.4.2.3. Data collection concerning immunization

Within the I-module some four different immunization statuses are distinguished: *ready*, *update*, *new* and *incorrect*. The categories *ready* and *update* in the basic package are actually the only categories that may occur in regular units and certainly in units that are possibly deployed of have recently been deployed. *Update* might occur in those cases where one is in the middle of a series of vaccinations or if in a particular case a certain immunization has expired. The only units where *new* can be explained, is at the various recruitment centres where at a certain moment there might be an influx of new recruits. The vaccinations are divided into two groups. The so-called basic package and the supplementary packages. The basic package is the same for every soldier and is supplied during the initial training. In addition, there are supplementary packages for the different deployment areas. The supplementary package is composed on the basis of reports and regulation of authorities, health care services and the World Health Organization (WHO). These vaccinations are only then administered when is it known whether a soldier will be posted and where to.

B.4.2.3.1. Basic package

The basic package is provided during the initial training of the soldier by means of a number of criteria. On the basis of an interview, a questionnaire and things like the child vaccination programme one received or demonstrable earlier vaccinations for certain diseases, it is determined which vaccinations are necessary. The curative doctor at the health care centre does the administering and the registration of the vaccinations. After administration of the vaccinations the doctor presents the soldier with the so-called yellow booklet, which has the details of the provided vaccinations. The doctor also takes care of the electronic rapportage in the I-module of all vaccination data, including previous vaccinations such as through the child vaccination programme. This way an overall picture of the vaccination history of a person emerges. Using the details as filled out by the doctor, the I-module determines whether a soldier complies with the requirements of the basic package. After completing his initial training, every soldier has to comply with the requirements of the basic package.

B.4.2.3.2. Supplementary package

The supplementary package is, per deployment area, determined on the basis of reports and regulations of authorities, health care services and the World Health Organization (WHO). Preceding a posting, the servicemen are informed which supplementary requirements they have to comply with for being posted. By means of the chosen supplementary vaccinations and the soldier's status in the I-module, it can be determined which vaccinations have to be given in addition. It can also be indicated which supplementary package is necessary, which vaccinations have been administered and using all this data the I-module decides whether the soldier complies with the requirements of the chosen supplementary package and which vaccinations are still possibly lacking. The supplementary package often involves a number of so-called series vaccinations. Only after having had the complete series one is fully protected against the disease in question.

Besides, there are also vaccinations that expire after a certain period of time; the protection against the disease is in that case insufficient. Therefore, when determining the degree of immunization, a large number of parameters have to be taken into account: basic and supplementary package, validity and series. All this is different from vaccine to vaccine. The rapportage function of the I-module shows the degree of immunization per administrative unit. Within the four different categories *ready*, *update*, *new* and *incorrect*, the degree of immunization is given in percentages per (administrative) unit.

B.4.2.4. Responsibilities

In the process for achieving a good degree of immunization, three parties are directly involved and they each have their own responsibility within the process. That is in the first place the soldier himself. The soldier is told during his training that he is responsible for his state of health and the degree of immunization is one of the factors in this. Therefore, the soldier has to make an appointment with the doctor in the health care centre in order to make sure that his degree of immunization complies with the requirements of the basic package. The making of subsequent appointments in order to maintain this degree of immunization is also a responsibility of the soldier. The second responsible is the commanding officer of the unit. He is responsible for the deployment of his unit and this goes for both ordnance as well as personnel. In this respect, he also has a controlling and supervising task. He has to make sure that his unit complies with all criteria that are demanded of this deployment and the state of health is one of these criteria. The (administrative) officer receives reports with regard to the degree of immunization of his unit and the standard he has to comply with. He can see which persons are insufficiently immunized and take action. Finally, there is also a part for the doctor. He also has a supervising and controlling task. The doctor has both sight on the degree of immunization of the individual soldier as well as of the units within his practice. The doctor advises the officer about the degree of immunization of the unit and the way in which this can possibly be improved. The doctor is the only person that also knows the so-called problem cases and he can address both the soldier as well as his immediate superior with regard to this. Ultimately, the aim is to achieve the highest possible degree of immunization within the health centre. The doctor can draw up reports in which the degree of immunization of soldiers, connected to the health care centre emerges. There are however no standards for this from the side of the organization. If the system works well, every soldier is at least immunized for the basic package. Because the validity of the vaccination is limited, there could be some fluctuation in the overall picture.

B.4.2.5. Management information

B.4.2.5.1. How is this defined?

In a working relationship with different expert doctors, the functionality of the I-module is defined. Different guidelines were used for this, such as the ones provided by the WHO, the Denmark government, the health care services and the Denmark Institute for the Tropics. The state of health indicator (immunization degree) is developed for rendering the implementation of the policy regarding vaccinations measurable. For the determination of this indicator no specific technology or method was used. The immunization degree developed from pragmatic use of the policy instructions and common sense. Rapportage was carried out per administrative unit. The choice to base this on the administrative unit was not an obvious one and steps have already been taken to change this into rapportage per actual unit. For defining the requirements and requests with regard to management information, no methods or techniques were used. This means that only limited rapportages are possible and these are generated on paper.

B.4.2.5.2. How does management information evolve?

The I-module is developed as a registration application for supporting the immunization process. The creation of management information is not included in the development. The only thing the I-module yields is a number of standard rapportages. From these standard rapportages only the immunization degree per unit can be regarded as management information. This 'management information' from the I-module consists of a list on paper sorted by (administrative) unit that gives only the immunization percentage within the categories *ready*, *update*, *new* and *incorrect*. The creating of this report takes several hours because the immunization degree has to be calculated separately for every individual soldier. Furthermore, the report is only available on paper. The rapportage is manually processed in reports to the higher management. This means that it takes the necessary time to get this information available. Apart from this, the I-module supplies some reports to the health care centre and a doctor can check which persons still need to be vaccinated. These are however not reports that are made regularly and worked with pro-actively.

B.4.2.5.3. Reliability of data

The doctor at the health care centre is responsible for entering the vaccination data in the I-module and therefore also implicitly for the determination of the immunization degree. Data does not always have to be entered right after a vaccination. There is some administrative backlog, caused by insufficient knowledge of the application at a number of users and the poor discipline of doctors and sometimes assistants for altering details. Besides, the yellow booklet, that includes all vaccinations and the I-module are not in line with each other. There is also no active monitoring of the expiration of an immunization. Some immunizations only have limited validity and a repeat vaccination has to take place in time. The expiration terms for some vaccines are three, five and/or ten years. These terms are not monitored and also not noted by the system and as a result vaccinations are not repeated on time. The expiration of immunizations during postings is also not taken into account.

Looking at the figures for the immunization degree of October 2003 we see that at the time of the rapportage 23,329 persons were in the army, divided over 195 administrative units with an average size of 120 persons. A more detailed breakdown is given in Figure B.4.2.1.

The immunization degree of the Royal Denmark Army and the Border Control service is 57.48% of a population of 23,329 persons. The division over the various statuses is shown in Figure B.4.2.2. In Figure B.4.2.3, assuming a binomial division, the distribution within the presented data is given. As can be seen, this distribution is very limited with 23,329 soldiers. The figures as given in the rapportage in all cases have a distribution of less than 0.7%.

B.4.2.6. The organization of IT today and tomorrow

B.4.2.6.1. Organization

Above the current organization of the use of IT within the Ministry of Defence is described. This is changing. The supply of IT will continue to be looked after by the Defense Telematics Organization (DTO). This organization provides exploitation and application management of tailor made applications.

Size of unit	Number of Units	Total Number of persons
= 1	10	10
< 10	8	30
< 25	9	170
< 100	90	5904
< 200	49	6554
> 200	29	10661
Totaal	**195**	**23329**

Figure B.4.2.1. Overall breakdown of number of persons per unit

The application management of the standard packages as used at the Ministry of Defence is executed by the suppliers of those packages.

With regard to the demand for IT; an organization of the demand is taking place from 1 January 2004:

(a) the responsibility for the information function lies at central level within the Ministry. The Directorate Information function and Organization (DIO) determines the necessary information systems and their functionality;

Immunisation degree – Royal Denmark Army and the Border Control (October 2003 Status)				
	Ready	**Update**	**New**	**Incorrect**
Percentage	57,48%	11,39%	1,40%	29,73%
Numbers	13410	2657	326	6936

Figure B.4.2.2. Immunization degree October 2003

Status	Chance of				Distribution	
	Succes	Failure	Number	Average	Numbers	%
Ready	57.48%	42.52%	13410	7708	57.25	0.43%
Update	11.39%	88.61%	2657	303	16.38	0.62%
New	1.40%	98.60%	326	5	2.12	0.65%
Incorrect	29.73%	70.27%	6936	2062	38.07	0.55%

Figure B.4.2.3. Summary of chance and distribution

(b) the responsibility for procurement of IT objects rests with the Directorate ICT Execution (DICTU). Based on the functionality as provided by DIO, the DICTU takes care of the acquisition and functional maintenance of the necessary IT facilities in the divisions of the Ministry. It controls the DTO as well as the other supply organizations.

In June 2004 the DIO and the DICTU fill in their tasks step by step. The DIO and DICTU interpret in 2004 all their tasks for the personnel applications. This also includes the above-described registration of immunization degree.

IT costs are directly on-charged by DTO. There is a fixed subscription rate for the connection to the network, for use of intranet/extranet/internet and personal productivity tools. This rate also includes exploitation and application management for the applications in question. Special requests regarding intranet/extranet are charged separately based on cost price. All other applications are on-charged according to use. To this purpose, a registration of use, of the configuration, of the authorization and of the calls is kept.

With regard to the licences of applications the costs for the user licence are on-charged by the DICTU.

B.4.2.6.2. The objects and processes

Each workplace within the Ministry of Defence has access to intranet, extranet and internet facilities. At every workplace MS Office XP has been installed. From every workplace one can use the applications as needed for the work, on the basis of one's authorization. The Ministry of Defence uses People Soft for secondary processes to do with personnel. In the field of finances, procurement and logistics my-SAP.com is used. All other applications are tailor made. These tailor made applications were developed by DTO and are maintained by DTO.

Questions

1. The Ministry of Defence (MOD) owns or is owner of a right to use all infrastructure and application objects. It is also responsible for all application management. If necessary it hires manpower of third parties for carrying out tasks in the demand and the supply organization.
   - State in which way MOD can internally on-charge the costs for IT.
   - Which organization does MOD have to set up for arriving internally at direct on-charging?
   - How could MOD benchmark its costs with other military organizations? What are the problems with these figures?
   - What is useful in using indicators? In which fields would this be possible without any problems within the Ministry of Defence? In which fields not?
   - Where could you apply activity-based costing in the MOD?
2. At the Ministry of Defence, to what extent should there be a relation between its strategy and the way in which on-charge of IT costs is achieved? Which type of strategy does the MOD have? What are the implications for the method to be used for on-charge of IT costs?
3. How would you optimise the organization of IT management from the cost perspective, if you were the Ministry of Defence? If you were DTO?
4. It does not transpire from the case study whether DTO, DIO or DICTU have set up competency management within their organization. Do you share the idea that competency management may be nice but is really not all that important for these three Defence divisions? If so, why? If not, why not and which competencies should they definitely set up?
5. Under which conditions, could competency management at IT tasks in DTO be successful? Which competency should DTO set up in that case? What will the career path of people working on these tasks look like? In your opinion, which competencies are important in the execution of tactical tasks for the front and back-office organization at DTO? Illustrate your answer with three examples.

6. Why is procurement of IT facilities important for the Ministry of Defence? About which definition of procurement do we speak in that case? What are routine products at the Ministry of Defence? What are strategic products? What is the importance of this difference?
7. What is the role of the internet in procurement of IT products within the Ministry of Defence?
8. How would you apply ISPL within the Ministry of Defence? How does risk management in procurement Ministry of Defence come up for discussion?
9. Which roles do you see at the Ministry of Defence in the management of service agreements? How do you view these roles in concluding contracts? What is the legal framework in the contract the Ministry has with the supplier of the package for personal productivity tools and for financial applications?
10. What are the reasons for DTO, respectively DIO and DICTU to record agreements in contracts and subsequently service level agreements? What are the reasons for the partners of the DICTU? What are critical success factors at concluding SLA's for the DICTU and the DTO? Why?
11. What is the problem of an SLA between the demand and the supply organization for example for the exploitation of IT facilities at the Ministry of Defence? Illustrate your answer by giving an example.
12. Specify a plan for arriving step by step at a service level agreement for the application management and exploitation of the People Soft and the SAP application for the DICTU with respectively DTO, SAP and People Soft.
13. Indicate which service levels you consider to be important for the management application for immunization? Do you recommend the Ministry of Defence to produce a user catalogue for its IT service products and services? Why? Why not? Who is making this?
14. How would you safeguard and monitor the concluded SLA's with the various outsourcing partners if you were the DICTU?
15. At security of IT facilities, reliability of the facilities is of major importance. Provide a calculation of the advantage of 99.5% availability, a response in 99.999% of less than 5 minute for asynchronous e-mail and almost 100% certainty on secure sending of e-mail for the Ministry of Defence. In this calculation we assume the following data:
    - one e-mail per employee (the Ministry of Defence has about 80,000 employees) per day is sent;
    - in the old organization there were different e-mail applications used within the Ministry of Defence, a 99.9% chance of deformation of the message

and a 98% chance the e-mail reached the recipient within one day. In 1% of all cases this never arrived.

– the value of an e-mail varies. Generally spoken, by sending e-mails, a mode of communication that is asynchronous by nature, messages are sent that reach the recipient and result in speeding up the elapsed time of actions. On average per e-mail 25 euro in costs, cause by delays in decision-making, not being informed etc. is saved.

– in the new situation every e-mail is logged and it is possible to analyze the send and receive pattern.

16. Which challenges are there to the Ministry of Defence at the demand-side of IT with regard to information security? What does this mean for the IT supply-side?

17. Indicate how the information and IT security is probably organized within the Ministry of Defence. Which does the Ministry have to do in order to comply with the ISO 17799 standard? Explain your answer.

18. Which level of continuity of IT facilities would you set up with regard to People Soft and SAP? What does this mean to the Ministry of Defence?

19. How does the immunization application score with regard to architecture of their security concerning the ten points of Saltzer and Schroeder?

20. Which actions did the Ministry of Defence take to arrive at standardization of IT application? Discuss the standardization of information (content) and the standardization of IT products and processes. Explain your answer.

21. Which advantages and which disadvantages are a result of this way of standardizing? Explain your answer. What is the importance of compliance to international standards to the Ministry of Defence?

22. In your opinion, what comes under utility computing at the MOD? How is IT portfolio management designed? At which Jeffery level does this portfolio management operate?

APPENDIX C

Concepts and abbreviations

INTRODUCTION

This list is divided into two parts. One part consists of the main terms in the field of IT management and the other is a list of terms and abbreviations as used in the book. The list of main terms provides in brief, the subjects and perspectives that define the field.

THE PRINCIPAL TERMS EXPLAINED IN BRIEF

The key concepts in IT management are:

1. *IT management* is keeping the infrastructure for the use of IT and the applications that use this structure in such a condition, that the information function will continue to comply with the requirements and needs of those that pay for this.
2. *Perspectives on IT management*. There are four perspectives on the field IT management. These are:
   - the perspective of authority: who owns the facility? Who manages it and who uses it? What are the mutual relations?
   - the perspective of the execution of tasks. These can be carried out at strategic, at tactical and at operational level. These may concern infrastructures and applications.
   - the perspective of change. Every year, there are new releases and versions of objects of the infrastructure and the applications. In addition, one starts to manage entirely new objects. Each change may pass through several phases. At completely new changes one still has to gain

563

experience and produce the management indicators. At new releases or versions of existing objects the procedure is fixed.

   –the perspective of system analysis. One may conclude service level agreements in which the functional and performance requirements for the management effort are recorded and in which is agreed in what manner one deals with one another. The infrastructure and/or applications to be managed are clearly defined.

3. *Objects of management.* The objects for which special management tasks are carried out are objects of the infrastructure, the applications and the organization. Objects of the infrastructure can be divided into:

   –objects of the technical infrastructure being storage, processing, transport and import/export facilities. In general these are computer centres, networks and workplace facilities.

   –objects of the informatics infrastructure. These include software building tools and tools for supporting IT management tasks. The applications to be managed in general are divisible into administrative and technical applications, personal productivity tools and electronic–commerce applications. Objects of organization are the structures and the tasks within those structures set up for servicing infrastructures and applications.

4. *Exploitation of infrastructures and applications.* In general, exploitation of IT facilities can be supported methodically by ITIL. ITIL can be applied for data, image as well as speech facilities. Every organization can interpret its own management using the ITIL description. Other methods in this area are eTOM, TMN and MOF. For maintenance of informatics infrastructures usually the method is chosen that is used for the management of applications.

5. *Management of applications.* Applications are the reason why owners invest and pay day in, day out for the maintenance of IT facilities. Management of applications includes two tasks: a functional, more user-oriented, requirements specifying task and an application management or more technical oriented task aimed at realizing specifications by specification of functions to be programmed, programming and testing of the software. Next, an application is taken into production and the exploitation of IT facilities starts.

In this book the term functional and application management will also be used for the maintenance and exploitation of IT infrastructures or part of these infrastructures. Functional management is situated within a demand organization. Application management and exploitation in (a) supply organization(s).

6. *Management costs.* The costs at IT management can be divided into investment costs and permanent costs. On the one hand, these costs are determined by the functional and performance requirements to the IT management and on the other hand, these are driven by cost-increasing factors such as the management of a large diversity of objects with corresponding functionality (lack of standardization); choosing for tailor made where a standard product could possibly also be used and organizations not changing alongside if the technique enables other ways of working. During the last few years infrastructures for example enable concentration of management of objects. With regard to IT management costs the concept total cost of ownership (TCO) emerges. This means that the total costs of an object to be managed are included over its entire life span. Therefore, IT management costs include among others an investment component and a component of fixed charges.

DEFINITIONS AND EXPLANATION OF SOME ABBREVIATIONS

ACM	Application cycle management, part of the method ASL
AM	Application management, technical development and maintenance of applications
Application	see information systems
ASL	Application Services Library, a set of methods for structuring maintenance of applications and infrastructures, especially suitable for larger organizations

ASP	Application Service Providing, an example of the third generation outsourcing, where the desired applications are called up from browsers at workplaces; the possibility for supplying these applications is created by a third party; they provide the use of the application and often also of the infrastructure at a price fixed in advance
IT management or more proactive IT service management	Providing the agreed functionality and performances at application of IT in information function
BiSL	Business Information Systems Management Library, structured method for functional management for larger organizations
BSC	Balanced Score Card, a method for balancing the information function, necessary for controlling the business processes in organizations
CAO	Collective Labour Agreement
CCTA	Central Computer and Telecommunications Agency, inventor and manager of the ITIL method; by now part of the OGC
CMM	Computer Capability Model, precursor of CMMI
CMMI	Capability Maturity Model-Integrated system/software engineering, a model for denoting the level of service; CMMI distinguishes five levels, being reactive, repeatable, proactive, geared to the business and innovative
CO	Sector continuity
CobiT	Control Objectives for Information and related Technology
CSF	Critical Success Factors
EFQM	European Foundation for Quality Management

ERP	Enterprise Resource Planning, integrated applications for supporting the operational management (Muntslag, 2001)
Encryption	For example transporting data over a network encrypted, so that people first have to decipher these data before they can understand them.
eTOM	Enhanced Telecom Operations Map
EX	Exploitation
Exploitation of IT facilities	Bringing and keeping infrastructures and applications in production in conformity with the functional and performance requirements as agreed with the owners of (a user right) of the service
FM	functional management, development and maintenance of applications and infrastructures from a functional point of view
HW	Hardware
IT	Information Technology
ICT	Information and Communication Technology
Information	Data that improves the knowledge of the recipient of this data
Information systems (also applications)	(in the narrow or 'management' sense because in the broader sense this could also include parts of the infrastructure): the programmes and procedures operating within an infrastructure and the people necessary for maintaining the data, programmes and procedures; this maintenance can be perfective, corrective, additive and/or preventive
Information function	Ensuring that the data needed for making decisions is available in organizations; this data has to be present in conformity with the requirements set in advance, which are called functional and performance requirements

Informatics infrastructure	defined as the whole of IT development and IT service management objects that services tasks in the field of development and maintenance of all IT objects that are part of the infrastructure. In practice these objects are compilers, case-tools, editors, linkers, database management programmes and IT service management tools for performance measures, on charge of costs, tuning, configuration management, help desk support, etc.
Infra	Infrastructure
Infrastructure	the complex of technical and informatics facilities necessary for providing the demanded IT facilities; this is therefore the technical infrastructure plus the informatics infrastructure. Infrastructure plus applications plus supporting processes form together the complete facility, that support the organizational processes.
INK	Institute Dutch Quality, Dutch organization that is part of the EFQM.
ISPL	Information Systems Procurement Library
I/O	Input and output of data
IS	Information system
ISACF	Information Systems Audit and Control Foundation
ISO	International Organization for Standardization
ISO-LCP	ISO life-cycle processes
ISPL	Information Services Procurement Library, a method for systematically arriving at procurement of IT services and products
IT	Information technology
ITIM	Information Technology Investment Model
ITIL	Information Technology Infrastructure Library
Legacy	the technology used in the infrastructure and/or applications is out-of-date, whilst the organization is dependent of this infrastructure and/or applications

OCM	Organization cycle management, part of the method ASL.
Organization (Bosman, 1996)	a system of production factors (including people and procedures) that combined pursues the achieving of one or more objectives
NEN	Dutch Normalization Institute, comparable to ANSI in the USA
NGI	Dutch Society for informatics, comparable to ACM and IEEE in the USA
NMF	Network Management Forum
PRINCE2	Projects in Controlled Environments, version 2, a method for project management
RFP	Request For Proposal
RFI	Request For Information
SLA	Service Level Agreement
SLM	Service Level Management
Service Level Management	A form of management of IT facilities, in which the focus is strongly aimed at organizing management tasks so the service level as agreed with the customers is achieved or more than achieved
SNO	Dutch for "service niveau overeenkomst," same as SLA or service level agreement
SW	Software
TM	Technical Management, see exploitation of IT facilities
TCO	Total Cost of Ownership
Technical infrastructure	This supports tasks in the field of storage, processing, transport and import and export of images, speech and data; for the execution of the tasks of the technical infrastructure servers, networks and workstations are needed; hardware for servers, networks and workstations combined with the corresponding operating systems and the network software are part of the technical infrastructure.
TMN	Telecommunication Management Network

APPENDIX D

Literature

SOURCES IN THE ENGLISH LANGUAGE

Sources used throughout the entire text

Applegate, L.M., R.D. Austin and F.W. McFarlan, *Corporate information strategy and management*. McGrawhill Higher Education, 2003. Website: www.mhhe.com/applegate.

Benko, C. and F.W. McFarlan, *Connecting the dots*. Harvard Business School Press, Boston, 2003.

Carr, N.G., *IT does not matter*. Harvard Business Review, 2003.

Eiserman, T.R., *Internet business models, text and cases*. Irwin, New York, 2003.

Gartner Group, Symposium IT expo, yearly Gartner Group conference Europe sessions, Cannes, 1996, 2001, 2002 en 2003.

Laudon en Laudon, *Management Information systems, managing the digital firm*, 8th edition. Prentice Hall, London, 2004.

Looijen, M., *Information systems, management, control and maintenance*. Kluwer Bedrijfsinformatie b.v., Deventer, 1998 (with supplement).

Slack, N., *Operations management*, 3rd edition. Prentice Hall, London, 2001.

van Bon, J., *IT service management, an introduction*, 2nd edition. van Haren publishing, Zaltbommel, 2004, ISBN 9077212280.

1. The basis of the field

Gilmore, J.H. and B.J. Pine, *Markets of one, creating customer unique value through mass customisation*. Harvard Business School Press, Boston, 2000.

Howes, T., *Setting the standard for utility computing, launch of the Data Center Markup Language*. Boston, 2003, www.dcml.com (case EDS).

Ross, J.W. and P. Weil, *Six IT decisions your IT people shouldn't make*. Harvard Business Review, November 2002.

Straub, D., *Foundations of net-enhanced organizations*. Wiley, 2004.
van Schaik, E., *A management system for the Information Business*. Prentice Hall, Englewood Cliffs, NJ, 1985.

2. Supplying IT products and services within an architecture

IEEE-SA Standards Board, Standard 1471–2000, IEEE Recommended Practice for Architectural Description of Software-Intensive Systems, 2000.
Mingay, S., *IS service delivery: Managing external chaos, minimizing internal complexity*. European Symposium, Cannes, France, November 2003.
Nolan Norton, Metamorphosis 2000, Enterprise architecture: Laying the e-foundation for 21st-century business. Congress, Munich, March 27–29, 2000.
Open Group, *The Open Group Architectural Framework (TOGAF)*. www.opengroup.org, 2001.

3. Task-focussed and simultaneous process-focussed IT supply

Davenport, Th.H., *Process innovation, reengineering work through information technology*. Harvard Business School Press, Boston, 1993.
Gouillart, F.J. and J.N. Kelly, *Transforming the organization*. McGrawhill, New York, 1995.
Hammer, M. and S.A. Stanton, *The reengineering revolution*, Harper Business, New York, 1995.
Harmon, P., *Business process change*. Morgan Kaufman Publishers, Boston, 2003.
Kaplan, R.S. and D.P. Norton, *The balanced scorecard*. Harvard Business School Press, Boston, 1996.

4. The demand-side: functional management (BiSL)

Fichman, R.G. and S.A. Moses, *An incremental process for software implementation*. Sloan Management Review, volume 40, number 2, 1999.
Weil, P. and Ross, J., *A matrixed approach to designing IT governance*. Sloan Management Review, Winter 2005.

5. The supply-side: application management (ASL)

Backer, Y., et al., *Application Services Library, a management guide*. Van Haren Publishing, Zaltbommel, 2003.

van der Pols, R., *ASL, a framework for application management*. Van Haren Publishing, Zaltbommel, 2004.

6. The supply-side: exploitation (e.g. ITIL/MOF-MSF/eTOM)

Keeton Powers, M., et al., *Microsoft solutions framework, delivering IT solutions* (chief editor: J. van Bon). Van Haren Publishing, Zaltbommel, 2004.

OGC, *Best practice for service support*. London, 2000.

OGC, *Best practice for service delivery*. London, 2001.

Pulturak, D., et al., *MOF pocket guide, IT service operations management* (chief editor: J. van Bon). Van Haren Publishing, Zaltbommel, 2003.

Telemanagement Forum, *Enhanced Telecom Operations Map* (e-TOM). Telemanagement Forum, GB921, March 2004, http://www.tmforum.org/browse.asp?catID=0

Telemanagement Forum, *e-TOM—ITIL applications note, using e-TOM to model the ITIL processes*, http://www.tmforum.org/browse.asp?catID=0

7. Organizing IT tasks and processes

Galbraith, J., *Organizational design: An information processing view*. Addison and Wesley, Reading, 1973.

Mintzberg, H., J.B. Quinn and R.M. James, *The strategy process, concepts, contexts and cases*. Prentice Hall, Englewood Cliffs, NJ, 1988.

Parker-Priebe, M.J., *Theory and practice of business/IT organizational interdepencies*. Thesis, University of Brabant, Tilburg, 2000.

Sahay, S., B. Nicholson, and S. Krishan, *Global outsourcing*. Cambridge University Press, Cambridge, 2003.

Schotema, R.P. (editor), *ASP—Application service providing*. Vieweg and Sons, Wiesbaden, 2000.

Scott Morton, M.S., *The corporation of the 1990's, information technology and organizational transformation*. Oxford University Press, Oxford, 1991.

van der Zee, H. and P. van Wijngaarden, *Strategic sourcing and partnerships*, Nolan, Norton Institute, Addison and Wesley, Amsterdam, 1999.

8. Controlling IT facilities (ICT governance) and the necessary information

Brown, J.S., *Research that reinvents the corporation*, Harvard Business Review, August 2002.

Christensen, C.M., *Innovation and the general manager*. Richard D. Irwin, Homewood, IL, 1999.

Davenport, T.H. and L. Prusak, *Working knowledge: How organizations manage what they know*. Harvard Business School Press, Boston, 2000.

Ghoshal, S. and L. Gratton, *Integrating the enterprise*. MIT Sloan Management Review, vol. 44, No. 1, herfst 2002, pp. 31–38.

Kuiper, A.P., P.M. Los and J.S. Sietsma, *The guide to IT service management, chapter 38, Knowledge management and the IT service management organization*. Addison-Wesley, Reading, 2002.

9. House in order: evaluate and improve

ISACF, *Cobit, executive summary*. Rolling Meadows, www.isaca.org (zie ook www.isaca.nl), 1998.

ITSMF UK, *OGC Questionnaire Phase-1*. Transfer Complete, http://www.itsmf.com/news/news.asp?NewsID=71, 2004.

Lescouhier, S., *An introduction to Cobit*. ITSMF Newsletter België, December 2000.

Niessink, F., *IT Service CMM, a pocket guide*. Van Haren publishing, Zaltbommel, 2004.

Rocheleau, R.A., *Enhancing availability using digital's availability analysis tool*. Digital equipment, Utrecht, 1996.

van Bon, J. (editor), *IT governance, a pocket guide, based on Cobit*. Van Haren publishing, Zaltbommel, 2004.

10. Innovation from customer and chain perspective

Davis, M. and J. Heineke, *Managing services, using technology to create value*. Irwin, New York, 2003.

Hammer, M., *The agenda*. Three Rivers Press, New York, 2001.

Fitzsimmons, J.A. and M.J. Fitzsimmons, *Service management, operations, strategy and information technology*, 4th edition. McGrawhill, New York, 2004.

Lovelock, C., *Services marketing, people, technology, strategy*, 4th edition. Prentice Hall, New Jersey, 2001.

11. The financial aspects

Brandt, A., *An unmanaged computer system can stop you dead*. Harvard Business Review, November/December 1982.

Brandt, A., *Make information services pay its way*. Harvard Business Review, January/February 1987.

Parker, M.M., R.J. Benson and H.E. Trainor, *Information economics*. Prentice Hall International Editions, Englewood Cliffs, 1988.

Treacy, M. and F. Wiersema, *The discipline of the market leaders*. Addison-Wesley, New York, 1995.

Venkat, V., *Offshoring without guilt*. Sloan Management Review, Spring 2004.

12. The personnel aspects

British Computer Society, *ISM 3 model*, http://www.bcs.org/BCS/Products/Corporate/legacy/IndustryModel/Resources/

13. Procurement of IT products and services (such as ISPL)

Heine, J., *Ten critical issues facing ICT asset managers*. Gartner Symposium ITxpo 2003, Cannes, 2003.

ISPL series of books (9 booklets) (available through the EXIN), ten Hagen & Stam, Den Haag, 1999.

Kraljic, P., *Purchasing must become supply management*, Harvard Business Review, September/October 1983.

Telgen, J., et al., *Lecture notes purchasing*. University of Twente, Enschede, 2004.

14. Controlling contracts using service level agreements

Lee, J.J. and R. Ben-Natan, *Integrating Service Level Agreements, optimizing your operational support system for SLA delivery*. Wiley, Indianapolis, 2002.

15. Securing IT facilities (such as ISO 17799)

Mingay, S., *Best practices and trends in business continuity management*. Gartner Symposium ITxpo 2003, Cannes, 2003.

Schneier, B., *Secrets and lies, digital security in a networked world*. Wiley, New York, 2000.

Stiennon, R., *Future of information security*. Gartner Symposium ITxpo 2003, Cannes, 2003.

Stiennon, R., *Intrusion detection is dead: Long live the firewall*, Gartner Symposium ITxpo 2003, Cannes, 2003.

16. Standardizing of content, process and product

Biegel, S., *Confronting the limits of our legal system in the age of cyberspace*. MIT Press, Boston, 2001.

Data center mark up language, *Simplifying data center complexity, white paper*. www.dcml.org, 2003.

Dewan, R., A. Seidmann and S. Sundaresan, Strategische keuzen bij IS-infrastructuren: Bedrijfsstandaarden versus decentrale optimalisati. 16th ICIS conferentie, Amsterdam, December 13–16, 1995.

Heine, J., *Measuring IT asset measurement performance: Metrics, methods and scorecards*. Gartner Symposium ITxpo 2003, Cannes, 2003.

Howes, T., *Setting the standard for utility computing*. DCML Technical Overview, www.dcml.org, 2003.

Jacobs, K., *Standardisation processes in IT, impact, problems and benefits of user participation*. Vieweg, Wiesbaden, 2000.

Kaplan, S. and M. Tripsas, *Thinking about technology: Understanding the role of cognition and technical change*. Congress Academy of Management (AOM), Seattle, 2003.

Mahoney, J., *Managing complexity: Sane strategies for IT leaders*. Gartner Symposium ITxpo 2003, Cannes, 2003.

Morris, J. and A. Davidson, *Policy impact assessments: Considering the public interest in internet standards development*. TPRC September 2003, zie www.cdt.org.

Spar, D., *The politics of innovation*. Harvard Faculty Seminar Series, serial number 10493, Boston, 2002.

17. IT Management en route to 2027 (ITIM, amongst other things)

Govekar, *IT operations and infrastructure, burning issues and advice*. Gartner Symposium ITxpo 2003, Cannes, 2003.

Jeffery, M. and I. Leliveld, *Best practices in IT portfolio management*. Sloan Management Review, Spring 2003.

Jones, N., *Connected enterprise, connected society*. Gartner Symposium ITxpo 2003, Cannes, 2003.

Linder, J., *Transformational outsourcing*. MIT Sloan Management Review, Winter 2004.

Mierits, L., *Communicating the business value of IT, a challenge whose time has come*. Gartner Symposium ITxpo 2003, Cannes, 2003.

Murphy, T., *Implementing a business value from IT program*, Gartner Symposium ITxpo 2003, Cannes, 2003.

Ross, J. and G. Westerman, *Architecting new outsourcing solutions, the promise of utility computing*. MIT CISR, October 2003, CISR WP 117 and Sloan WP No. 4458-01.

Sharma, Chetan and Nakamura, Yasuhisa, *Wireless Data Services, business models and global markets*. Cambirdge University Press, Cambridge, 2003.

Venkat Venkamatran, N., *Offshoring without guilt*. MIT Sloan Management Review, Spring 2004.

Willcocks, L. and V. Graeser, *Delivering IT and e-business value*. Computer weekly professional series, Butterworth and Heinemann, Oxford, 2001.

Appendix A. short cases about the contents of a chapter

Lucas, H.C., *The T-form organization*. Jossey Bass, San Francisco, 1996.

O'Brien, J.A., *Management information systems, managing information technology in the E-business enterprise*, 5th edition, McGraw-Hill, Boston, 2002.

Appendix B. extended cases for group assignments

Davenport, T.H., et al., *Just in time delivery comes to knowledge management*. Harvard Business Review, July 2002.

McFarlan F.W. and R.D. Austin,*CareGroup*, revised 26/2/2003. Harvard Case 9 303-097, 2003.

Saloner, G. and A.M. Spence, *Creating and capturing value*. Wiley, New York, 2002.

Appendix G. websites about the topic IT management (see also appendix G)

Internet addresses: Buyers outsourcing guide 2003, IT beheer 9, 2003.

SOURCES IN OTHER LANGUAGES THAN ENGLISH USED THROUGHOUT THE ENTIRE TEXT

Amerongen, S., P.A. Anthonio and Th.J.G. Thiadens, *E-business en beheer van ICT-voorzieningen.* Solidium, Culemborg, 2000, 1st edition, Anthonio/Nederlof en partners 2001, 2nd edition.

Giesberts, C., *Kiezen voor een aspiratieniveau van het beheer van een portaal.* doctoraalscriptie bij de belastingdienst. Universiteit van Twente, 2002.

Looijen, M., *Beheer van informatiesystemen.* Kluwer Bedrijfsinformatie b.v., Deventer 2000, 5th edition.

Mintzberg, H., *Mintzberg over management.* Veen, Amsterdam, 1991.

Ruijs, L. and W. de Jong, *ICT-dienstverlening, van ICT beheer naar ICT Service Management.* Academic Service, Den Haag, 2003.

Thiadens, Th.J.G. and F. Verdonk,*De beheerprocessen simpel geïmplementeerd.* ten Hagen & Stam, Den Haag, 2001.

Thiadens, Th.J.G. and H. Spanjersberg, *Beheerst beheren.* Het Expertise Centrum, Den Haag, 2000.

Thiadens, Th.J.G. and A.P. Kuiper, *ICT service management.* ICT-reeks, ten Hagen & Stam, Den Haag, 2003.

Thiadens, T., *Beheer van ICT-voorzieningen, infrastructuren, applicaties en organisatie.* Academic Service, Schoonhoven, 2002, 4th edition. Website www.ict-management. com.

van Bon, J. (editor), *IT beheer jaarboek.* ten Hagen & Stam, Den Haag, 1997–2003, diverse edities.

van der Pols, R., *Nieuwe informatievoorziening, informatieplanning en ICT in de 21ste eeuw.* Academic Service, Schoonhoven, 2003.

2. Supplying IT products and services within an architecture

Bakkeren, W., C. Hofman and A. Ligthart, *Een goede architect kent de bouwplaats.* Informatie, November 2003.

Berg, M.V.D., J. Luijpers, M. van Steenbergen and R. Wagter, *Dynamo, architectuur in het E-tijdperk.* Iquip Informatica, Diemen, 2001.

Boeters, A. and B. Noorman, *Kwaliteit op maat, IT-projecten beheersen met de RADAR-methode.* Kluwer Bedrijfsinformatie, Deventer, 1997.

Ruijs, L., et al., *Op weg naar volwassen ICT dienstverlening.* Perform-series, Academic Service, Schoonhoven, 2000.

Truijens, J. and J. Winterink, *Management (in) control met informatiearchitectuur. Management en Informatie*, 11th volume, 2003, no. 1.

van der Aart, F.S. and H. Verniers, *Beheren onder architectuur biedt nieuwe perspectieven. IT management year book 2000*. ten Hagen & Stam, Den Haag, 2001.

3. Task-focussed and simultaneous process-focussed IT supply

Alofs, T., *De end-to-end service organisatie*. Informatie, January/February 2002, volume 44.

van den Berg, H., et al., *Processen vertalen vanuit de strategie*. Informatie, May 2003, volume 45.

Cremers, M., *Drie eeuwen business process management*, Informatie, May 2003, volume 45.

Dekkers, M., *Analyse methoden geen bezuinigingsgereedschap*. Automatiseringsgids 11/7/2003.

de Vries, E., *ICT enabled distribution of services, front office information and multi-channeling*. Thesis, Amsterdam, 2003.

Dohmen, L., *Meetbare praktijkeffecten van IT-service management*. Informatie, January/February 2002, volume 44.

Oosterhout, M., et al., *Rendement uit processen*. Informatie, May 2003, volume 45.

van der Aalst, W., et al., *Formele methoden in business process management. Informatie*, May 2003, volume 45.

Verdonk, F. and Th.J.G. Thiadens, *De processen simpel geïmplementeerd*. ten Hagen & Stam, Den Haag, 2001.

Vos, G.C.J.M., F. Aertsen and A.A.Th. de Schepper, *Dynamiek in logistiek*. ten Hagen & Stam, Den Haag, 2002.

Wijngaard, J., *Dictaat Logistiek en operations management*. Post doctorale controllers opleiding, Rijksuniversiteit van Groningen, 2004.

4. The demand-side: functional management (BiSL)

Bal, C.M.R. and M. Boreel, *IP Vint: Wie niet snel is, moet slim zijn, productiviteit van automatisering nader beschouwd*. IP, Diemen, 1995 (CMM-model).

Delen, G.P.A.J. and M. Looijen, *Beheer van informatievoorziening*, Cap Gemini publishing, Rijswijk, 1992.

Deurlo, K., F. van Outvorst and R. van der Pols, *Een nieuw functioneel beheer model*. IT beheer jaarboek. ten Hagen & Stam, Den Haag, 2002.

Donatz, B. and F. van Outvorst, *Functioneel beheer bij pakketten*. IT beheer jaarboek. ten Hagen & Stam, Den Haag, 2003.

PinkRoccade, *Checklist functioneel beheer*. Bilthoven, 2004.

van der Pols, R., *Een nieuwe rol voor het informatiemanagement*. IT beheer jaarboek. ten Hagen & Stam, Den Haag, 2003.

van der Pols, R., *Functioneel en applicatiebeheer, presentatie EMIM politie*. Universiteit van Amsterdam, Warnsveld, 1/3/2004.

van der Pols, R., *BiSL, een framework voor Functioneel Beheer en Informatiemanagement*, Van Haren Publishing, Zaltbommel, 2005.

van Dolder, C., *Perspectief: functioneel beheer*. IT beheer 2, February/March 2004.

5. The supply-side: application management (ASL)

Congres Wereld van IT beheer, 2001: Service management in de dealing room van ABN AMRO.

Deurloo, K., R. van der Pols and R. Sieder, *ASL Self-Assessment*. ten Hagen & Stam, Den Haag, 2004.

Meijer-Veltman, M., *ASL en CMM*. Informatie, volume 44, October 2002.

Meijer-Veltman, M., *ASL en ISO 9001:2000*. Informatie, volume 45, March 2003.

van der Pols, R., *ASL, een framework voor applicatiebeheer*. ten Hagen & Stam, Den Haag, 2001.

van der Pols, R., et al., *Application Services Library*. Informatie, June 2002.

6. The supply-side: exploitation (e.g. ITIL/MOF-MSF/eTOM)

Bouman, J.F., ICT service manager zoek een andere baan! In: J. van Bon (editor), *De wereld van IT beheer*. ten Hagen & Stam, Den Haag, 2002.

de Vos, J., et al., Kennismanagement: hoe haal je voordeel uit wat je al weet? In: J. van Bon (editor), *De wereld van IT beheer*. ten Hagen & Stam, Den Haag, 2001.

Jansen, P., *IT-service management volgens ITIL*. Addison-Wesley, Amsterdam, 2003.

Schreuder, K., et al., Wat doet ITIL met mensen? In: J. van Bon (editor), *De wereld van IT beheer*. ten Hagen & Stam, Den Haag, 2001.

van Hemmen, L., *Ondersteunende modellen van netwerkmanagement*. IT management select, 1997/1.

van Hemmen, L. and O. Roelofs, *Virtueel service management.* Informatie, volume 45, March 2003.

7. Organizing IT tasks and processes

de Bruijn, F., *Trends in IT management.* de Wereld van IT beheer, Nieuwegein, 2004.
de Koning, D., *IT-afdeling moet op zoek naar (nieuwe) balans.* IT beheer 8, 2003.
Heuschen, R. and C. Bell, *Outsourcing als evolutionair process beschouwd.* IT beheer, February/March 2004.
Mintzberg, H., *Mintzberg over management.* Veen, Amsterdam, 1991.
Strikwerda, J., *Shared service centra: van kostenbesparing naar waardecreatie.* Van Gorcum, Assen, 2003.
Uijlenbroek, J.J.M., *ICT-sturing in complexe organisaties, Het Expertise Centrum, onderzoek voor het Ministerie van Verkeer en Waterstaat, lezing op 'de wereld van IT-beheer'.* ITSMF, February 1999.
van Dalen, H., *Philips Semiconductors Shared ICT services.* de Wereld van IT beheer, Nieuwegein, 2004.
van Starreveld, L. and Van Nimwegen, *Bestuurlijke Informatieverzorging, deel 1: Algemene grondslagen.* Stenfert/Kroese, Groningen, 2002, 5th edition.
Vogd, F., et al., *Utility computing.* De wereld van IT beheer, Nieuwegein, 2004.

8. Controlling IT facilities (ICT governance) and the necessary information

de Best, B., *Generieke en specifieke Acceptatie criteria.* Verslag afstudeerproject, Open Universiteit, Heerlen, 2000.
de Best, B., *Generieke en specifieke Acceptatie criteria.* Q-force, Utrecht, 2000.
de Best, B., *Whitepaper, Is ITIL balanced?* Q-force, Utrecht, 2000.
Boxel, L.A.P., *ICT service assessment.* Scriptie, Open Universiteit, Heerlen, 2003.
Daamen, C.E. and P. Kuiper, *Gedegen communicatie op basis van stakeholder management.* IT beheer 10, 2003.
Delen, G.P.A.J., et al., *World class IT, van service gericht naar business gericht met uw ICT organisatie.* KPMG consulting, De Meern, 2000.
Geertsema, J.B., *Information management organisatie bij EMMTEC services.* Doctoraalscriptie bij Emmtec, Universiteit van Twente, Enschede, 2002.
Zomer, T., *Wij geven te weinig uit aan IT.* IT beheer, number 4, May 2001.

9. House in order: evaluate and improve

Aarts, W., *Werken met ISO9001:2000*. Samson, Deventer, 2000.

Accountantsdienst Ministerie van Binnenlandse Zaken en Koninkrijksrelaties, *presentatie CobiT model*, 15 March 1999, Driebergen, 1999.

ASL Service Libarary werkboek, *ASL zelfevaluatie*. ten Hagen & Stam, Den Haag, 2003.

de Wijs, C., *Information systems management in complex organizations*. De Wijs, Voorburg, 1995.

Kleyn, G. and B. van Strijen, *Risicomanagement in IT-projecten*. Kluwer Bedrijfswetenschappen, Deventer, 1994.

Lescouhier, S., *An introduction to Cobit*. ITSMF Newsletter België, December, 2000.

Mayjer-Veltman, M., *ASL en ISO 9001:2000*. Informatie, volume 45, March 2003.

Peters, L., N. Bakker and M. van Vuur, *Meten is weten, sturen is de kunst*. IT beheer 6, 2003.

10. Innovation from customer and chain perspective

Chrafih, A., *Dienstverlening in een informatiecentrum*. Scriptie Erasmus, Rotterdam, 2003.

Looijen, M., *Beheerstappenplan*. *Jaarboek Wereld van IT beheer 1999*, red. J. van Bon, ten Hagen & Stam, Den Haag, 1999.

11. The financial aspects

Kersten, B. and H. Verniers, *Masterclass, samenvatting kosten & baten*. Congres Wereld van IT beheer, Nieuwegein, 2004.

Penninx, W. and H. Groen, ICT kosten, theorie en praktijk. In: *ICT service management, best pratices*. ITSMF, Van Haren Publishing, Zaltbommel, 2004.

PinkRoccade, *Costscan*. Bilthoven, 2002.

Renkema, T.J.W. and E.W. Berghout, *Investeringen in informatiesystemen*. Bedrijfskunde, volume 68, 1996, no. 1, pagina 32–44.

Renkema, T.J.W., *ICT baten in beheer*. Congres Wereld van IT beheer, Nieuwegein, 2004.

Thiadens, Th.J.G., *Kijken naar grote ICT projecten*. EMIM politie, Universiteit van Amsterdam, Amsterdam, 2004.

Thiadens, Th.J.G., *Praatjes over kosten*. PinkRoccade Attribit, Bilthoven, 2002.

van der Burg, J., *Kantoor-efficiëntie, Customer intimacy versus operational excellence*. Scriptie, Open Universiteit, Heerlen, 2004.

van der Pols, R., *Nieuwe informatievoorziening, Informatieplanning en ICT in de 21ste eeuw*. Academic Service, Den Haag, 2003.

van der Zee, H., *Quantitaive and qualitative control of quality and benchmarking of IT*. Informatie, volume 40, May 1998.

van Dijk, P., et al., *Benchmarking en ICT costmanagement*. Congres Wereld van IT beheer, Nieuwegein, 2004.

van Haalen, D., *Inzicht in de kosten van ICT services*. IT beheer, November 2002.

Vercouteren, W.J.J.C., Beheersing en verlaging van ICT beheerkosten: de vergelijking van twee kostenmodellen. In: *ICT service management, best practices*. ITSMF, Van Haren Publishing, Zaltbommel, 2004.

Schrage, M., *The Innovation subsidie*. Sloan Management Review, Spring 2004.

Wiggers, P., et al., *Workshop ICT portfolio management*, Congres Wereld van IT beheer, Nieuwegein, 2004.

12. The personnel aspects

Coul, J., Op de, *Taken, functies, tollen en competenties in de Informatica*. NGI-uitgave, ten Hagen & Stam, Den Haag, 2001.

Exin, Frameworks, versie 3.0, www.ict-competenties.nl (zie ook www.career-space.com), Utrecht, 2002.

Kamphuis, R., *Het proces zelf is de helft van het doel*. IT Beheer, magazine voor IT service en beveiliging, nummer 3, November 2000.

13. Procurement of IT products and services (such as ISPL)

Braam, G., *Het optimaliseren van de ICT procurement organisatie, de gevolgen van interne en externe factoren op de inrichting en positionering van de ICT procurement functie*. Scriptie Erasmus, Rotterdam, 2003.

Griffioen, W., *Professionalisering ICT-klant/leveranciersmanagement*. Scriptie Erasmus, Rotterdam, 2002.

Harink, J., *Internet-technologie in inkoop, de kinderschoenen ontgroeid*. Thesis, Universiteit van Twente, Enschede, 2003.

van Berkel, J., et al., *Aanbesteden van ICT projecten*, Papernote no. 14, Het Expertise Centrum, Den Haag, 2003.

14. Controlling contracts using service level agreements

Boddeke, M., *Sturing op het koppelvlak van Continuïteit en Exploitatie*. Afstudeerverslag, Open Universiteit, Heerlen, 2003.

Broos, L.C.P. and W.H. van Holst, *Rechten voor IT beheerders*. Congres Wereld van IT beheer, ten Hagen & Stam, Nieuwegein, 2004.

Davids, I. and A. Faas, *Grip op uw ICT dienstverlening*. IT beheer 8, 2003.

Delen, G. and E. Beulen, *Contracten, kijk al aan de start naar de finish*. IT beheer 8, 2003.

de Jong, P., IT service à la Carte. In: J. van Bon (editor), *De wereld van IT beheer*. ten Hagen & Stam, Den Haag, 2003.

de Lange, E., *Contractuele kant van outsourcing; hands on. op*. Congres Wereld van IT beheer, ten Hagen & Stam, Nieuwegein, 2004.

Kotterman, G. and B. Hoondert, *Beheerkosten in de greep*. IT beheer 1, 2004.

Lugtigheid, P.C. and E. Wesselman, Service level management op basis van ABC. In: *World class IT: Praktijkgids ICT sourcing* (redactie G. Delen, Tutein Nolthenius), Den Bosch, 2003.

van Boxel, L., *ICT service assessment*. Afstudeerverslag, Open Universiteit, Heerlen, 2003.

van der Zanden, H., and M. Vogelaar, *Betere SLA's werpen vrucht af*. IT beheer 4, 2003.

15. Securing IT facilities (such as ISO 17799)

Brouwer, A., *Waarom informatiebeveiliging*? Seminar PinkRoccade, Bilthoven, 2004.

Bruls, W., *Blauwdruk verenigt disciplines*. Informatie, May 2004.

de Roos Lindgren, E. and P. Overbeek, *Lezing informatiebeveiling Executive master of Information management voor de sector Openbare Orde en Veiligheid*. Universiteit van Amsterdam, Warnsveld, March 2004.

Driessen, B., *Praktische organisatie van continuity*. IT beheer 7, 2003, Informatie, May 2004.

Moons, J. and C. de Backer, *Draadloze netwerken*. Informatie, May 2004.

Overbeek, P., E.R. de Roos Lindgren and M. Spruit, *Informatiebeveiliging onder controle*. Prentice Hall/Pearson Education, Amsterdam, 2000.

Overbeek, P., *Trends in security*. IT beheer 1, January 2004.

Rorive, K., *Voorkom complexiteit in beveiliging netwerk*. IT beheer 9, 2003.

Ruts, B., *Beveiliging van data in vijf stappen*. IT beheer 1, 2004.

16. Standardizing of content, process and product

Biegel, S., *Confronting the limits of our legal system in the age of cyberspace*. MIT Press, Boston, 2001.

Hendriks, P., *Kwaliteitszorg van software ontwikkeling*. Informatie, November 2000.

17. IT Management en route to 2027 (ITIM, amongst other things)

Akershoek, R. and F. Vogd, *It does not matter*. Congres Wereld van IT beheer, Nieuwegein, 2004.

Bloem, J. and M. van Doorn, *Realisten aan het roer, naar een prestatie gerichte governance van IT*. VINT, Amsterdam, 2004.

de Bruijn, F., *Trends in IT management*. Congres Wereld van IT beheer, Nieuwegein, 2004.

Creyghton, E. and W. Verbruggen. *Incrementele aanpak offshore outsourcing*. Informatie, volume 45, April 2003.

ITSMF, *IT service management, best practices, deel 1*. Van Haren Publishing, Zaltbommel, 2004.

Turlings, P., *Subscription management, the next generation kantoorautomatisering*. IT beheer jaarboek, ITSMF, Amersfoort, 2002.

Weggeman, M., *Organiseren met kennis*. Scriptum management, Amsterdam, 1997.

Appendix A. short cases about the contents of a chapter

Abcouwer, A.W. and J. Truijens, *Wat doet de baas eigenlijk*? PrimaVera paper, Universiteit van Amsterdam, 2004.

Bakker, R.J.W., *Triton bij Ahrend*. IT beheer praktijkjournaal, April 1997.

Bellini, P., *De dealing room, close encounter van business en IT-support*. ABN AMRO, ITSMF lustrum congres Noordwijk, ITSMF, Almere, 2000.

Drouven, F., *'De wereld van IT beheer' verovert de wereld*. Symposium world class IT management, ITSMF, Amsterdam, 2000.

Gompers, R., *Ervaringen met competentie management bij de e-bank. IT-beheer*, November 2000.

Goudriaan, R.E., *Informatiebeveiliging in een wereldwijde organisatie*. Implementatie BS7799 bij de ING Groep, De wereld van IT beheer 2001, ten Hagen & Stam, Den Haag, 2001.

Ruijs, L., et al., *Op weg naar volwassen ICT dienstverlening*. Perform-reeks, Academic Service, Schoonhoven, 2000.

van Nunen, J., et al., *Ketensynchronisatie in de retail, het antwoord op ECR*. Adviesgroep logistiek, marktgroep consumer benefits, Deloitte and Touche, Amsterdam, 2002.

Appendix B. extended cases for group assignments

Alberts, L., *BISML bij de Orbis zorggroep*. Lezing dd. 1/6/2004, PinkRoccade, Bilthoven, 2004.

Kamps, J., *Managementinformatie in de Nederlandse militaire gezondheidszorg*. Scriptie Open Universiteit, 2004.

Nationaal Ziekenhuis Instituut, *Ziekenhuisinformatiemodel*. Den Haag 1983.

APPENDIX E

Explanation ITIL service delivery and support processes

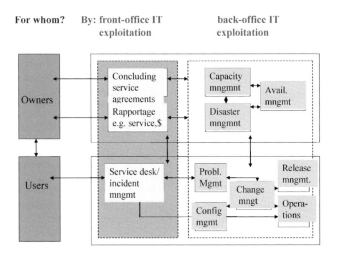

For whom?	By: front-office IT exploitation	back-office IT exploitation

SERVICE SUPPORT

In the field of service support the following tasks can be distinguished:

Service desk

This is often the common ground between the user of the service and the IT service supplier. All contacts with this supplier at service delivery level primarily go through the service desk. That is why a customer friendly, service-focussed attitude is of the greatest importance. This is where users can call in with all sorts of queries. This could concern incidents. Small incidents and incidents for which a quick 'work around' is known, are solved by the service

591

desk on the phone. Those incidents that cannot be solved within an agreed short period of time (for example 10 minutes) or cannot be solved on the phone are passed on to Problem management. A tool in the functioning of the service desk is a progress monitoring system. All reported incidents are recorded in this, together with a brief description of the problem. All the next links in the management chain record the state of play in this, so the service desk has an up-to-date overview of the progress of a specific incident at any given time and can inform users about the state of affairs of the incidents.

Because of its direct contact with the customers, the service desk has a better idea of the use of IT. Users ask the service desk to solve their problems. However, at the same they may also convey, the meagre response; that certain application functions simply do not work, that other functions do not fit the need or that a service could be more useful if it was provided in a different manner. The questions, complaints and remarks from users come in on the phone, fax or through e-mail. By means of a network connection the user can track the completion of a query or a complaint if this cannot be done immediately. Over the past few years, service desks have step by step turned into central contact points. The work in the service desk developed into more than just writing down a call. The service desk tracks how a complaint is dealt with, service rapportages are generated and records are kept whether the user was satisfied with the way in which their complaint was dealt with. A visit to an efficient service desk provides immediate insight into and an overview of the prominent operational problems of the infrastructure, the applications and the IT organization.

Problem management

Problem management includes the experts with regard to contents of the technical infrastructure. They try to diagnose the incident as reported. By doing this, the reported incident can often be reduced to a known fault. If they do not manage to find a diagnosis independently, the experts with regard to contents bring in the supplier of the component in question. If the fault that causes the incident is known and, possibly in cooperation with the supplier, a solution has been found then this is passed on to Change management.

Change management

Faults can be resolved by means of a change in the technical infrastructure. The technicians of Change management apply these changes. For this specifically, skill is of the utmost importance, and not just faults but also new requests of the users or preventative maintenance may lead to changes. In this case, Change management cannot be accessed directly but is obtained by Tactical management through a set change procedure.

Release management

Release management ensures that only tested and correct versions of authorized software and hardware are brought into production. The installation of new versions should only take place within the framework of a change and should therefore be geared to change management.

With regard to the installation of new networks, central servers and their operating systems, Configuration and Change management are cooperated with. That is where one implements the hardware and software at workplaces, in network hardware and central servers that have been released for production. Release management determines which hardware and software is to be implemented. This is where, after thorough testing and after performing an exploitation test at applications, it is decided which releases and versions of software are to be implemented. The management of the organization indicates which guidelines and standards are applicable.

Release management and the organization of the distribution of software are tasks that are often underexposed. That is to say, control does not always take place on controlled innovation of hardware and software, whilst in configurations applications, system software and applied hardware often have to be attuned to each other. To this purpose, there is sometimes some catching up to do. However, it is also possible that, because of requested EDP audit accounts regarding transaction using certain packages, an infrastructure is required that is not entirely 'state of the art.' Because of this, it might be necessary for the management organization to keep knowledge about 'legacy' systems in-house for managing these packages. Implementation of such a package in that case requires the management that makes this choice to be fully aware of this.

Configuration management

Configuration management has two important goals: ensuring that only authorized components are included in the technical and informatics infrastructure and providing information on the technical and informatics infrastructure.

With regard to the first goals, Change management and Release management for example have to report all changes in the infrastructure to Configuration management. This includes amongst other things, other workstations or peripherals connecting to the technical infrastructure. With regard to the second goal, it is necessary to set up and utilize an application in which the data about the components of the infrastructure and the connected workstations and peripherals are recorded. All other processes in the operational management consult this application.

A check on the functioning of configuration and change management is performed by asking after the architecture of the IT configuration, the number of different makes and types of pc's that are used, the number of different suppliers one procures products and services from etc. A streamlined organization will limit itself in the number of suppliers, will have a transparent IT architecture and has clear standards for the workplace configurations. In such an environment one may find indicators for performing certain activities. In such an environment the planning is clear and the costs are predictable.

SERVICE DELIVERY TASKS

ITIL includes the following processes for being able to guarantee the quality of the IT services provided:

Service level management

This is the process that ensures by means of good collaboration between provider and customer, the corresponding and safeguarding of an optimum level of IT services. The IT services are laid down in a standard service agreement (SLA). Change of this agreement is only possible after consultation of provider and customer. This means that service level management predominantly consists of studying the rapportages, taking stock of users' remarks about the quality of the standard services and of possible requests with regard to changes in the applications and the infrastructure.

Capacity management

The purpose of capacity management is taking care of the amount of available IT resources being optimally geared to the demand of customers. Being able to comply with agreed response times is also included in this. In order to being able to set-up a proper planning of the required system capacity, one needs to known the system use over a longer period of time. Collecting this data (with the aid of monitoring) and analysing this data is part of capacity management.

Availability management

This is the process that ensures that the agreed availability level is guaranteed by means of the right application of resources, methods and techniques. At capacity and availability management, one often weighs up the realising of customers requests and the costs involved in this. The double executing of servers, network parts and workplaces may improve availability and capacity, however the owner does have to pay for the costs involved in this.

Disaster management

The process ensures that the agreed continuity level can also be guaranteed in case of disasters. A disaster is in this case, an unplanned situation in which it is not expected that the duration of the non-availability of the IT services will exceed the agreed threshold values. Based on risk analysis, a so-called disaster recovery plan is drawn up and safeguarded. When considering disaster recovery there is a similar consideration as in capacity and availability. Taking care of back up and recovery in-house, as opposed to hiring recovery facilities elsewhere.

Financial management

Financial management is the process that provides an insight into the costs involved in IT services. Based on this data, it is for instance possible to determine whether the price-performance ratio of the IT services needs to be improved. This data is also used as a basis for on charging the cost of the management to the various organization divisions.

The Tactical management has to provide rapportages about each of the aforementioned divisions periodically to the organization divisions that make use of the IT services.

APPENDIX F

Levels on which the IT demand and supply organizations can operate (*Giesberts, 2000*)

LEVELS

After studying models such as the Capability Maturity model Integrated (CMM-I), the model of the European Foundation for Quality Management (EFQM), the world class IT management model and the IT service management CMM, Giesberts chose for reasons of practical usability to derive a model for the level on which an organization executes its IT tasks from the EFQM model.

This level can be determined by projecting a description of the levels onto the IT organization to be examined. In doing this, the following view on the execution of IT tasks is the guiding principle:

> *The execution of IT tasks demands the set-up of processes at operational, as well as tactical and strategic level. Repeatable execution of tasks should be based on a description of the processes. The improvement of processes is controlled by means of qualitative and quantitative measuring of supplied functionality and performances. These measures are periodic and periodically reported. This way, organizations can execute their IT tasks; have a structured training and evaluation programme for their employees. In this case, we speak of competency management.*

Looking at this view on the execution of tasks in IT organizations the following operating levels are defined:

Level 1: Activity-oriented operating of an IT organization

Every employee in the IT demand and supply organization strives to carry out his job in the best possible way. At this level skill is highly valued and supported by training. In case of complaints the IT organization tries to remedy these. This phase is typically product-focussed. The organization has function descriptions but no process descriptions. Serious events are reported. Knowledge is not structurally recorded or transferred. Training is aimed at increasing skills. Tasks are carried out from an operational set-up and are mainly problem solving. Specialists are the most important employees of the organization. The customer is not part of the picture.

Level 2: Process-oriented operating in an IT organization

The cohering activities have been regrouped into processes and are described. There is mutual dependency. The individual steps in the process are identified and tasks and responsibilities are fixed. Performance indicators act as a means for control. Processes are improved on the basis of problems that have been ascertained.

The operational processes are described, including standards and criteria and are reproducible. Costs and planning are safeguarded using methods and aids. Process owners are responsible for progress of the processes. The performances of the processes are measured systematically. Resources are made available for making improvements. Products have to comply with the requirements before these are taken into exploitation. Staff skills are improved and proposals for improvements are stimulated.

Level 3: System-oriented operating of the IT organization

The improvement of the IT organization as a whole is systematically worked on. The feedback loop is applied. Customer focus is dominant for the policy, which is aimed at rather preventing instead of resolving problems.

The responsibilities and the mutual coherence between the various set-up processes and the other departments are in the picture and known. The policy for set-up and control of IT tasks is together with the employees, assessed at advisability and feasibility and translated into measurable objectives. Progress is measured and evaluated. Audits and trend analyses are used for carrying out improvements proactively and in cooperation. The requirements and requests of external customers are seen. An integral training plan is in place and the IT organization knows the staff's needs in the long term.

Level 4: Chain-oriented operating of the IT organization

Together with partners in the chain, one strives for maximum added value. It is determined per partner who is most suitable for executing a specific task. Operating systems are connected. Innovation is paramount.

There is structural exchange of information between clients, users, customers and suppliers. This forms, together with evaluations of the in-house performances, a means for controlling the IT organization. One matches oneself against the best organizations in the branch. Expectations of customers and suppliers play a large part in the drawing up of the policy. There is open (external) communication about the policy and its realization. External parties are involved in the evaluation of mutual performances. Staff policy is an integrated part of the organization policy.

Level 5: Transforming the IT organization and excelling

In its market segment, the IT organization is right at the top. The process of continuous improvement is anchored in the structure and the culture of the organization. Based on a long-term view, the sails are trimmed with the wind in time and new activities are started for setting up the organization for these.

The organization anticipates future developments and adjusts its processes accordingly by collecting information actively and structurally. At outlining a policy one looks further than the in-house organization. One looks across borders. One is open to all relevant information, also from society. Communication takes place openly. Continuous improvement is embedded in all processes. The employees are able to direct their own training and careers.

APPENDIX G

Relevant Websites

GENERAL

- www.itsmf.nl (Dutch site) site of the IT service management forum. This is an association of companies aimed at passing on knowledge in the field of IT service management. The ITSMF site has links to:
  - Management events
  - Management themes
  - Management methods
  - literature
- http://nl.itsmportal.net (Dutch site): portal with information on IT management subjects
- www.ict-management.com (site with a Dutch and an English section): site with links to presentation material supporting the teaching of IT management, when using this book, 'Manage IT.' Lecturers can ask for a password to get suggestions about solutions for the cases in this book.
- www.sei.cmu.edu/cmmi/: site of the software engineering research institute of the Carnegie Mellon University about CMMI
- www.cio.com: reference to a site that can be used to look at the application of IT from a management perspective
- www.exin.nl (site in Dutch): information about ITIL foundation exams
- www.isaca.org: site of the Information Systems Audit And Control Association & foundation, which publishes *CobiT*, the control objectives for information and communication technology
- www.gartner.com: independent advice group for ICT
- www.aberdeengroup.com: site of the Aberdeen group
- www.helpdeskinst.com: site of the helpdesk institute
- www.kwintes.nl (Dutch site): site of the Quantifying Information technology research in the Netherlands (Dutch site)

– www.ink.nl (Dutch site, English counterpart: http://www.efqm.org/): site about the INK model, that is equal to the EFQM model.
– www.ict-competenties.nl (Dutch site):about the interpretation of ICT competencies
– www.career-space.com: competency profiles as set up by several suppliers with subsidy from the European commission
– www.efqm.org: information on the INK/EFMQ model
– www.aslfoundation.org (Dutch site with English section): articles and best practices on application management (BiSL originates from the same organization, but the site www.bisl.nl is only Dutch)
– www.pugnl.nl (Dutch site, but there is an English counterpart): background articles and best practices about PRINCE2. There is also a Prince user group in the United Kingdom. The web address is http://www.usergroup.org.uk/members.htm
– www.i-tracks.nl (Dutch site): about a new structure in ICT training
– www.tmforum.org: telemanagement forum with information on the enhanced telecommunications operations management (e-TOM)

EXAMPLES OF SITES WITH TOOLS

– http://www.hps-inc.com/: process simulation tool from the Forrester school (ithink)
– www.ciscoretail.com/sbnd/: based on requirements a network is configured, giving attention to architecture and security aspects
– www.quint.nl/index.asp?page_id=qqq_home (Dutch site): test for examining the implementation of ITIL in an organization
– www.itsmf.com/bestpractice/selfassessment.asp: ITIL self-assessment

EXAMPLES OF SITES ON SECURITY

– http://www.veiligophetweb.nl/?page=9&catid=6&object=104931 (Dutch site): Site of the Safe Internet Foundation (SIF). SIF is the advocate for the end user of the digital highway. SIF investigates, publishes, carries out projects and seeks publicity for improving the quality and especially the security of the internet

- www.gvib.nl (Dutch site): site of the Dutch society for information security
- www.ordb.org/submit/: test of the security of an IP-address
- www.cert.org: security at the Carnegie Mellon University
- www.nen.nl (site both in Dutch and English): site about the code for information security and ISO
- www.govcert.nl (site both in Dutch and English): virus alert service

EXAMPLES OF SITES ON PROCUREMENT OF IT FACILITIES

- www.ispg.nl: site about IT procurement
- www.ogc.gov.uk: site of the Office of Government Commerce (basis of ITIL and procurement methods of the British government)
- www.buyitnet.org: The BuyIT Best Practice Network is an independent not-for-profit group with a mission to *"help UK organisations realise the business benefits from Information & Communications Technology by identifying and promoting best practice in e-business"*
- http//simap.eu.int/: European procurement rules (also www.ez.nl)
- www.caucusnet.com: Network of technology purchasers (mainly IT technology) in the USA. These purchasers pass on information about their experiences in negotiating with suppliers

SITES ABOUT STANDARDIZATION

- http://www.iso.org/iso/en/iso9000-14000/basics/general/basics_1.html: site of the International Standardization Organization
- www.opengroup.org: organization of suppliers with sets for standards in the field of architecture, security etc.
- www.standards.org: site of the Singapore government that provides insight into the most recent international ICT standards
- www-i4.informatik.rwth-aachen.de: site of the informatics chair of the university of Aachen (Germany) with links to all international organizations active in the field of ICT standardization

−www.dcml.org/aboutDCML.asp: site about the Data Center Mark up Language (DCML). DCML provides a standard model for fashioning and describing computer center environments
−www.cdt.org: interest group of independent organizations at standardization. Website of the center for democracy and technology. Dutch equivalent www.bof.nl

SITES OF MAGAZINES

−www.itservice.nl (Dutch): IT service magazine
−www.itbeheermagazine.nl (Dutch): IT service and security magazine
−www.computable.nl (Dutch): weekly for ICT with amongst other things, articles on management
−www.informatie.nl (Dutch): monthly, including articles on ICT management
−www.automatiseringsgids (Dutch): weekly including articles on ICT management
−www.outsourcing-journal.com: site of the outsourcing journal

Index

This index refers to the theory covered in chapters 1–17. It does not refer to the material in the appendices of this book.